# Hellenistic Poetry and Art

*by the same author*

FROM MYCENAE TO HOMER
GREEK ART AND LITERATURE 700–530 B.C.
GREEK THEATRE PRODUCTION

# Hellenistic Poetry and Art

T. B. L. Webster

NEW YORK

BARNES & NOBLE, INC.

*Publishers · Booksellers · Since 1873*

*First published in 1964*
ⓒ *T. B. L. Webster, 1964*
*Printed in Great Britain by Butler & Tanner Ltd*
*Frome and London*

To
D. B. T.

# Contents

———————◆———————

# List of Plates

# Acknowledgements

I am deeply grateful to my wife and to Dr J. R. Green, who have read my manuscript and saved me from many errors besides suggesting many improvements. For the errors which remain they are in no way responsible. For photographs and leave to reproduce I am indebted to the following:

Mr Walter C. Baker of New York; Alexandria Museum; Allard Pierson Stichting, Amsterdam; American School of Classical Studies in Athens; Antikensammlungen, Munich; Boston Museum of Fine Arts; British Museum; Fratelli Alinari; German Archaeological Institute in Athens; Istanbul Museum; Kunsthistorisches Museum, Vienna; Musée Alaoui, Tunis; Musée du Louvre, Paris; Ny Carlsberg Glyptotek, Copenhagen; Staatliche Museen, Berlin.

# *Preface*

———◆———

This book has been written chiefly for my own satisfaction, to complete a parallel history of Greek literature and art from Homer to the Roman period. Literature here is restricted to poetry because I did not feel that I could write satisfactorily about Hellenistic prose or fit it into the same framework. Poetry and art raise sufficiently formidable problems of interpretation and presentation, and for them I shall be satisfied if I have presented a useful collection of comparative material.

Chronological problems are serious, and too many pages are concerned with expounding them, and the result is too often a statement of the line taken rather than a solution. For poetry the recurrent question is what constitutes imitation, where can we say with certainty that this poem must be later than that poem because the writer of this poem was remembering, quoting, parodying, or rebutting that poem. Perhaps it is never safe to date by such echoes, but if the date can be established by other means a good echo is interesting evidence of the later poet's knowledge and intention. Thus it is comparatively easy, as well as interesting, to establish chains of echoing epigrams from the late fourth century into the Roman period, and we can watch what started as a symposion game becoming a literary convention. It is comparatively easy also and important to establish recollections of earlier poetry which the reader was meant to observe, whether to hear an overtone or to mark a contrast. The really difficult question is the relative chronology of Apollonios Rhodios, Theokritos, Kallimachos' *Aitia* and *Hekale*. The evidence of echoes is fully recorded by Pfeiffer in his magnificent edition of Kallimachos. His conclusion that Kallimachos is always the originator I have with great hesitation queried[1] (the discussion will be found in Chs. III, IV, V). But whether the priorities can be finally established or not, it is much more important to recognize the very great and original merits of Apollonios.

The main phases of Hellenistic art are comparatively clear: the

[1] Cf. in general *Wiener Studien*, 66, 1963, 68.

followers of Praxiteles and the followers of Lysippos in the early third century, the Pergamene school in the late third and early second century, the new classical style on the mainland of Greece in the second half of the second century, the Neo-Attic style and mechanical copying in the first century. Sites such as the Athenian agora through the whole period, the Chatby cemetery at Alexandria, Pergamon, Delos, and in the West Lipari and Tarentum for more limited periods, give dates for major works and establish the chronological series of terracottas and pottery by which other undated works can be dated. Plenty of problems remain and wildly different dates have been proposed for works as individual as the Laokoon and the Zeus from Aigeira; in such cases one can only choose whatever stylistic analogy seems most convincing.

Some of the difficulties arise because artists can echo their predecessors as well as poets. Scholarship in art runs parallel to scholarship in literature, and the scholar-poets of Alexandria can be matched with two names of scholar-artists, Antigonos of Karystos in the late third century and Pasiteles in the early first century. The common source is respect for the past, which shows itself first in the rare archaistic works of the late fifth century and later manifests itself very obviously in the Attalids' creation of 'a new Parthenon' in Pergamon and in the Neo-Classical gods and goddesses of late second-century Greece. The kings had their art collections as well as their libraries, and their taste went back at least to the beginning of the fifth century. The temples also contained many works of art, and Herodas' women, visiting the Asklepieion, enjoyed what they saw, like Theokritos' women visiting the palace of Ptolemy Philadelphos for the Adonis festival. Whether access to temples was so easy earlier is perhaps uncertain; there were, of course, pictures in the Stoas in Athens and the Lesche of the Knidians in Delphi; it is curious that we hear so little of their visitors in classical times. But now there would seem to be a general interest in classical as well as Hellenistic art, and we shall find that the poets share this interest. The considerable number of direct and indirect reflections of works of art in poetry is one of the justifications for this book.

Learned poetry implies that the readers will understand at any rate the most obvious allusions and this means that they must have access to the sources of the allusions; in fact that books must have been fairly readily obtainable; for this the early papyri give some evidence.[1] In the modern world reproductions of works of art go hand in hand with the dissemination of printed books. For copying of works of art on many scales and in many materials and media there is ample evidence from the beginning of the first century B.C. Before that the second-century Myrina terracottas which copy earlier or contemporary sculptures and painting and the third-century Calene bowls which are decorated with reliefs cast from classical silver-ware[2] are certain instances of reproductions which any man could have owned. The little Dioskorides mosaics, dated about 100 B.C., are copies of third-century paintings but the technique is so fine that such mosaics can hardly have been common. Nevertheless it is difficult to believe that there was not some way of disseminating pictures like the plaster casts used for silver-ware. In general it is probably fair to say that the artist, like the poet, knew more of the art of the past and respected it more than he ever had before.

The broad sequence of artistic styles – elegant, violent, new classical, Neo-Attic – has some analogies in the history of poetry, and realistic art, pastoral art, learned art have obvious parallels in realistic poetry, pastoral poetry, and learned poetry, but to shape this book as a parallel history of styles seemed to me to have disadvantages which outweighed the advantages. One of the few cases where poets and artists were certainly working together is in dramatic production and I have emphasized this wherever possible. The Homeric bowls, some silver cups, and the relief in the British Museum with the Apotheosis of Homer were clearly made by artists working in the closest touch with scholars or poets; but more often, as with the Pergamene gigantomachy, we can appreciate that scholarship has been realized in a work of art but we have lost the texts which would elucidate the detail. Moreover in attempting to write a parallel history of style the danger of pressing analogies too far is very real, particularly in a period like the Hellenistic age when poets and artists are concerned more with exploiting the technical possibilities of their own media – allusion, vocabulary, dialect, rhythm,

[1] Cf. C. H. Roberts, *Mus. Helv.*, 10, 1953, 264, particularly 266 ff.
[2] Cf. G. M. A. Richter, *A.J.A.* 63, 1959, 241.

and sound in poetry; volume, motion, and texture in sculpture; colour effects and spatial illusion in painting – than with expressing common ideals or ideas.

The sequence of styles therefore will remain in the background as a useful scheme of reference. A truer but less tidy picture is gained by trying to see what poetry and art was produced in the main centres and noting, as they occur, the cross-references both between the arts and between the centres. The story must start in mainland Greece; obvious stages are Alexandria and Pergamon; from the end of the third century mainland Greece was in direct contact with Rome; finally we have to look at the reception of Greek poetry and art in Rome itself, remembering at the same time the particular contribution of the cities of Sicily and South Italy, many of which had a Greek civilization going back to the seventh century or earlier.

B

# Note on Abbreviations

In addition to the usual abbreviations for Journals the following will be found in the text and notes:

1. *Literature*

A.P. = *Anthologia Palatina*

K = Kock, *Comoediae Atticae Fragmenta*

Kaibel = Kaibel, *Comicorum Graecorum Fragmenta*

L.G.C. = Webster, *Studies in Later Greek Comedy*

M = Morel, *Fragmenta poetarum Latinorum*

N = Nauck, *Tragicorum Graecorum Fragmenta*

P or Powell = Powell, *Collectanea Alexandrina*

Pf. = Pfeiffer, *Callimachus*

P. Oxy. = *Oxyrrhynchus Papiri*

P.S.I. = *Papiri greci e latini, Pubblicazioni della Societa Italiana*

R = Ribbeck, *Scaenicae Romanorum Poesis Fragmenta*

2. *Inscriptions*

I.D. = *Inscriptions de Délos*

I.G. = *Inscriptiones Graecae*

O.G.I.S. = Dittenberger, *Orientis Graeci Inscriptiones Selectae*

S.E.G. = *Supplementum Epigraphicum Graecum*

S.G.D.I. = Collitz, *Sammlung griechischer Dialektinschriften*

S.I.G. = Dittenberger, *Sylloge Inscriptionum Graecarum*

3. *Art*

Bieber, *Hell. Sc.* = Bieber, *Hellenistic Sculpture*

Lippold, *Gr. Pl.* = Lippold, *Griechische Plastik*

Lullies = Lullies and Hirmer, *Greek Sculpture*

Pfuhl, *M.u.Z.* = Pfuhl, *Malerei und Zeichnung der Griechen*

Winter, *K.i.B.* = Winter, *Kunstgeschichte in Bildern*

4. *Dramatic Monuments*

Bieber, *Hist.* = Bieber, *History of the Greek and Roman Theater*

*M.N.C.* = Webster, 'Monuments illustrating New Comedy', *Bulletin of the Institute of Classical Studies (London)*, Supplement 11

*M.T.S.* = Webster, 'Monuments illustrating Tragedy and Satyrplay', *Bulletin of the Institute of Classical Studies (London)*, Supplement 14

## CHAPTER I

# Mainland Prologue

◆

## The Late Fourth Century

The death of Alexander in 323 and the death of Julius Caesar in 44 may be regarded as the beginning and the end of the Hellenistic age. In this period Greek poetry and art passed through a series of phases and spread far beyond its earlier spatial confines; long before the end of the period the effects on Roman poetry and art are already visible and by the end of the period the new Graeco-Roman poetry and art of the imperial age begins.

The story is immensely complicated even if the intricacies of political history can be largely omitted. The Hellenistic Kings are our concern in so far as they attracted or repelled poets and artists, and as early as Lykophron Rome had become a force to be remembered by Greeks. The political history seems to show continuous and complicated wars; the history of art and literature is a rich and continuous international development. This first chapter is chiefly concerned with those elements in mainland poetry and art which influenced Alexandria in the time of the early Ptolemies, and therefore it can end with some account of Aratos' *Phainomena*, which was loudly heralded by Kallimachos as fulfilling his ideal of poetry. Inevitably this prologue overlaps the last chapter of *Art and Literature in Fourth-Century Athens*,[1] but that chapter was confined to Athens and dealt with prose as well as poetry; here the scope is wider and the emphasis is different.

An inscription in Delphi dated at most ten years before our period begins preserves a paian to Dionysos written in aeolo-choriambic metre by Philodamos of Skarpheia on the coast of Lokris. Dionysos is so peculiarly the god of the Hellenistic age that it is worth looking at this early account of him. Much is difficult and unclear on the battered stone.[2] Dionysos is begged to come in the spring and bless

---

[1] Athlone Press, 1956, abbreviated in what follows as *A.A.L.*

[2] Text: J. U. Powell, *Collectanea Alexandrina*, 165; *S.G.D.I.*, 2742; cf. *S.I.G.*³, 270; *R.E.*, s.v. Philodamos; Daux, *Chronologie*, no. E 1.

the city of Delphi. (This is then a spring return of Dionysos, as we know it also at the Anthesteria in Athens.[1]) When he was born in Thebes all the gods danced and men rejoiced. His worship spread to Orchomenos and Euboea (this is near Philodamos' own Lokris), 'and all the holy blessed song-fraught land of Delphi danced, and you stood on the folds of Parnassos among the Delphian maidens showing your starry form'. (Sophocles had already called Dionysos 'leader of the fire-breathing stars' in the *Antigone* (1146), but stars, as we shall see, had a special significance for the Hellenistic age.) The god came to Eleusis and was called Iacchos, 'and opened to men a harbour from their woes' (Demeter is not even mentioned; this association of Dionysos with the mysteries is found in the same chorus of Sophocles' *Antigone*, and it was given a new twist, as we shall see, for Demetrios Poliorketes). Dionysos came to Thessaly, Olympos, and Pieria, and the Muses 'wreathed their heads with ivy and sang round him, calling him immortal, glorious Paian for ever, and Apollo led them' (we shall see, as we proceed, that Dionysos becomes the patron of all kinds of poetry in the Hellenistic age, and here he has become, like Apollo and Asklepios, a god of healing.) The stone here becomes illegible, but evidently Apollo was the link which took the poet back to Delphi and Apollo's regulations for the cult in Delphi, ending with the instruction to set Dionysos on a chariot drawn by golden lions (this is an allusion to his Eastern journeys) and to prepare a fitting grotto for the god.

Dionysos' grotto will concern us later as one of the elements in Greek pastoral poetry; here two roughly contemporary terracottas[2] from the Athenian agora are relevant. The first (pl. I*a*) is a plastic vase in the shape of a cave with a vine growing round it adorned with bunches of grapes, in which the infant Dionysos stands; the 'grotto' of the paian is the cave of the Nymphs, in which the young Dionysos grew up. The other terracotta (pl. I*c*) is a woman seated on a rock with a tympanon on her knee, a maenad in the hills above Delphi or elsewhere. Dionysos is one of the gods associated with wild country; the other is Pan: a short trochaic hymn to Pan from Epidauros[3] has

[1] Pickard-Cambridge, *Dithyramb etc.*[2], 21, 37, 82 n. 3.

[2] D. B. Thompson, *Hesperia* 23, 1954, 83, on Agora P 12822; *Hesperia* 31, 1962, 251, on Agora T 2180.

[3] *I.G.*, IV, 1[2], 130, Maas, *Epidaurische Hymnen*, 130.

been dated to the late fourth or early third century in spite of the curious punning on the name which makes Pan the foundation of all things. For us it is relevant because Pan is described as 'leaping from the shady caves – fair dancer, fair-faced, beautiful with his golden beard'. This is the Pan who is described in Alexandrian pastoral epigrams. A pretty poem by Anyte is probably an inscription for a cup dedicated by a rustic spring: 'To bristle-haired Pan and the Nymphs of the farm the shepherd Theodotos dedicated this gift under the rock, because when parching summer had worn him out, they rested him, giving sweet water in their hands' (A.P. XVI, 291).[1] Another, which reads like an inscription for a picture or statue, brings us even nearer to the terracotta of the maenad seated on the rock; A.P. IX, 745:[2] 'Look at Bromios' horned goat. How haughtily his bright eye looks down his shaggy jaws, proud that often in the mountains the Naiad took the hair about his cheeks in her rosy hand.'

Anyte of Tegea in Arcadia was a writer of lyric, but all that survives is a number of delightfully simple and straightforward epigrams. Her portrait[3] was made by Euthykrates of Sikyon and Kephisodotos of Athens, the son of Praxiteles, which shows both that her popularity was considerable and that she lived in the late fourth century. Her poem on the spear dedicated by the Cretan Echekratidas (A.P. VI, 123) seems to be the model for the preceding epigrams by Kallimachos and by Nikias so that her work was evidently known in Alexandria.

Another Arcadian epigram of the late fourth century is by Perses of Thebes (A.P. VI, 112):[4] 'Three Mainalian stags' heads with enormous horns are dedicated under your portico, Apollo, they were killed from horseback by the hands of Gyges, by Dailochos and Promenes, the children of good Leontiades.' It has been shown that Leontiades was a Theban who lived in exile during the period that his city was destroyed, and the same may well have been true of the poet. We

[1] Cf. IX, 313, 314; XVI, 228, 231.
[2] Cf. VI, 312.
[3] Overbeck, *Schriftquellen*, 1341.
[4] Cf. Wilamowitz, *Hellenistische Dichtung*, 137. Cf. also Perses' epitaph on two woodmen, A.P. VII, 445.

may perhaps remember here the large kantharos (pl. II)[1] found in the Athenian agora which was dedicated to Dionysos and Artemis: it is one of the few examples of what is called West Slope ware with a picture; Artemis with her hounds is spearing a feline in front of a country shrine beyond which stands a large stag; it is an anticipation of later pastoral art, as these epigrams anticipate later pastoral poetry. Perses also wrote an epitaph which describes a grave stele (*A.P.* VII, 730): 'Unhappy Mnasylla, why on your tomb, as you weep for your daughter, stands this painted relief of Neotima, from whom once travail tore her soul, and she lies with a deep cloud over her eyes in the arms of her mother? Alas, Aristoteles, her father, not far away kneads his head with his right hand. Unhappy ones, not even in death did you forget your woes.' This is almost a description of the stele of Plangon found at Oropos and now in the National Museum at Athens,[2] except that there the man is on the left and therefore his *left* hand is to his head, and an extra woman is added, the nurse who holds the dying woman instead of the mother. It is often difficult to decide who is living and who is dead on grave-reliefs and in fact Plangon's stele bears also the name of the man, which presumably means that both of them are dead. Perses' epitaph names all three: Neotima, the daughter who died in childbirth, Aristoteles, the father, and Mnasylla, the mother; the relief evidently was not made until the mother died. The later Attic grave-reliefs 'show an obvious emotion which was scarcely seen before', and it is this unrestrained grief which Perses expresses.[3] The typical epitaphs of the early third century, as we shall see, are more restrained (and not therefore less effective); in the same way the emotional exuberance which characterizes grave-reliefs and sculpture of the second half of the fourth century does not appear again so clearly until Pergamene art of the late third and early second century.

In the fourth century this emotional exuberance is associated particularly with the sculptor Skopas and perhaps with Bryaxis, if he is

---

[1] Agora P 6878, Buschor, *Griechische Vasen*, fig. 281; T. L. Shear, *Hesperia* 6, 1937, 375, fig. 39.

[2] Athens, N. M., Conze, no 309; K. Friis Johansen, *Attic Grave Reliefs*, 50, fig. 26.

[3] *A.A.L.*, 86 ff. I have not included with Perses Adaios of Macedon in spite of *A.P.* VII, 694 because I do not feel convinced that he is pre-Augustan.

the sculptor of the Mausolos and the Demeter of Knidos. This style can be clearly distinguished from the dramatic style of Leochares (if the Ganymede and the Apollo Belvedere are rightly associated with him), from the sunny charm of the school of Praxiteles, and from the realism of the Sikyonian sculptor Lysippos, who combined a new boldness in three-dimensional composition with a new veracity in surface treatment. Four of Lysippos' pupils should be mentioned. Eutychides and Chares worked in Antioch and Rhodes, and we shall return to them later. Teisikrates made a portrait of Demetrios Poliorketes which has been recognized in a bronze statuette,[1] a copy of the first century B.C. (pl. IIIb). The young king stands with one foot on a rock, an attitude which is probably meant to recall Lysippos' statue of Poseidon, because Demetrios claimed to be a sea-king; he wears the military chlamys, but he has the bull horns of Dionysos on his forehead; he looks to the sky in an attitude reminiscent of Alexander and his chlamys is probably the famous cloak embroidered with stars; as a new Dionysos he is also leader of the stars. The fourth pupil of Lysippos, Euthykrates, made the statue of Anyte;[2] it is not clear whether he co-operated with Kephisodotos of Athens or whether they both made portraits of the poetess. For such a commission their styles were not so far apart that collaboration would be impossible.

Kephisodotos was the son of Praxiteles and with his brother Timarchos continued the sunny elegant style which distinguished his father. They made a portrait statue of Menander for the theatre of Dionysos in Athens[3] and an Asklepios and Hygieia for the temple of Asklepios in Kos, to which we shall return.[4] The clearest idea of this post-Praxitelean art can be formed from the Athenian terracottas of the late fourth and early third century (pl. I), which formed the

[1] Naples 1606. Lippold, *Gr. Pl.*, 295, pl. 105/1; Bieber, *Hell. Sc.*, 50, fig. 149; Ath. 535f. (Douris); Overbeck, *Schriftquellen*, 1525, Pliny, *N.H.* 34, 67.

[2] Overbeck, *Schriftquellen*, 1341.

[3] Overbeck, *Schriftquellen*, 1337–8; add Dio Chrys. *Or.* XXXI, 628 R; *I.G.*, II², 3777; Lippold, *Gr. Pl.*, 300; Bieber, *Hell. Sc.*, 51, figs. 150–7; H. Heintze, *Röm. Mitt.* 68, 1961, 80; G. M. A. Richter, *Latomus* 20, 1955, 38; 36, 1959, 34; *Antiquities in Dumbarton Oaks* no. 4. The mosaic portrait in Mytilene (*Ergon* 1962, 155, fig. 186) seems to me to confirm the identification of the bust in Venice (Bieber, fig. 156).

[4] See below, p. 158.

models for the well-known Tanagra statuettes.[1] We have already noticed the child Dionysos standing in his vine-clad cave and the maenad seated with her tambourine on a rock, but we must at least mention the hedgehog with figs on its spines (for which Mrs Thompson compares *A.P.* VI, 45 and 169), the charming ladies and the flying Erotes, who belong to the world of the symposion, the soldier, and the actors and masks of tragedy, satyr play and comedy. They have a simple elegance like that of Menander and many early Hellenistic epigrams.

Later and quite different from the Paian of Philodamos with which we started is the Paian of Isyllos,[2] who came from the Bosporos and was made a citizen of Epidauros. The group of connected inscriptions among which it is preserved is dated epigraphically about 300. After the statement that his dedication is to Apollo Maleatas and Asklepios, Isyllos starts with a political maxim in trochaic tetrameters: 'If the people educate men aright to aristocracy, the people is itself the stronger; for it is supported by their valour. If anyone having been well educated touches wickedness sailing in foul water, the people is safer if it punishes him.' The conception of the people as both helped by an aristocratic governing class and checking their excesses is rather the conception of balanced democracy as propounded by Isocrates in the *Areopagiticus* (20, 26). This maxim Isyllos vowed that he would inscribe, if the law which he proclaimed established the truth of the maxim (this, I think, is the meaning of his rather curious phraseology). The next section in hexameters gives the law, which Isyllos discovered 'as an undying ever-flowing present for the immortal gods'. The best men of Epidauros, who had in their hearts the patriotic virtues of valour and honour, were to go in procession with long hair and white robes, some wearing laurel wreaths to Apollo, others with olive wreaths to Asklepios, to pray for health, good order, peace and blameless wealth, and that Epidauros should always have men of gentlemanly spirit. 'So broad

---

[1] D. B. Thompson, *Hesperia* 21, 1952, 116; 23, 1954, 72; 26, 1957, 108; 28, 1959, 127; 31, 1962, 244; 32, 1963, 88.

[2] *I.G.*, IV, 1², 128; Powell, op. cit., 132; Diehl, *Anth. Lyr.* VI, 281; Wilamowitz, *Isyllos von Epidauros*, 1886. It has been suggested that Bosporos is the name of a village in the Argolid.

ruling Zeus would spare us.' Then a short section explains that Apollo Maleatas is senior to Asklepios (four hexameters and one pentameter). Then in prose he states that Apollo in Delphi had sanctioned the inscribing of the paian. This paian is the song which the good men sang: it is a simple and inoffensive song in free Ionic metre giving the pedigree of Asklepios – Malos married Erato; Phlegyas married Malos' daughter, Kleophema; their daughter, Aigla-Koronis, was taken by Apollo and bore him Asklepios: 'Hail Asklepios, patron of your mother's city Epidauros, and send health clear-seen for our souls and our bodies.' Difficult questions about Koronis' fidelity to Apollo and Asklepios' misuse of his powers are carefully omitted. Finally a hexameter section tells the story which gave Isyllos his special position. Asklepios had saved Sparta from Philip; on his way he appeared in shining golden armour to the boy Isyllos, who had come to his shrine to be cured, and had promised to return after the victory to cure him. Isyllos duly reported his vision to the Spartans, and they instituted a cult of Asklepios the Saviour. Philip of Macedon failed to capture Sparta in 338, and Sparta did not enter his alliance. Between 338 and the carving of the stone about 300, Isyllos had proposed his maxim and his law, and he believed that his law was effective in promoting a pro-Spartan aristocracy in Epidauros. He is no great poet, but he provides an interesting glimpse of 'Spa' mentality in religion and government. The great prosperity of Epidauros began in the fourth century: the temple and tholos belong to the middle of the fourth century and the theatre to the third century. However scornful Wilamowitz may be about this small-town outlook at a time of world conquest, it seems to have worked and Epidauros continued to flourish.

Besides Philodamos, who wrote the paian to Dionysos, we hear of two near contemporaries who came from Skarpheia, an otherwise little known town. Both were comic actors. The earlier was called Lykon, who was a favourite of Alexander (Ath. 538f). He has the further interest that Phalaikos wrote an epitaph for him in the hendecasyllabic metre which bears his name (*A.P.* XIII, 6):[1] 'This

---

[1] Cf. Wilamowitz, *Griechische Verskunst*, 142; *Hellenistische Dichtung*, 134, for the identification and the text. Cf. Phalaikos' two other inscriptional epigrams in unusual metres, *A.P.* XIII, 5, 27.

fine portrait of the Laughing Comedian, wreathed with ivy and garlands for Dionysos' procession, I stand as a memorial to Lykon. A reminder of all his brilliance on earth, his charm in talk and wine, and for those hereafter a pattern of his looks is dedicated here.' Like Perses' epitaph on Mnasylla the poem describes the statue or relief on the tomb. The first line and the last line (particularly the word *paradeigma*) show that it is an ideal portrait – like but more beautiful as Aristotle said (*Poetics* 1454b 10). They also show that the actor was not wearing his mask: it was either pushed back on his head so as to leave his wreathed forehead bare, or he carried it.[1] Kallimachos copied the metre, and he also echoed the sentiment 'charm in talk and wine' in his own pseudo-epitaph (*Ep.* 35 Pf). Another foretaste of the Alexandrian epigram is a dedication in elegiacs of a yellow chiton with a golden belt to Dionysos by Kleo, who could defeat all the men in drinking.[2] Phalaikos may have composed the epigram as an actual text for the dedication or it may be a poem composed to be sung at the symposion by men who knew Kleo.

## Drama

The other comic actor from Skarpheia, Aristodemos, brings us to Athens and Menander because he acted in Menander's *Dyskolos* at the Lenaia in 317/6. A full treatment of New Comedy is impossible here,[3] but an attempt must be made to sketch briefly its chief characteristics, the dramatic personalities of its chief authors, its attitude to external events, and its spread over Greece in our period. New Comedy is social comedy in the modern sense, the kind of comedy in which characters like ourselves achieve conjugal felicity by surmounting a series of obstacles. The phrase 'like ourselves' points the difference between New Comedy and Middle Comedy, which Aristotle about 350 could still describe as having characters 'worse than ourselves'. It is true that many of the elements of social comedy, love-affairs, intrigues, procurers, parasites, and nurses can be traced back into

[1] Cf. below, p. 21, n. 3, CT 1.
[2] Ath. 440d. Cf. Aelian, *V.H.*, II, 41 (end).
[3] For details, cf. my *Studies in Menander*[2], Manchester, 1960; *Studies in Later Greek Comedy*, Manchester, 1952. Abbreviated as *S.M.*, *L.G.C.*

Middle Comedy and that elements of Middle Comedy, the running slave, the heavily-laden porter, knockabout, and description of feasting and the equipment for feasting can be traced forward into New Comedy and clear examples are visible in the *Dyskolos*.

Apart from the details of plot and character-drawing (in which we cannot check Middle Comedy, because only shortish fragments survive) the difference between 'worse than ourselves' and 'like ourselves' is shown in appearance and language. Again the new masks for lovers and young hetairai introduced in the Middle Comedy period are no longer ugly and distorted, and the padding of all characters and the phalloi worn by male characters become less obtrusive in the third quarter of the fourth century, but the essential change was made by giving all male characters chitons which reached to the middle of their thighs or further and by restricting padding to characters who were meant to appear fat.[1] Where we can compare masks and costumes of New Comedy with faces and costumes of contemporary terracottas, reliefs, and statues, it is clear that 'like ourselves' is a reasonable description of the external appearance of comic characters.[2] Merely because it is verse the language of New Comedy cannot be naturalistic in the modern sense: it avoids however both the heights and the depths of Aristophanic language (and as far as we can test it of Middle Comedy); it is closely modelled to the needs of the particular character at the particular moment, and in Menander at least is extremely subtle and flexible; it has in fact the stylistic elegance of contemporary Attic terracottas. In language and costume New Comedy is nearer to Euripidean Tragedy than Old Comedy or Middle Comedy had been, but although we know desperately little about new tragedy as distinct from revivals of classical tragedy (and what little we know is more easily considered in connection with the Alexandrian Pleiad) the new tragic masks with a tower of hair over the forehead and exaggeratedly emotional treatment of brows and nose and the elaborate clothing clearly distinguished the tragic actor from the comic actor,[3] and the archaic

[1] Cf. *Monuments illustrating New Comedy* (= *M.N.C.*), 5, 14, 17, 21 ff.

[2] Cf. statuettes, etc. referred to in preceding note with terracottas referred to above, p. 6 n. 1.

[3] Cf. *Monuments illustrating Greek Tragedy and Satyrplay* (= *M.T.S.*), 8, 11.

strictness of Hellenistic tragic iambics[1] must have set new tragedy far apart from the more naturalistic and varied speech of New Comedy.

The comic poets themselves, as we can see particularly from Menander, used classical tragedy rather as we use Shakespeare: a scene can be modelled on a tragic prototype (like the Arbitration scene in the *Epitrepontes*), a character can quote or allude to tragedy for a particular effect.[2] A slave comes out with a string of tragic quotations to make his announcement of a shammed death convincing. An old man rages in tragic tones when he believes that his mistress has seduced his son. Knemon (*Dysk.* 154) in his fury at trespassers wishes he were Perseus, because Perseus 'was winged and did not need to meet those walking on earth, and because he possessed a possession with which he could turn to stone all who bothered him'. Knemon's vagueness about Perseus' winged sandals and the Gorgon's head would tell the audience that he had seen Euripides' *Andromeda* a long time ago. Menander knew his classical tragedy in two ways: he saw a revival every year on the stage (the change from the revival of a single old tragedy to a competition in which three actors produced each an old tragedy seems to have taken place just after his death)[3] and in the Peripatetic school tragedy was used as a source of examples for ethical situations and for rhetorical technique.

Menander was a pupil of Theophrastos and must have learnt from him both literary criticism and ethics. Aristotle's[4] definition of a plot as a sequence of necessary or probable incidents from a beginning through a middle to an end and his further definition of poetic universality ('a man of a certain kind will probably or necessarily speak words or perform actions of a corresponding kind') were put into practice by Menander. Now that we have a complete play in the *Dyskolos* we can see how neat his construction is. Of course the conventions have to be accepted: the agora of Athens, the harbour, and the country are too far to be visited between scenes but near enough to be visited between acts; we must not therefore measure the distance from Phyle to Athens and ask how Getas got to Athens and came back with the cook before the end of the second act, which

---

[1] Maas, *Greek Metre* 1962, 66, 76.        [2] Cf. *S.M.*, 155 f.; *Dyskolos* 153 ff.
[3] *A.A.L.*, 115.
[4] *Poetics*, Ch. 7–9. On stage conventions see *Rylands Bulletin* 45, 1962, 235 ff.

starts while it is still comparatively early morning. The three-door stage of the Lykourgos theatre is a reality which the dramatist can use, and we must not point out either that there were never any houses on either side of the Nymphs' cave at Phyle or that the cave could never have taken a large picnic party. But granted the conventions the *Dyskolos* gives us a series of necessary or probable incidents, which arise from the meanness and bad temper of Knemon, the young Sostratos' disregard for proprieties in the pursuit of his love, the charity of Gorgias, and the arrogance of the cook. Menander adds a conception of Knemon which may well owe something to Peripatetic ethics: his bad temper and meanness are due to his perception that all men only pursue selfish gain; if all men lived like him there would be neither lawsuits nor wars. It is an impractical ideal, but still an ideal. And the premise that all men only seek selfish gain has been proved false in one instance, because Gorgias has saved him without any thought of gain. In some plays Menander advertises his ethical approach by putting the prologue in the mouth of a personification: the speech of Agnoia in the *Perikeiromene* has been described as a sermon on an Aristotelian text.[1] The text is the distinction of crimes in *Nicomachean Ethics* V, 8, and it is reasonable to suppose that Orge (Rage) and Methe (Drunkenness) delivered similar sermons in the plays named after them. For the *Dyskolos* Aristotle also provides a text: in discussing the good in the first book of the *Nicomachean Ethics* (1097b 8), Aristotle says, 'by self-sufficient we do not mean sufficient for himself alone, for the liver of a solitary life, but also for parents, children, wife, and even friends and fellow-citizens, since man by nature lives in a city'. If the audience remember this passage, they must think that Knemon's conception of self-sufficiency is too narrow; even when he is shocked out of it by his tumble and charmed out of it by Gorgias, he only widens it to include his daughter, his wife, and his stepson, and that only for a moment.

What as far as we know, Menander could not have learnt from the Peripatetics and may have derived from Sophocles rather than Euripides, is the technique of portraying a character: here the *Dyskolos* is masterly and the technique is easier to appreciate because the play is complete. The picture of Knemon as bad-tempered is given

[1] M. Tierney, *P.I.R.A.* 43, 1936, 247.

indirectly by Pan and by Pyrrhias before he appears and justifies it in his treatment of Sostratos. The daughter and Gorgias add the strain of meanness, while at the same time the Daos–Gorgias–Sostratos triangle beautifully fixes their own characteristics. The borrowing scene shows both strains in Knemon as well as awaking the antipathy of the cook and the slave Getas. The scene with Simike shows Knemon's bad temper and meanness again, but curiously produces a moment of pity in Getas (603), which foreshadows Knemon's apology. The cook is heartlessly exultant when Knemon falls into the well. Gorgias leaps to the rescue, and only then does Knemon's great speech give his full measure. He and Gorgias, like Polemon in the *Perikeiromene* and Charisios, Habrotonon, and Syriskos in the *Epitrepontes*, have the peculiar Menandrian characteristic of belying the prediction which the audience would naturally make from their masks.

How much of Menander's skilful craftsmanship was shared by his contemporaries and successors is difficult to say, when we have only Latin adaptations by which to judge them. The *Hekyra* of Apollodoros of Karystos, which seems to have been written rather after 279, is the one play in which we seem to see the Menandrian sympathy carried further and where we inevitably think of the cast in terms of Tanagra terracottas. In Diphilos the good characters are good and the bad characters are bad, so that the shading is much less subtle; but the *Rudens* with its spectacle and brilliantly interwoven themes is a most engaging comedy. Philemon's *Mostellaria* has a beautiful succession of comic scenes, in which the slave Tranio is driven from one rash position to another, and this rather than the moralizing of the *Trinummus* would seem to be the kind of comedy in which Philemon excelled.

New Comedy is not political or personal in the sense that even Middle Comedy was political and personal. There are nevertheless a number of harmless references to personalities and political events.[1] Occasionally a reference has some bite in it, and even the harmless references tell us that the comic poets were aware of the outside world. Archedikos' attack on Demosthenes' nephew Demochares seems to have been in the lifetime of Antipater and therefore before

[1] Details are given in *L.G.C.*, 102 ff.

319; this is in the old manner. The allusions to the Gynaikonomoi, sumptuary officials probably introduced by Demetrios of Phaleron, are mild. The expulsion of the philosophers after Demetrios Poliorketes had captured Athens in 307 was welcomed by a character in the *Hippeus* of the aged Alexis, who also called for libations to Antigonos, Demetrios Poliorketes, and Phila in the second edition of the *Krateuas* in 306. Stratokles, the politician who had been most responsible for the flattery of Demetrios Poliorketes, was perhaps actually brought on the stage by the comic poet Philippides, who accused him of manipulating the calendar so that Demetrios could be initiated and of turning the Parthenon into a whore-house, as a result of which the peplos, offered to Athena at the Panathenaia and on this occasion decorated with figures of Antigonos Monophthalmos and Demetrios, was split by the wind as it was carried across the agora, and the vines were destroyed by frost. Philippides had the protection of Lysimachos, the ruler of the North East, and Demetrios was involved in the Ipsos campaign. Demetrios Poliorketes recaptured Athens in 294, and a comic poet Demetrios attacked Lachares, the ally of Cassander who had been the leading spirit in the government: in this play the cook has cooked for Seleukos, Agathokles, and Lachares; his hirer threatens to strip him, as Lachares stripped the statue of Athene of her gold.

Another comic poet, Antiphanes (he may be the comic actor known from the records of 299/8), speaks of 'pouring in a double portion of wine for the holy goddess and the sweetest king'. The 'holy goddess' is Demeter, and Demetrios is almost equated with her as a god. The equation is made in the song[1] which was sung to greet Demetrios in 291 (and this was presumably Antiphanes' source). The song is of great interest because it gives us some impression of how the gay and courageous king appeared to the Athenians. He was met by 'processional choruses and *ithyphalloi* with dance and song'. The *ithyphalloi* are described in the next century by Semos of Delos as wearing masks of drunkards and long thin chitons, when they

---

[1] Ath. 253c; Powell, op. cit., 173; Diehl, op. cit., 249; Ehrenberg, *Aspects*, 179 ff. Probably to be ascribed to Hermokles if it is a paian (Ath. 697a), and Semos describes the *ithyphalloi* in his work *On Paians*. On the *ithyphalloi* see Pickard-Cambridge, *Dithyramb, etc.*[2], 137, 140 f.; E. W. Handley, *Menander; Dyskolos*.

c

escort the phallos-pole into the orchestra of the theatre and sing in their special metre (which in the song to Demetrios alternates with iambic trimeters); that ceremony was presumably part of the Greater Dionysia. Here they sing of Demetrios because he is the new Dionysos. They welcome Demeter and Demetrios: 'she has come to celebrate the mysteries of her daughter and he is cheerful, as the god should be, and beautiful and gay' (we remember Dionysos' visit to Eleusis in Philodamos' paian). 'His appearance is noble, his friends are round him, as if his friends were stars and he was the sun' (again we remember the starry form of Dionysos in Philodamos' paian). 'Hail, son of the strongest god Poseidon and Aphrodite.' (Demetrios was the son of Antigonos. Antigonos had been a sea-king and Demetrios was a sea-king, and therefore had Poseidon on his coins. He may be called the son of Aphrodite because he was successful in love or more generally because of his extraordinary charm.) 'The other gods are either far away or have no ears or do not exist or do not listen to us at all, but you we see here, not wood or stone but real.' This is a very genuine account of the despair of the times, when the normal gods had not only proved themselves ineffective but had their existence or their relevance called in question by philosophers. Then the singers pray for peace from the ravages of the Aetolian Sphinx. The Aetolians at this time were allied with both the Boeotians and Pyrrhos of Epirus against Athens, so that they were near enough to be dangerous and they had been supported by the supporters of Lachares. It is at least possible that Demetrios' son, Antigonos Gonatas, was in Athens with him now and laid the foundations of his Athenian friendships which will occupy us later.

Demetrios Poliorketes had not much longer to rule, and soon after this Ptolemy's fleet caused a revolution in Athens; Demochares and Philippides returned; Philippides was concerned in negotiations with Lysimachos and spent largely on the entertainment of the Athenians. A reflection of Demetrios Poliorketes has been seen in the vain and erotic soldier of the *Miles Gloriosus*; he is in the service of Seleucus and claims to have defeated 'the grandson of Neptune' – either Demetrios or his son; the original must date from a time when Demetrios was not in Athens, perhaps soon after Ipsos rather than now. The secret treaty between the young Antigonos and Pyrrhos is twice mentioned in comedy. In 280 Demochares took advantage of the discomfiture of Antigonos to persuade the Athenians to erect a statue to Demosthenes in the agora.[1] The statue is known in copies and gives a good idea of the grim, humourless, nervous orator. But this revolution has not left any echo in the surviving fragments of comedy, and from 280 to 270 there is nothing to note except the toast to Ptolemy Philadelphos, Arsinoe, and Homonoia in Alexis' *Hypobolimaios*, which shows the poet in extreme old age uniting Egypt with the ideal of Athenian democracy. Philemon's visit to Egypt must also have been about this time, and Poseidippos wrote an *Arsinoe*, although we cannot say what relation the title bore to Ptolemy Philadelphos' queen.[2]

Except for the rare cases of direct attacks on local politicians Attic New Comedy only contains such references to outside events as would be either recognized or passed over as irrelevant in other Greek cities. The upper-class life which was so elegantly depicted had its parallels in every Greek city, and the evidence suggests a wide spread of both comedy and tragedy over the Greek world in the Hellenistic age. Alexandria had its own tragedians and imported Attic comedy, but of the tragic Pleiad the names of Aiantiades, Homeros, and Dionysiades can be found in the Attic victor list,[3] and Sositheos the tragic poet may be related to the actor honoured in an Attic inscription.[4] We have plenty of evidence for drama all over the Greek world, but much less for what plays were produced in this period. In Athens itself, besides the competition of new tragedies and comedies (details survive of new comedies produced at the Lenaia in 290/88),[5] a competition between three old tragedies, three old satyr plays, and three old comedies is attested for the middle of the third century and probably started soon after 290.[6] In the two years recorded the old plays seem to have been produced by the competing actors, as no producer's name is recorded; the tragedies included a

[1] Plutarch, *Vit. X Orat.*, 847a. Rome, Vatican, Braccio Nuovo 62, Winter, K.I.B., 319/8, 9; Bieber, *Hell. Sc.*, 66, figs. 214–29; Lippold, *Gr. Pl.*, 302, pl. 108/2.

[2] See below, p. 124.

[3] *I.G.*, II², 2325.

[4] *I.G.*, II², 1320 (presumably he is also the actor recorded at the Lenaia in 2325).

[5] *I.G.*, II², 2319.

[6] *A.A.L.*, 115; Meritt, *Hesperia* 7, 1938, 116; the *Atlas* (old satyr play) may be that illustrated on a fourth-century Apulian vase, Bieber, *Hist.²*, fig. 43.

play by Sophocles, the satyr plays included the *Hermes* of Asty-damas, and the three comedies were by Menander, Philemon, and Diphilos. Lucian recounts the disastrous effects on the young men of Abdera in the early third century of a performance of Euripides' *Andromeda*.[1] One of the two mosaics by the Samian artist Dios-korides has been plausibly identified with the opening scene of Menander's *Synaristosai*, and the mosaic probably records a third-century performance by the Ionian-Hellespontine guild.[2] The double-sided mask, one side pale with love, the other sunburnt, worn according to Kallimachos by the Rhodian actor Agoranax[3] would have been extraordinarily suitable for Sostratos in the *Dyskolos*: Pamphilos in this play, whatever it was, must have had a similar part. The inscription[4] of a tragic actor, who was also a boxer, in Tegea, which can be dated between 276 and 219, records his victories at the City Dionysia in Athens with Euripides' *Orestes*, at the Soteria at Delphi with Euripides' *Herakles* and Archestratos' *Antaios*, at the Heraia of Argos with Euripides' *Herakles* and *Elektra* (?), and at the Naia at Dodona with the *Acheloos* of Euripides and the *Achilles* of Chairemon.

This evidence suggests that performances of new and old plays went on side by side. The actor from Tegea acted one old tragedy in Athens like the actors in the record of the mid-third-century com-petition. The contemporary statuette from the Athenian agora gives a good idea of his appearance when he played Herakles.[5] At the Soteria in Delphi he played Euripides' *Herakles* and Archestratos' *Antaios*. This is our only evidence for what plays were produced at the Soteria, and as Archestratos is unknown, it seems probable that he was a contemporary tragic poet and that one old tragedy and one new tragedy was produced by this troupe. We have records for four consecutive years, probably from 260 to 257.[6] The Soteria was founded to commemorate the defeat of the Gauls by the Aetolians

---

[1] *De Conscr. hist.*, 1. For dramatic terracottas from Abdera see my *Monuments illustrating Tragedy and Satyrplay* (= *M.T.S.*), XT 1–2.

[2] See below, p. 185.     [3] Kallimachos, *Ep.* 49 Pf. See below, p. 122.

[4] *S.I.G.*[3], 1080.     [5] *M.T.S.*, AT 13.

[6] *S.I.G.*[3], 424; *S.G.D.I.*, 2563–6; Dinsmoor, *Athenian archon list* 1939, 140; Daux, *Chronologie*, G. 21, 23–5 (dates 257/2).

in 279. In the next year the Amphiktyons passed a decree[1] giving the Artists in Athens freedom from taxation and military service, which the Amphiktyons were prepared to guarantee wherever the actors might be. This probably renewed old privileges (which had already been granted to the Athenian 'as to the Isthmian-Nemean guild)[2] and was not necessarily connected with the institution of the Soteria, although obviously it may have been coupled with an invitation to the Athenian artists to participate in the Soteria. One of the delegates named in the Amphiktyonic decree is the Athenian tragic actor Neoptolemos. His name has been restored as the first tragic actor in a fragmentary record of the Soteria, which probably precedes the four consecutive years.[3] The heading states that Pythokles, son of Aristarchos of Hermione, was priest appointed by the technitai and that the assembly of the technitai contributed the contest to the god and to the Amphiktyons. The records of the Soteria for the four years give the names and cities of the competitors and are dated by the Delphic archon, the priest, and the Hieromnemones. Pythokles is no longer priest but in the second year is one of the chorus of men. The priest in each year is Philonides, son of Aristomachos of Zakynthos. As he occurs in a Delphic document between Delphic officials, he must himself be a Delphic official and is presumably the priest of Apollo Soter for the festival. But he is also a well-known comic actor; his father was acting at Athens in 299. He himself appears in the victor lists for the Dionysia and the Lenaia, and he acted at Delos in 263. In the first year recorded at Delphi, besides being priest, he also acted in comedy with another Zakynthian and an Eleian and with a Boeotian flute-player, who performed again two years later for a comic troupe and three years later for a tragic troupe; the Eleian also appears in the Athenian comic actor lists. Philonides' troupe has no *didaskalos*; this may be simply an omission, or it may mean that Philonides only played old comedy and produced it himself. *Didaskalos* means 'trainer', but in the Athenian

---

[1] *I.G.*, II[2], 1132; *S.I.G.*, 399.

[2] *S.I.G.*[3], 460; Daux, op. cit., F 27 (probably 280/79).

[3] *S.I.G.*[3], 489; Bousquet, *B.C.H.* 83, 1959, 168. The restoration of Neoptolemos is doubtful. Pythokles in *I.G.*, IV, 682 (= Kaibel 926) is a descendant of the imperial epoch. Our Pythokles was probably priest a year earlier, *B.C.H.* 1928, 259.

records the verb 'trained' is used with the poet's name. Therefore the *didaskalos* in Delphi was probably a poet, who produced his own play; if we had the record for the tragic actor from Tegea, it would probably show Archestratos as *didaskalos*; Dionysios of Athens who appears as *didaskalos* of comedy in the second and third recorded year is probably the comic poet, who referred to Seleukos in one of his plays.[1] In the first year there are four comic troupes of three actors and three tragic troupes of three actors, each with flute-player and *didaskalos* (except for Philonides). The comic troupes share the services of seven comic choreuts; the tragic troupes perhaps use the 'chorus of men' as their chorus. The first tragic actor Oikiades of Kassandreia played at Delos in 270. The third tragic troupe led by Ouliades of Miletos played again next year with a different flute-player and *didaskalos*. The *didaskalos* of the second comic troupe, Kephisodoros of Boeotia, appears in the next year as *didaskalos* for another troupe and two years later as a comic choreut, which shows that the boundary between composing and performing is fluid. This gives the general picture: the remaining years provide several further names of comic and tragic actors who are known from the records of Athens, or Delos or both.[2]

The theatre at Delos was already built in the fourth century (although it underwent a great deal of rebuilding in the third century and later) but the records start in 284 and run to 170.[3] They record the competing *choregoi* for the Dionysia and the performers (including twice comic poets as well as comic and tragic actors) who 'gave a display for Apollo'. No obvious relationship can be seen between the numbers of *choregoi* for the Dionysia and the numbers of actors or poets who gave a display for Apollo; it rather looks as if the latter was voluntary and not obligatory. We cannot therefore say whether the plays at the Dionysia were new plays or old plays, but perhaps when new plays were produced the poet normally also gave a display for Apollo. In 280 Ameinias, Philemon, and Nikostratos are

[1] Kock iii, 493, no. 450, cf. Körte, *R.E.*, s.v. Dionysios.

[2] Conveniently listed by Dinsmoor, op. cit., 112 n. 18, although some of his cases are doubtful.

[3] Summarized in my *Griechische Bühnenaltertümer*, 41. On Nikomachos, cf. Habicht, *Ath. Mitt.* 72, 1957, 224.

presumably the comic poets known from the Athenian lists (this will be Philemon II), and in 263 the comic poet Nikomachos is called an Athenian; but these are the only dramatic poets listed here in the early third century, so that probably the normal practice at Delos was to produce old plays and the actors were the producers.

In 263 a tragic actor Theodoros performed at Delos. He gives us another cross-reference, as he is presumably the tragic actor whose name is inscribed under the statue of Tragedy on the choregic monument[1] at Thasos; under the statue of Comedy the name of Philemon is inscribed; he is presumably Philemon II, who will therefore have been actor as well as poet. The monument, which is near the temple of Dionysos, was semicircular and had statues of Dionysos, Tragedy, Comedy, Dithyramb, and Nykterinos; the last two have the names of flute-players inscribed, so that presumably the Nykterinos like the Dithyramb is a choral composition; perhaps the noun to be supplied with the adjective Nykterinos is Nomos and it was written for night rites of Dionysos. The names presumably give us the four kinds of performance at the Dionysia in Thasos. Three pieces of sculpture are preserved; an over life-size head of Dionysos with long hair (the style is post-Praxitelean), the body of Comedy in high-girt chiton and himation with heavy folds (the contrast of chiton and himation, simply shown without the complications of later transparent drapery, is not unlike the contemporary statue from Rhamnous[2] (pl. IIIa), which however is much solider and has a much less interesting pose: it was made by Chairestratos for two citizens of Rhamnous, one of whom had been a choregos for comedy). The third piece of sculpture from the Thasos monument is an astonishing mask of a blind old man (Teiresias?), which was held in the hand of Tragedy. Another semicircular base[3] in the precinct of Dionysos carried statues of Dionysos and the Muses. Here again we see the close association of Dionysos with the Muses as in the paian of Philodamos. This group also can be dated in the early third century. It is contemporary with the very fine proskenion theatre.[4]

---

[1] Thasos Museum. P. Devambez, *Mon. Piot* 38, 1941, 113; *M.T.S.*, tS 1.

[2] Athens, *N.M.* 231. Winter, *K.i.B.*, 344/1; Lippold, *Gr. Pl.*, 302, pl. 108/1; Bieber, *Hell. Sc.*, 65, fig. 516; *I.G.*, II², 3109.

[3] F. Salviat, *B.C.H.* 83, 1959, 288, 302, 324.     [4] F. Salviat, *B.C.H.* 84, 1960, 300.

Performances in Euboea[1] were regulated by a law, which can be dated between 294 and 288. The government of Chalkis sends a messenger to the technitai (possibly the Athenian guild?) to announce acting contracts at Chalkis and the other cities of Euboea. Agents are appointed to give the artists their contracts, to arrange for their pay and rations; provision is also made for judging the contests and for fining the technitai if they fail to keep their contracts. Much is obscure, but the productions certainly included cyclic choruses of men and boys as well as tragedy and comedy, and the 'didaskaloi of the tragic and comic actors' were presumably poets so that new tragedy and comedy was produced at these festivals. These official arrangements ratify earlier arrangements which cannot be dated. (The theatre at Eretria goes back to the fourth century, and was rebuilt with ramps and high stage in the third century.)[2]

The evidence of international acting suggests that plays and acting conditions must have been much alike over the Greek world. The tragic actor from Tegea acted at Athens, Argos, Delphi, Dodona; actors whom we know in Athens also competed at Alexandria, Delphi, Delos, and Thasos. The actors came from many different places between Tarentum in the West and Sinope in the East, and only one of the twenty-two Delphi troupes in the four years has three actors from the same city (Athens). The poets were equally diverse in origin: Menander was an Athenian, but Diphilos came from Sinope, Philemon from Syracuse, one Apollodoros from Gela and the other from Karystos in Euboea, Lynkeus from Samos, and Poseidippos from Kassandreia. To this evidence for international dramatic activity we can add the direct evidence of the remains of theatres and the representations of actors in many different materials. A good case can be made that the essential change from acting on a low stage in front of the *proskenion* to acting on the roof of the *proskenion* was made in the early third century B.C.[3] This set the actors in a frame but separated them from the chorus, who remained in the orchestra. In New Comedy the chorus only sang interludes, and it is possible that in

[1] *I.G.*, XII, 9, 207, with *Supplement*, p. 178.
[2] Bieber, *History*[2], 68, 118.
[3] Cf. my *Griechische Bühnenaltertümer*, 20; G. M. Sifakis, *B.I.C.S.*, 10, 1963, 31.

Athens the choruses were sung by the *ithyphalloi*.[1] In new tragedy also the chorus only sang interludes; of old tragedy one can only say that this separation would be much less embarrassing for Euripides and Sophocles than for Aeschylus, who was probably seldom revived. The evidence for the introduction of the high stage early in the third century is good for Athens, Epidauros, Sikyon, Corinth, Thasos, and Priene, and some theatres in the West.

The great change in tragic costume was the introduction of the *onkos* mask and the moulding of brows and nose to show emotion: in Athens the change can probably be dated about 330/20, and although the evidence from elsewhere is much less good than for comedy, the *onkos* mask is represented on Gnathia vases from Tarentum of the earliest third century and on the Pompeian wall-paintings of tragic actor and tragic poet, which probably copy paintings in Alexandria of the late fourth and early third century.[2] For comedy the evidence is much fuller: decent costume with the standard Early Hellenistic masks are attested outside Athens for Halai (Boeotia), Lipari, Tarentum, and Alexandria in the late fourth century, and for Corinth, Amphipolis, and Asia Minor in the early third century.[3] We shall see later that when the slave mask changes with a change of emphasis on the slave's part this change too is quickly reflected in masks all over the Greek world. Drama was international and the great comic poets of the late fourth century, particularly Menander, created social comedy, an art form which lasted with variations through the Hellenistic period into the Roman period, and shows no sign of dying today.

## Antigonos Gonatas and His Poets

The discussion of drama in its various manifestations has taken us well beyond the time of Demetrios Poliorketes and indeed the limits of this chapter. It is now time to say something of the non-dramatic

---

[1] Cf. E. W. Handley, *Menander's Dyskolos*. In the *Dyskolos* the chorus are called *Paianistai* and Semos describes the *ithyphalloi* in his work *On Paians*.

[2] *M.T.S.*, GV 8, 9; NP 33, 36.

[3] *M.N.C.*, BT 1; GV 684; ET 1, 2; CT 1; XT 1; NM 1, 2. For Lipari see L. Bernabo Brea, *Meligounis-Lipari*, II (forthcoming).

poetry and art which can be associated with Demetrios' son and successor Antigonos Gonatas. The Macedonian capital Pella[1] has suddenly become real for us through the discovery of houses with magnificent mosaics; probably they were residences of important officials rather than private houses; here we have scenes in a style reminiscent to some extent of the Alexander mosaic and quite different from the elegance of post-Praxitelean art. The Alexander mosaic is a much later copy of a great fourth-century painting; the Pella mosaics are original pebble mosaics from two houses of the late fourth or early third century B.C. The very beautiful floral borders (in the neighbouring palace of Palatitsa[2] a whole room is decorated with a floral mosaic of the same style) are like a contemporary pebble mosaic in Epidamnos,[3] which in its turn has been compared with the floral ornaments on the great Apulian vases of the last third of the fourth century. Cassander may have brought artists from Epidamnos to Pella. The connection with Tarentum and Apulia is obscure, but the figure style in the mosaic of the deer-hunt is also not unlike the figure style of Apulian vases and the source of both may lie in the Sikyonian school of the Peloponnese,[4] particularly in the work of Pausias. These freely executed florals, in which flowers of different sorts and tendrils spring from an acanthus leaf, belong to a tradition which runs parallel to the symposion decoration of ivy-sprays, vine-sprays, and garlands; both develop through Pergamene art to the garlands surrounding Roman mosaics and the floral decoration of Roman silver cups;[5] these free floral designs may be like the 'flowers' of Pausias and the 'flowers' which a second-century epigrammatist noted as surrounding a painting of Apelles.[6]

The subjects of the Pella mosaics include, from one house, Dionysos on a Panther, a pair of Centaurs, and a lion-hunt, and from the other, two men killing a deer (signed by Gnosis), Helen and

---

[1] P. M. Petsas, *Archaeology* 1958, 247; *Archaeology in Greece* 1957, 14, 1961/2, 18; *B.C.H.* 86, 1962, 809; M. Robertson, *Greek Painting*, 169. Alexander mosaic, Naples 10020; Pfuhl, *M.u.Z.*, fig. 648; Rumpf, *M.u.Z.*, pl. 48; *Ath. Mitt.* 77, 1962, 229; *A.A.L.*, pl. 12.

[2] *Archaeology in Greece* 1956, 19.     [3] Rumpf, *M.u.Z.*, 139, fig. 16.

[4] Cf. *A.A.L.*, 83.     [5] Cf. below, p. 298.

[6] C. H. Roberts, *Journal of Juristic Papyrology* 4, 1950, 215; T. B. L. Webster, ibid. 5, 1951.

Theseus, and an Amazonomachy. Dionysos is young, slim and naked, and sits on the panther's back with his right hand round its neck and a thyrsus in his left hand, which makes a diagonal in the other direction. The clean outline of his head and the treatment of his hair recalls much earlier vases by the Jena painter,[1] and the likeness may not be wholly illusory because the Jena painter has been thought to show the influence of Sikyonian *chrestographia*, which descended by another route to Pella. This is Dionysos on his Eastern journeys, a subject which we have met already in the rather earlier paian of Philodamos. For Dionysos with his satyrs and maenads Macedonia has also provided a superb illustration in a bronze krater[2] from a late fourth-century tomb just north of Salonika; the body is decorated in relief with Dionysos and Ariadne among satyrs and maenads and on the shoulder with plastic figures of Dionysos, maenads, and a reclining Papposilenos. The style is claimed as Sikyonian, and the shape and decoration again recalls Apulian vases.[3] The swirling satyrs and maenads clearly derive from Attic compositions of the late fifth century, which are echoed later in Pergamon and later again in Neo-Attic reliefs.[4] The originals belong to the time of Euripides' *Bacchae*, and it is at least possible that Archelaos already had examples in his palace and that the bronze krater was felt to echo these, just as the Pella mosaic with male and female centaur seems to have been a remote echo of a famous painting by Zeuxis.[5] The dance of satyrs and maenads is an enduring symbol of Dionysiac ecstasy, whatever that ecstasy may have meant to each succeeding generation.[6]

The lion-hunt shows the same clean style as the Dionysos mosaic, but here it is possible that Alexander's lion-hunt, when Krateros diverted a lion which was attacking him, was intended.[7] The artist

[1] E.g. Jena 390. Rumpf, *M.u.Z.*, pl. 43/4; Hahland, *Vasen um Meidias*, pl. 22c; Beazley, *A.R.V.*, 880.

[2] *Archaeology in Greece* 1961/2, 15; *B.C.H.*, 87, 1963, 802, pl. 16–20.

[3] E.g. Boston 03.804, *A.A.L.*, pl. 9.     [4] Cf. below, pp. 208, 248.

[5] Lucian, *Zeuxis* 3; Overbeck, *S.Q.*, 1663.

[6] Cf. below, pp. 166, 196. On an Orphic cosmogony of the same date and place, cf. Kapsomenos, *Gnomon* 1963, 223.

[7] Krateros dedicated a bronze group by Lysippos at Delphi with the king attacking the lion and himself coming to the king's help: Pliny, *N.H.* 34, 64; Plutarch, *Alex.* 40 (Overbeck, *S.Q.*, 1490–1). Cf. also below, p. 179.

has shown the muscles of the two male figures by inner markings, like a red-figure vase-painter, and his Krateros derives ultimately from the statues of the Tyrannicides.[1] The cloaks of the two men and the lion's body are however fully shaded. The figures stand out like figures in relief against the dark blue background, and the ground is a narrow strip of grey green in front. The mosaics from the other house have a similar convention, except that in the deer-hunt and the Theseus and Helen the front strip is rocky. The convention is perhaps not so dissimilar from the Alexander mosaic as it appears at first sight. That is, it is true, a crowded battle but the battle is accommodated on a fairly narrow shelf in front of a light background, which is as flat as the dark backgrounds of Pella. The deer-hunt signed by Gnosis is a variant of the age-old group of two warriors about a fallen warrior,[2] of which the Pella Amazonomachy is a more normal example. Gnosis has balanced the diagonal which runs from the left hunter's right elbow down the deer's body to the right hunter's left foot by another diagonal, which runs from the light rock on the left through the hound to the flying petasos of the right hunter. The right hunter largely repeats the pose of the right hunter in the lion-hunt, but Gnosis has introduced far more shading on his male bodies than the artist of the lion-hunt. The Rape of Helen is a centrifugal three-figure composition; the scheme is again traditional; it is used by the Meidias painter for the Rape of the Leukippids.[3] Theseus with Helen in his arms moves to the left towards his charioteer Phorbas, who is ready to drive off to the left; Helen holds out her hands to Deianeira, who starts away to the right. Why Deianeira is chosen is unknown. It is curious to find this Attic legend in Pella, and presumably the Amazonomachy should be interpreted as Theseus' Amazonomachy too. Perhaps they reflect the deep respect of the Macedonians for Attic culture.

This is the Pella of Cassander rather than the Pella of Demetrios

[1] The group erected 477 by Kritios and Nesiotes (Lippold, *Gr. Pl.*, pl. 34/3; Winter, *K.i.B.*, 218/1–3). Echoed in the late fifth and fourth century on vases, e.g. Hahland, *Vasen um Meidias*, pl. 6a, Boston 98.936.

[2] Cf. the early sixth-century Euphorbos plate, British Museum A 749, Pfuhl, *M.u.Z.*, fig. 117; Rumpf, *M.u.Z.*, pl. 7/4.

[3] British Museum E 224; Beazley, *A.R.V.*, 831/1; Pfuhl, *M.u.Z.*, fig. 593.

Poliorketes and Antigonos Gonatas, but the glimpse is a valuable one of the high civilization of these Macedonian nobles. In this Pella presumably the epigrammatist Poseidippos grew up, since he was in Alexandria before 280, and he provides another link between mainland Greece and Egypt.[1] Another set of pictures perhaps brings us closer to Antigonos, the frescoes of the big hall in the villa of Publius Fannius Synistor near Boscoreale.[2] Many interpretations have been given of these pictures, and both dating and locality of the originals is conjectural. Professor Robertson's remodelling of Studniczka's interpretation of the pictures on the West wall is attractive. Studniczka saw Menedemos of Eretria, Antigonos Gonatas, and Phila. Robertson sees a philosopher, perhaps Zeno, personified Macedonia, personified Persia; the seated figures are feminine and they sit on rocks; they should therefore be personifications. The identification with Persia has been challenged. Mrs Thompson says, I think rightly, that the seated woman is wearing not a tiara but a kerchief. She cannot therefore be Persia. If the kerchief is particularly worn by dancers and such dancers are associated with Dionysos, Demeter, and Kybele, Kybele may be the right choice as her patron, and Kybele's dancer may have seemed suitable at Pella to personify Hellenized Anatolia. One step further may perhaps be taken: the seated woman with her hand on her fingers is seeing a vision,[3] and the vision is connected with Macedonia and the old man, a vision perhaps of Greek culture coming to the East. The treatment of space as a narrow shelf before a plain background suggests that the original was not painted too long after the making of the Pella mosaics. The figures have the monumentality and solidity of early third-century sculpture like the Themis of Rhamnous (pl. IIIa) and the Demosthenes of Polyeuktos.[4] If we ask for a time when such a picture would have been topical in Pella, the top date would seem to be Antigonos' marriage with Phila,

---

[1] Cf. below, p. 54.

[2] Pfuhl, *M.u.Z.*, figs. 716–18; Rumpf, *M.u.Z.*, pl. 52/1; M. Robertson, *J.R.S.* 45 (1955), 58, with bibliography; D. B. Thompson, *Troy, Supplementary Monographs 3*, 52 n. 128.

[3] Cf. the picture of the tragic poet from Pompeii (? Philikos by Protogenes), below, p. 128.

[4] Cf. above, p. 15.

the sister of Antiochos I of Syria, in 276, and the bottom date the death of Zeno in 261. (The interpretation of the corresponding East wall seems to me much less certain, but Robertson's suggestion of the marriage of Alexander with the daughter of Dareios is attractive; the pictures on the North wall probably derive from originals of a different date and place.) The young Antigonos saw Zeno whenever he could and invited the philosopher to come to Pella. Zeno was too old but sent his pupil Persaios, and the poet Aratos of Soli went to Pella at the same time.

Aratos came from Soli in Cilicia. The certain dates that we have for him are his hymn to Pan after Antigonos' victory over the Gauls in 277 and his poem to Phila when Antigonos married her in 276. According to the Suda 'he heard the grammarian Menekrates of Ephesos, the Philosophers Timon and Menedemos, living in the 124th Olympiad' (284/80, the other *Lives* put him one Olympiad later), 'when Antigonos was king of Macedonia, and he lived with him and died with him, a contemporary of Antagoras of Rhodes and Alexander the Aetolian'. Menekrates of Ephesos was a didactic poet, known to Varro as a writer on agriculture and to the scholiast of Euripides' *Rhesus* 528 as a writer on astronomy: no source except the Suda mentions his connection with Aratos and it has therefore been doubted.

Timon of Phleious is tied to Aratos by the story (Diog. Laert. IX, 12, 113) that Aratos asked him how he could safely possess the poetry of Homer, and he answered that Aratos must discover old copies which had not been emended. As Timon is said (loc. cit. 110) to have testified in his iambics to his acquaintance with Ptolemy Philadelphos and Antigonos, it is a natural suggestion that when he spoke of emending Homer he was referring to the edition of Zenodotos and that he met Aratos at the court of Antigonos. Timon also described the Museum of Alexandria (Ath. 22d) as 'a bird cage of the Muses in which many book-vines, well-propped, struggle endlessly'. Here one should first remember the Just and Unjust Argument of Aristophanes' *Clouds* who were brought on in cages like fighting-cocks (Schol. 889). The scholar-poets are vines, because they are supposed to be servants of Dionysos, and vines on poles, because they are supported by Ptolemy. The quarrel may well be the early stages of the quarrel between Kallimachos and Apollonios Rhodios. It is good satire and precious evidence for knowledge of Alexandria in mainland Greece.

Timon appears as a pleasantly irreverent poet who parodies Homer to mock philosophers past and present: Athenaeus has preserved a number of other satiric hexameters: Prodikos is 'a silver-snatching season-reckoner' (406e), Plato's characters are 'the figments of one who knows plastic dolls' (503e), a friend of Menedemos is 'Dinnermad, with the eyes of a corpse and a heart unwreathed' (162f) – as well as the basic parody of the Homeric line (A 225) 'wine-heavy with eyes of a dog and heart of a deer', he alludes also to the corpselike students of the *Clouds* (and many succeeding comedies) and to the rolled (*kylistos*) garland that banqueters should wear. Epikouros is 'son of a schoolmaster, most dissolute' (588b) and 'indulges his belly than which nothing is more wanton' (279f) – again the phrase comes from Attic comedy (Epikrates, K. ii, 284/5). Zeno gives his name to an unexciting soup (158b).[1] Ariston of Chios is a parasite of Persaios, because Persaios is the companion of Antigonos (251c), Dionysios of Herakleia, who gave up the Stoic doctrine of the nonexistence of pain in his last illness, 'when ready to sink, took to drink' (281e). This brings Timon down to about 250, and his drinking bout with Lakydes (438a) is unlikely to have been before 240, but he lived to be a very old man. The style, parody of Homer laced with reminiscences of Old and New Comedy, is effective for satire (445e): 'or a heavy ox-smiter sharper than Lykourgos, who smote Dionysos' without-rhythm-drinkers and cast out their horns and wine-insatiate draughtswomen'. The 'draughtswomen' are ladles, and the ox-cleaver and the name give the reference to Lykourgos' assault on the Maenads in the *Iliad* (Z 130 ff). We do not know the context: Timon may be attacking the drunken Epicureans, but he is more likely to be mocking some pompous ascetic like Zeno. Aratos had the sense not to adapt this style to astronomy; Lykophron, Leonidas, and Euphorion were less cautious in using it for serious poetry. The one poem of Aratos which may show the influence of Timon is the scathing pseudo-epitaph on the epic poet Diotimos, *A.P.* IX, 437, 'I lament Diotimos, who sits on the rocks saying Beta

---

[1] Was this the soup with which Crates embarrassed him? Cf. *A.A.L.*, 118.

and Alpha to the boys of Gargara'. This is Timon's spirit but not Timon's style.

Of the philosophers irreverently treated by Timon, Menedemos, Zeno, Persaios, and Dionysios of Herakleia were contemporaries; Dionysios may well have been Timon's pupil but can hardly have been his teacher (the reports state both). Aratos[1] and Persaios went together to Antigonos when the king summoned Aratos; this must have been when Antigonos asked Zeno to come but he refused because of his age and sent Persaios instead: the date was probably when Antigonos consolidated his kingdom in 277/6. It follows that Zeno's acquaintance with Antigonos and with Aratos was earlier and that Antigonos had probably met Aratos in Athens before he summoned him to Pella. Menedemos, whom the Suda names with Timon, wrote the decree which the Eretrians passed in praise of Antigonos' victory over the Gauls; he seems to have gone to Pella later and died there not long after Eretria was captured by Antigonos in 270. Aratos may well have been there then, but according to Diogenes Laertius (II, 18, 10) it was in Eretria that Menedemos 'greeted Aratos, Lykophron, and the Rhodian Antagoras', and these meetings were presumably earlier than 277/6. Here again there are links with Alexandria: Menedemos served on an embassy to Ptolemy, and Lykophron went to Alexandria to catalogue the comedy manuscripts in the library. Lykophron came from the neighbouring town of Chalkis and wrote a satyr-play called *Menedemos*, in which the satyrs complained of the frugal meals provided by the philosopher. Presumably it was produced in the beautiful theatre at Eretria under the Law which regulated productions in the early third century.[2] It will, however, be better to consider this play with Alexandrian drama. As the *Alexandra* seems to have been written in Alexandria and has been credibly dated between 272 and 264, Lykophron probably left Euboea about the time that Aratos went to Pella.[3] Alexander the Aetolian,[4] who dealt with the tragedies and satyr-plays in the Alexandrian library, is mentioned as a contemporary of Aratos but is associated with Antigonos and not with

[1] The chief sources besides the Suda are the other ancient lives quoted by E. Maass, *Commentariorum in Aratum reliquiae* 1898 (1958), 77, 147, 323.

[2] Cf. above, p. 20.      [3] See below, p. 131.      [4] See below, p. 130.

Menedemos; he may therefore have gone to Alexandria rather after 276.

The third poet who visited Menedemos and is named as a contemporary of Aratos was Antagoras of Rhodes.[1] The pleasant story in Athenaeus (340e), that Antigonos found him cooking in camp and asked if Homer could have written up Agamemnon's campaigns if he had cooked conger-eels, shows that Antagoras was Antigonos' official poet but does not give a date, and Plutarch expressly refers it to the older Antigonos (*Mor.* 182F). The pretty inscription for the bridge on the Sacred Road to Eleusis (3P = *A.P.* IX, 147) may be considerably later than the bridge itself, which is dated about 320. The short poem to Eros (1P), inquiring as to his parentage since his designs for men are as often good as bad, was circulated under the name of Krantor, a member of the Academy, and must therefore have been written before Krantor's death about 275. A date in the early third century would allow of its echo in Kallimachos' *Hymn to Zeus*, which has been plausibly dated about 280;[2] this gives us another link with Alexandria, and Krantor's death was celebrated by Kallimachos' young friend, Theaitetos. The nature of Eros had been the Academy's concern since the time of the *Symposium* and *Phaedrus*,[3] and the new poem to Eros is written in that spirit: Antagoras asks whether Eros is the first of the gods born by Erebos and Night or the son of Kypris or of Gaia or of the Winds. Soon after 268 Krates, the head of the Academy, died, having recently succeeded his friend Polemon. Antagoras (2P = *A.P.* VII, 103) wrote their epitaph: ' "In this tomb godlike Krates and Polemon are hidden", say, stranger, as you pass, "men great-hearted in like-mindedness, from whose holy lips sacred words came and the pure life of wisdom adorned them for a divine eternity, obedient to unalterable tenets" '. Von der Mühll has rightly stressed the echo of the famous Thermopylae epigram in the first and last lines: 'Stranger, tell the Spartans that we lie here, obedient to their words'. The two philosophers, however, fought not for freedom but for truth, and this made them equally worthy of divine honours. The Academy worshipped the

[1] Texts in J. U. Powell, *Collectanea Alexandrina*, 120 f. On fr. 1, cf. von der Mühll, *M.H.* 19, 1962, 28.
[2] See below, p. 98. [3] Cf. *L.G.C.*, 55, for reflections in Middle Comedy.

D

Muses, and therefore their lips were holy and their words sacred; and Speusippos in his epitaph on Plato (*A.P.* XVI, 31) had given 'his godlike soul' a place among the gods. Their 'like-mindedness' was also not only personal but traditional: Eudemos dedicated an altar of Solemn Friendship in honour of Plato, and Aristotle's poem on it praises Plato's private life and his words.[1] This then is a traditional poem for two traditionalists, who regarded the *dogmata* of the school as unalterable, and the story that Antagoras abused Krates' revolutionary successor, Arkesilaos, publicly in the agora is credible.[2] If, as seems likely, Antagoras was attached to the younger Antigonos, neither Arkesilaos' attacks on the Stoics nor his flirtations with Eumenes of Pergamon would have pleased him. Whether Antagoras wrote a *Thebais* (4P) is doubtful: no fragments survive, and the story that the Boeotians heard a reading of it without applause is also told of Antimachos, whose *Thebais* is well attested. To us Antagoras appears as a pleasant and simple poet, attached to the Academy in Athens but also welcome in Eretria and Pella.

Like him Aratos moved between Athens, Eretria, and Pella, but in Athens his friend was Zeno rather than the Academy. Besides the *Phainomena* two epigrams survive, one the pseudo-epitaph on Diotimos already discussed, the other (*A.P.* XII, 129) on the beauty of the boy Philokles praised by Rhianos of Crete, who was a contemporary of Eratosthenes and therefore considerably younger than Aratos; if this epigram is really his, it must be one of his later works. The story of Timon's advice to Aratos to find old copies of Homer is naturally connected with the tradition that Aratos edited Homer. He is credited with an edition of the *Odyssey*, and one *Life*[3] adds that he is said to have gone to Syria and lived with Antiochos and was required by him to edit the *Iliad*. The visit to Antiochos I is well attested and presumably took place between 276, when Phila, the King's daughter, married Antigonos, and Antiochos' death in 262.

---

[1] Jaeger, *Aristotle*, 106.

[2] Aelian, *V.H.*, XIV, 26.

[3] Maass, 78. It is unwise to add another theory where there are so many; but it must be noted that the Boscoreale philosopher (above, p. 25) is more like Aratos than Zeno, and the picture might represent the transference of Greek poetry and scholarship in the person of Aratos to the East.

Of the rest of Aratos' life we only know that he died at Pella before Antigonos himself died in 239.

The *Phainomena* is said to have been commissioned by Antigonos, but, as Professor Kidd says in his excellent article on the poet,[1] 'it is more likely that Aratos conceived his poem in the stimulating environment of Athens'. This does not rule out Antigonos' commission, because the association of Zeno with both Antigonos and Aratos goes back before 277/6. Antigonos certainly captured Athens in 281 and there may have been other occasions when he was there. The date of the *Phainomena* is tied up with the date of Apollonios Rhodios' *Argonautika*, which seems to echo it more than once;[2] the first line is probably echoed in Theokritos' *Ptolemaios* (XVII, 1), which is dated between 278 and 270; the appreciations in the epigrams of Kallimachos (27 Pf.) and Leonidas (*A.P.* IX, 25) give no useful date; Kallimachos' praise was repeated in his *Against Praxiphanes*,[3] and this implies that Praxiphanes had attacked Aratos (the attack is in fact indicated in the clumsy Latin of the *Life of Aratus*; (*Callimachus*) *adsistens ei ab infantia propter Praxiphanem Mytilenum*[4] means, or rather translates a Greek text which meant 'defending him from the charge of lacking eloquence because of Praxiphanes'). Praxiphanes was an old man in 270 and the attack should be earlier rather than later. There seems no reason why the poem should not have been in wide circulation by 275. It would not have taken long to write, since it is largely a versification of two prose texts, the *Phainomena* of Eudoxos and the *Semeia* of Theophrastos.[5]

The success of the poem was instantaneous and enduring. Antigonos greeted it with the pun: 'you have made Eudoxos more-Eudoxos (more glorious)'. For Kallimachos subject and style were Hesiodic, the verses were 'fine' (*leptoi*), evidence of 'earnest sleeplessness'; the author was very learned and an excellent poet. The

---

[1] *A.U.M.L.A.* 15, 1961, 5 ff. Cf. also W. Ludwig, *Hermes*, 91, 1963, 425 ff.

[2] See below, p. 69.

[3] Cf. K. O. Brink, *C.Q.* 40, 1946, 13, 20, 25; Callimachos, fr. 460 Pf.; Maass, op. cit., 78, 149.

[4] On such misunderstandings, cf. S. Lundström, *Lund Årsskrift* 51, 1955, 151 f.

[5] On the complicated relationship of the existing *Semeia* to the Theophrastan original see Regenbogen, *R.E.*, s.v. Theophrastos, 1412.

commentaries began with Attalos and Hipparchos in the second century, and translations into Latin were made in the first century. Granted that a description of the constellations and of weather-signs is desirable in poetry, Aratos has done his job extremely well. In an age when books were difficult to obtain verse had the advantage of being memorable. And the stars had a peculiar fascination for Aratos' contemporaries. Their importance for sailors and farmers was of course immemorial. The scientific study of the stars and their movements became increasingly important from the time of Eudoxos in the mid-fourth century. The occasional equation of rulers with stars we have already mentioned in connection with Demetrios Poliorketes. The stars might also be recording angels of human conduct, a belief rare earlier but clearly seen in the *Epinomis* ascribed to Plato and in the prologue speech of Arcturus in Plautus' *Rudens*, translated from Diphilos' play which was produced in the last ten years of the fourth century.[1] This treacherous path leading to astrology Aratos disregarded nor did he consider an astral equation for Demetrios' son Antigonos, although thirty years later the Alexandrian astronomer Konon discovered Berenike's Lock among the stars and was duly lauded by Kallimachos. Nor had he any interest in the scientific study of the most complicated stellar movements practised by Eudoxos and his successors: in fact he refuses to discuss the movements of the planets (453 f.): 'the other intermingling Five stars, in no way like, whirl on every side of the Twelve figures. Nor looking at others could you tell where they come. For they are all vagrants, and great are the years of their revolution and greatly distant the signs of their coming together into one. Nor have I any courage for them. May I suffice to tell the circles of the unwandering stars and their signs in heaven.'

This is a transition passage from the earlier description of the constellations to the description of the Milky Way, the Tropics of Cancer and Capricorn, the Equator, and the Ecliptic. From this he passes to the rising and setting of the constellations. As the ancient commentators[2] still note agreements with Eudoxos in this later passage, Aratos' refusal to tell of the planets marks where he left out a

---

[1] Cf. Fraenkel, *C.Q.* 36, 1942, 12.
[2] Cf. Maass, op. cit., 16, 17, 19, 20, 23–4.

passage of Eudoxos' *Phainomena*. The commentators also say that the earlier description was written with the globe at rest but the description of the risings and settings with the globe turning.[1] The celestial globe was introduced into Greece by Eudoxos; modern scholars often assume that Aratos used it, but he does not mention it in his text, and the statement of the commentators would be correct if he was following a text of Eudoxos which itself started with his globe at rest and continued with the globe in motion.

The transition from the rising and setting of the constellations to the weather-signs is abrupt. The last rising is the rising of Eridanos, the River (728). 'Already too rising from the water the first curve of the River could be seen by a sailor on the clear sea, as he waits for Orion himself, in case he might give him a sign either of the measure of the night or of his sailing. For in all ways the gods tell men most things. Do you not see? When the moon appears tiny with her horns in the evening, she teaches that the month is beginning.' In this transition Aratos makes his own position clear: by stars and weather-signs the gods have told men most of the things that they need to know, and this knowledge is vital for the sailor – how vital the countless epitaphs in the Greek Anthology for sailors lost at sea show clearly. At the end of the poem (1142), when he has recounted the weather-signs given by sun, moon, stars, animals, birds, trees, fires, and lamps, he says, 'Do not despise any of these. It is good to consider sign on sign. If two agree, expectation would be more certain; with a third you would be confident . . . if you study all these year by year, your views about the heavens would not be casual.'

Thus the link between the passages from Eudoxos and Theophrastos is Aratos' purpose, to tell the sailor and the farmer the signs from which they can predict seasons and weather. In several places his poem can be compared with his prose sources, and they show, first that he is extremely faithful to his sources and secondly that he is a very skilful literary craftsman who uses metaphor, simile, assonance, and alliteration, word-pattern, and particularly variation of terms, to turn prose into poetry: very good examples are given in Professor Kidd's article.[2] A single short example: Eudoxos writes 'under the head of the Great Bear the Twins lie, in the middle the

---

[1] Maass, op. cit., 80.                    [2] Op. cit., 11 f.

Crab, and under his hind feet the Lion'. In Aratos (147 f.) this becomes: 'Under his head Twins, under middle is Crab, under hind-feet Lion shines fair'. Aratos has kept as close as possible to his source: he omits articles, he uses a poetic word (κρατί) instead of the ordinary word for head, and adds the Homeric tag 'shines fair' at the end. A glance at Nikander[1] shows how different this could have been, and this efficient craftsmanship with its rejection of difficult words must have been in Kallimachos' mind when he called Aratos' verses 'fine': it is the fineness of Early Hellenistic epigram rather than the subtlety most associated with the word in Alexandria.

'Hesiodic the song and manner' writes Kallimachos, who himself copied Hesiod when he claimed to have received the *Aitia* from the Muses on Helikon in a dream (fr. 2 Pf. and Schol.). The comparison with Hesiod is a compliment to Aratos in Kallimachos' mouth, just as it would have been (or was?) depreciatory in the mouth of Praxiphanes. Aratos himself never mentions Hesiod directly, but the echoes are clear enough to make the comparison easy and probably Aratos wished it to be made. Particularly in the Weather-signs the clipped sentences, the direct addresses to the reader, the many references to ploughman, husbandman, and goatherd recall the older poet, and both have a clear appreciation of the dangers of the sea.[2] One echo, which is not noted by the ancient commentators, is significant for the difference between the two men. Early in the Weather-signs Aratos has emphasized the small trouble and large reward of observing those stars which are sure signs of storm (765): 'for often even on a calm night a man puts his ship in shelter fearing the morning sea. Sometimes it comes on the third day, sometimes on the fifth, sometimes the disaster is there without warning. For we have not yet learnt everything from Zeus, but many things are still hidden, which Zeus will give us later if he wills. For openly he helps the race of men, from every side appearing and in every way showing signs.' Many things are hidden but the signs are there to be interpreted and with Zeus' will we shall interpret them. This is the confident voice of the man who recognizes the march of science; it is an

[1] See below, p. 193.
[2] The ancient commentators compare l. 154 with Hes., *Op.* 643 and l. 299 with Hes., *Op.* 686 (Maass, 367, 399).

echo and refutation of Hesiod (*Op.* 42): 'the gods have hidden and keep hidden from men their livelihood', from which Hesiod deduces the need for hard work and just dealing, a whole way of life, whereas Aratos restricts himself to a particular set of problems, which can be solved by careful observation of the signs provided by the gods.

The passage quoted, like the transition passage (732), states the gods' care for men. Earlier in the account of the constellations (408) we find that 'ancient Night, lamenting the troubles of men, made the Altar a great sign of a sea storm. For she hates the destruction of ships and displays different signs in different quarters, pitying men in the waves.' Night here has become the dispenser of Zeus' aid, because it is in Night that the constellations shine, and Aratos calls her 'ancient Night', because she comes very early in Hesiod's *Theogony* (123) as the child of Chaos. She is united with Zeus as a friendly goddess who gave the Greeks victory over Troy in Aeschylus' *Agamemnon* (355) and she appears occasionally in fifth-century art.[1] The religious interpretation in these passages has nothing to do with Eudoxos or Theophrastos, but is Aratos' own conception, which comes out clearest in the prologue and in the passage about the Maiden (*Parthenos*). The constellation Maiden holds an ear of corn in her hand (96 ff.). She may be the daughter of Astraios (this is a concession to Hesiod), but there is a story that she used to dwell among men and meet them face to face and they called her Dike (Justice). In that golden age there were no serious quarrels or war and the Cruel Sea was far away. In the silver age she dwelt alone on the mountains, and 'whenever she filled the hills with men, she cursed them' and told them that they were much worse than the golden age and would produce worse children, who would start wars. When the bronze race was born Dike flew off to heaven 'and settled in this place where she shines every night on men as the Maiden'. The framework and some of the details of the three ages come from Hesiod (*Op.* 197). But we have no earlier evidence than Aratos for the identification of Dike and the Maiden. In the golden age Aratos makes her behave as a Homeric or Hesiodic king dispensing justice to her people with her councillors in the agora. For the silver age Aratos perhaps remembered Arete (Excellence) dwelling on a mountain with a steep and

---

[1] Cf. S. P. Karouzou, *J.H.S.* 75, 1945, 43.

rough path up to it (*Op.* 289), but probably also Hesiod's own meeting with the Muses on Helikon (*Theog.* 24), when their first words to him were: 'Shepherds of the field, foul reproaches, mere bellies'. Presumably also Aratos had some feeling that early settlements were on the hills. The mountain on which she dwells is not defined. Many readers would know the *Parthenion oros* in Arcadia where Telephos was exposed, and the identification seems to have been made in Pergamon.[1] Eratosthenes however completely rejected Aratos and identified the Maiden of the constellation with the Attic princess Erigone.[2] This one considerable expansion in the description of constellations (the treatment of the Horse (216 f.) is much shorter; so is the story of Orion (636 f.)) must have been important in Aratos' eyes; probably he had to give so many examples of god's beneficence in giving signs that he felt the need to say something of the moral government of the Universe and so wrote his history of Dike, finally placing her in the stars where she is unattainable but remains both an eternal warning and an eternal inspiration, as well as guaranteeing the signs. The conception is certainly in harmony with the closing lines of Kleanthes' slightly later *Zeus Hymn*:[3] 'Grant that they may have judgment, trusting in which thou governest all things with Justice (Dike)'.

If this is right, Aratos by reserving his allusion to the moral government of Zeus for this digression has been able to devote the prologue entirely to Zeus' responsibility for the signs which he is going to describe in his poem. 'Let us begin from Zeus, whom we humans never leave unsaid. Full of Zeus are all roads, all the market places of men, and full are the seas and harbours. In all ways we all need Zeus. For we are his breed. In his kindness to men he gives favourable signs, and wakes the people to work, reminding them of their livelihood. He tells when the clod is best for oxen or hoe, he tells when the seasons are favourable for digging round the trees and sowing all kinds of seeds. For he himself fixed the signs in the sky, distinguishing the stars, and considered for every year the stars which might give the surest signs, that all things might grow for men surely in their seasons. Therefore men worship him first and last. Hail, father, great wonder, great blessing to men, you and the for-

[1] See below, p. 194.          [2] See below, p. 137.          [3] See below, p. 216.

mer breed. Hail, Muses, sweet ones all. I pray, as is right, to tell of the stars; make my whole song a sign.' This is a very accomplished piece of writing with its pattern of repetitions and keywords. The ancient commentators recall the prologue of Hesiod's *Erga* where he calls on the Muses to sing of Zeus. They also interpret 'Full of Zeus are all roads etc.' as meaning full of Zeus because Zeus is air, and it would be only a slight modification of this interpretation to substitute for air the Stoic notion of fire. Wilamowitz[1] anticipates when he says 'Zeus must help man everywhere'; Aratos means rather that human activity on land and sea is full of Zeus because human souls are parts of the universal fire and yet they all need Zeus. The relationship between Zeus and men is phrased in the old form 'we are his breed', which recalls the Homeric 'father of gods and men', and Zeus, like the Homeric Odysseus, is kind as a father. Then follows the announcement that Zeus made the constellations to give signs of the seasons.

Aratos' basic idea that the heavenly bodies are signs given by the gods to enable them to define the seasons is an old one. Probably Aeschylus already knew an explanation of the regular motions in terms of divine forethought when he made Prometheus claim to have taught men to distinguish the seasons by the rising and setting of the stars (*P.V.* 454). The teleological passage in Xenophon's *Memorabilia* which expressly mentions the sun and the seasons (IV, iii, 4) is ascribed to Diogenes of Apollonia, who lived in the third quarter of the fifth century.[2] The teleological conception is of course completely compatible with Zeno's account of the universe arranged by creative fire like a well-ordered constitution, in which the heavenly bodies are themselves composed of percipient and intelligent fire. The case however for supposing that Aratos was influenced in the phrasing of this prologue by his acquaintance with Zeno rests not so much on the conception itself (which we cannot trace word for word in Zeno) as in the emphasis on Zeus instead of god or the gods or the divine, the idea that all human activity is full of Zeus, and the fact that Zeno's successor Kleanthes echoed Aratos in his *Zeus Hymn*.

[1] *H.D.* II, 263.
[2] See Jaeger, *Theology of the Early Greek Philosophers*, 168 f. Cf. however, Hueffmeier, *Philologus* 107, 1963, 131.

The *Phainomena* was immediately successful. It had repercussions in Alexandria, in Pergamon, in mainland Greece, and in Italy. It had a rich following of commentaries and imitation. It probably started or at least renewed the fashion for finding stories in the stars, and the figure of the Maiden encouraged an optimistic view of divine government.

## CHAPTER II

# Philitas and the early Epigrammatists

———◆———

Theokritos, looking back about 270 to a day in Kos which marked his acceptance into the select band of pure poets, says that he did not then regard himself as a better poet than Sikelidas from Samos or Philitas (VII, 40); Lykidas congratulates him on not trying to emulate Homer. This suggests that Sikelidas, better known as Asklepiades, and Philitas were then still alive and that the battle between long and short poetry had already begun, but we cannot date the day in Kos, and we must not demand more historical realism of Theokritos than is likely to be found in a poet, particularly an ancient poet; all we can safely say is that about 270 Theokritos regarded Philitas and Asklepiades as old masters of short poetry, whom he had succeeded.

Philitas is dated back by the ancient lives to the time of Philip and Alexander, and was the educator of Ptolemy Philadelphos. This puts his birth 340/30 and shows that he was still alive about 290. Zenodotos is also said to have been his pupil. Zenodotos was born under the first Ptolemy Soter, was Librarian under Philadelphos, and educated Philadelphos' children. As he seems to have been succeeded by Apollonios of Rhodes about 260, he was presumably born early in Soter's reign, perhaps about 320. The other man who is named as a friend and acquaintance (perhaps *gnorimos* may mean pupil here) of Philitas is Hermesianax of Kolophon, who seems to have been dead by 286.[1] Kallimachos is also named as a contemporary in the *Life of*

---

[1] Pausanias 1, IX, 7. For the date of the attack on Kolophon see *C.A.H.* VII, 91. The bronze statue of Philitas mentioned by Hermesianax does not date Philitas' death; it may have been given him in his lifetime, e.g. when he was appointed tutor to Philadelphos. The notices about the librarians as tutors of the young Ptolemies are confusing: (1) Philitas, who was not librarian, was the tutor of Philadelphos (Suda), (2) Zenodotos, the pupil of Philitas and librarian, also educated the children of Ptolemy (Suda), (3) Apollonios Rhodios, librarian between Zenodotos and Eratosthenes, became teacher also of the first king (*P. Oxy.* 1241). It is generally assumed that Zenodotos taught the children of Soter; but if he did not become librarian until after the death of Demetrios of Phaleron at the beginning

*Aratos* but may have been as much as thirty years younger. It is generally assumed that Philitas died young, but the evidence is an epigram which said that he was destroyed by the Megarian fallacy and evening studies and the story that he was so thin and light that he had to weight his shoes with lead;[1] this is, surely, a comic transference of thinness of style to thinness of body. He may therefore have lived until 280 or later, and there is no reason why he should not have been alive for Theokritos' day in Kos.

His works provide no dates except in so far as we can perceive echoes in Apollonios, Theokritos, and Kallimachos. The comic hero of Straton's *Phoinikides*,[2] faced with a cook who uses Homeric words, says that he needs a book of Philitas to discover their meanings. The passage gives no useful date (even if, as I think, it originated with Philemon rather than Straton, because Philemon did not die until 263), but it shows that Philitas wrote a dictionary of difficult words. This may be the work called *ataktoi glossai*, which is quoted many times in Athenaeus: the examples he gives are mostly of ordinary words with strange local meanings – the Megarians call cups *gyalai* (467c) and the Syracusans call crumbs *kypella* (483a). Professor Turner[3] has also associated with Philitas a third-century list of compound adjectives drawn from epic and lyric poetry (including Antimachos) and in some cases used by later Hellenistic poets; they are arranged 'by rough groupings based on one or other elements of their formation or of meaning'. Both these works would obviously be useful to poets who affected a rarefied style, and may well have been the result of Philitas' 'evening studies'.

His *Demeter* was in elegiacs: the fragments show conventional

---

of Philadelphos' reign (as would seem likely from Diogenes Laertius V, 78), he must rather have taught the children of Philadelphos. They are usually assigned to Apollonios, which involves emending 'first king' to 'third king', Euergetes, but here again is the difficulty that Euergetes was born between 288 and 280 and must therefore have been grown up if Apollonios took over about 260; the solution may be that the title went with the librarianship, whether there was a prince to educate or not.

[1] Ath. 401e and 552b; 597b, l. 78 (Hermesianax) is emended to give this sense.
[2] Cf. *Studies in Later Greek Comedy*, 145; Treu, *Philologus* 102, 1958, 235.
[3] *Hibeh papyri* II, no. 172.

complaints by the goddess and conventional consolation.[1] The *Hermes* was in hexameters and told of Odysseus seducing one of the daughters of Aiolos. This is presumably a piece of mythological invention, a phenomenon to be remembered in dealing with Alexandrian poetry. The reason for the title is unknown. Odysseus (fr. 7) addresses his *thymos* as in the *Odyssey* – 'besmirched with many difficulties, you never meet with calm weather, and new pains are continually in uproar about you'. This owes something to Archilochos, but the elaboration is Hellenistic and is closely copied by Apollonios (4, 447). These two poems were presumably short epics. The other fragments ascribed to definite works come from the *Paignia* or *Epigrammata*, except for one from the *Hermeneia* and one from the *Telephos*. The fragment (fr. 17) of the *Hermeneia* (which is unintelligible as a title) describes 'a wretched dirty chiton, and about his thin waist a belt of black rushes'.[2] It may be a description of a poor fisherman (cf. fr. 20) and possibly 'he dwelt at the mouth of black-rocked Byrina' in Kos (fr. 24). It anticipates the descriptions in Kallimachos' *Hekale* and the pseudo-Theokritean *Halieis* and the poor fishermen of Hellenistic art.[3] In the *Telephos* (and the title may be merely a dedication to Philitas' father, who was called Telephos) he placed the marriage of Jason and Medeia in the house of Alkinoos, here he differs from Antimachos, who had placed the marriage in Kolchis, and agrees with Timaios, who placed it in Kerkyra; Timaios may have been his source, and Apollonios then dramatically substituted for Alkinoos' palace the secret marriage in the cave.[4] Perhaps the lines (fr. 13) 'the gods will reveal the earth some time but now only the precinct of the swift winds can be seen' describes a storm on the Argonauts' voyage. If so, the *Epigrammata* (to which this fragment is ascribed) included narrative poetry.

One of the *Epigrammata* (fr. 12) is a two-line epitaph, as also is one

[1] *P. Oxy.* 2258 adds a rare word for a bow also used by Kallimachos. (Compare also fr. 21 with Kallimachos fr. 236.) *P. Oxy.* 2260 adds the pentameter to fr. 23, '(I or he) would see also the divine hill of Eleusis': possibly also from the *Demeter*? Texts of the known fragments are found in J. U. Powell, *Collectanea Alexandrina* 1925, 90 f.; Diehl, *Anth. Lyr.*, VI, 49.

[2] The reading is unclear but the sense is certain.

[3] Cf. below, p. 168.

[4] Cf. *Schol.*, Ap. Rhod. IV, 1141, 1153.

of the *Paignia* (fr. 11). Presumably therefore *Paignia* and *Epigrammata* are alternative names for a collection of short poems, and the epitaph – without definition of person or place – belonged to this kind of verse. The riddle about the fawn's voice is symposion poetry (fr. 16): 'may the fawn speak, having lost her life, if she has avoided the blow of the sharp thorn'. The fawn's bones were used for flutes, but were supposed to be useless if the fawn had impaled itself on a thorn. The last of the *Paignia* (fr. 10) at least comes near to pastoral: 'no stupid rustic will take me, an alder, from the mountains, lifting his mattock, but one knowing the ordering of words, who has laboured much to learn the path of all stories'. The clear reminiscence of Alkman (fr. 13D 'You were not a rustic etc. but from Sardis') does not give much help. Wilamowitz[1] remarks that 'raising a mattock' is no way to fell a tree but must be a general description of the rustic. The 'alder' therefore may be corrupt and may conceal an adjective agreeing with the mattock. A woman then is speaking and a woman who prefers a learned poet to a rustic. Wilamowitz says it is Bittis. It is safer to say that Philitas puts the words in the mouth of a woman who prefers a poet to a rustic: this intermingling of statements about poetry with statements about love Philitas passes on to Kallimachos (*Ep.* 28). Philitas and Bittis are found in Hermesianax (Ath. 597b, 75 ff.) in a poem to which we shall return: 'the Koans set him in bronze under the plane-tree singing of swift Bittis'. As we shall see, it is a likely conclusion that the love-affair was a fiction but that Philitas did sing of Bittis. 'Under the plane-tree' could be combined either with 'set him in bronze' (Powell) or 'singing of swift Bittis'. The latter seems more likely, and Hermesianax (and the maker of the bronze) had in mind a line of Philitas (fr. 14) 'to sit beneath the old plane-tree'. If this is right, the line presumably comes from a poem about Bittis; as Hermesianax calls her swift, she is probably a Nymph and the poem may well have been a pastoral,[2] in which Philitas described or impersonated a shepherd or a goatherd sitting under a plane-tree and singing of Bittis.

[1] *Hell. Dicht.*, i, 115. Cazzaniga, *R.I.F.C.* 40, 1962, 238 interprets this as literary criticism: alder = Demeter = Philitas' *Demeter*, i.e. no unlearned person shall destroy my poetry.

[2] Fr. 22 has also been claimed for pastoral and certainly alludes to Komatas or Aristaios, but the sense is doubtful and we have no context.

The fragments of Philitas are scanty but sufficient to show why his successors held him in such veneration. As tutor to Ptolemy, he could set the standards for Alexandrian poetry. The short epic on a usual or an unusual story had a future, and realistic description is one of its ingredients. Short poetry also includes the fictional epitaph, the poem for the symposion, and the pastoral. These are our immediate concern, but before leaving Philitas let us note his influence on the library. Although the first impulse and the early collecting was due to Demetrios of Phaleron, Zenodotos was Philitas' pupil and worked on Homer. Kallimachos, the cataloguer, was a poet. Lykophron and Alexander the Aetolian, who were summoned to help Zenodotos, were poets. Apollonios, who succeeded Zenodotos, was a poet, and his successor, Eratosthenes, was a poet. Thus the interaction between learned poets and the library was continuous.

Hermesianax of Kolophon is a much less important figure. He was a friend of Philitas and lived to know of his statue in Kos but not to see the sack of Kolophon in 286.[1] He wrote three books of elegiacs called after his mistress, Leontion. He had predecessors for this in Mimnermos and Antimachos, and like Antimachos searched mythology for lovers. In the first book the Kyklops is in love with Galateia (fr. 1); here the source is Philoxenos. Daphnis is in love with Menalkas and Menalkas with Euhippe (fr. 2–3); these pastoral affairs are set in Euboea; and, if the date is right, the poem must be earlier than Theokritos' account of Sicilian Daphnis. The second book has the story of Arkeophon, who falls in love with Arsinoe, daughter of Nikokreon of Cyprus (fr. 4), and perhaps the story of Leukippos (fr. 5) and of Nanis, the daughter of Kroisos (fr. 6). Two of these strange stories are given a historical setting (Nikokreon and Kroisos are historical characters), and two of them are aetiological: Arsinoe was turned to stone and the Leukippos story explains a place called Kretinaion in Ephesos. Both characteristics look forward to Kallimachos' *Aitia* (and aetiology also forms a major part of Apollonios' *Argonautika*). Of the third book ninety-eight lines have been preserved by Athenaeus (597b). Here the love-affairs of poets and philosophers are catalogued: Philitas is the last poet and Aristippos the last

[1] Cf. above, p. 39. Fragments are in J. U. Powell, op. cit., 96 f.; Diehl, *Anth. Lyr.* VI.

philosopher (but the poetry may have been cut short by Athenaeus). Hesiod was in love with Eoie; Homer with Penelope; Mimnermos with Nanno; Antimachos with Lyde; Alkaios with Sappho; Anakreon also with Sappho; Sophocles with Theoris;[1] Euripides with a servant of Archelaos; Philoxenos was in love with Galateia; Philitas with Bittis. These show clearly enough that Hermesianax is not concerned with truth but with amusement; only the love-affairs of Nanno and Lyde are true and were inserted because the poems called after them are predecessors of the *Leontion*; the rest are fiction, and we need not believe in Argiope as the beloved of Orpheus or Antiope as the beloved of Mousaios or Bittis as the beloved of Philitas. Argiope and Antiope are probably inventions; Bittis was probably a character in a poem of Philitas (as suggested above), like Penelope in the *Odyssey*. Anakreon's Lesbian girl (5D) accounts for his affair with Sappho; the sources for the love-affairs of Alkaios, Sophocles, and Philoxenos were Attic comedy.[2] The reader was supposed first to be mystified by Argiope and Antiope and then diverted by the extravagance of the rest, to whom Nanno and Lyde gave an appearance of security. The poem is a warning not to take even Alexandrian learning too seriously.

Asklepiades of Samos, known also as Sikelidas by Theokritos (VII, 40) and Hedylos (Ath. 473a), is treated as an acknowledged master by both. Theokritos names him in the same breath as Philitas. Otherwise we have no certain external evidence for his date.[3] Individual epigrams have echoes in Apollonios Rhodios, Poseidippos, Theokritos, Kallimachos, Leonidas, and Mnasalkas, and this tends to make him an older rather than a younger contemporary of these poets. The only mention of the royal family by Asklepiades is in the epigram ascribed both to him and to Poseidippos (*A.P.* XVI, 68): 'This is a portrait of Kypris. Let us see whether it is not Berenika. I am in doubt to which it should be called more like.' Berenike II, the

---

[1] The text is corrupt. Theoris is likely; there is no excuse for importing Erigone (Gulick).

[2] Cf. *Gk. Art and Lit.* 700/530, 51; *Introduction to Sophocles*, 14 f.; *Studies in Later Greek Comedy*, 21.

[3] Both he and Poseidippos have been possibly identified in a Delphic inscription of 276/5, C. A. Trypanis, *C.R.* 2, 1952, 67.

wife of Euergetes, is too late; this must be Berenike I, the wife of Soter, who was born about 340, and though all allowances must be made for compliments, it must have been written at latest very early in the third century. (It is echoed by Theokritos, XVII, 36 f.)

The ascription of this and other epigrams to two alternative authors and particularly the number of epigrams in the anthology shared by Asklepiades, Hedylos, and Poseidippos, has led to the suggestion of an early anthology of epigrams by these three writers, who are run together into a single couplet in Meleager's *Garland* (45): 'both Poseidippos and Hedylos, wild-flowers of the meadow, and the anemones of Sikelidas'. This anthology has been supposed to be the *Soros* or 'Heap', which is known to have contained poems of Poseidippos.[1] The evidence is weak, but a papyrus of the mid-third century[2] contains an anthology which certainly included Poseidippos. The first poem describes the marriage of Arsinoe, and evidently introduces the anthology as a wedding gift. Lasserre argues for the marriage of Arsinoe I (not later than 281) rather than the marriage of Arsinoe II (between 278 and 274). The poems seem to be described as 'leaves and flowers from a fountain'; the imagery points in two directions, towards the symposion, at which the drinkers are garlanded with flowers, and towards the conception of this kind of poetry as something essentially pure and fine;[3] the choice of the word *krene* 'fountain', i.e. artificial, rather than *pege* 'spring', i.e. natural, is surely intentional.[4] The title of the other supposed anthology, *Soros*, means a heap of winnowed grain (as at the end of the seventh *Idyll* of Theokritos): the grain is the result of a long process of purifying labour and again suggests something pure and fine. The papyrus anthology is called *Symmeikta Epigrammata*. *Epigrammata* should, of course, mean inscriptions, whether dedications or epitaphs. Thousands survive, and good poets were often employed to write them.

[1] For evidence and literature see most recently F. Lasserre, *Rh. Mus.* 102 (1959), 326, who notes that the mss. of Theokr. *Ep.* 18 have *Soros* for the wise sayings of Epicharmos.

[2] Milne, *British Museum* no. 60, interpreted by F. Lasserre, *Rh. Mus.* 102, 1959, 222. The other names are doubtful, and even if correctly restored, there is no evidence that they refer to poets included in the anthology.

[3] Cf. on Kallimachos, *Hymn* II, 105 f., below, p. 101.

[4] Cf. R. E. Wycherley, *C.R.* 51, 1937, 1.

E

Such short poems were now being composed as literature without any intention of having them inscribed; one of Philitas' two epitaphs was called a *Paignion* and one an *Epigramma*. We need not hesitate to translate the title as *Epigrams*, but the old meaning should be remembered, as the inscribed epitaph or dedication is a reality, to which the literary epigram approximates. *Symmeikta* seems from its uses elsewhere to mean 'mixed' rather than 'blended'; it emphasizes the variety of the contents rather than the choice of each epigram to suit its neighbour.

Thus in the early third century, besides collections of shortish poems by a single author like the *Leontion* of Hermesianax (to which in form Kallimachos' *Aitia* is a successor), there were collections of mixed epigrams, partly approximating to inscribed dedications and epitaphs, and partly deriving from the symposion, which aimed at a certain purity of style. The symposion had its own traditional literature, drinking songs, in which one singer might cap the verse uttered by his predecessor, and recitations of high poetry old or new, literary discussions, variety turns. It was the party of young men attended by girl musicians, which took place in the *andron*. The *andron* had elaborate furniture, drinking services, and rugs; the walls might be decorated with wreaths and theatrical masks and hung with figured tapestry; the floor might be covered with pictorial mosaics.[1] In the *andron* of a rich house there might also be statues large or small (Lysippos made a Herakles 'to be placed on a table').[2] Perhaps we may also say that the pastoral was not as alien to this setting as it seems: vines with hanging bunches of grapes and branches of ivy with fruit were a common decoration (real vines and ivy, or painted, or in mosaic) and converted part of the room into a rustic grotto: round the great symposion tent of Philadelphos[3] was a garden roofed with branches of myrtle and laurel, and the ground was covered with flowers.

The early anthologies were literary versions of symposion poems and of inscriptional poems. Some of the poems could well (and

---

[1] Cf. *Rylands Bulletin* 45, 1962, 764. The mosaics at Pella, cf. above, p. 22, belonged to particularly splendid examples of the *andron*.

[2] Cf. de Visscher, *Herakles Epitrapezios*, 1962.

[3] Ath. 196d. Contrast Studniczka's interpretation, *das Symposion Ptolemaios II*, 1924, 71.

indeed may) have been inscribed on stone, some express perfectly the life of the symposion; others are more obviously contrived. It is not easy and perhaps it is not profitable to try and define which poems are immediate reactions to an occasion and which are artificial compositions; some very good poems are nevertheless demonstrably answers to earlier poems and in that sense contrived. Asklepiades of Samos[1] is an early master of this kind of poetry and so is usually the originator where his poems can be compared with others. Very little survives in metres other than the elegiac, but because the Asclepiad is called after him he must have written in this metre. A fragment in choliambics (Schol. E. *Hec.* 127) is possibly aetiological. An epitaph (*A.P.* XIII, 23) in catalectic iambic tetrameters and trimeters might well be an inscription.

The large number of elegiac poems may be divided into symposion poetry and inscriptional poetry, but some which formally belong to the latter class belong by content to the former. Here we are particularly concerned with poems which established a type to be followed. Preparations for the symposion, the symposion itself – the room, the participants, the course of events – and the succeeding Komos, is a sequence which can be illustrated from comedy.[2] In *A.P.* V, 181, where the lover quarrels with his slave about prices and then orders expensive perfume, Asklepiades recalls many comic passages; he varies the formula in 185 and it is taken up by Poseidippos in 183.[3] The symposion itself is taking place in XII, 135: 'Wine is the proof of love. Denying to us that he was in love, Nikagoras was convicted by his many toasts. He wept and bent his head and looked downcast and his tied wreath fell.' Nikagoras' story later took a happier turn, because Hedylos in V, 199, parodies a dedication epigram in describing how Aglaonike dedicated her sandals and breastband to Kypris after she had been put to sleep by Nikagoras;[4] this is perhaps the inspiration of Kallimachos' poem about the gifts

---

[1] Cf. the recent study by Albini, *P.P.* 81, 1961, 410.

[2] Cf. *Rylands Bulletin* 45, 1962, 268.

[3] The first words of 181/10 are repeated by Poseidippos in quite a different kind of epigram 213.

[4] The relation here is like that between the two poems about Pythias: V, 164 by Asklepiades, 213 by Poseidippos (which in one phrase echoes 181 by Asklepiades).

dedicated by the old courtesan (XIII, 24 = 38 Pf.). But the falling wreath of Nikagoras is echoed in another epigram of Kallimachos (XII, 134 = 43 Pf.): 'the roses from his wreath casting their petals were all on the floor. He is in some fierce fire. By the gods, my guess is not out of step. I am a thief and I recognize the thief's tracks.' As with Hedylos, Kallimachos has made Asklepiades more pointed and sharp: 'casting petals' is the technical term for pelting the athletic victor with flowers and contrasts the lover's sickness with the health of the athlete. The whole of such a disastrous symposion is described by Theokritos in *Idyll* XIV.

Another little collection of love epigrams which belong together perhaps starts from XII, 46, Asklepiades: 'I am not twenty-two, and I am weary of living. Erotes, why this cruelty, why inflame me? If I die, what will you do? Clearly, Erotes, you will play with knuckle-bones as before, ignorant.' The chubby child Erotes (the Cupids of Roman and the *putti* of Renaissance art) are new in Hellenistic art and sometimes they play with knucklebones;[1] a particular twist to this idea is given by Apollonios, when he makes Ganymede play knuckle-bones unsuccessfully with Eros (3, 114 ff.). The child Eros can also symbolize the love of or for a child, because Eros and the boy beloved may be indistinguishable (Asklepiades XII, 75 echoed by Poseidippos XII, 77), and Asklepiades, 'Little Eros, flown away from his mother, still easy to catch' (XII, 105, cf. 162) recalls the boy-loves trying out their wings in Theokritos' *Adoniazousai* (XV, 120 f.) or the earlier Eros snuggling up to his mother on a mould for silver ware.[2] This, however, is a digression from the Erotes who will 'ignore' Askle-piades' death. They are equally careless of Poseidippos (XII, 45): 'Yes, yes, shoot, Erotes. I am there, one target for many. Do not spare me, ignorant ones. If you defeat me, you will be famous archers in heaven, masters of a mighty quiver.'[3] Asklepiades answers

---

[1] Cf. Neutsch, *Ganymed*, 18f. The child Erotes with short wings date from the last quarter of the fourth century, *J.H.S.* 71, 1951, 228.

[2] D. B. Thompson, *Hesperia* 8, 1939, 309, fig. 17. For terracotta Erotes, cf. Charbonneaux, *Les Terres-cuites Grecques*, pl. 56.

[3] A very similar pick up of a single word in a key position links V, 186 (Posei-dippos) to V, 158 (Asklepiades). In V, 161 Hedylos has elaborated not the language but the imagery of V, 44 (Asklepiades, who took the image from Alkaios, 73 L–P).

back (XII, 166): 'This that is left of my soul, whatever it is, Erotes, let it at least have peace. Or do not shoot me with arrows but with thunderbolts and turn me finally into ashes and cinders. Yes, yes, shoot, Erotes. For stiff with misery, I want, if anything, to have this from you.' Theokritos picks this up in Simichidas' song in *Idyll* VII, 117: 'Erotes like blushing apples, shoot with your arrows lovely Philinos, shoot him for me'. But there is a remoter echo of the first line of Asklepiades' poem in an epigram of Kallimachos (XII, 73 = 41 Pf.): 'Half of my soul is still alive; half I do not know if Hades or Eros has snatched, it is gone'. This whole sequence shows very clearly how these poets responded to each other.

The unhappy lover is usually the man: and we need not fear to accept Asklepiades' unhappiness as his own, as in one poem (XII, 50), which has a clear reminiscence of Alkaios, he addresses himself. 'Drink, Asklepiades. Why these tears? What is wrong with you? You are not the only victim of cruel Kypris . . .' But once in a poem, which also recalls Alkaios,[1] he speaks in the character of a woman: 'Archeades used to cuddle me. Now, poor wretch, he does not even turn to me in fun, nor is honeyed Eros always sweet. But when he torments he is often a god even more desirable to lovers.' Theokritos' Simaitha is, of course, a large-scale development of this theme, but it is probable that Asklepiades reflects a very old symposion custom, and when men dressed up as women at the symposion, they sang of women's loves; professionally also a song on such a theme could be sung by the *magodoi*.[2]

Inscriptional poetry – epitaphs, dedications, and book-titles – also echoes from poet to poet. It is sometimes difficult to decide (and perhaps not worth trying to decide) whether a similar real occasion has produced a similar poem or whether one or both poems are purely literary and divorced from any real occasion. Thus Asklepiades' poem on a tomb by the sea (VII, 284) is closely echoed by Leonidas (283) and more remotely by Poseidippos (267); his poem

---

[1] 10 and 380 L–P; Page, *Sappho and Alcaeus*, 291. On the Asklepiades poem, cf. G. J. de Vries, *Mnemosyne* 16, 1963, 57.

[2] For the evidence, cf. A. Rumpf, *Studies presented to D. M. Robinson*, II, 84 f. The evidence runs from the mid-sixth century to the late fourth. On the *magodoi* see below, p. 127.

on a cenotaph (500) is echoed by Theaitetos (499) and Kallimachos (271 = 17 Pf., 521 = 12 Pf.). Modern taste would probably suppose the first trio to be literary contrivance and the second trio, which are very simple and give the father's name as well as the dead man's name, to be real epitaphs. If this is right (and it may not be), then real epitaphs followed certain conventional patterns (and inscriptions show that this is true). On the other hand some poems which have the form of epitaphs were certainly literary. Asklepiades has three very different examples. In V, 153 'the welcome face of Nikarete, smitten by Desires, often appearing at the upper window, was withered, dear Kypris, by the bright lightning of Kleophon's sweet glance before her door'. In form this is an epitaph for a woman struck by lightning, but the lightning (as long before in Sophocles, fr. 474 P) comes from her lover's eyes. 'Smitten by Desires' picks up the archer Eros of other epigrams. The whole is a very compressed account of a serenade. Asklepiades' epitaph on Ajax (VII, 145) is the earliest of several which follow it in the *Anthology*: 'Here I unhappy Arete sit by this tomb of Ajax with shorn locks, my heart smitten with great grief, if among the Greeks crafty Deceit has more power than I'. 'Here' and 'this tomb' perhaps implies a picture, and a picture of Virtue (*Arete*) as a mourner seated on the tomb of Ajax is a possible decoration of the *andron*. The third literary epitaph (IX, 63) is a praise of Antimachos' *Lyde*: 'I am Lydian (Lyde) in race and name, but I am nobler than all the women descended from Kodros, because of Antimachos. Who has not sung me, who has not read Lyde, the joint writing of the Muses and Antimachos?'[1] The poem starts as an epitaph for the Lydian girl, whom Antimachos made as noble as the descendants of the founders of Kolophon; then the girl becomes the book, and the poem ends with the praise of Antimachos. We have noticed allusions to Antimachos in Philitas, and Hermesianax (also of Kolophon) calls the poem 'holy'. Asklepiades simply praises the *Lyde*; he does not emphasize any particular virtue in it. It would seem therefore that the *Lyde* had not yet been challenged within the group of writers of short poems; Kallimachos' attack came later. Asklepiades' other poem on a poet takes a different form; it is a development of the book-title, a form used brilliantly

[1] Cf. M. Gabathuler, *Hellenistische Epigramme auf Dichter* 1937, 51.

later by Kallimachos; Asklepiades uses it for Erinna[1] (VII, 11): 'This is the sweet labour of Erinna, not long, for she was a girl of nineteen years, but more powerful than many others. If Hades had not come too soon, who would have had so great a name?'

The third form of inscription which recurs in these poems is the dedication. Asklepiades' poem on Lysippos' Alexander (XVI, 120): 'The bronze man with his eye on Zeus looks as if he will say: "The earth I subject to myself; You, Zeus, keep Olympos"' corresponds to Poseidippos' poem on Lysippos' Alexander, not necessarily the same statue (XVI, 119): 'The Persians are no longer blameworthy. Cattle are allowed to flee a lion.' These are a pair of literary extensions of the dedication which would be inscribed on the base of the statue.[2] So too a dedicated mask would have its inscription; Asklepiades wrote a poem on a comic mask dedicated to the Muses by a boy who had won it as a prize for writing well (VI, 308): why the mask of old Chares should cause such amusement to the children escapes us because we do not know the comedy to which Asklepiades alludes. This poem was echoed by Kallimachos, whose schoolboy dedicated a mask of Dionysos to the Muses (VI, 310 = 48 Pf.). Finally, Asklepiades can use the dedication, as he uses the epitaph (V, 153), to describe a love-affair (V, 145): 'There, garlands, remain, hung by these doors, not dropping your petals in haste. I drenched you with my tears. For rainy are lovers' eyes. But when you see him as the door opens, pour my rain on his head that his brown hair may drink my tears.' So the inscriptional epigrams lead us back to the symposion, and the symposion is the centre of Asklepiades' poetry.

Hedylos of Samos, who was possibly associated with Asklepiades in an early anthology and answered, as we have seen, at least two of his epigrams, wrote of Asklepiades in the symposion (Ath. 473a):[3] 'From dawn to night and from night again to dawn Sokles drinks from four-chous jars. Then suddenly he is gone. But by wine his play is much more honeyed than Sikelidas (Asklepiades). He is also

---

[1] See Gabathuler, op. cit., 50. On Erinna C. M. Bowra in *Greek Poetry and Life*. On the 'Book-Title' as a form see Gabathuler, 110.

[2] V, 203 (Asklepiades), 202 (Poseidippos) are another pair of dedications.

[3] Cf. Gabathuler, op. cit., 52. The list of gourmands in Ath. 344f. also clearly belongs to symposion poetry.

much stronger. And how his charm shines! So, my friend, write and drink.' Sokles is a young poet (like Theokritos on the day in Kos) who is measured against the old poet as a writer of symposion poetry. Hedylos says of himself (Ath. 473a): 'in wine I could find a new word, fine and honeyed'. The important points in these two poems are first that both are called *Epigrams* and clearly the word is used simply in the sense of short poetry, secondly that this short poetry advertises itself as symposion poetry (so Kallimachos (VII, 415 = 35 Pf.) describes himself as 'skilled in song and skilled in laughter attuned to wine'). A wry comment on the symposion, written later in Hedylos' life, is given by *A.P.* XI, 414: 'Limb-loosing Bakchos and limb-loosing Aphrodite produce a daughter, limb-loosing Gout'. Thirdly, its keywords are 'fine' (*lepton*) and 'honey-sweet', both words used of Aratos by Kallimachos (IX, 507 = 27 Pf.) and parallel in imagery to the pure water of the poem on Arsinoe's marriage which forms the introduction to the early anthology.[1] Lastly, if it is right to see in the first poem Hedylos comparing a younger contemporary Sokles with an older contemporary Asklepiades, the early dating of Asklepiades is confirmed, because Hedylos himself, who is called 'Samian or Athenian', was presumably born during the Athenian occupation of Samos, which ended in 322 B.C.[2] He was the son of Hedyle who wrote a *Skylla*, in which Glaukos was in love with Skylla, whereas in Hedylos' poem he was in love with Melikertes; Hedyle's mother was Moschine, the Attic writer of *iamboi*. He came therefore from a poetic family, which is firmly attested as Athenian. The Glaukos poem was presumably one of the new short epics on an unusual subject. Hedylos probably was not born many years before 322 as the other date for him is not earlier than the late 270's.

This date is given by the dedication for Arsinoe Zephyritis (Ath. 497d). Arsinoe was worshipped as Aphrodite of the West wind between her marriage (278/4) and her death in 270, when she was deified in her own right. Hedylos' epigram is an appeal to young drinkers to come and look 'at this *too* in the temple of Arsinoe'. The object is a golden trick-cup made by Ktesibios in the shape of a

---

[1] Cf. above, p. 45. And compare for 'fine' the 'thinness' of Philitas, above, p. 40.
[2] Ferguson, *Hell.Athens*, 20. On Hedylos, Athenaeus 297a.

dancing Bes who blew a trumpet when the wine flowed. 'This *too*' suggests that there was a set of poems on dedications in the new temple, and the appeal to the young men contrasts this poem with the appeal to the 'holy daughters of the Greeks and workers of the sea' who are invited to visit the temple by Poseidippos (Page, *G.L.P.*, no. 104); Poseidippos also wrote a poem celebrating the building of the temple by the admiral Kallikrates (Ath. 318d). Kallimachos wrote a dedication for a nautilos shell given by a girl from Smyrna to Arsinoe Zephyritis (5 Pf.). Probably all four epigrams were written about the same time for a fashionable new temple; all four circulated as literature, but they may also have been inscriptions in the temple. Three very pretty dedication poems for Kallistion also link Hedylos (Ath. 486b) with Poseidippos (*A.P.* XII, 131) and Kallimachos (*A.P.* VI, 148 = 55 Pf.): in Hedylos, having won a drinking bout with men, she dedicates a glass cup scented with myrrh (perhaps the prize for the drinking bout?) to Aphrodite, who is begged to preserve her for further lovers (the 'spoils of sweet desires' in the last line echoes 'soft booty of maiden desires' in his Nikagoras Epigram (V, 199), discussed in relation to Asklepiades). Poseidippos simply prays Aphrodite to be kind to her because she never sent a lover away from her door. In Kallimachos she dedicates a lamp with twenty wicks, brighter than the evening star, to Sarapis at Kanopos. Another heavy drinker is celebrated in a dedication poem by Hedylos (VI, 292): 'Bands, purple undergarment, Laconian robe, golden ornaments – all these Nikonoe drank up. The girl was a lovely shoot of Erotes and Graces. Therefore to the judge of the beauty contest, Priapos, she dedicates this fawn-skin and golden jug.' In form a simple dedication, the poem also tells that what she lost by drinking Nikonoe could recoup in a beauty contest. 'The shoot of Erotes' is old imagery which goes back through Ibykos to Nausikaa in the *Odyssey* (6, 157). Priapos, however rude his lower parts, has a 'femininely ogling eye' in an epigram (V, 200) which Wilamowitz[1] ascribes to Hedylos, and 'his lovely head is bound with yellow ivy' in an epigram by Theokritos (*Ep.* 3). Wilamowitz supposes that Priapos symbolizes the sexual desires of Nikonoe's lovers; but perhaps Hedylos is thinking of Alkaios' beauty contest

[1] Op. cit., I, 145.

(130 L–P), which took place in a country shrine, and Priapos is a country god who could survey the contest and therefore be called the judge. Lastly, two literary epitaphs should be mentioned. One (Ath. 176c) is on Theon, a flautist who used a single pipe: he had a son in his old age and he is called 'the charm of the mimes on the *thymele*'. (Presumably this means that he accompanied drama and implies both that 'mime' is not yet a technical term and that the distinction between *thymelikoi* and *skenikoi*, performers in the orchestra and performers on the stage, had not yet been made in Alexandria.) 'He fluted the drunken frolics of Glauke', a poetess whose works were known to one of Theokritos' rustics (*Idyll* IV, 31). The other epitaph (*A.P.* XI, 123), which is purely literary, is brilliant satire on a doctor: 'Agis neither purged Aristagoras nor touched him. He only came in, and Aristagoras was gone. Where is aconite so strong? You coffin-makers, pelt Agis with ribbons and wreaths.' Agis is to be treated as an athletic victor by the coffin-makers. It is perhaps fanciful to suggest that Hedylos remembered Medeia's treatment of Talos here (Ap. Rh. 4, 1673).

The third of the three poets who may have been associated in the early anthology called the *Soros* was Poseidippos of Pella. Many of his poems have already been mentioned in connection with Asklepiades or Hedylos. Besides the date of 281 suggested for the other early anthology *Symmeikta Epigrammata* in which he was certainly included and the date in the late 270's for the poems on Arsinoe Zephyritis, the poem on the Pharos can be dated 282/1 (Page, *G.L.P.*, no. 104a) and he was honoured in an Aetolian decree of 264/3 (*I.G.*, IX², 17). He also wrote an epigram on a woman who blew the trumpet in the first great Pompe in Alexandria (Ath. 415b); this is presumably the great procession described by Kallixenos and dated in the late 270's. He seems therefore to have been well established in Alexandria by 280 and may well have been born in the last quarter of the fourth century. Lasserre[1] has suggested that the introductory poem of the *Symmeikta Epigrammata*, describing the marriage of Arsinoe was written by him; this cannot be proved. But the image of the pure fountain water in that poem agrees well with the image of the cicada

[1] *Rh. Mus.* 102, 1959, 243. Poseidippos is perhaps also mentioned in a Delphic inscription of 276/5, C. A. Trypanis, *C.R.* 2, 1952, 67.

in *A.P.* XII, 98 (both images are part of the stock in trade of Kalli-machos): 'The cicada of the Muses, Desire tied on a thorn and wanted to put to sleep, by putting fire under its sides. But, long exercised in books, the soul cares for nothing else, blaming the cruel god.' The cicada is the pure singer and here presumably the learned singer. The poem, which is in form a literary epitaph on a cicada, is given a curious twist at the end, because the soul does not die but reviles its persecutor; here poetry is a cure for love, as Theokritos recommends (*Id.* XI, XIII). The same shape is given to another literary epitaph (Ath. 596c): 'Doricha, your bones are dust . . . but the fresh pages of Sappho survive, speaking of your name as blessed, which Naukratis will guard here as long as a Nile ship goes to the sea'. We cannot tell whether this is earlier or later than the lovely Kallimachos poem (*Ep.* 2): 'One told, Herakleitos, of your death . . . but your Nightin-gales live', which uses the same shape in all seriousness.[1] Poseidippos' poem is surely not a commissioned inscription for a cenotaph in Naukratis[2] but a literary joke (like the poetical love-affairs in Her-mesianax). The poet knew his Sappho and knew therefore that Sappho hated Doricha; the only poem of Sappho which mentions her suggests that she was not a Naukratite but a Lesbian hetaira, and it is possible that Herodotos confused her with Rhodopis;[3] whether Poseidippos knew this or not we cannot say, but he must have known that Sappho abused her. (He also mentioned Doricha in a work called in one place *Aithiopia* (Ath. 596c) and in another *Asopia* (Ath. 491c); the title has been emended to *Aisopeia* on the ground that Aesop was a fellow-slave of Rhodopis according to Herodotos (2, 134); whatever the true interpretation may be, this would seem to have been a poem on a larger scale than those we possess.)

Poseidippos also shows his knowledge of Sappho in a symposion poem (V, 134): 'Attic pitcher, pour the dewy juice of Bakchos, pour. Let our bottle party receive the dew. Let the wise swan of Zeno be

---

[1] Poseidippos' epitaph on the three-year-old boy who fell into a well may be in-scriptional (VII, 170). The epitaph on the glutton Phyromachos (Ath. 414e) is clearly literary and owes much to Comedy. The poem on the glutton Theagenes (Ath. 412e) is a parody of a statue dedication, cf. Papothomopolos, *R.P.* 36, 1962, 252.

[2] Gabathuler, loc. cit., 53.

[3] 15 L–P. Cf. *Greek Art and Literature, 700–530 B.C.*, 51.

silent and the Muse of Kleanthes. May our concern be bitter-sweet love.' 'Bitter-sweet' is Sappho's adjective for love (130 L–P). The abandonment of this poem[1] conflicts with the 'cicada' poem and with another, XII, 120: 'I am well armed, and I will fight with you, and I will not give in, though I am mortal. But do you, Eros, attack me no more. If you find me drunk, carry me off and sell me. As long as I am sober, I have Reason to fight on my side against you.' Wilamowitz sees autobiography here: the young man of Pella went to Athens and had begun to study but changed over to poetry, but this is to read too much into the poem and the chronology is doubtful.[2] Poseidippos knows his philosophical catchwords like *logismos* and he knows the names of two Stoics, what he wants from Attica is not philosophy but a wine-jug (he may remember the Attic cups of Pindar's Thrasyboulos, fr. 108B).[3]

If we cannot reconstruct the love-life of Poseidippos, we can say a little more about his attitude to poetry. A very fragmentary poem on papyrus (*P. Tebt.* I, 1902, no. 3) praises someone's writing because of the 'wisdom of the words'; 'he is like a brother to me and the friend (?) of all who know beauty'. Here again 'wisdom' (*sophie*) is one of Kallimachos' words for poetry (e.g. fr. 1, 18). The man is a poet because the verses are addressed to the Muses, and he is a contemporary. His name is lost in the first line, and all we can say is that of the obvious candidates Asklepiades, Kallimachos and Theaitetos fit the gap more easily than Hedylos or Theokritos; Asklepiades is most likely because of his association with Poseidippos in early anthologies. This poem is an extended book-title. The other poem which mentions poets is a symposion poem (XII, 168):[4] 'For Nanno and Lyde pour two and for amorous Mimnermos and for modest Antimachos. Mix the fifth for me, and the sixth, saying, Heliodoros, "for everyone

---

[1] Cf. also V, 211.

[2] Op cit., I, 148. Kleanthes and Zeno together are unlikely to have been famous much before 280; the *Lagynos* is called Attic because it was a common word in New Comedy (Ath. 499b); under Philopator (cf. Studniczka, op. cit., 15) it became very popular as a one-man jug like the *chous*.

[3] The curious poem (*A.P.* IX, 359) on the many disadvantages of life ends with the old Greek theme 'it is best not to be born', but the individual disadvantages listed seem to derive from such books as Theophrastos' *On Marriage*.

[4] See Gabathuler, loc. cit., 52 f.; Giangrande, *Rh. Mus.*, 106, 1963, 255.

who is in love". The seventh for Hesiod, and the eighth say for Homer, and the ninth for the Muses, the tenth for Memory. I will drink a cup full over the brim for Kypris and another for the Erotes; sober or drunk I am not without charm.' The text is corrupt in the last two lines, but the sense must be roughly as given: Poseidippos claims to write good serious poetry as well as good symposion poetry. The choice of poets is interesting: Mimnermos for his Nanno and Antimachos for his Lyde. This is like Hermesianax' list. Then Hesiod comes before Homer; Gabathuler rightly notes the great interest Hesiod had for the Alexandrian poets. Antimachos again here is a favoured poet, and elsewhere Poseidippos (*Schol.*, Ap. Rhod. I, 1289) followed Antimachos in saying that Herakles left the Argonauts because he was too heavy for the boat. Unfortunately nothing more than the bare fact is known, but this tells us two things: first that Poseidippos agreed with Antimachos rather than Apollonios and secondly that he, like Asklepiades, could combine a respect for Antimachos with the new ideal of fine and pure poetry.

The poem on the Pharos (Page, *G.L.P.*, 104a) is in form a dedication. 'O Lord Proteus, the saviour of the Greeks, the watcher of Pharos, Sostratos, son of Dexiphanes of Knidos, set up. For in Egypt there are no peaks and mountains as in the islands but the harbour mole stretches out low. Therefore, cutting the straight and steep sky, this tower is clear from countless miles by day. All night the sailor running with the wave will see a great fire burning from the top, and could speed even to Bull's Horn, and he would not miss Saviour Zeus, O Proteus, who sails this way.' It is a neat poem with its echo of Proteus and Saviour from the first line to the last. Strabo (XVII, 791) says that the Pharos was a white-stone tower of many storeys, 'dedicated by Sostratos of Knidos, for the safety of sailors, as the inscription says'. The text of the inscription, which is given by Lucian (*Quom. hist.* 62), gives the dedication 'to the saviour gods'. The saviour gods must be Ptolemy I and Berenike: then the Saviour Zeus at the end of Poseidippos' poem flatters the dead Ptolemy. Many of the pictures of the Pharos[1] show a male figure on the top (presumably the fire was in the torch which he seems to be holding in his

---

[1] O. Kurz, *Begram et L'Occident*, 101, figs. 359–62; R. G. Goodchild, *Antiquaries Journal* 41, 1961, 218; Harden and Toynbee, *Archaeologia* 97, 1959, 191, 206; Picard,

hand) and two Tritons below him. In the poem the fire seems to have been on the top of the tower and the Tritons are not mentioned. Presumably the poem was written before these statues were added; Picard illustrates a late silver cup showing the Pharos without a statue and a Roman relief showing it with a fire burning on the top; these must go back to Early Hellenistic originals.

Another literary inscription is the poem on Lysippos' *Kairos* (XVI, 275), which is a dialogue between the statue and the spectator. The opening words 'Where did the sculptor come from?' at least suggest that the statue did not stand in Sikyon, and Kallistratos[1] may have been guessing when he wrote 'Lysippos put it out for the Sikyonians to see'. Poseidippos must certainly have seen the statue (or a replica by the artist) since a copy so early is hardly likely. The same dialogue form is adopted by Kallimachos for his much longer poem on the statue of Delian Apollo (fr. 114), which is probably later if it was not written until the 60's.[2]

Finally a curious poem preserved on wooden tablets of the first century A.D. (Page, *G.L.P.*, no. 114): the poet appeals to the Muses to sing of his old age and to Apollo to give an oracle that he may be honoured in Macedonia, the islands, and Asia. He wishes for a statue in the market place. He is sitting in the darkness, shedding hot tears. Then with a curious twist: 'let no one shed a tear. But may I go on the mystic path to Rhadamanthys . . .' It is a curiously inconsequent poem, but as the poet calls himself Poseidippos of Pella, he probably really did write it in old age when he was living in Greece.[3] The final prayer is paralleled in Theaitetos' epitaph on Krantor (Diog. Laert. IV, 25) and in the anonymous epigram on Philikos (Page, *G.L.P.*, no. 106).

Poseidippos and Hedylos certainly overlapped with the productive period of Kallimachos and Theokritos; Asklepiades overlapped for a shorter period as it is unlikely that he was writing for many years

---

*B.C.H.* 76, 1952, 61. (The poem on the fountain, Page, *G.L.P.*, no. 105a was also associated with Poseidippos by Körte because of the likeness of its last line to the Zephyritis poem, Page, no. 104b8.)

[1] Overbeck, *S.Q.*, no. 1464.

[2] See below, p. 98. Cf. also Kallimachos, *A.P.* VI, 351 = 34 Pf.

[3] Cf. H. Lloyd-Jones, *J.H.S.* 83, 1963.

after 280. These three set the forms of the Alexandrian epigram and expressed its ideals, as fine, pure, clever, symposion poetry. This overlap makes it impossible to say how far the vocabulary and imagery used to describe this poetry is the invention of Poseidippos and Hedylos; fineness (*leptotes*) certainly goes back to Philitas. The earliest poem where the imagery of purity has been detected is the *Marriage of Arsinoe* which has been dated to 281: by this time Kallimachos was already writing and may have influenced the phraseology. The explicit establishment of this ideal may have been followed quickly by criticism of the wrong kind of poetry, the long and obscure. For this we have early evidence in the *Thalysia* of Theokritos; whether the passage (VII, 45f) should be dated to the day in Kos perhaps as early as 280 or to the time of the composition of the poem, not later than 270. There is no trace of this criticism of long poetry in Asklepiades and Poseidippos, but instead the positive statement of the Scholiast (to Kallimachos, fr. 1, 1) that they blamed Kallimachos for dryness and shortness. This disingenuous attack may have been provoked by Kallimachos' attack on Antimachos' *Lyde*; but why did Kallimachos attack the *Lyde*, which seems to have been revered by Philitas and Hermesianax as well as by Asklepiades and Poseidippos? He regarded it as long and obscure instead of short and fine. A possible reason is that as Apollonios wrote on Antimachos and based his *Argonautika* to some extent on the *Lyde*,[1] Kallimachos decided to exclude Antimachos from the roll of short and fine poets. Timon's reference to the endless struggles in the bird-cage of the Muses must refer to the early 70's and may reflect these quarrels.

The epigrams of Theokritos and Kallimachos will be discussed with their other poems. But here it may be noted that many of them fall readily under the same headings as the epigrams which have been described. Theokritos' epigrams can be divided into epitaphs and dedications, inscriptional and literary; he has left us no symposion epigrams. He has no literary book-titles but instead five poems on poets.[2] One is a literary epitaph on Hipponax, the other four are

---

[1] Cf. Wyss, *Antimachi Colophonii Reliquiae*, XIX, XLVIII. On Timon see above, p. 26. Wilamowitz, *Hell. Dicht.*, i, 147 regards *A.P.* V, 202/4 as an obscene parody of Kallimachos, *Hymn* V, 2; the epigram is attributed to 'Asklepiades or Poseidippos'.

[2] See Gabathuler, op. cit., 74 f.

inscriptions, two literary on Archilochos and Anakreon and two, because they name the dedicators, were probably commissioned for statues of Epicharmos and Peisander. The epigram (22) on Peisander is in hendekasyllables. The rest all recall metres used by the poets themselves. The Hipponax epitaph (19) is in choliambics: 'the honest man may sit on his tomb' anticipates Kallimachos' later use of the fierce poet as a peace maker.[1] The Anakreon poem (17) is in alternating iambic trimeters and hendekasyllables: the latter may allude to the Anacreontic line since the hendekasyllables can be seen as an Anacreontic with three extra syllables at the beginning: 'he was a superb lyric poet and loved young men'. For Archilochos (21) Theokritos chooses a long asynartete line (cf. Archilochos fr. 112D) followed by two iambic trimeters, a metre which Archilochos invented:[2] his iamboi were famous, he was tuneful and skilful at making elegiacs (this is probably the sense of ἔπεά τε ποιεῖν) and singing to the lyre. This is neat but very pale beside Kallimachos (fr. 380): 'the anger of a dog, the sting of a wasp, and poison on both sides of his mouth': Archilochos would naturally be more sympathetic to Kallimachos than to Theokritos. The commissioned inscription on Epicharmos (18) praises him as a provider of maxims and as the inventor of comedy (a claim without foundation but the Syracusan Theokritos could not be expected to see that). The metre is trochaic tetrameter catalectic, Reizianum, iambic trimeter, Reizianum. If the Reizianum here may be regarded as an allusion to the end of an anapaestic tetrameter catalectic, Theokritos has used or alluded to the three normal metres of Epicharmos.

This particular form, dedication of a portrait real or imaginary, Kallimachos does not use. He puts his literary allusions into other kinds of epigram. The sixty surviving epigrams can be divided into symposion poetry, epitaphs inscriptional and literary, book-titles, and dedications inscriptional and literary. Some have been discussed already; others are better related to Kallimachos' other poetry. A few may be noted here as adding something new within existent categories. Three epigrams go rather outside the normal run of symposion poems. In *Ep.* 1 Kallimachos advises Dion to listen to a story of Pittakos and marry a wife in his own class; perhaps this is nearest to

[1] Cf. below, p. 100.    [2] Cf. A. M. Dale, *C.Q.* 13, 1963, 47.

Poseidippos' philosophical poem about the difficulties of living (*A.P.* IX, 359). The second is the prayer to Dionysos for victory in poetic competition (*Ep.* 8). The third is the statement that producing drama is disastrous for friendship (*Ep.* 59). In all these Kallimachos says what he wants without any reference to wine or love. Two of the literary epitaphs (*Ep.* 21, 35) show a new shamelessness in self-advertisement: the first is an epitaph for his father and the second for himself. One of the dedications (*Ep.* 62) parodies the dedications of successful weapons,[1] and particularly a poem by Anyte (*A.P.* VI, 123) on a spear dedicated by a Cretan soldier: Kallimachos' Cretan dedicates a bow and so gives peace to the goats on Mount Kynthos. Kallimachos' light, stinging poems are the first epigrams in the modern sense of the word.

Herakleitos, the subject of Kallimachos' most moving literary epitaph (*Ep.* 2), has left a single very good epitaph on a mother of twins (*A.P.* VII, 465): 'The earth is new dug, on the faces of the stele the garlands of leaves shiver half dead. Traveller, let us read the writing and see whose smooth bones the stone says it covers: "Stranger, I am Aretemias (? Artimmias). Knidos my country. I came to the bed of Euphron. I had my share of travail. I bore twins and left one to guide my husband's old age. One I take away to remind me of my mate." ' Theaitetos, whom Kallimachos consoles for lack of success in drama by praising his purity and wisdom (*Ep.* 7), is known by several epigrams[2] – an epitaph on Krantor, the Academic philosopher who died about 275, who 'pleased men but pleased the Muses still more . . . a holy man . . . and may he live there in prosperity' (Diog. Laert. IV, 25), the epitaph on Ariston of Kyrene, who died at sea (*A.P.* VII, 499, very close to Asklepiades and Kallimachos, as we have seen), the epitaph on the eighty burned to death at a symposion in the house of Antagoras (VII, 444), and a very attractive dedication for a picture or relief in the same dialogue form as Poseidippos' epigram on Lysippos' Kairos, VI, 357: ' "May you be blest, children. What race

---

[1] Cf. the inscriptional epigram Chamoux, *B.C.H.* 82, 1958, 571, 'A shield is a fitting dedication to Enyalios, but this Nike Eupolemos says he dedicates as a fair favour for Magas the King'.

[2] Cf. Gow, *C.R.* 9, 1959, 5. Add also to the epigrams mentioned Diog. Laert. 8, 48, *A.P.* VII, 727.

F

are you? What pretty name was given you who are so fair?" "I am Nikanor, my father Euptoietos, my mother Hegeso, and I am a Macedonian by race." "And I am Phila, and this is my brother. By our parents' vow we stand here." ' The likeness of the first line to Theokritos XVII, 66, 'may you be blest, boy' probably means that it was a common Alexandrian prayer. Nikias, the doctor to whom Theokritos addressed several poems, has also left a number of epigrams – an epitaph on a cicada (VII, 200), and a prayer to a bee (IX, 564), a pair of dedication poems for spears, obviously dependent on Anyte (VI, 122, 127, cf. 123), a dedication of a 'watery' veil to Eileithyia (practically the same adjective occurs in Theokritos' distaff poem for Nikias, A.P. VI, 270 with Theok. XXVIII, 11), three pretty country dedications – a fountain (IX, 315), a Hermes (XVI, 188), and a Pan (XVI, 189) – which are written in the style and spirit of Theokritos.

The other contemporaries of Kallimachos and Theokritos who wrote occasional epigrams may be left until after they themselves have been discussed. The other great epigrammatist, Dioskorides, belongs later, to the time of Ptolemy Philopator.

## CHAPTER III

# Apollonios Rhodios

Apollonios Rhodios is not an easy author for the modern reader. He lacks the immediacy which makes Homer and the tragedians so alive. However many times the stories may have been told before, Achilles and Thetis in the *Iliad*, Odysseus and Penelope in the *Odyssey*, Agamemnon, Medeia, and Oidipous in tragedy are completely convincing as persons in a setting which is entirely devised for them. This is, of course, what Aristotle saw; Aristotle's influence on Menander is clear, but the essence of Aristotelian criticism escaped Apollonios. The *Argonautika* seems to lack the organic unity recommended by Aristotle; its climax comes suddenly in the third book and the poem ends with the arrival of the Argo at its home port; the problems which face Jason and Medeia, although they have been foreshadowed, remained unsung. Yet, if as seems likely, it was the critic in the Aristotelian tradition, Praxiphanes,[1] who gave Apollonios a refuge in Rhodes, some defence in terms of unity, perhaps the unity of a common exploit, must have been found for the *Argonautika*.

To understand Apollonios we must try to see him with the eyes of his Alexandrian contemporaries when they had accepted his work. The ancient *Lives*[2] do not tell a clear story. What seems to emerge is that Apollonios was an Alexandrian by birth and a pupil of Kallimachos, that an early unsuccessful reading of his poetry sent him to Rhodes where he became an honoured citizen and polished his

---

[1] On Praxiphanes, cf. K.O. Brink, *C.Q.* 40, 1946, 11. The most sympathetic account of Apollonios is perhaps that of J. F. Carspecken, *Y.C.S.* 13, 1952, 110 f., who sees the story as the action of a group of ordinary men engaged in heroic action and the story ends when the group action ends.

[2] Cf. C. Wendel, *Scholia*, 1 f. The chronology proposed by E. Delage, *Biographie d'Ap. Rhod.*, 1930, seems acceptable. The librarianship is given by *P. Oxy.* 1241 (*Callimachus*, II, xcvii, no. 13). A discussion of the recent scholarship by H. Herter in *Bursiansjahresbericht* 285, 1955, 222. Professor Pfeiffer warns me that in the second *Life* 'was thought worthy of the libraries' may refer to Apollonios' epic rather than to himself.

poems, that he returned to Alexandria and was so successful that he became librarian of the Mouseion and was buried with Kallimachos. The period of his librarianship is approximately fixed as 261/46. Kallimachos (like Theokritos and Aratos) was primarily associated with Ptolemy Philadelphos but lived on into the reign of Ptolemy Euergetes, who succeeded in 246 B.C.; Apollonios in the *Life* is only connected with Ptolemy Euergetes. This may mean that his Rhodian period was known to have fallen in the reign of Philadelphos. But we have no evidence for the length of the Rhodian period nor can we say that residence at Rhodes necessarily meant losing touch with Alexandria. Kallimachos' criticisms of long poetry occur in the prologue of the *Aitia* when he had lived 'no small number of decades', in the second hymn (105 ff.), which according to the ancient commentator praised Ptolemy Euergetes, and in an epigram (28) which cannot be dated. Apollonios is not mentioned in any of these poems nor by the ancient commentators on the *Aitia*, who name Kallimachos' critics. Apollonios is only mentioned in connection with the *Ibis*; ancient sources which have as much validity as the *Aitia* commentary say that Kallimachos attacked Apollonios under the guise of that dirty-feeding bird; the *Ibis* cannot be dated. There are therefore two possibilities: *either* Kallimachos' late criticisms of long poetry were directed at Apollonios and caused him to give up the librarianship and retire to Rhodes where he polished and published the *Argonautika*;[1] *or* Kallimachos' late criticisms of long poetry were primarily a vindication of his own position as a writer of short poetry (a vindication which was perhaps necessary because of Apollonios' successful return) but earlier in the *Ibis* he had attacked Apollonios directly and caused him to retire to Rhodes. The second theory seems to accommodate more readily the traditions about Apollonios himself, his early period with Kallimachos, his return to Alexandria, and his burial with Kallimachos. Whichever theory is true, we have one negative and one positive fact: Apollonios was *not* accepted as one of the early circle of Alexandrian poets who were famous in the early years of Ptolemy Philadelphos; he was nevertheless an Alexandrian poet who learnt in Alexandria and whose work was finally accepted in Alexandria.

[1] Cf. A. Lesky[2], *Gesch. der gr. Litt.*, 781 f.

After its preliminary difficulties the *Argonautika* was accepted. The few lines that are quoted from an earlier edition are minor variants and tell us nothing; Professor Hermann Fränkel[1] has convincingly dissociated them from the story of the unsuccessful first reading, and suggested that they come from an earlier private copy or copies.

Our *Argonautika* is the successful *Argonautika*, according to one theory not completed for some considerable period after 246 B.C., according to the other far advanced (if not completed) in 261. If the first theory is correct, our *Argonautika* was written long after Kallimachos' *Aitia* and Theokritos. On the second theory the question of priority arises; according to this theory the unsuccessful first reading cannot have been later than 265. Our only dates for Theokritos suggest that he was writing in Alexandria between 273 and 270.[2] The preface to the *Aitia* dates the second edition to Kallimachos' old age, but we have no evidence as to how early he started the first edition, although he is so firmly connected with Ptolemy Philadelphos that 283 is a top date. The important problems are the relation of Apollonios to the Hylas and Amykos poems of Theokritos and the relation of Apollonios to the *Aitia*.

Mr Gow[3] has argued strongly that in the thirteenth *Idyll* (Hylas) and in the second part of the twenty-second (Amykos) Theokritos took episodes from the first and second books of the *Argonautika* and rehandled them according to the principles of Kallimachos. Professor Pfeiffer[4] says that it is clear that Apollonios used the *Aitia* again and again for his own purposes, and he is not convinced that Theokritos was using Apollonios. The Amykos story is certainly an old part of the Argonaut story, so that both Theokritos and Apollonios were using a common source. The Hylas story is itself old, but it does not seem to have been brought into connection with the Argonauts before;[5] the Scholiast on Apollonios (1, 1289) notes nine versions of the Argonaut story in which Herakles was not left behind while searching for Hylas but for some other reason: they include Hesiod,

---

[1] *O.C.T.*, v–vi.     [2] A. F. Gow, *Theocritus*, xvii ff.

[3] *Theocritus*, xxii ff., 231 ff., 382 ff. On p. 591 he suggests a later dating.

[4] *Callimachus*, II, xlii, and commentary to individual fragments.

[5] Cf. Roscher, s.v. Pfeiffer argues that fr. 596 of Kallimachos does not necessarily refer to Hylas; if it refers to Hylas, it is probably a criticism of Apollonios.

Pherekydes, Antimachos, Ephoros, Herodoros, and the epigram-matist Poseidippos (one of the Telchines in *Aitia* I). The earliest refer-ences to Hylas as occurring in the Argonaut story are therefore Apollonios (1, 1207 f.) and Theokritos. It seems unlikely that Theo-kritos, who is only interested in Herakles and Hylas, would have given the story a new setting; he is more likely to have taken the new setting from Apollonios. There are five close resemblances between the two poets; the Argo is like an eagle in Theokritos (24) and like a hawk in Apollonios (2, 933); 'water for supper' is Hylas'. quest in both; in both the Nymphs are dancing; in Theokritos 'love scatters the tender wits of all of them', in Apollonios Aphrodite 'scares the wits' of the spring Nymph only; in Theokritos Herakles rushes up like a lion hearing the cry of a fawn, in Apollonios Polyphemos hastens like a wild beast hearing the bleating of sheep. These parallels are close enough to show that one poet knew the other's work, but they do not show which was the earlier. Theokritos lays his emphasis on Herakles' love for the boy, Apollonios (1, 1227 f.) has the won-derful picture of the Nymph falling in love with the boy as he shines in the moonlight.

The parallels between the two versions of the Amykos story (2, 1–97) are not so striking: they amount to six points of detail from which neither priority nor connection can be convincingly argued.[1] Here Theokritos follows what can be proved to be an earlier ver-sion, in which Kastor and Polydeukes meet Amykos by a spring; this is known from the fourth-century Ficoroni cista.[2] Apollonios alters the setting: Amykos challenges the Argonauts as soon as they disembark. The Amykos story cannot therefore be used for dating Apollonios. The fact that Theokritos quite unnecessarily sets the Hylas story in the Argonaut story suggests that Apollonios had already made this innovation, and therefore that at least an early version of this part of the *Argonautika* was known by 270.[3]

Professor Pfeiffer is convinced that Apollonios used the *Aitia* and

---

[1] Theokr. 22, 27 with Ap. 2, 231; 33 with 1, 1184; 44 with 2, 4; 65 with 2, 14; 94 with 2, 38; 104 with 2, 107. Cf. H. Fränkel, *T.A.P.A.* 83, 1952, 25 ff.

[2] Pfuhl, fig. 628; Beazley, *E.V.P.*, 5, 57; Bieber, *H. Sc.*, fig. 718. Cf. below, p. 252.

[3] Wilamowitz, *Hell. Dicht.*, II, 184, accepts two very doubtful echoes of Apol-lonios in *Idyll* VII of Theokritos.

*Hekale* of Kallimachos, and this case has to be examined. It is natural to take first the poems about the Argonauts. The iambic fragment (198) about the hydrophoria in Aegina only shows that Apollonios (4, 1765) and Kallimachos both knew this rite. The *Aition* of Theiodamas (fr. 24) is told at length; Apollonios (1, 1220) cuts it short; there is no point of contact except subject matter and no reason to suppose that Kallimachos put the death of Hylas in the Argonaut story. The *Aition* of the anchor stone at Kyzikos (fr. 108–9) also shows contact of subject matter; Kallimachos names the harbour Panormos but Apollonios (1, 953) leaves it nameless. The *Aition* of the ritual jokes at Anaphe (fr. 7–21; 716) is much more important; it is told by Apollonios late in the fourth book (4, 1694–1730). Kallimachos starts the story with the return of the Argonauts from 'Aietes the Cytaean' (the same formula is used by Apollonios, 2, 1094); he saw what his daughter (Medeia) had done and sent his men in pursuit as in Apollonios (4, 212 ff.); but Apsyrtos was killed in the palace (fr. 8) instead of much later as in Apollonios; the Argo went home by the route by which she had come (fr. 9) and not by the much more complicated route provided by Apollonios; the Kolchians divide in Illyria (fr. 11) as in Apollonios; the chase continues to Phaeacian Corcyra (fr. 12). Both poets tell of the later Corinthian foundation of Corcyra: Kallimachos ends with a line 'this was going to be completed long afterwards', which Apollonios uses in a different context of the future fate of the Boreads (1, 1309). Drepane in Corcyra according to Kallimachos is apparently the sickle of Demeter (fr. 14); Apollonios notes both this explanation and the other that Drepane is the sickle of Kronos (4, 984); both explanations can be traced earlier than the Alexandrian poets. Then the mist falls on the ship (fr. 18), and first the Dioskouroi pray for help, then Jason prays to Apollo, promising gifts to Pytho and Ortygia and reminding Apollo that his oracle had caused the voyage and that the Argonauts had honoured Apollo as Embasios, god of embarkation. In Apollonios (4, 1701) only Jason prays, and he promises gifts to Pytho, Amyklai, and Ortygia but says nothing of the oracle; his promises are partly a verbal repetition of his promises to Apollo at the altar of Apollo Embasios at the beginning of the voyage, when also he reminded Apollo of the oracle (1, 411). Both poets land Apollo on the Melanteian rocks; then the next morning the Argonauts sacrifice to Apollo Aigletes and name the island Anaphe; the Phaeacian maid-servants of Medeia laugh at their poor offerings and the men chide them, thus founding the present-day rite. The two accounts are undoubtedly close. Professor Pfeiffer maintains that Apollonios had read the *Aitia* and used Kallimachos' poem not only for the Anaphe story in his fourth book but also in his first book for Jason's earlier promises to Apollo, for Jason's reference to the oracle and for the single line ending the story of the Boreads. Dr Haendel[1] argues that Apollonios shows his virtuosity as a follower who is yet independent by replacing Kallimachos' line by another in the Anaphe story and using Kallimachos' line elsewhere. This seems a great deal of trouble to take over a very undistinguished line, which might well occur to both poets independently. It would however be much easier to sup-pose that Kallimachos knew Apollonios' first two books, perhaps in their earliest form, and used them freely to expand Jason's prayer in the Anaphe story. We have seen that Theokritos also seems to have known the first two books. The three divergences from Apollonios – the death of Apsyrtos (which Apollonios puts late to make a further trial for Medeia), the Argo's route home, and the explanation of Drepane – all come in Apollonios' fourth book; this may actually have been written later than the Kallimachos poem, or Kallimachos may here have intentionally followed a more canonical version. On the final part of the story, the marriage in Corcyra, the mist, the Melanteian rocks, the sacrifice and the badinage the two poets are in complete agreement. In assessing this we must remember not only that Kallimachos was the poet of the *Aitia*, but that Apollonios also was passionately interested in aetiology. Nothing prevents our sup-posing that they both worked on aetiology in the library before Apollonios' withdrawal. There are over thirty historical explana-tions of present names or practices in the *Argonautika* and only four of these are known to have been treated also by Kallimachos. Apol-lonios presumably worked out the aetiology for his Argonaut story in Alexandria, and it seems at least possible that Kallimachos bor-rowed from his first version.

[1] P. Haendel, *Beobachtungen Zur Epischen Technik des Apollonios Rhodios*, Munich 1954.

Most of the aetiology of the *Argonautika* is relevant, in the sense that something which happened on the voyage is said to be the cause of something which still happens. But when the Argonauts are delayed with Phineus by the Etesian winds (2, 498 ff.), Apollonios tells us at length that Kyrene was the mother of Aristaios, who ultimately settled in Keos and made an altar of Zeus Ikmaios and sacrificed in the mountains to Seirios and Zeus son of Kronos; therefore the Etesian winds blow for forty days and in Keos the priests still make sacrifices before the rising of the Dog Star. In Kallimachos' *Akontios and Kydippe* (fr. 75, 32) Apollo commends Akontios to his father-in-law by saying that he is descended 'from the priests of Aristaios Zeus Ikmios, whose care it is on the mountains to soothe bitter Maira when she rises and to beg the wind from Zeus'. The facts are the same but the names are changed: Ikmios instead of Ikmaios, Maira instead of Seirios, and Aristaios has become a title of Zeus. Kallimachos quotes the fifth-century Kean writer, Xenomedes; and he may also have been Apollonios' source. Even here, when the irrelevance makes Apollonios' dependence more likely, the variations suggest that he does not depend on Kallimachos but perhaps on Kallimachos' source.

The other reminiscences of Kallimachos which have been noted consist of single words or pairs of words, and in most cases it is very doubtful whether, if in fact there is borrowing, we can say which way the borrowing goes.[1] Two passages in the *Hekale* are, however, worth considering. Aratos' *Phainomena* was known early in Alexandria (probably well before 270), and it seems very likely that Apollonios remembered his ὑψόθεν ἐμπλήξῃ δεινὴ ἀνέμοιο θύελλα (423) when he wrote in a simile (1, 1203) ὑψόθεν ἐμπλήξασα θοὴ ἀνέμοιο καταΐξ. Kallimachos ends a line in the *Hekale* (fr. 238, 29) θοὴ βορέαο καταΐξ εἰσέπεσεν, and thus provides the last and most elegant development of the phrase made by Aratos. If Apollonios' priority is established here, other parallels in the *Hekale*, if valid at all, are likely to be reminiscences of Apollonios.[2]

A single rare word has been claimed as evidence for the priority of

---

[1] Cf. Pfeiffer on fr. 40; 43; 52; 75, 25; 80, 10–11; 103; 384, 5; 470b; 602; 676.
[2] On Aratos, Wilamowitz, *Hell. Dicht.*, II, 183. On the *Hekale*, cf. Pfeiffer on fr. 238, 9; 260, 27, 50; 292; 301, and *J.H.S.* 75, 1955, 71.

Kallimachos in a passage of the *Hekale*, where morning is not indicated by a simple dawn formula but by a description (fr. 260, 63 ff.): 'Soon came frosty dawn, when the hands of the robbers cease to prey; for the morning lamps already shine, and the drawer of water sings his song, and the man who lives by the roadside is wakened by the creaking waggon-axle, and the metal-working slaves within torment the ear.' Apollonios (4, 109 f.) uses the same rare word *anchauros* as an adjective of the night in a similar passage, where he describes the hunters going out before first light. Both found a rare Cyprian word; Apollonios used it as an adjective and Kallimachos used it as a noun. We cannot say that either copied the other.

Both passages belong to the general class of elaborate descriptions[1] substituted for simpler indications of time. Homer had shown the way in the *Iliad* (11, 86): 'when the woodcutter prepares his meal . . .', the Greeks broke through the Trojans; *Odyssey*, 12, 439, 'when a man gets up to his meal from the agora, deciding many quarrels for men who seek decisions', then the planks appeared from Charybdis. Between Homer and the Hellenistic poets Hesiod (*Op.* 581) described dawn as the time for beginning agricultural work, and the chorus of Euripides' *Phaethon* speak of the birds, the herdsman, the horses, the hunters, and the sailors, who put to sea at dawn. The two Hellenistic poets develop the rare Homeric practice under the influence of later and fuller poetic description of activities at different times of day.

Apollonios in these descriptions sometimes emphasizes the effect of light: even in (4, 109) 'the white rays of dawn smite the path'; so also (1, 519) 'when gleaming dawn beheld with bright eyes the high peaks of Pelion and the shores were clear, washed by the wind-driven sea'; (1, 1280) 'when bright-faced dawn shines from heaven, rising from the East, and the paths are bright and the dewy plains shine with a clear glow'; (2, 164) 'when the sun rising from the East lit up the dewy hills'; (3, 1223) 'dawn rising cast its light above the snowy Kaukasos'; (4, 1170) 'Dawn coming up with her divine eyes began to dissolve black night through the sky, and the shores of the island smiled and the dewy paths of the plains from afar'. The eyes of dawn

[1] Cf. also Kallimachos, fr. 21, 3; 177, 5; 238, 15, 20; Ap. Rhod. 1, 1172; 2, 165; 3, 744, 1340; 4, 109, 1312, 1629, and the passages discussed in the text.

give rather than receive light; hills, shores, and roads reflect the light. In the evening (1, 450) 'the fields are new-shadowed beneath the peaks'. This suggests that Apollonios saw like a painter, and we shall have later to consider whether other descriptions provide further evidence: we have already noticed the boy Hylas shining in the light of the full moon (1, 1231).

The Hellenistic audience must have enjoyed aetiology, and they had a learned interest in mythology even where it did not explain a present usage. Apollonios sometimes says that he knows earlier accounts;[1] more often he gives the story, and from our point of view it is a digression from the straight line of the Argo's voyage; such are the story of Dipsakos (2, 652), of Herakles and the girdle (2, 774 ff.), of Prometheus' eagle (2, 1248), of Boutes and Eryx (4, 917). But the Hellenistic audience presumably enjoyed the digressions.

Another kind of knowledge which the Hellenistic audience expected from its poets may be broadly termed scientific. Aratos versified the astronomy of Eudoxos, and we have noted the occasional reference to him by Apollonios. Wilamowitz[2] records the passages where Aratos shows his knowledge of Empedokles; Orpheus' song in Apollonios (1, 496 f.) starts with an Empedoklean cosmogony, and the beast-men of Kirke are compared with primeval monsters which also sound Empedoklean (4, 677). The curious geography of the Argo's return voyage (4, 259 f.) is based on a recent scientific writer called Timagetos; but Apollonios allows Jason to acquire the necessary knowledge from a Kolchian called Argos, who knew a map left by the Egyptians when they colonized Kolchis: we know the story of Sesostris' world conquests and his inscriptions (the origin of Apollonios' map) from Herodotos (II, 102 f.), but Apollonios may have had a source nearer both in time and place. More obviously connected with modern Alexandrian geography are the descriptions of the Thermodon (2, 972) and the Rhone (4, 627) and the descriptions of people like the Mossynoikoi (2, 379, 1015) and the Chalybes (2, 1001). There is a touch of imaginative insight in the story of the shepherds who retreated to the hills because they thought the ships were sea-monsters (4, 316), an insight which some of the Pergamene sculptors of Gauls also possessed.

[1] E.g. 1, 59; 2, 904; 4, 984, 1381.     [2] *Hell. Dicht.*, II, 265.

Alexandrian medical observation and discovery has also left its mark: Professor Solmsen[1] has recently pointed out that when Apollonios describes the pain of Medeia's love as 'about the fine nerves and right up to the lowest part of the brain' (3, 762) he is alluding to the discovery of Herophilos and Erasistratos that the nerves originated in the brain. At a lower level Apollonios' description of the starving Phineus (2, 197 ff.) is a medical description: 'standing up from his bed, like a harmless dream, leaning on his stick he went out on crooked feet, feeling the walls; and as he went his joints trembled with weakness and age. His flesh was shrivelled and dry and squalid; only the skin held the bones together. When he came out of the hall, his knees were so heavy that he sat down on the threshold of the courtyard. A purple torpor enveloped him; he felt the earth come up from below and swim round; he lay dumb in a strengthless swoon . . . Then with great difficulty drawing his breath from the depth of his chest he prophesied to them.' The account of snake-bites (4, 1505 ff.) shows the same kind of interest.

This survey of Apollonios as a learned poet has shown three elements of more general interest – his feeling for effects of light, his insight into the emotional reaction of the primitive shepherds, and his power of accurate description. If we look for these qualities in his similes we are led immediately into another question: how does he compare with Homer when it is fair to compare him with Homer? Like Homer, Apollonios uses a large number of short comparisons and a large number of long similes. He clearly imitated the earlier poet, and in particular he liked those similes where a whole situation in the modern world illustrates a whole situation in the ancient world. The range of comparisons is much the same: wind, weather, sea, torrents, trees and plants, lights, animals, insects, birds, snakes, and a number of unique comparisons among which craftsmen of various kinds are common. The range of application differs from Homer partly because Apollonios has far less fighting than the *Iliad*, partly because he has more miraculous events to describe, partly and most interestingly, because he is more interested in psychology. His similes may be classified as close to Homer, conceivable for Homer, new in application, new in subject matter.

[1] *Mus. Helv.* 18, 1961, 195.

It would be tedious to list all the similes which are close to Homer. The Minyans fight like wolves (2, 123); they fall on the Doliones like hawks on doves (1, 1049); Jason proposing to fight the earth-born is like a boar (3, 1351): Jason, like Paris, is compared to a war-horse (3, 1259, cf. *Iliad* 6, 506). In the *Odyssey* (6, 100) Nausikaa and her girls playing ball on the sea shore are compared to Artemis and her nymphs hunting; Apollonios borrows and greatly elaborates the comparison for Medeia and her girls going out to meet Jason (3, 876). He thinks again of the girls playing ball when he wants a parallel for the Nereids throwing the Argo from hand to hand (4, 948), and perhaps the same passage was in his mind when he compared the oarsmen keeping time to Orpheus' lyre with a chorus of young men dancing to the lyre in honour of Apollo (1, 536).

Many of the other similes could easily have been Homeric: Jason withstanding the bulls like a rock withstanding the sea (3, 1293, cf. *Iliad* 15, 618), the Boreads pursuing the Harpies like hounds pur-suing a hare (2, 278, cf. *Iliad* 15, 579), the Lemnian women crowding round the Argonauts like bees buzzing round flowers (1, 879, cf. *Iliad* 2, 87). Apollonios' craft similes are used in the same way as the simile of the drill in the ninth book of the *Odyssey* (384) – to explain one physical process or event by another which is better known: the dead giants are like ships' timbers laid in rows by the shore so that they may become soft enough to receive wedges (1, 1003); the noise of the blows on the cheeks of Amykos and Polydeukes in the boxing match was like the noise of joiners hammering wedges into ships' timbers (2, 79); the roof of shields put over the Argo to keep off the Stymphalian birds was like a roof of close-fitting tiles along the walls of a house (2, 1073); the fire-breathing bulls are like the roaring fire which leaps intermittently from a furnace as the smith's bellows blow or cease to blow (3, 1299). The principle is the same but the comparisons and applications are new. Apollonios in the much more complicated and sophisticated society of the Hellenistic age still has an unspoilt eye for craftsmanship and in this shows his kinship with the Alexandrian scientist.

Sometimes Apollonios applies Homeric comparisons to different subject matter. It would be interesting to know whether he expected his audience to remember the original and therefore often to make the further comparison that private emotion can be as destructive as war. Jason comes to Medeia as beautiful and as devastating as Seirios (3, 957); so Achilles in his shining armour appears to Priam before his last battle with Hektor (*Iliad* 22, 26). Medeia and Jason stand silent like oaks or pines on a calm day; then the wind stirs the trees to move endlessly; so they too were going to speak long beneath the breezes of Eros (3, 967). Perhaps he remembered the Homeric comparison (*Iliad* 14, 398): 'nor does wind cry so loud about the lofty foliage of the oaks, the wind which roars very loud in its anger, as was the voice of the Greeks and Trojans shouting terribly as they rushed upon each other'. If one remembers the Homeric passage, one must think the lovers are very different from the soldiers but their conversation too is destructive as well as passionate. Homer uses the poor woman weighing wool as a comparison to explain both the quivering balance of the engaged armies and the desperate urgency of the battle (*Iliad* 12, 433). In Apollonios the poor wool worker appears twice: first, the blaze which she lights in the morning so as to be able to work before dawn is compared to the disastrous blaze of love in Medeia's heart (3, 291). Later, Medeia's sleepless misery after her appeal to Arete in Corcyra is compared to the misery of a widow spinning at night with her children crying around her. Homer does not often use similes to explain emotions, and when Medeia's heart warms and melts like the dew on the roses in the dawn light (3, 1019), the audience surely is meant to remember how Menelaos' spirit was warmed like the dew on the ears of corn when Antilochos gave him the horse (*Iliad* 23, 597). The memory would point the likeness and unlikeness between the tough warrior's sudden gratitude and the girl's sudden joy at hearing Jason speak to her.[1]

Among the similes which are new in subject matter I only mention those which show Apollonios' interest in light effects. 'Medeia's heart ranges within her breast as a gleam of the sun darts about the roof, rising from water which has been newly poured in a cauldron

[1] Other psychological similes which adapt similes in Homer: 1, 1265 (*Iliad* 22, 300); 2, 27 (lion); 4, 12 (deer); 4, 460 (*Iliad* 5, 597); 3, 656 (*Odyssey* 8, 523). In general on the comparison between Apollonios' similes and Homer see J. F. Carspecken, *Y.C.S.* 13, 1952, 53 ff.: he notes that the density of similes is the same in the *Iliad* and the *Argonautika*.

or pail. It leaps this way and that shaken by the swift whirlpool' (3, 755). Professor Hermann Fränkel[1] has suggested a Stoic origin for this comparison but gives no evidence before Epictetus; it seems possible that the Stoics borrowed from Apollonios. When Jason and Medeia reach the tree holding the fleece, the fleece is like a cloud blushing in the flaming rays of the rising sun (4, 125). And when Jason lifts the fleece joyously, he is like a girl in a high room holding a fine fabric under the light of the full moon (4, 167). Finally, Lynkeus thinks he sees Herakles in the furthest distance, as one sees or thinks he sees the moon dim as the dawn breaks (4, 1479).

The similes have already shown one passage where an event in Apollonios clearly recalls an event in Homer: Medeia driving with her maidens to the temple of Hekate (3, 870 ff.) recalls Nausikaa driving out with her maidens to do the washing. There is, however, an intentional contrast: Medeia has only achieved a precarious balance after a night of misery; she has with difficulty reached the stage where she can behave like Nausikaa. In other passages the reminiscence is uncomplicated by contrast. Hera beautifies Jason before he meets Medeia (3, 919 ff.) just as Athene beautifies Odysseus when he has met Nausikaa; Jason like Odysseus is aided by a divine mist (3, 210 ff.) to reach the palace, which he then admires, again like Odysseus.[2] Phineus (2, 311) plays the part of Proteus in the *Odyssey*, and Lykos' reminiscences of Herakles (2, 774) recall the Homeric Nestor. On a much smaller scale when Jason's mother, Alkimede, laments before Jason goes, the line σεῖο πόθῳ μινύθουσα δυσάμμορος (1, 286) awakes an echo of Odysseus' mother in the Nekyia (202) ἀλλά με σός τε πόθος σά τε μήδεα, φαίδιμ᾽ Ὀδυσσεῦ, σή τ᾽ ἀγανοφροσύνη μελιηδέα θυμὸν ἀπηύρα.

Apollonios also introduces characters already known from Homer, the Sirens, Arete and Alkinoos, Kirke, Thetis, Hera. Apollonios knows the pedigrees of the Sirens and their shapes (4, 891); instead of earplugs of wax, their song is drowned by Orpheus' lyre but even so Boutes is a casualty. Apollonios has transposed the incident into a more heroic key, and perhaps has called attention to the fact by

---

[1] *A.J.P.* 71, 1950, 125; *Mus. Helv.* 14, 1957, 17.
[2] Note however that Apollonios has made the palace a contemporary palace with bronze Corinthian capitals in the courtyard (G. Roux, *R. Ph.* 37, 1963, 84).

naming Orpheus' song εὐτροχάλοιο, which echoes the κηροῖο μέγαν τροχὸν of *Od.* 12, 173. Arete and Alkinoos are put in a real Corcyra instead of a fabulous Phaeacia (4, 982 f.). Apollonios has accepted from Homer the high status of Arete, whom Odysseus was told to approach first (6, 304, cf. 7, 66); king and queen discuss high policy in bed, and the queen, while the king is still asleep, sends a messenger to Jason to force the king's hand: Arete is the same sort of skilful manipulator as Kandaules' queen in the Gyges tragedy.[1] The same kind of modernization can be seen in Kirke: this Kirke has been frightened by a dream into burning all her drugs, but she is easily recognizable as the sister of Aietes (4, 662), she purifies Jason and Medeia after the murder of Apsyrtos (which Medeia does not mention) and she sends them away. That is all: she knows the truth and she disapproves, but she cannot deny her niece the ordinary rights of a suppliant. The terrible but alluring magician of Homer has become a nervous aunt.

Thetis is summoned by Hera because her aid is needed to get the Argo through Skylla and Charybdis. Hera needs a lesser god as she needed Hypnos for the Deception of Zeus (*Iliad*, 14, 231). Hera's transaction with Hypnos is simple: she goes to see him and first offers a golden throne and then puts the price up to marriage with one of the younger Graces. In the *Argonautika* (4, 782) she summons Thetis to see her and relies on the polished rhetoric of the great lady: 'I could get the Argo through the Planktai, but I need your help for the Symplegades. I brought you up. You were loyal to me when Zeus made love to you and I gave you a wonderful wedding. Achilles is going to marry Medeia in the end. Therefore you must help, even if Peleus has been a fool.' So Thetis has to meet Peleus again to tell him that the Argo can safely sail (4, 852): 'She stopped near him, touching his arm; and no one could see her clear, but she appeared to his eyes alone and said: "Don't stay any longer on the Tyrrhenian shores . . . Don't point me out to anyone when you see me coming with the Nereids, but keep it to yourself or you will make me even more angry than before." She spoke and vanished into the depths of the sea, and a terrible grief struck him, because he had not seen her since she left his house and bed in anger, when Achilles was a child.' The

[1] *Ox. Pap.* no. 2382.

opening recalls the scene in the *Iliad* (1, 193) where Athene prevents Achilles from drawing his sword on Agamemnon. By this reminiscence Apollonios marks the difference from the scenes in the *Iliad* where Thetis and Achilles appear as mother and son, although the mother has special capabilities; here Thetis is a goddess and Peleus is a mortal, and with the same kind of insight that he shows for the shepherds who have never seen a ship, Apollonios has sketched this relationship. A similar sympathy has produced two other unexpected and successful incidents: the Moon, lovesick for Endymion, laughing gleefully because Medeia, who as a sorceress has often used her, is to suffer all the agonies of love (4, 54), and the Hesperides lamenting bitterly because Herakles, whom they describe in no complimentary terms, has shot the snake which guarded the golden apples (4, 1398 ff., 1430 ff.).

When the Homeric Hera borrows Aphrodite's charms to deceive Zeus (14, 188), she tells her a lie; she says she wants Aphrodite's charms to reconcile Okeanos and Tethys. Apollonios' Hera needs Aphrodite's help to make Medeia fall in love with Jason. This passage (3, 36) opens with reminiscences of the polite welcome given in the *Iliad* to Thetis by Hephaistos (18, 369). The heroic scene is set but the action is Hellenistic. Aphrodite is surprised that her aid is needed for a heroic expedition, and when she is told what is wanted, complains that Eros is an impossible child. Eros is found playing dice with Ganymede. Aphrodite bribes him with a ball made for the infant Zeus. He comes down to Earth, and crouching at Jason's feet shoots his arrow into Medeia's heart. The scene with the goddesses is enchanting, particularly Hera's parting remark: 'Don't fight with your boy. He'll be better when he grows up.' This Eros is the incarnation of Sappho's adjective *amechanon*, 'irresistible'. He is not himself characterized as a lover like some fourth-century Erotes.[1] He is a winged boy who can do whatever he likes. An ordinary boy like Ganymede has no chance against him; the diceing scene is known from a Roman gem which goes back to an early Hellenistic original, but whether it inspired Apollonios or *vice versa* cannot be said.[2] Asklepiades speaks of a plurality of Erotes playing with dice, but

---

[1] Cf. *Art and Literature in Fourth-century Athens*, 103 ff.
[2] B. Neutsch, *Ganymed*, 18 f. Cf. above, Ch. I.

G

they are Hellenistic *putti*. The tiny Eros shooting from Jason's feet
might well be derived from a work of art: a small, shooting Eros is
carried by Aphrodite on a fourth-century mirror.[1]

In the scenes on Olympos Apollonios, like Homer, portrays the
gods as behaving like ordinary men and women, but their behaviour
is now Hellenistic. One passage about a god, however, is quite
different (2, 669). The Argonauts have disembarked at dawn after
rowing all night. 'To them Leto's son, coming from Lycia to the
distant land of the Hyperboreans, appeared. Bunched golden locks
swung on either side of his cheeks as he went. In his left hand he
wielded a silver bow, a quiver hung down his back from his
shoulder. The whole island shook beneath his feet and the waves
washed on the shore. They were possessed by helpless wonder as
they saw.' Dr Rieu[2] has suggested that Apollonios understood the
special receptivity of tired men. In any case he has realized magnificently in words the kind of conception that the Early Hellenistic
sculptor had in mind when he created the original of the Apollo
Belvedere.

The connection here between 'the utterly grievous weariness', the
vision, and 'the helpless wonder' may be interpreted as psychological, and Apollonios' description of Medeia is certainly a psychological study. It is true that Eros shoots her with his arrow at the
beginning, that Hera had kept her at home (3, 250) and Hera inflicted
her with fear when she had saved Jason from the bulls (4, 11), but
this is all epic machinery: the descriptions are of psychological events
and their physical concomitants, even once in modern medical terminology (as we have seen). At the first sight of Jason she is speech-
less, she glances at him continually, her heart beats quickly and pain-
fully, she changes colour. She watches him through her veil (gesture
well known from contemporary art) as he departs; her mind goes
with him and recalls every detail of his appearance; she is terrified
that he may be killed (3, 444–71). At night she dreams first that
Jason had only undertaken to tame the bulls in order to carry her off;

[1] Paris, Louvre. Züchner, *Klappspiegel*, no. 17; Metzger, *Representations*, 343.
Cf. also the Apulian squat lekythos, Taranto 4530, Arias-Hirmer, 238, with
Aphrodite suckling an Eros, two Erotes wrestling, and a box of Erotes.
[2] *Apollonius of Rhodes; the Voyage of the Argo*, 23.

then she tames them herself, but her parents say Jason ought to have done it; finally they leave the choice to her; she chooses Jason and they scream in anger, which wakes her up (3, 616–32). This is quite different from the symbolic dreams of tragedy, of Atossa, Elektra, or Iphigeneia. It is the real, inconsequent dream of an overwrought girl.[1] Then follows the long night of unhappiness and agonized indecision, which drives her nearly to suicide. Then she pulls herself together and drives out, like Nausikaa, to meet Jason, give him the ointment, and lose herself again in love, which turns to repentance when she gets home. The story goes on with her fears and her flight from her parents to Jason, when she helps him get the fleece. From that moment she is desperate; she plans and lures Apsyrtos to his death, she appeals to Kirke, to Arete, and to the Argonauts. Her story ends with the necessary marriage; but a Fury had marked the murder of Apsyrtos (4, 475) and Medeia's return is to be an evil to the house of Pelias (4, 242). Apollonios' audience knew the Euripidean sequel, and he has drawn his Medeia convincingly as she develops from first love to the desperation which arises from her need to save her own position. Even in her first love she wishes for a moment for Jason's death (3, 464) and the idea recurs in the long night of indecision with the idea of suicide and with the fear that her deception of her parents will be discovered.

Besides all this, Apollonios has shown her as a magician, her careful tendance of Hekate, her collection of herbs and her skill in using drugs and instructing others in their use. We see her at work when she hypnotizes the snake which guards the fleece, first invoking Hypnos and Hekate, then dripping narcotic over its eyes, and she goes on until Jason, who has taken down the fleece from its tree, calls her away (4, 164). Apollonios (4, 1673) expresses his wonder at her telepathic treatment of Talos: she invokes the Keres into her own mind, she bewitches his eyes with their malignant eyes, she 'gnashes' grievous wrath against him, she casts forth destructive images in her fury – and Talos knocked his ankle against a rock and ichor poured out. Both stories are old, but they are brilliantly retold, and Apollonios observes the magician as accurately as he observes the girl in love or the old priestess who is prevented by the crowd from speaking to

[1] On dreams, cf. del Corno, *Rendiconti Ist. Lombardo* 96, 1962, 334.

Jason or the old Polyxo who insists on making her speech in Lemnos (1, 311, 670).

The same power of observation is found in other descriptions, and this makes Apollonios' chief claim on the modern reader. It is seen in the description of Dindyma in the first book (1, 1112 f.), of Cape Acherousias, of the boar, and of Prometheus and his eagle in the second book (2, 728, 815, 1247 ff.) and many other passages. Here I would end with passages which recall works of art. Jason's cloak (1, 725) is a rich Hellenistic textile and the individual subjects can be paralleled, the forge of the Kyklopes, Amphion and Zethos building Thebes, Aphrodite holding the shield of Ares, the battle of Teleboans and Taphians, Pelops and Hippodameia, Apollo and Tityos, Phrixos and the ram. The departure of the Argo (1, 519) is a brilliant pageant of sight and sound, starting with the clear dawn light on the mountains and the shores, and ending with Cheiron waving his hand while his wife shows the little Achilles to his father. The education of Achilles and Jason by Cheiron and his family is, of course, an old story,[1] but it may well have been Apollonios who first brought them to see the Argo off. From the time of Homer in literature and from at least the sixth century in art the divine spectator of a human event was often represented, and divine spectators, interested gods and personifications of localities became increasingly common in classical and fourth-century scenes. Apollonios uses this tradition brilliantly here, again in the second book (911 f.) where Sthenelos rises from his tomb 'as he was when he went to war' to view 'men of his own kind', and again in the fourth book (956 f.) when Hephaistos watched the Argo passing the clashing rocks, leaning his shoulder on the staff of his hammer, while Hera in fear for the outcome threw her arms round Athene. If one thinks of these scenes in terms of Early Hellenistic art they come alive, and it is this power of vivid description more than anything else which for us still makes Apollonios a poet.

[1] Cf. Beazley, *Development of Attic Black Figure*, 51.

## CHAPTER IV

# Theokritos and Herodas

◆

Ancient sources say that Theokritos was a Syracusan and that he lived in the time of Ptolemy Philadelphos, but tell us practically nothing else.[1] His appeal to Hiero II of Syracuse can be dated with fair certainty 275/4; he was not in Sicily when he wrote it (XVI, 106): 'Uncalled I would abide, but if they call I would confidently go with my Muse'. The epigram (18) written for a bronze statue of Epicharmos need not have been written on the spot, but it at least shows that Theokritos kept up relations with Syracuse.[2] As it was a dedication to Dionysos, Gow suggests a connection with the theatre of Hiero II, which however is now dated after 238; the statue must have belonged to an earlier theatre and does not therefore give us any date for Theokritos. The other firm date is 274/70 for *Idylls* XV, XVII, both of which belong to the Alexandria of Ptolemy Philadelphos and Arsinoe II. *Idyll* VII describes a day in the past in Kos and implies that Theokritos is already in receipt of Ptolemy's patronage (91 f.); it was therefore also written in the late 70's. The day in Kos was in the lifetime of Asklepiades and Philitas (40), but that need not put it far back: Aratos (probably not the poet of the *Phainomena*) was having an unfortunate love-affair as also in *Idyll* VI, which may therefore be contemporary. *Idyll* VI consoles Aratos with the story of Polyphemos and Galateia: the same story is used in *Idyll* XI to console the doctor Nikias. Whether Theokritos became a friend of Nikias in Kos or Alexandria we do not know (Nikias was a fellow-pupil of Erasistratos, which perhaps suggests Alexandria), but the two Polyphemos poems should not be far apart. Theokritos also rewrote the Hylas story (XIII) as another consolation

---

[1] What follows is largely dependent on the edition of Mr A. S. F. Gow; for dating see his introductions to the relevant idylls. I have only considered those poems which Gow regards as genuine. On *Idyll* I see now R. M. Ogilvie, *J.H.S.* 82, 1962, 106. Cf. also R. Stark, *Maia* 5, 1963, 359 ff.

[2] Cf. above, p. 60.

for Nikias; later Nikias went back to Miletos and married; one poem (*Idyll* XXVIII) certainly and *Epigram* 8 probably belong to this later period. Theokritos claims grey-hair in one poem (XXX); but as we do not know at what age he started to write this does not help us. In fact nothing compels us to put any poem before 280 B.C. or after 270. If Kallimachos refers to him in *Epigram* 52, he was presumably still a young man when he came to Alexandria, but the reference is not certain.

Theokritos was a Syracusan, who wrote in Kos and Alexandria. He appealed to Hiero II in 275/4; he wrote an epigram for the statue of Epicharmos in Syracuse; the spindle which he sent to Nikias' wife (XXVIII) was made in Syracuse. Gorgo and Praxinoa, who go to see the festival of Adonis (XV), are like him Syracusans living in Alexandria; one of his epitaphs also is for a Syracusan who died in a foreign land (*Epigram* 9). Sicilian and South Italian colouring appears in the Pastoral poems: the story of Polyphemos and Galateia, with which Aratos and Nikias are consoled, is set in Sicily and derives from the late fifth-century poet Philoxenos, who wrote it in Syracuse. Nikias is told the story directly by Theokritos (XI). For Aratos (VI) the story is divided between two neat-herds, Damoitas, who does not appear elsewhere, and Daphnis, a mythical Sicilian neat-herd, who is the subject of *Epigrams* 2–5 and of Thyrsis' lament in *Idyll* I; and Thyrsis himself, who also appears in *Epigram* 6, claims that he comes from Aetna.

Thyrsis is a Sicilian shepherd with a name which would be very suitable for a satyr, but the cup which he wins came from an Eastern ferryman (I, 57).[1] Here then Theokritos does not trouble to be consistent: the shepherd should be Sicilian, but the audience will appreciate the local reference. So too *Idyll* IV is set in Kroton and the local athlete has the name of the sixth-century Milon, but the neatherd can sing songs of two contemporary Eastern singers (31), V is set in Thourioi, Komatas has a mythical name but owns a cup made by Praxiteles and Lakon refers to the river Haleis in Kos, VII is set entirely in contemporary Kos but Lykidas expects to hear Sicilian pastoral poetry (72 f.) sung by Tityros, who has a satyr name. Tityros is also the goatherd companion of the goatherd of

[1] Cf. Gow, ad loc.

*Idyll* III who is described as if he were a satyr and sings a town serenade to a nymph in a cave: Amaryllis is probably considered Western as she is also named in IV (36). Only *Idyll* X is a consistent picture of contemporary country life: the reaper in love with the dark Syrian girl and the overseer who sings a traditional reaper's song; even here the contrast between the two probably owes something to New Comedy. In the other pastorals we must not ask too precisely whether the characters are mythical or real, whether they are satyrs or rustics, whether they are in the West or in the East. They belong to a world which is for one reason or another as unreal as it is tuneful. Here in desirable settings of trees, rocks, and springs, recalled to business occasionally by the antics of their animals, rustics converse or contend with dialogue or song in meltingly beautiful hexameters (or elegiacs). Except for the realistic X, all these poems have a strong Western colouring and it is tempting to suppose either that Theokritos was writing pastoral before he went to the East or if he was young when he came East that he started composing with a nostalgic eye for Sicily and South Italy: into his Western poetry, when it became popular in the East, he then introduced local references and learned allusions, like the mythical lovers in *Idyll* III, 40 ff. and Melanthios (the goatherd of the *Odyssey*) at the end of *Idyll* V.

The most difficult to interpret of all these poems is *Idyll* VII: on the way to a harvest festival in Kos, Simichidas, who is undoubtedly Theokritos, meets Lykidas and has a contest with him. Simichidas says that he has some reputation but is no match for Sikelidas (= Asklepiades) of Samos or Philitas. Lykidas says that Simichidas is a good singer, quite unlike the foolish bards who try to imitate Homer.[1] So far, it is at least clear that Theokritos proclaims himself the successor of Philitas and Asklepiades as an exponent of short poetry, which includes pastoral; both Philitas' Bittis and Hermesianax' pastoral love poetry were earlier. Lykidas then sings (52 f.): 'if my love Ageanax reaches Miletos safely, I shall have a celebration in which two shepherds, one from Acharnai, one from Lykope, will pipe, while Tityros sings of Daphnis and Komatas'. Simichidas then sings of Aratos' unhappy love. He prays that Pan

[1] Cf. above, p. 39.

(from Thessaly) may bring Philinos to him and that the Erotes (from Miletos and Caria) may wound Philinos with their arrows. Lykidas then gives Simichidas his throwing-stick and they part. A further point is now clear: although both men say that they are singing pastoral, neither song would naturally be called pastoral: both start from real contemporary love-affairs; Lykidas' celebration includes two Sicilian pastoral songs; the only pastoral element in Simichidas' song is Pan. The poem therefore not only proclaims Theokritos' adherence to the school of Philitas but also suggests an extension of the range of 'pastoral'.

Simichidas, Sikelidas, Philitas, Aratos (the addressee also of *Idyll* VI) are known figures; it is a temptation to try and identify the others, particularly Lykidas. Two recent articles have proposed two very different solutions for the whole poem. F. Lasserre[1] has noted a number of parallels between the two songs and epigrams in the Anthology, particularly with poems by Kallimachos, Leonidas, and Asklepiades. The most convincing parallel is the reminiscence in Simichidas' prayer to the Erotes to wound Philinos (118–19) of similar appeals by Asklepiades and Poseidippos (*A.P.* XII, 166 and 45). Lasserre goes further; he supposes that the two songs are a kind of parody on a recently published anthology called the *Soros* or heap, and that the end of the poem is allegorical: the wine is the new poetry, the winnowing fan is Theokritos' idyll and Demeter's heap is the new Anthology. It is difficult to prove or disprove these suggestions. The allusions to contemporary epigram can be gratefully accepted but need not mean more than that Theokritos is claiming his place among this band of poets by using the familiar technique of picking up phrases in their poetry.

The interpretation of the last lines depends on the date of the *Soros* of Poseidippos, which we do not know. But without going so far as Lasserre, it is tempting to see a reminiscence of the 'flowers and pure fountain' of the *Marriage of Arsinoe*[2] and to suppose that twenty-five years later Kallimachos was thinking of this poem, when in the second *Hymn* (110) Apollo tells him that Demeter's bees only bring her pure water. The prayer that the poet may plant again the winnowing fan on the heap belongs more naturally to a real harvest

[1] *Rh. Mus.* 102, 1959, 307.  [2] Cf. above, p. 45.

festival than to an allegorical harvest festival, but may also be a prayer that the poet may join this band of poetic rustics.

M. Puelma,[1] who also accepts the conclusion as allegorical, has discussed the Homeric parallels to the phraseology in the Lykidas scene. 'Lykidas was very like a goatherd' (14). This formula or variations of it are used in the *Odyssey* when Athena appears in human form (3, 796, etc.); she was very like Mentor, etc. Puelma argues that Lykidas therefore is characterized as an ideal goatherd. His repeated smiles (19 f., 42 ff., 128 f.) again recall the smile of the god greeting a man (*Od.* 13, 287, etc.). The ideal goatherd is also the master poet, and he presents Simichidas with his throwing-staff as a *xeneïon ek Mousân*, 'a gift from the Muses', Simichidas is thereby made a member of the company to which Lykidas belongs, a company which serves the Muses (128 f.). The scene is then a consecration of Simichidas like the consecration of Hesiod in the *Theogony*. This is convincing, but the essential difference must not be forgotten: Simichidas is already a poet and has already been taught by the Nymphs as he pastured his herds (91 ff.). So Lykidas does not so much consecrate him as reconsecrate him as a member of the Koan circle. Contemporaries would be able to say whether the ideal goatherd concealed a real poet but we cannot; we must be content to say that in *Idyll* VII Theokritos recalls that in Kos he was accepted into the circle of Alexandrian poets with a new kind of pastoral.

The other poems include the same kinds of poetry which are found in Kallimachos: minor epics, aetiology, occasional poetry, poems to patrons, mimes. As an elaboration of a heroic incident, the Hylas story (XIII) belongs to the minor epics. Formally it is a consolation to a friend in love like *Idyll* XI. The question of Apollonios' priority has already been discussed.[2] Theokritos makes more of Herakles' love and of its issue in training the boy to be like himself, he enlarges on the vegetation, substitutes a chorus of three nymphs in the water, 'Eunika and Malis and Nycheia with spring in her eyes', for Apollonios' chorus who dance for Artemis, makes them all three fall in love with Hylas, and finally makes Herakles walk to

[1] *Mus. Helv.* 17, 1960, 144 ff. Commentary on l. 20, G. Roux, *R.P.* 37, 1963, 76 f.
[2] Cf. above, p. 65.

Phasis. This last line is not so much a correction of Apollonios as a
hint to Nikias that however much he indulges in love-affairs he will
have to return to his ordinary life as a doctor in the end. The other
two minor epics are straight narratives. *Idyll* XXII is a 'hymn' to the
Dioskouroi; after an introduction describing chiefly their help to
sailors, there follow first the boxing match of Polydeukes and
Amykos (expanded from Apollonios), then Kastor's duel with
Lynkeus. This is a pedestrian poem. On the other hand the *Herak-
liskos* (XXIV) is charming. Various versions are known, and we cannot tell how faithfully Theokritos used his source: the long period,
eight or ten months, between the birth of Herakles and the strangling
of the snakes is likely to have come from Sophocles rather than
Euripides.[1] The numerous pictures do not help us here because they
cannot tell us the age of the babies. Theokritos has written a human
story in which the only heroic elements are the snakes (launched
apparently through the lattice work of the doors),[2] the light sent by
Zeus (which in the *Amphitruo* (1096), probably following Euripides
here, accompanies the birth) and the strength of Herakles. This insertion of miraculous events in an ordinary human situation is very
much in the manner of Apollonios Rhodios. Here Alkmena puts the
babies to bed in a bronze shield and rocks them to sleep with a cradle
song. Iphikles screams when the snakes come. Alkmena wakes and
wakes Amphitryon. As he gets ready the supernatural light goes out
because Herakles has already killed the snakes. Amphitryon rouses
the household, and then they put the babies to bed again and go to
bed themselves. Alkmena summons Teiresias in the morning and he
prophesies Herakles' future and gives instructions for purifying the
house. The poem continues with a summary account of the education of Herakles. Its charm lies in the domestic scene of the earlier
part; the relationship between Alkmena and Amphitryon rather
recalls Apollonios' Arete and Alkinoos.

Three poems may be classed as aetiology. They are not announced
as aetiology like the poems of the *Aitia*, but in each lines are inserted which refer to a modern rite.[3] The pretty poem of the two

[1] Cf. *Studies in Later Greek Comedy*, 86 f.      [2] Cf. Gow on l. 15.
[3] On the *Aitia*, cf. Gow, ad loc. Wilamowitz rejects the Theokritean authorship
of XXVI.

lovers (XII) alludes at the end to a kissing competition at Megara (30 f.). The very attractive description of the girls at Helen's wedding (XVIII) contains lines (43 f.) in which the girls say that they will be the first to place wreaths on a plane-tree and to pour oil beneath it, and the tree will be inscribed: 'Worship me. I am Helen's tree'. This clearly alludes to a tree-cult. And the strange description and justification of the rending of Pentheus (XXVI) seems best explained as giving the aetiology for the slaying (or mock slaying) of a child at some Dionysiac festival.

Some of the occasional poems in a variety of metres and dialects have been already mentioned.[1] The epigrams raise the usual question: which are actual inscriptions and which are literary exercises? Some epitaphs (7, 9, 11, 15, 16, 20, 23) seem to be tomb-inscriptions; the Hipponax (19),[2] although in form an epitaph, is certainly literary and it probably takes with it the inscriptions (17, 21) for supposed statues of Anakreon and Archilochos. On the other hand the inscription for the statue of Epicharmos (18) seems to have been a commission, and the inscription (22) for the statue of Peisander, set up by the people 'many months and many years later', sounds like a real inscription. There is no reason either to doubt the dedicatory inscriptions (8, 10, 12, 13, 24), including the bankers' sign (14).

This leaves us with the first six epigrams: 1, a dedication of flowers to the Muses and Apollo, is literary because it does not name the dedicator and it is extended to include the sacrifice of 'this white, horned goat here'. But where is 'the white, horned goat, nibbling the terebinth'? It is tempting to think that he is in a picture (like Anyte's goat)[3] and then it is very tempting to see 3 as inspired by a picture of Pan and Priapos assailing a sleeping Daphnis, and 5 by a companion picture of three musicians (including Daphnis) and a sleeping Pan.[4] These poems, with the settings of the Pastorals themselves, must be considered later as evidence for rustic landscape painting in Alexandria. They need not be regarded as poems composed to be inscribed under pictures; the pictures may in fact be imaginary, but they must at least be possible decorations for an *andron* in Alexandria or the point of the epigrams would be lost.

[1] Cf. above, p. 59.     [2] Cf. above, p. 60.     [3] Cf. above, p. 3.
[4] Risch. *Mus. Helv.* 19, 1962, 200 notes that 3, 6 quotes Sappho 2 L-P.

The other three epigrams are also pastoral in that the characters come from the Pastorals: 2 is a dedication by Daphnis, 6 is an epitaph on Thyrsis' kid. 4 is an elaborate literary dedication: a goatherd is asked to go to a shrine of Priapos, which has a setting worthy of the end of VII, and sacrifice a kid to Priapos so that the speaker may be rid of his love for Daphnis; if Priapos refuses and the speaker succeeds with Daphnis, the sacrifice will be a heifer, a goat, and a lamb. Here Theokritos has combined the pastoral setting and characters with the neat form and unexpected end-twist of the symposion epigram.

Of the two poems to patrons, the poem to Hiero II (XVI) is a competent performance embodying many of the ideas which Pindar put in his poems to Hiero I but has little appeal to us today, except for the pretty conceit at the beginning, when Theokritos' Graces (poems that ask for patronage) come barefoot home complaining and stay at the bottom of the empty chest with their heads on their chilly knees. The poem to Ptolemy Philadelphos (XVII) is much more immediate; this is a court which the poet knows and for which he is grateful. The ancestry of Philadelphos, the association of Berenike with Aphrodite,[1] the birth of Philadelphos and the rejoicing of Kos (a theme which recurs in Kallimachos' hymn to Delos), the prosperity of Egypt, the extent of Ptolemy's power and military authority, his patronage of Dionysiac festivals, his worship of his parents and his marriage with his sister Arsinoe are themes of present interest to him and his audience. Near the beginning (28 f.) Herakles, the ancestor of both Ptolemy Soter and Alexander, going home drunk with nectar from the feast of the gods, gives to one of them his bow and quiver and to the other his iron club and 'they escort the bearded son of Zeus and his arms to the ambrosial chamber of white-ankled Heba'. This must surely be the description of a picture or tapestry in the palace.

Two of the mimes (XV and XIV, with which the realistic X should be included) pick up themes from this idyll. Mime is a convenient term for a realistic representation of contemporary life: it is not meant to imply anything about the origin of the poems (we have no evidence that the *Adoniazousai* (XV) resembled Sophron in more

[1] Cf. fr. 3 and Ch. II, p. 44.

than its title) or about the method of performance; if these poems were performed at all, they were presumably recited by Theokritos. The tapestries which the women admire in the palace (78) may well include the drunken Herakles, and Berenike has been immortalized by Aphrodite here as there (106). This is Arsinoe II's Adonis festival, and the professional singer describes the tableau of Aphrodite and Adonis and then the song which will be sung the next morning when the image of Adonis is taken to the sea. The song is the climax of the two Syracusan women's visit to the palace; the poem starts with Gorgo calling for Praxinoa to take her to the festival. After the enchanting business of getting Praxinoa ready, the two women with their servants struggle through the crowds encountering various people on the way until they get into the palace; after the song they hurry home to feed their husbands. The two women are beautifully observed.

A succinct praise of Ptolemy as a good paymaster for soldiers as well as a patron of the arts ends *Idyll* XIV, which is a realistic dialogue between two friends; one has had a disaster in love which he recounts, and his friend encourages him to enlist with Ptolemy. The opening lines may be a reminiscence of comedy, and the picture of the Athenian Pythagorean (5) is known from many comic fragments. The theme of the young man in love who goes to war is also a theme of comedy. Theokritos may have started from Comedy rather than life, but the description of the party is entirely realistic and is unlikely to be second-hand. Similarly in *Idyll* X, which in spite of its country setting can be reckoned among the mimes, the overseer's scorn for the reaper in love may recall the opening of Menander's *Heros*, but the realization in the two songs owes nothing to comedy.

The fourth of these poems, the *Pharmakeutria* (II), may owe a detail or two to Sophron but nothing more.[1] The love-affair which starts at a festival (66 f.) is again a well-known theme of comedy. But again the details are Theokritos' own. The magical practice of the love-sick Simaitha can be paralleled from the magical papyri; the girl wavers between magic to destroy Delphis and magic to

---

[1] A very good detailed commentary is given by H. Hommel in *W.S.* 69, 1956, 187.

bring him to her door. At one moment the barking of the dogs and the silence suggest that Hekate will appear (35 f.). When the rites are over, she tells to the Moon the story of her love: how utterly she was prostrated by the beauty of 'shining-skinned' Delphis with a beard like helichryse and breast shining brighter than the moon. Finally she sent her maid to ask him to come. When he came, she chilled colder than snow, sweat poured from her, she could not speak, and she went stiff like a doll. Delphis treated her with ironic gallantry but she now believes him to be unfaithful. Like poetry for the Cyclops in *Idyll* XI, magic and the moon do their work for Simaitha, and she is prepared at the end to bear her load of longing. When she says farewell to the Moon, she transfers to her the epithet 'shining-skinned' which she had before used of Delphis. There are some pointers to Apollonios Rhodios in this poem, and it is possible that Theokritos thought of Delphis and Simaitha as an everyday parallel to his Jason and Medeia; the physical prostration of the women is closely parallel,[1] but it may be objected that both poets had a common source in Sappho. Delphis' breast is brighter than the moon, and Apollonios' Hylas shatters the spring-nymph as the full moon shines upon his beauty (1, 1229 ff.); Theokritos uses this point here instead of in the Hylas story.

All the mimes remind us of Attic comedy, but they differ from comedy in three obvious points: performance, which is presumably by recitation; scale – a moment of comedy is elaborated into a complete scene; metre and dialect, both of which are alien. The mimes of Theokritos are not isolated: *Hymns* V and VI of Kallimachos, to which we shall return, and the *Mimiamboi* of Herodas which we must now consider exhibit the same characteristics. Herodas is practically unknown outside the preserved papyrus text, and therefore we have only internal evidence for his place and date.

Herodas has been chary of local indications. II, 95 f. firmly localizes the procurer's speech in Kos, and he goes on to say that Asklepios came here from Trikka. This is the cue for localizing IV in Kos, although Kynno's opening line 'Lord of Trikka, Kos and Epidauros' seems to exclude Kos. Presumably she is using a traditional invocation made elsewhere. The archaeology (see below) fits

[1] Cf. 88 f. with Ap. Rh. 3, 297; 106 ff. with 3, 961 ff.

well enough with Kos. We know nothing of the Gerenia (V, 80); a connection with Nestor and therefore an Ionian city has been suggested, but Gerenia was also a centre of the Asklepios cult founded, like Kos, from Trikka. The indications in VIII (40) 'as we perform in choruses of Dionysos' and (79) 'to sing to the sons of Xouthos' have been said to point to Athens, but such choruses were not restricted to Athens and 'sons of Xouthos' should rather be 'Ionians'; in any case the phrase may only mean 'sing in Ionian dialect'. The only clear indication of date is given in I, 26 ff., where the beauties of Egypt include a precinct of the *Theoi Adelphoi*, which was constructed by 272/1 B.C.[1] Such other indications as there are (e.g. the artists named in IV) point earlier rather than later, and there seems no valid reason for dating any of these poems much after 270.

The poems are all pieces of about a hundred lines composed in *skazons*. Some are monologues; some are dialogues with a third and fourth speaker occasionally intervening. The name *mimiamboi* implies no more than that the pieces are dramatic in form and iambic in metre. The metre, language, and dialect come from the sixth-century Ephesian poet Hipponax. But the men and women of Herodas are not local notorieties like the men and women of Hipponax. The titles are general: the procuress, the procurer, the schoolmaster, women making dedication and sacrifice to Asklepios, the jealous woman, intimate women, the cobbler (only the *Dream* stands by itself and is autobiographical). The titles suggest Middle Comedy, and this may not be a false lead. The pieces are not in any sense scenes from comedy, at any rate as we know it. They are rather elaborations of ideas from comedy, sometimes using material from comedy, and sometimes quoting comedy. The individual characters are all possible in comedy, and where we have no parallel, this may well be due to our lack of material. It is the scale, metre, and language rather than the situation or the people or the viewpoint from which they are seen, which differ from comedy. The difference in

---

[1] The date is given by *P. Hibeh*, ii, 199. 'The good King' is Philadelphos in his human capacity. The separate chronological question raised by VIII is discussed below. In the following account I have used the editions of Herzog-Crusius, Headlam-Knox, Nairn. A fragment of VIII 67–75 has been identified in *P. Oxy.* 2326 by A. Barigazzi, *Mus. Helv.* 12, 1955, 113.

scale is partly due to the need to make these poems self-contained; but Herodas contents himself with a minimum of background, and the lack may sometimes have been unsatisfactory even for a contemporary audience.

The *Procuress* (I) is perhaps closest to comedy. The situation, a procuress trying unsuccessfully to tempt a young woman to desert her absent husband and sell herself to the young man who has engaged the procuress' services, is certainly possible in comedy. The opening scene of Menander's *Synaristosai*, where the procuress withdraws her daughter, gives one element; the scene in Menander's *First Adelphoi*, where Antiphon tries to withdraw his daughters from their absent husbands, provides another element. The imaginary description of the husband's life in Egypt matches the real description of the returned husbands' life in Asia in the *First Adelphoi*. The lover is said to have fallen in love with Metriche at a festival, like many lovers of New Comedy. Metriche is awaiting supplies from the country like many wives of New Comedy. The old woman likes her cup of wine like the procuress of the *Synaristosai*. The scene is probably longer than a similar scene in comedy would be. Comedy would perhaps not have time for the byplay with the slave-girl at the beginning, but this occurs several times in Herodas, as also in the *Adoniazousai*: it is a measure of Metriche's character that she is gentle with her slave-girl. Why Metriche welcomes the old woman as a long absent friend, we are not told; we should perhaps assume that she is the local gossip. The old woman slanders the husband and proposes the new lover. Metriche refuses indignantly, but gives the old woman a strong cup of wine which sends her away happy, hoping that the two hetairai whom she owns (?) (is her daughter Philainion a third?) may remain young as long as she lives.

The *Procurer* (II) is also close to comedy. In form it is a prosecution of a ship's captain, who has taken one of the procurer's girls, set fire to his house, and damaged the girl – a theme from Diphilos' *Synapothneskontes* and Menander's *Second Adelphoi*. Herodas may also have had the speech of the procurer in Menander's *Kolax* (99 f.) in mind, and one line 'He is now Thales, but before he was Artimmes' is very closely modelled on a line from another speech in the *Kolax* (133). The leading theme of this speech is the contrast between the law-abiding poor metic (the procurer) and the law-breaking rich metic (the ship's captain); (the contrast in their dress, *tribon* and *chlaina* is well-known in comedy): the whole tradition of the city of Kos demands that the rights of the poor foreigner be safeguarded. But the procurer can never resist either a chance to do business or a jab at his adversary's origins. The *Shoemaker* (VII) is a parallel portrait. Here no comic parallel survives, but one may well have existed in Euboulos' *Cobbler*. This is dialogue between the Cobbler and Metro, who brings other women to buy from him. The cobbler is magnificently proud of his own creations, but in the end allows Metro to get a considerable reduction for her friend.

The rest, like the first, are essentially portraits of women. The *Schoolmaster* (III) is much more a portrait of the pupil's mother than of the schoolmaster or the boy; the schoolmaster does nothing but beat the boy; the mother wants nothing but continued punishment for the boy, but Herodas gradually develops the whole situation: the grandmother is illiterate, the father is old and deaf and short-sighted, they are poor and live in a tenement; the mother is clearly trying to educate the boy out of his social station, and the boy has taken refuge in gambling and violence. Aristophanes' *Clouds* has a different but equally ill-matched trio of father, mother, and son, and Middle Comedy may have provided closer parallels. Equally unattractive is the jealous woman (V). She must be well off, as she has three male slaves and a female slave. Nothing is said of her husband. She is jealous because she suspects her favourite male slave of pursuing another woman. This is a reversal of the usual comedy situation in which the old master is in love with the young slave-girl; this is the tyrannical wife of comedy, but she is herself in love with a male slave. The slave's defence (27): 'I am human, I sinned', is practically a quotation of Menander's *Phanion* (fr. 432), and his mistress hopes that he will cringe as low as Daos (68, interpreted Knox). The woman first proposes to beat the slave and then to have him branded; she only gives this up when the woman-slave, whom she brought up and loves as much as her own daughter, reminds her that the festival of the dead is nearly due. Herodas likes the unexpected twist, which shows a new facet of character (the *Shoemaker* is a masterpiece of this technique), and the reference to the Gerenia was no doubt

H

clearer to his audience than it is to us. The *Intimate Women* (VI) contrasts two women, one rather bad-tempered and ready to fly into abuse at any moment, the other more peaceable but persistent in her demand for an instrument of excitement (cf. Ar. *Lys.* 109), which the other has obtained. The *baubon* is known from comedy: the text for many of these women might be found in Praxagora's speech in the *Ekklesiazousai* (221 f.). It is surprising, perhaps, to find it a prized possession of respectable married women – at the end the visitor (like Gorgo in the *Adoniazousai*) goes off to feed her husband, and the other woman sees to her chickens.

The *Women who dedicate and sacrifice to Asklepios* (IV) also contrasts two women, the efficient Kynno, who knows exactly what should be done and can show the sights of the temple, and the simple Kokale, who makes the dedication and goes into raptures over all that she sees. The general theme, performance of a rite with description by an expert, recalls the last two hymns of Kallimachos (V, VI). The division into outside and inside the temple recalls the division into outside and inside the palace in the *Adoniazousai*. Ancestors in comedy are possible: Aristophanes' *Peace* has a protracted scene of sacrifice, and a night in the temple of Asklepios is described in detail in the *Plutus*. For us the great interest of this piece lies in the ceremony itself, in the description of the statues outside the temple and the paintings inside the temple, and in the reaction of Kokale to these works of art. Like the women in the *Adoniazousai*, Kokale's only standard is likeness to life (27 ff.): the girl looking at the apple will die if she does not get it; the boy strangling the goose would talk if he were not stone; Batale's portrait is so good that you do not need to see her herself; the boy's flesh is tender and hot; the painted silver fire-box would tempt a thief; Apelles' ox has a terrifying look in its eye. The progress of the rite would be clear to those who did it every day: it starts with Kynno's prayer to the deities of the temple, after which she tells Kokale to hang her votive tablet on the right of the statue of Hygieia. Presumably her slave Kydilla takes the sacrificial cock to the Neokoros (41). The women then go inside the temple. The Neokoros announces the success of the sacrifice (80). Kynno then instructs Kokale to give him the leg of the bird, to give the snake its offering, and to wet her cakes, in return for which she is to receive holy bread; of this the efficient Kynno claims her share.

These delicate, somewhat tart little scenes, except for the fact that they are written in *skazons*, seem strangely unlike Hipponax as we know him. Yet it is as a second Hipponax that Herodas advertises himself in his *Dream* (VIII). The description of the dream itself is sadly mutilated, but the main lines can be made out from the interpretation at the end. The poem starts with the usual abuse of two female slaves: one is to drive the sow to pasture, the other to find wool for a sacrifice. A third slave is to interpret the dream (but in fact the speaker interprets for himself). The dream starts: 'I seemed to be dragging a goat through a long gully, it was a well-bearded and well-horned goat'. Then the text is corrupt for fifty lines. It seems however that some goatherds took the goat, sacrificed it (possibly because it nibbled a vine), and divided the flesh. A young man, with a fawnskin round his middle, a *kypassis* on his shoulders, a wreath of ivy on his head, and buskins, told them to blow up the goatskin like the skins that Odysseus received from Aiolos, and jump on it, the best dancer to be the winner as in the choruses of Dionysos. Only the narrator succeeded in jumping twice on the skin. Some praised him, others reviled him and an angry old man tried to drive him away (possibly in the eight missing lines, 50–7, the old man succeeded in jumping once on the skin). The narrator appeals to the young man, who orders them both to be beaten (?). Then follows the interpretation (67 ff.): dragging the goat from the gully means that Herodas received his gift of poetry from Dionysos; the forcible sacrifice of the goat means that Herodas will have many critics; the successful jumping and the beating (?) shared with the angry old man means that Herodas will be the glorious successor of Hipponax as a writer of *skazons* in Old Ionic.

This fascinating poem belongs to the long succession of poetic initiations. Nearest in time are Kallimachos' dream that he received the *Aitia* on Helikon and Theokritos' account of his acceptance in the *Thalysia* (VII). Kallimachos' dream has a direct reference to Hesiod's initiation, and Kallimachos feels himself a successor of Hesiod. Herodas' dream seems to be a variation of Archilochos' initiation: Archilochos was driving his father's cow to market when the Muses appeared to him and substituted a lyre for the cow. The likeness to Archilochos' story suggests that Herodas too received his poetry from a god; the equipment of the young man is the equipment of Dionysos, so that it is Dionysos who adjudicates the dispute between Herodas and Hipponax. Dionysos, as far as we know, has no particular connection with Hipponax, but Herodas identifies the goat with his poetry as a gift of Dionysos (67 f.), and Dionysos adjudicates the dispute. Dionysos is the god both of the drama and of the symposion; both are relevant to the *Mimiamboi*, if they were symposion recitations.

Herodas represents himself as a rustic and represents his critics as goatherds. In the *Thalysia* (VII) Theokritos describes his acceptance in Kos by the ideal goatherd Lykidas as the poet of an extended form of bucolic poetry which included 'mime'. The only poem of Herodas which is certainly localized (II) is set in Kos, and there is no strong reason against the supposition that the whole set were written in Kos. The critics are poets; this seems the natural interpretation of 'many will pluck my works among the Muses' (71). In the dream they are goatherds. They would seem therefore to be the bucolic school of Kos, Theokritos and his friends.

Finally, Herodas follows the traditional conception of Hipponax as an angry man. Kallimachos' Hipponax is surprisingly a peace maker, but in a poem (*Iambos* I) probably written after 250. Herodas' poem should be earlier, but this dating raises another chronological point. Latte[1] must surely be right in supposing that Eratosthenes in his *Erigone* provided an origin in Ikaria for the custom known from comedy of dancing on inflated goatskins (*askoliasmos*). It is sometimes said that Herodas was using Eratosthenes, who arrived in Alexandria in 247. There are however difficulties in this suggestion: it is not certain (although likely) that Herodas' goat nibbled vine-shoots as in the Eratosthenes story (the essential words are lost, 20–2). The young man who ordered the jumping is not Ikarios (as in Eratosthenes) but Dionysos. And Herodas explains that the best dancer should be the winner 'as we do in the choruses of Dionysos'; he may in fact be alluding here to a comedy of Euboulos, *Amaltheia* (K. ii, 166/8): 'Put the skin in the middle and jump

[1] *Hermes* 85, 1957, 385.

on it and laugh at those who fall off'. Probably, therefore, Herodas is himself giving an origin for the jumping, which is quite independent of Eratosthenes and precedes the *Erigone*.[1] Then the poem also precedes Kallimachos' new conception of Hipponax in *Iambos* I, and there is no reason also why Kallimachos should not have had Herodas' dream in mind when he wrote in *Iambos* XIII: 'I did not go to Ephesos or mix with the Ionians, Ephesos, which kindles those who are going to write skilful Skazons.' This poem of Kallimachos is later than 270/65 but how much later we do not know. Herodas in the *Dream* claims to be a second Hipponax who is going to write for Ionians, and he may himself have visited Ephesos. We need not therefore suppose that Herodas was writing for any long period before or after 270. What he claims in the *Dream* is that he has defeated the pastoral poets of Kos with another and equally artificial kind of mime – themes from comedy transmuted into sketches written in the Old Ionic of Hipponax.

[1] The version of Herodas' dream is not unlike the scene on a Roman mosaic in Berlin illustrated by Herzog (Herzog-Crusius, *die Mimiamben des Herondas* 1926, pl. 16, quoting Jahn, *A.Z.* 1847, 131). On the mosaic Dionysos and Ariadne look on while satyrs jump unsuccessfully on the skin in the presence of two Muses; an extremely fierce white-haired satyr puts his hand on the shoulder of a young satyr, who looks as if he is going to jump but may, on the other hand, have jumped successfully. If this version was known to Herodas, either in poetry or in art, it could very well have been the origin of the *Dream*.

## CHAPTER V

# *Kallimachos*

———◆———

Kallimachos certainly lived through the reign of Ptolemy Philadelphos and died in the reign of Ptolemy Euergetes. He came from
Cyrene to Alexandria; he was first a schoolmaster in the suburb of
Eleusis, then was in charge of the catalogue at the Library. The fixed
points for his production are given by Pfeiffer:[1] *Epigram* 20 is very
early, about 300, and was written at Cyrene; it probably takes
*Epigram* 54, also for a Cyrenaean, with it. *Hymn* I, according to
Wilamowitz,[2] contains a reference to Philadelphos early in his reign,
i.e. about 280 B.C.; this therefore will have been written soon after
Kallimachos came to Alexandria. The *Galateia* (fr. 378-9) is probably not long after 278 B.C. The *Marriage of Arsinoe* (fr. 392) is
about 276/5 B.C., and the *Deification of Arsinoe* (fr. 228) in 270 B.C.
The *Hymn to Delos* (IV) is dated by Wilamowitz[3] 269/5, after the
death of Arsinoe and before the outbreak of the war with Antigonos
Gonatas. If, as he argues, Kallimachos had visited Delos when he
wrote this hymn, fr. 114 (probably from bk. III of the *Aitia*), fr. 203
(*Iambos* XIII), and *Ep.* 62 derive from the same visit: fr. 178 (*Aitia*)
in which Kallimachos denies knowledge of seafaring should be
earlier.

Theokritos' dated poems belong to the years 273/70, and according to our argument[4] presuppose a first edition (in whatever form) of
Apollonios' *Argonautika*, as do also the *Aitia* and the *Hekale* of Kallimachos. The likely echoes of Theokritos in Kallimachos are two in
the *Hekale*, one in the third book of the *Aitia*;[5] the introduction to

---

[1] *Callimachus*, II, xxxvii.   [2] *Hell. Dicht.*, II, 1. Cf. McKay, *Mnem.* Supplt. VI, 13.

[3] Op. cit. 62. On the reference to the Gauls, here l. 184 and fr. 379, cf. the poem
explained by Bartoletti, *S.I.F.C.* 34, 1962, 21 ff., combining a Florentine papyrus
with Page, *G.L.P.*, no. 110. Cf. also Peek, *Maia* 15, 1963, 199.

[4] Cf. above, p. 65.

[5] Fr. 73 with Theocr. XVIII, 47; fr. 274 with I, 30 and particularly II, 78; fr. 292
with XV, 34. Perhaps also fr. 67, 13 with Theocr. XIII, 45; *Hymn* VI, 90-4 with
Theocr. II, 90, 106.

the eleventh idyll is clearly echoed in *Epigram* 46, which is itself dated well before 240, because, as Pfeiffer notes, the doctor consoled in that epigram has a son who is referred to as an authoritative person in a papyrus of 240. It is at least tempting to put fairly near 270 B.C. some other poems recalling the manner rather than the wording of Theokritos, particularly *Hymns* V and VI which have the same spirit as Theokritos' *Adoniazousai* (XV).¹ Four further epigrams may also belong here; *Ep.* 30 (note also the name Kleonikos) and 43 recall the unhappy lover of Theokritos XIV; *Ep.* 22 is bucolic, not only in matter but also in the bucolic anaphora, which is found again in the first book of the *Aitia* (fr. 27); *Ep.* 52 may be a compliment to the young Theokritos.

After 265 B.C. we have no firm dates again until the beginning of the reign of Euergetes in 246 B.C. It can at least be suggested that most of the last two books of the *Aitia*, the *Hekale*, and the third hymn belong here; and *Iambos* IV with its pair of birds has perhaps a reminiscence of the *Hekale*. For the last period *Hymn* II is dated by its reference to Euergetes (26).² The *Coma Berenices* belongs to 246/5 B.C. with fr. 388 rather earlier and fr. 387 rather later. The prologue of the *Aitia*, written when Kallimachos had lived 'many decades', must belong to this time, and the reference to Parmenion's Serapieion in the first *Iambos* may place this here too.³ Possibly also the Sosibios poem (fr. 384) is very late; it is as frigid as the *Coma Berenices*.

The late dating of the first *Iambos*, if it can be maintained, is extremely interesting as it may be Kallimachos' last word on literary disputes. He pictures Hipponax returning from the dead to summon the *philologoi* to the new Serapieion to hear the story of the Seven Sages: Thales was offered the cup which had been bequeathed to the wisest, and passed it on to Bion; so it went the rounds until it came back to Thales, and he dedicated it to Apollo at Branchidai. The

---

¹ Wilamowitz, op. cit., 33 dates *Hymn* VI rather before 270 B.C., because l. 9 is echoed by fr. 228, 45 f.; but the echo may go the other way. *Hymn* V is also early if it is parodied in *A.P.* V, 202/4.

² Pfeiffer, II, xxxviii. Contrast K. J. McKay, *Mnem.* Supplt. VI, 16, 24.

³ Cf. B. R. Rees, *C.R.* 75, 1961, 1; A. Rowe, *R.B.*, 39, 489 ff. On Hipponax and Kallimachos, cf. A. Ardizzoni, *Annali Cagliari* 28, 1960, 7 ff. The date of the Serapieion is, however, put back to Alexander by Bradford Welles, *Historia* 11, 1962, 286. Kallimachos may refer to the rebuilding under Ptolemy III.

Alexandrian scholar-poets are not only told the story of the Seven Sages by a revenant; they are also told it among the statues of wise men in the Serapieion, if Professor Rees' attractive interpretation is right. Euhemeros in the poem is a statue, presumably one of a group like the remarkable collection of Homer, Pindar, Demetrios of Phaleron, Orpheus, Hesiod, Protagoras, Thales, Herakleitos, and Plato from the Exedra of the Serapieion at Memphis; similar groups are known in mosaics, which presumably derive from Hellenistic paintings.[1] The presence of two Early Hellenistic figures, Euhemeros and Demetrios of Phaleron, in these groups of classical and mythical figures shows how strongly the Alexandrians felt themselves the heirs of the whole tradition of Greek poetry and wisdom. Thales at Memphis is explaining a globe with his stick; Thales in the first *Iambos* is also an astronomer and is scratching geometrical diagrams on the ground with his stick. The metre and the language and the manner of this poem come fom Hipponax, but Kallimachos has given the expression an Alexandrian obscurity: Thales is drawing a figure invented by his junior, Pythagoras; Pythagoras is therefore called by the name of the Trojan war hero, Euphorbos, whose incarnation Pythagoras claimed to be. This learned allusion is matched by an equally learned vocabulary. But this learnedness is varied with direct flashes: 'my good man, don't wrinkle your nose. I have not much time myself.' But the general purpose must be a demand to cease hostilities, and the revenant Hipponax, who in his lifetime drove the sculptor Boupalos to suicide by his abuse, as he reminds us at the beginning, is the most powerful possible advocate. The solidarity of learned poets is also the message of the fourth *Iambos*, the story of the two trees, which may also belong to this time, if it is later than the *Hekale*.

The hostilities themselves are mentioned during this late period at the end of *Hymn* II, in the prologue to the *Aitia*, and in *Iambos* XIII, which is certainly later than the Delian hymn (270/65) and may have been composed as a pendant to *Iambos* I.[2] The *Diegesis* to

---

[1] Lauer and Picard, *Les Statues ptolémaiques du Serapieion de Memphis*, 1955; K. Schefold, *M.H.* 14, 1957, 33; G. M. A. Richter, *Coll. Latomus* 44, 1960, 671, also on the mosaics.

[2] Dawson, *Y.C.S.* 11, 1950, 148.

*Iambos* XIII says that Kallimachos answered those who blamed him for the variety of his poems by saying that he copied Ion of Chios and that nobody blames the craftsman for making many different sorts of object. What is left of *Iambos* XIII gives first the criticism – Kallimachos writes Ionic without going to Ephesos, mixes old and new vocabulary, mixes dialects – then the answer that no one made a rule 'one poet, one genre', then probably the passage about the craftsmen (36) and Ion of Chios (41 f.). The Muses loved him, but now the poets abuse each other so violently that the Muses fly past for fear of being abused. 'Do not wonder then if I sing limping iambics, although I have never been to Ephesos.'¹ The charge against Kallimachos is variety of metre, dialect, and vocabulary; his counter-charge is mutual abuse and lack of inspiration.

The abuse poured out by rival poets in *Iambos* XIII is personified by Phthonos and Momos of *Hymn* II (105): 'Envy said in Apollo's ear, "I do not like the singer who does not sing as the sea." Apollo kicked Envy out and said: "The Assyrian river's stream is great but carries most of the filth of the land and much rubbish on its waters. Demeter's bees do not bring water from everywhere but the little water, finest flower, which wells clean and undefiled from a holy spring." Farewell, Lord. May Criticism dwell where Envy is.' Viewed with the charge, the defence is an admission of writing many kinds of poetry, a claim that each poem is comparable to the finest, purest spring water, and a countercharge that the large poem contains a lot of filth and rubbish (this elaborates the lack of inspiration alleged in *Iambos* XIII). It sounds as if Kallimachos has been in danger of losing some position and that, although Phthonos has been defeated, criticism (Momos) remains. Wilamowitz² suggests that the reference may be to Apollonios' withdrawal to Rhodes; chronologically this seems unlikely, and as the scholiast (on l. 26) says that Kallimachos gives divine honours to Euergetes as a scholar, the patronage of Euergetes would seem to be what Kallimachos achieved against his rivals and detractors; with the new king as

---

¹ 63 μὴ θ[αυμάσῃς νυν ἦν τὸ χωλὸν] ἀείδω.

² *Hell. Dicht.*, II, 87. Erbse, *Hermes* 83, 1955, 425, cannot believe that Kallimachos could compare the work of his pupil to the large and dirty Assyrian river; I do not understand this view.

his patron he could adopt towards others the lofty attitude of the first *Iambos*, and call his own song 'stronger than the evil eye' as he does in *Epigram* 21 (perhaps the concluding epigram of a collection of epigrams). In the context of the historical situation, Berenike of Cyrene's defeat of Demetrios, and her marriage with Euergetes, the whole hymn makes sense: Kyrene as the bride of Apollo defeating the lion (90 f.) is a divine parallel to the story of Berenike, Demetrios, and Euergetes, just as Apollo's rejection of Phthonos is a divine parallel to Euergetes' giving patronage to Kallimachos in spite of his detractors. We should not simply identify Apollo and Euergetes: we should rather say that the human event has a divine parallel (which in the case of Apollo and Kyrene lies in past history). A rather similar kind of near-identification is to be seen on the later Archelaos relief:[1] Homer's fame is eternal and ubiquitous, but Time and the World are given the faces of Ptolemy Philopator and Arsinoe, because they made the Homereion in Alexandria and so ensured Homer's immortality in the Greek-speaking world. Apollo may work through Euergetes but he is also for Kallimachos the god of poetry; the *Hymn to Apollo* is therefore a very personal poem. Like *Hymns* V and VI it is a dramatic presentation, and here too the god is going to appear. The other two hymns describe a ritual procession with statue or emblem, but here the laurel, the walls, the doors, the palm-tree, and the swan all feel that the god himself is coming (like Hekate in Theokritos II) and the young men must sing. It is their song that Kallimachos gives in his hexameters, an elegant cult hymn, telling of Apollo's powers and prowess and so leading to the founding of Cyrene, which Apollo pointed out to Kallimachos' ancestor Battos and promised to 'our kings', presumably Philadelphos and Euergetes (65 ff.). Such a hymn from the time of Homer's Delian hymn could always finish with a *Sphragis* containing a reference to the poet, and this tradition formally justifies the allusion to Kallimachos' own position at the end.

Apollo is quoted again in the late prologue of the *Aitia* (1, 21): 'when I first put the tablet on my knees, Apollo said to me: "The victim must be fat but the Muse fine (*leptalee*); don't take the highroad but the untrodden path, even if it is narrower".' Originality

---

[1] Pl. IV. *M.T.S.*, no ES 1. Cf. below, p. 145.

is emphasized more obviously here than in the *Hymn*, but there too the clean spring is only known to Demeter's priestesses, just as here Kallimachos claims to sing among those who love the shrill sound of the cicada and not the braying of asses. After Apollo's advice the poem comes to its conclusion with a curse upon old age and an assertion that the Muses will not desert their own when he grows grey: this is the confident spirit of the first *Iambos*. The beginning part of the poem with the ancient commentary goes into greater detail: 'The Telchines grumble at my song (ignorant of the Muse, they are not beloved by her), because I never completed a single continuous song in many thousands of verses to reverend kings or former heroes, but spin my song small, like a child, though the decades of my years are not few. I say this to the Telchines: "Prickly tribe, knowledgeable at wasting away your own hearts, I am truly oligostichic. Bounteous Demeter defeats the tall oak; the fine (*lepton*) sayings taught that Mimnermos is the sweeter of the two poets, the large woman failed. Let the Massagetai shoot far at their man. Koan nightingales like ours are sweeter. Away, horrid children of the evil-eye. Judge wisdom again by art not by the Persian measure. Don't ask me to father a loud sounding song. Thunder does not belong to me but to Zeus." '[1] Here the contrast is very clear between the short fine poems (*leptos*), which vary in dialect and metre, and the single continuous long poem, which the jealous critics say that Kallimachos has not written. (The scholiast on *Hymn* II, 106, says that the *Hekale* was written in answer to such criticism; if this is true, the criticism must have been made much earlier and the answer was evidently not accepted.)

The poem is more valuable still for its examples of ideals and critics. Kallimachos admires Mimnermos and Philitas. He dislikes Antimachos' *Lyde*, as we know from an epigram (fr. 398): '*Lyde*, a

---

[1] I have translated with Pfeiffer's supplements except in ll. 13, 16, where I have accepted from Puelma (*M.H.* 11, 1954, 107 f.) for 13 κλαγγὸν . . . φέροιτο and in 16 Κῷαι, with the direct reference to Philitas. In l. 9 Puelma rightly sees a contest of plants, as in *Iambos* IV. Here the corn yields to the wind and is saved, the oak crashes. Corn is chosen (rather than the willow (?) of S. *Ant.* 710 ff.) because of Philitas' *Demeter*. Cf. also Wimmel, *Hermes* 86, 1958, 346. On the *Lyde* see most recently Del Corno, *Acme* 15, 1962, 57 ff.

thick and unclear book'. In this poem (12) the large woman, un-favourably contrasted with Mimnermos' 'fine sayings', must be the *Lyde* (and the reader is meant to supply Mimnermos' Nanno as a small woman). The objection to the *Lyde* is presumably that what started as a poem lamenting the loss of the poet's beloved became a jumble of mythology, the Argonauts, Bellerophon, Oedipus, the Sun's cup, etc. But for Hermesianax these were 'holy books' (Ath. 13, 598a), for Asklepiades (*Anth. Pal.* IX, 63) 'the joint writing of the Muses and Antimachos' made Lyde more noble than any Ionian aristocrat, and Poseidippos (*Anth. Pal.* XII, 168) names her in the same breath as Mimnermos' Nanno. Asklepiades and Poseidippos are named by the scholiast on *Aitia* fr. 1 as two of the Telchines, the jealous critics. If it is surprising to find two elegiac poets, Asklepiades and Poseidippos, attacking Kallimachos, the answer must lie partly in the dispute over the *Lyde*. The other author known to us in the scholiast's list is Praxiphanes of Mitylene. Praxiphanes was himself attacked by Kallimachos in a prose work, *Against Praxiphanes*. Praxiphanes was a pupil of Theophrastos, and Professor Brink[1] convincingly argues that as a Peripatetic he would believe in the long poem with organic unity covering its digressions, and the scholiast sums up his list of critics by saying that they blamed Kalli-machos because his style was emaciated and he had no length. With length goes the full-bloodedness of the grand manner, which allows digressions within the general scheme; 'emaciated' and 'thick' deprecate the qualities which 'fine' and 'full-blooded' appreciate. The fragment of Kallimachos' *Against Praxiphanes* (460) throws another name into the battle: 'Kallimachos mentions Aratos as his elder not only in the epigrams but also in *Against Praxiphanes*, praising him as learned and a first-rate poet'. The epigram (27) cannot be dated: 'Hesiod's the song and the manner. Not the fur-thest of singers I fear the man of Soli copied but the most honey-sweet of poems. Hail fine sayings, sign of Aratos' sleeplessness.'[2]

---

[1] *C.Q.* 40, 1946, 19 f. with testimonia and fragments. Note that Praxiphanes' *On Poets* was a dialogue between Plato and Isokrates; and Kallimachos (fr. 589) attacked Plato's poetic judgment. In Alexandria itself Neoptolemos of Parion was a 'middle of the road man' (C.O. Brink, *Horace on Poetry*, 74).

[2] The text of the last line is uncertain but the sense is clear. ἔσχατος is rare in the sense of 'best'; yet the contrast between Hesiod and Homer seems desirable here; I

For Praxiphanes Aratos presumably came into the same category as Empedokles does for Aristotle (*Poet.* 1447b, 17, 'there is nothing shared by Homer and Empedokles except metre; therefore Homer may be called a poet and Empedokles a physiologist rather than a poet'). Kallimachos answers: he was copying Hesiod and not Homer. Hesiod was Kallimachos' own model; at the beginning and end of the *Aitia* (fr. 2; 112) he tells of Hesiod receiving his song as he pastured his sheep on Helikon and in the earlier passage he claims that in a youthful dream he himself received the *Aitia* from the Muses on Helikon. One other epigram should be quoted here. The beginning of the Aratos epigram suggests a book-title; *Epigram 6* is also a parody of a book-title for Kreophylos' *Sack of Oichalia*; the best that can be said of the poem is that it is called Homeric. And with this can be associated *Epigram* 28:[1] 'I hate the cyclic poem and the high-road and the prostitute; I don't drink from the fountain; I loathe everything public. Lysanias, you are beautiful, yes, beautiful. But before Echo has got this out, someone says, "Another has him".' In this parody of a love poem the comparison of the cyclic poem to high-road and public fountain recalls the prologue of the *Aitia* and *Hymn* II. It looks as if 'cyclic' already means (as in Horace, *A.P.* 136) not only conventional but poem of the Epic Cycle; it would thus cover both Kreophylos and Antimachos.[2]

The epigrams are not dated. The prologue of the *Aitia* is a late affirmation of Kallimachos' doctrine. Of the critics listed by the scholiast Poseidippos was writing as late as 264/3, but Asklepiades is associated as much with Ptolemy I as with Ptolemy II and Theokritos equates him with Philitas (VII, 40). The *Phainomena* of Aratos must have been published soon after his arrival at Antigonos' court in 276 B.C., if Apollonios Rhodios already knew it when he wrote the first version of the *Argonautika*. Praxiphanes need not, of course, have criticized it immediately; the two firm dates for Praxiphanes

---

suppose Kallimachos wants to stress the distance between everyone else and Homer. Better perhaps W. Ludwig, *Hermes*, 91, 1963, 425: 'not the worst but the sweetest'. On the 'book-title' epigram, cf. Gabathuler, 110. Cf. also above, p. 31, on Aratos.

[1] The Petersen-Mair punctuation of the last line must be right.

[2] It is very firmly attached to Antimachos by the scholiasts on Horace (B. Wyss, *Antimachi Colophonii Reliquiae*, lxvi).

are the Delian inscription dated epigraphically (270/60 B.C.) and the fact that he was Theophrastos' pupil before 288/7 B.C.; Professor Brink[1] puts his birth about 340 B.C. It seems therefore unlikely that the work which Kallimachos answers in *Against Praxiphanes* was written much later than 270. Another piece of early evidence for the clash of two poetic ideals is in Theokritos, not only in his rewriting of Apollonios in *Idylls* XIII and XXII but in his criticism of the 'birds of the Muses' who 'toil vainly, crowing against the Chian singer' (VII, 47). The echoes of Theokritos in Kallimachos have already been noticed, and it is at least possible that the love epigram (52) is a pretty compliment to an ally. On the evidence of *Idyll* VII Theokritos had declared himself by 270, and Timon's knowledge of the struggles in the bird-cage is certainly not later.

The prologue to the *Aitia* is therefore a late stage in an action which had been going on for thirty years. The name Telchines suggests not only malice but Rhodes. Among the known critics of the scholiast's list only Praxiphanes could be called a Rhodian, and he may have migrated to Rhodes before the death of Theophrastos.[2] If Praxiphanes was in Rhodes from about 290 onwards and as an Aristotelian was in favour of long poetry, was it to him or to his entourage that Apollonios went when he retired from Alexandria and did Kallimachos include Apollonios in the Telchines? One of the links between the two may have been a veneration for Antimachos, whom Apollonios edited and used as a source (cf. Wyss, xix, xlviii) and whom Praxiphanes as a Peripatetic would venerate out of loyalty to Plato. Praxiphanes, like Asklepiades, was probably dead before the prologue to the *Aitia* was written but Apollonios was still Librarian when Kallimachos feared that he would not get the patronage of Euergetes. Apollonios' name is not in the scholiast, but this may only mean that there was no record of his having attacked Kallimachos in writing, and does not exclude the possibility that Kallimachos meant the name Telchines to include the Rhodian writer of long epic. The *Ibis* (fr. 381–2) is our evidence that Kallimachos did attack Apollonios, but this may belong rather to the earlier date before Apollonios retired to Rhodes.

Kallimachos claims for himself short poetry, in many metres

[1] Loc. cit., 23 with T 1, F 5 and 6.          [2] Brink, loc. cit., 22 with T 3, 7.

(Pfeiffer's index lists sixteen), original, learned, only appreciated by connoisseurs. One quality more he gives in his own epitaph (*Ep.* 35): 'You walk past the tomb of Battiades who was skilled in song and skilled in laughter attuned to the wine'. Gabathuler suggests that this may be the concluding epigram of a collection (like 21). He claims not only serious poetry but also the light touch evident in the asides in the first *Iambos*. Although some of his poetry is obviously pretty, occasional verse (e.g. *Iambos* XII, fr. 227, 399–401), his light touch makes him sometimes difficult for us to interpret, particularly in the *Epigrams*. The poem to Theokritos (52) is a pretty compliment rather than an exaggerated declaration of love. And none of the symposion poems (*Ep.* 1, 8, 25, 28, 29, 31–2, 41–2, 44–6, 52, 59) need be taken very seriously whether they have an obvious literary reference or not: *Ep.* 43 with its Aristotelian terminology might be the apology of any young hero of Menander and ends with a near-quotation of the *Dyskolos* (303). But is the poem to Lysanias (28) primarily a condemnation of Lysanias or a condemnation of long poetry? Is the ninth *Iambos* primarily aetiology or primarily a condemnation of Philetades? And does the charming poem about Orestes (59) imply that Kallimachos lost all his friends by writing an unsuccessful drama? The Suda credits him with dramas, and another epigram (8) prays Dionysos for the short word 'I conquer'. The epigram on Theaitetos (7), who is probably the epigrammatist of that name, is a mock epitaph, but the ideal of pure poetry which theatre audiences reject is Kallimachos' own ideal. It is not an easy ideal, and in *Iambos* III, another difficult poem in which it is not clear to us whether the real object of attack is a prostitute or the society which lets the poet starve, he writes: 'It would have been profitable to toss my hair to the Phrygian flute in honour of Kybele or in a long frock to wail Adonis as a slave of the goddess. But I madly turned to the Muses: I must eat the bread I baked.' Theokritos' Adonis festival does not contain a male performer, but Galloi are well known from the Anthology, and later in the third century Dioskorides contrasts the success of Aristagoras dancing Gallos with the disaster of his own poem on the *Temenidai*.[1]

---

[1] *A.P.* XI, 195. Cf. below, p. 143. For Galloi, cf. *A.P.* VI, 51, 234 and Gow, *J.H.S.* 80, 1960, 88. For Gallai, cf. Kallimachos, fr. 761. The Simon of *Ep.* 38 was a

Herakleitos had lived true to the high ideal, and his 'nightingales' will live (*Ep.* 2). It is not technically an epitaph because it was meant for the circle of Herakleitos' friends, not for his tombstone; but it has the same simplicity and seriousness as the poems which may be accepted as epitaphs, e.g. *Ep.* 9, 12, 14–20, 26, 40, 58, 60, 61. Take for instance *Ep.* 15: ' "Timonoe". But who are you? By the gods I should not have known you, if the name of Timotheos your father had not been on the stele and Methymna, your city. Your husband Euthymenes surely grieves deeply in his widowhood.' Here the genuine feeling suggests a real epitaph; but the poem (13) in which the dead man says that Ploutos is a myth and life is cheap in the underworld is epigram rather than epitaph (cf. 3, 4, 7, 11, 21–3, 30, 35, 43, 61, some of which have been already discussed), and the eleventh *Iambos* is aetiology cast into the form of an epitaph. The same problem arises with the dedications: the interpretation of the pinax with a standing hero as the gift of a man who was angry with a cavalryman (24) is surely a joke (cf. also 47). The dedication for a temple in Thermopylae (39) was presumably commissioned by the Naucratite who dedicated his tithe[1] there. But did the Rhodian comic actor Agoranax, who dedicated the double-sided mask of Pamphilos, commission Kallimachos to say that the mask was 'not totally ravaged by love, but half like a roast fig and the lamps of Isis' (49)?[2] The other mask epigram (48) – the tragic Dionysos in the schoolroom, which gapes twice as wide as the Samian Gaping Dionysos – is also surely occasioned by seeing Dionysos in a school-room and is not a dedication written for the mask.

In the *Epigrams* Kallimachos wears his learning lightly. The scanty prose fragments (403–64) give some idea of the extent of this learning: he wrote among other things on Contests, Winds, Barbarian customs, National names (which seems to have been a lexikon of names given in different parts of the Greek world), Wonders of

---

Bacchic dancer if Bentley's emendation of l. 5 is correct, but the final words may be sound, 'poor dear, she was bold'.

[1] Cf. *Ep.* 5, 33, 37, 38, 55, 56, 57. On *Ep.* 2, cf. Snell, *Glotta* 37, 1958, 1, on metre, alliteration, assonance.

[2] Mair's text, οὐχ ἕν . . . δεδαγμένον, should be accepted here. See above, p. 16. Cf. *Ep.* 34, 51, 53, 54, 62.

the world (chiefly rivers), Names of months, Foundation of cities and changes of name, Nymphs, Birds, and the hundred and twenty volumes of *Pinakes*, which was a catalogue of all writers giving their lives and their works. This learning shows more obviously in the *Hymns* and the *Hekale* than in the *Epigrams* and most obviously in the *Aitia* and the *Iamboi*.

The *Hymns* are hymns only in two senses: their subjects are gods and a cult place, and like the Homeric hymns all except one are in hexameters. The Homeric hymns were meant for performance at a festival; these hymns are literature to read, and though they have a dramatic setting this setting must not be examined too closely. In the second *Hymn* as we have seen the poet imagines the holy place quivering in anticipation of Apollo's appearance, then he writes the choral hymn to the god ending as such hymns may with the poet's own view of his art. The introduction suggests Delphi and the hymn ends with the slaying of Pytho, but the emphasis is on Cyrene and even in the introduction the palm-tree is Delian. Perhaps we should think of a temple of Apollo in Cyrene and the audience would know the statue with golden chiton, himation, lyre, bow, quiver, and sandals. Kallimachos is only interested in the gold and gives no hint of the posture of the statue. In the other statue-poems also we have no evidence that he made his readers see the statue: *Iambos* VI gives the dimensions and cost of the Olympian Zeus; the Leukadian Artemis (fr. 31b), the Hera at Samos (fr. 101) and the Delian Apollo (fr. 114) interest him because of their unexpected attributes.

The fifth and sixth *Hymns*[1] have no personal reference but are more like the *Adoniazousai* of Theokritos. The identification must not be pressed too far, but essentially the speaker of *Hymn* V (the only hymn in elegiacs) purports to be a priestess of Athena at Argos instructing and talking to the girls who are to bathe the statue of Athena. Of course she speaks of the statue as if it were the goddess; that is natural for the priestess. She tells the girls to come out because the horses of the goddess' chariot are already neighing. She tells

---

[1] K. J. McKay ('Poet at Play', *Mnem.* Supplt. VI, 1962; *Erysichthon*, Leiden, 1962) should be consulted for detailed interpretation, his general treatment of Kallimachos' humour in these poems is excellent. For Alexandrian Eleusis, *P. Oxy.*, 2465.

I

them not to bring cosmetics because Athena did not use cosmetics at the Judgment of Paris. 'Come out, Athena.' She tells them the story of Eumedes. 'Come out, Athena.' She warns all of the dangers of river-water today because Athena is to bathe in it. 'Come out, Athena.' She tells them the story of Teiresias who saw the goddess bathing. 'At last Athena is coming.' This is essentially a simple poem: the stories come from Kallimachos' learning but they are the right stories for the Argive priestess to tell her girls. The speaker of *Hymn* VI purports to be the instructor of the women who sing to the Basket of Demeter as it goes in procession from the Alexandrian Eleusis. Because this is a festival designed to bring plenty she refuses to tell them of the wanderings of Demeter but tells them instead of the punishment of Erysichthon which is again treated in a highly individual and ironic way. The scheme here is the same as in *Hymn* V.

The first *Hymn* is a hymn to Zeus to be sung at the libation; in so far as it has a setting, the setting is a symposion. It is a learned poem: the Arcadian story of the birth of Zeus is to be preferred to the Cretan story. Zeus did not divide the world with his brothers; he won his kingdom by force; he is the god of kings, and therefore of Ptolemy Philadelphos. The *Hymn to Artemis* (III) is in form like a Homeric hymn. 'We sing of Artemis . . . Farewell, Queen, and kindly accept our song.' But except for the brief solemn passage about the city of unjust men (122 f.), when Artemis takes over the functions of the Hesiodic Zeus (*Op.* 225 ff.), the learned list of islands, nymphs, and cities, and the farewell with its four mythological examples of the disaster which ensues from dishonouring Artemis, the poem, as Professor Herter[1] has shown in detail, may be described as a pleasant trifling with Homeric themes. The technique is known from Apollonios Rhodios: not only translation into Hellenistic terms (as in the *Hekale* and the divine scenes at the beginning of Apollonios' third book) but direct contrast with the original, as when Apollonios turns Kirke into a nervous aunt. The tone is set in the second line, where Artemis is introduced as hunting hares. Then she appears as a child on the knees of Zeus and makes her demands: behind this scene is Thetis' appeal to Zeus. When she goes to get her weapons from the Kyklopes the contrast with Thetis' visit

[1] *Kallimachos und Homer*, Bonn, 1929.

to Hephaistos is clear: child and monsters instead of goddess and god; and the metalwork which is being made when she arrives is Poseidon's horse-trough instead of tripods for the banquets of the gods. Once (53) a piece of Alexandrian science intrudes; the Kyklops' eye is compared to a shield with four (instead of the Homeric seven) ox-hides, because Herophilos had recently discovered the four skins of the eye. After the serious passage about the unjust city, Herakles on Olympos (144 ff.) is pure comedy: a traditional glutton, he urges Artemis only to shoot the largest animals including oxen. The succeeding sections on islands, nymphs, and cities are full of learning. Not only learned but whimsically obscure is the passage about the dancers (170 ff.): 'when the nymphs surround you in dance . . . may not my oxen be ploughing another man's field . . . for the Sun never passes by that fair dance but stops his chariot to watch and the days lengthen'. This involved way of emphasizing the beauty of the dance recalls two lines in the *Aitia* (ff. 75, 10 f.), where instead of saying 'in the morning the oxen were going to be sacrificed', he says 'in the morning the oxen were going to rend their hearts, seeing the sharp knife in the water'. This is the 'narrow path' of originality in expression.

The fourth *Hymn*, to Delos, is the longest and perhaps the least interesting: in shape it is like a Homeric hymn and it is packed with learning. It has its political reference to Ptolemy Philadelphos and the Gauls (160 ff.). It has its Homeric reminiscences. Delos 'a fitter coursing ground for gulls than horses' (12) clearly recalls Homeric Ithaka (*Od.* 4, 605 ff.). In the Homeric hymn to Apollo the story is told shortly (III, 30): all the places visited by Leto refuse her except Delos, who stipulates that Apollo shall build his temple there. All the goddesses are there except Hera and Eileithyia, whom Hera has kept on Olympos. The goddesses send Iris to offer Eileithyia a gold necklace; Eileithyia comes and Apollo is born. What the Homeric hymn does in ninety lines takes two hundred in Kallimachos. Hera puts Ares on Haimos and Iris on Mimas to watch and threaten all the places visited by Leto. (Not long before in the *Deification of Arsinoe* (fr. 228) Kallimachos had sent Charis to the top of Athos to look over the sea and discover the meaning of the smoke rolling over the sea from Arsinoe's pyre.) Leto visits the places one by one. Twice the unborn Apollo speaks to threaten Thebes (88), to warn her off Kos (162) (because Ptolemy Philadelphos is to be born there), and, extremely late, to suggest Delos as a suitable place. Before this Peneios (121) had been prepared to receive her in spite of the threats of Hera and Ares, but she refused this sacrifice and turned to the islands who fled in terror before Iris. 'They all at her bidding fled in a body down the stream, whichever island Leto approached' (159). There seems to be a contradiction between this conception of islands that run away and the other conception of Delos as the wandering island among fixed islands (190 ff.). Presumably Kallimachos would answer that the island nymph is not bound to her island, as when the islands dance round Delos,[1] but the juxtaposition of the two conceptions is unfortunate and perhaps argues a lack of visual imagination in the poet. Delos defies Hera's anger. Iris flies to tell Hera. Then (228) she sits beneath Hera's throne, like one of Artemis' hunting dogs, ears pricked, always ready for orders; she sleeps beside the throne with her head lolling on her shoulders. This is one of the few passages where Kallimachos seems to be thinking of a work of art.[2] Hera, after a taunt at Zeus' women who give birth on deserted rocks, pardons Asterie (Delos) in spite of her criminal conduct, because in the past she preferred the sea to Zeus. This is in Kallimachos' best manner.

The one poem in which Kallimachos employs his technique on a larger scale is the *Hekale*. Its length has been estimated at a thousand lines, and the scholiast to *Hymn* II, 106 says that it was an answer to those who charged him with being incapable of writing a large poem. Even if the estimate is right, it is considerably shorter than any of Apollonios' four books. The ancient *Summary* tells us that Theseus, having escaped the plot of Medeia, was carefully guarded by his father, having unexpectedly returned from Troizen. Wanting to go and attack the bull of Marathon, he had to escape secretly in the evening. Suddenly a storm broke and he took refuge in the hut of Hekale. In the morning he went out and overcame the bull and returned to Hekale. He found her dead and lamented her. He rewarded her by bringing together the people into a deme which he called after her and established a precinct of Zeus Hekaleios. Plutarch,

---

[1] Cf. Beazley, *Vases in Poland*, 62 for the island dance in the fifth century.
[2] Cf. below, Ch. VIII, p. 173.

*Thes.* 14, adds the point that Hekale vowed a sacrifice to Zeus if Theseus returned. The *Priapea* 12, 3 says that Theseus actually found her on the pyre. Ovid tells us that she was never married (*rem. Am.* 747). Statius (*Theb.* xii, 581) speaks in a single sentence of Marathon, Crete, and Hekale's tears. Many fragments survive, and it is justifiable to follow every hint in placing them.

The poem starts with Hekale living on the Eastern slopes of Pentelikos, honoured because she is hospitable, comely in her broad shepherd's hat, with a shepherd's crook in her hand and a stick of heath to prop her aged steps.[1] The picture recalls the realistic old figures of Hellenistic art, but perhaps Kallimachos felt that he was getting too sentimental (having used all his powers of alliteration and assonance in this description)[2] and pulled himself up with the word ποιηφάγον (fr. 365), normally used of 'grass-eating' animals but here of the old woman, whose diet was vegetables. How he managed the transition to Theseus is unknown; perhaps Hekale foresaw the storm because of the snuffs on the wick of her lamp (fr. 269), and perhaps the poet addressed Adrasteia here (fr. 299, 687) because Hekale's life was near its end.

Theseus, like Hekale, is described: he wears a new Thessalian hat and a long chiton (fr. 304, 293). Presumably the various fragments referring to the Argolid come here and his journey was narrated, perhaps with considerable aetiological digression.[3] Medeia recognizes him and tries to poison him, but Aigeus has also recognized him and prevents him drinking: someone curses Medeia.[4] Here the story evidently follows the same lines as in Plutarch's *Theseus* (ch. 12). The account of Theseus' recognition tokens, sword and boots, is given by the poet, partly in narrative, partly as a speech by Aigeus to Aithra, which continues to within thirty lines or so of the point where Theseus sets out to find the Marathonian bull.[5] This

[1] Fr. 230 + 490 + 231, 552, 342, 292, 355.

[2] Cf. Pfeiffer on fr. 281, 283–4, 303–4, 323, 725; McKay, *Mnem.* Supplt. VI, 1962, 42, 77, 83 ff., 110.

[3] Fr. 277, 278–80, 285, 288, 307, 339, 237.

[4] Fr. 232, 345, 364, 233.

[5] Fr. 235, 236, 238. In fr. 238 Pfeiffer argues that the opening lines end Aigeus' speech and then Aithra's reactions are described. On the other side of the same papyrus (i.e. not much more than thirty lines on) Theseus has already set out.

must therefore be a flashback to the time when Aigeus was with Aithra in Troizen, and perhaps fr. 359, Aigeus 'picks up his armour and says', marks the return to the story: Aigeus forbids Theseus to leave Athens. As far as we can appreciate this part it is elegant narrative with Homeric echoes and a fair proportion of rare words.

The papyrus resumes with a description of clear weather while it was still midday; in the evening when daughters ask their mothers for the evening meal (a Hellenistic elaboration of the simple term, evening; so later the poet gives an elaborate description of dawn) then the storm gathered over all the mountains of Attica and the North wind fell upon the clouds. Surely the effect which Kallimachos wants here is that the storm, coming over Parnes, thyme-clad Aigaleos, rough Hymettos, chases Theseus up the road, and therefore Theseus has already started 'while it was still midday'; this is not really inconsistent with the Summary's 'about evening' because it is evening before Theseus has got far.[1]

Theseus finds shelter in Hekale's hut: 'Be the craftsman of my life and conqueror of my hunger' (fr. 267). Pfeiffer has shown that the model here is Odysseus' visit to Eumaios in the second half of the Odyssey, but this is Hellenistic genre-painting with all the colours of assonance and alliteration and with rare words. Hekale answers 'There is water and earth and a baking stove' (fr. 268).[2] He takes off his cloak, she sits him down, she makes up the fire, she heats water for washing, she gives him olives, vegetables, and bread.[3]

A papyrus fragment (fr. 253) gives on one side the end of Theseus' speech and on the other side part of Hekale's answer. Theseus told her who he was and that he was going to Marathon but perhaps not much more, before he asked who she was. She probably accused him of waking sleeping tears (fr. 682, perhaps also fr. 313 belongs here). She had been well off and of good family (fr. 254). She was turned out of her property and complained to the kings, and she was

[1] Fr. 321, 338, Boreas; fr. 319, 335, 566, weather; fr. 336, the beasts creep into their holes.

[2] It is not clear where the other fragments about pottery belong, fr. 341, 344. And does Theseus say 'But though you are ugly and have white spots on your eyes' (fr. 289)?

[3] Fr. 239–46, 248–52. Also 270, 286, perhaps 334, 495.

brought from Kolonos here, where she lives among poor farmers (this seems a possible way of putting the fragments together and may fill the gap in fr. 253).[1] She goes back to her prosperity:[2] 'I was watching the oxen circling my threshing-floor, when a chariot brought him from Aphidnai, like the kings who are sons of Zeus or god himself. I remember he had a fair cloak, held by golden pins, work spider-fine.' The abrupt introduction without a name shows that the man from Aphidnai must be a known character, and Pfeiffer's suggestion of Aigeus seems almost certain. Then she goes on to describe the fine down on his face, like helichryse (fr. 274), and his fair hair, which waved about his head, whereas Theseus' hair is cropped close (fr. 361, 376, 281). Nevertheless the likeness is amazing (fr. 367). Here too the background is Homeric, the youthening of Odysseus in the sixth book of the *Odyssey* and Helen's recognition of Telemachos in the fourth. Perhaps she leads on to the rest of the story by wishing she had never met Aigeus (fr. 619).

We cannot here be far from two overlapping papyri, which place nine book fragments.[3] Hekale speaks of two children whom she brought up in every kind of luxury. Then a gap probably of at least twenty-five lines, in which presumably the sentiment 'God did not give mortals laughter without tears' (fr. 298) belongs. Then, 'Did I refuse to hear death calling me a long time ago that I might soon rend my garments over you too.' There are two possible interpretations: 'I failed to die when one (or both) of the children died, and therefore now I shall have also to see you, Theseus, die', or she transposes herself into the past 'I failed to die when the first of the children died in order that shortly after I might see you, X (the other child), die'. With the second interpretation the death of the first child (and therefore probably the front of *Ox. Pap.* 2377) must come in the gap.

[1] Fr. 275, 329, 300; 272, 287, 290, 303, 489, 721.

[2] Bartoletti, *S.I.F.C.* 31, 1959, 179, having re-examined *P.S.I.* 133, is convinced that fr. 255 belongs here as the first preserved line of the verso (fr. 253, 8).

[3] *Ox. Pap.* 2376-7. Loeb fr. 284A. The fragments so placed are certainly 337, 366, 247, 284, 350, 294, 368, 639, 327. It is uncertain whether the front or the back of 2377 comes first; if the front comes first *Ox. Pap.* 2376 must have had at least forty-four lines to a column even if 2377 only had thirty-five. It is therefore rather more likely that the front of 2377 comes after the back, and I have assumed that order.

With the first interpretation Hekale fears that Theseus, who is so like the young Aigeus of long ago, will be killed by the Marathonian bull of which he had just told her. Hekale goes on to speak of Kerkyon, who fled from Arcadia and dwelt near, a bad neighbour to us. 'May I dig out his eyes and eat him raw!', and presumably soon afterwards 'May I die when I hear of him dead' (fr. 591). Hekale does not know that Kerkyon has already been killed by Theseus, and this is a wish which comes true, because she dies the day after Theseus has told her. On the first interpretation Hekale's narrative may be broken here, and Theseus may tell her of Kerkyon. Then she goes on to describe the death of the other child: 'this was my blackest day' (fr. 348). The front of *Ox. Pap.* 2377 has something about Peteus, son of Orneus, about fetching horses from Eurotas, possibly about Cape Malea, and about sailing with a hostile omen, and something about kings. It is a reasonable conjecture that the second child was sent on an expedition by Peteos and died in a disaster at sea. But who were the children? Ovid's evidence that Hekale was never married must be trusted. She may have been raped by Aigeus or another; but her account of bringing up the children sounds more like a nurse than a mother. A possible clue is given by fr. 527:[1] 'whom a concubine bore to him'. The children may have been illegitimate sons of Aigeus whom he left with Hekale to bring up. At the end of this scene Hekale presumably reproached herself for garrulity (fr. 310, 483).

Hekale went to bed (fr. 256). Theseus perhaps lay outside with his head on a stone (fr. 375). Hekale saw him get up (fr. 257) and presumably then prayed to Zeus for his safe return (Plutarch). Theseus went to Marathon and captured the bull, which had tried to escape up a valley.[2] As he brought the bull back, the villagers were terrified, but he told them to send a messenger to Aigeus; then they sang a paian and pelted him with leaves, and the women wound their girdles round him (fr. 260). Is it perhaps here that someone sings a hymn to Aithra among the assembled women? (fr. 371).

After a gap of twenty-two lines the crow is speaking and the crow

---

[1] The ascription and restoration of this fragment is quite uncertain: τοὺς αὐτῷ σκοτίους ἔτεκεν γυνὴ ἐμπελάτειρα is possible.

[2] Fr. 349, 363, 283, 309, 258, 259.

goes on speaking till nearly dawn. It follows therefore that Theseus spent the night wherever the victory was celebrated (Marathon?) and only next day found Hekale on her pyre. (It is true that on fr. 351, which is tied to this passage by *P. Oxy.* 2398, the Suda says 'Hekale said', but as there is no break in front of this passage and the lines continue with another story about the crow, this must be a corruption for 'Kallimachos said in the *Hekale*').[1] The preserved sequence then is the crow's account of Pallas, Erichthonios, and the daughters of Kekrops.[2] This is followed by another gap of twenty-two lines in which belong certainly fr. 261, 'I met Athena as she was coming to the Acropolis' (and told her that the daughters of Kekrops had disobeyed her), and probably frs. 320, 332, 374, Athena's anger. The crow goes on 'Athena's anger is always heavy. I was there when I was quite young eight generations ago.' This ends the Erichthonios story. Then after a gap of about twelve lines, now reduced by the two lines of *P. Oxy.* 2398, the crow continues with the prophecy of the Thriai that the crow will be turned black for informing Apollo about Koronis. Then the crow and her listener go to sleep before dawn. The listener may be the owl, which seems to speak in the first person in fr. 529 (cf. also 326, 608).

But how does the crow come into the *Hekale*? Gentili[3] suggests that as the crow's story quotes two instances of punishment for bringing bad news, the occasion must be the bad news of Hekale's death. The last word before the Koronis story is κακάγγελον, 'messenger of evil', and this is the end of the difficult passage which seems to be an interlude between the two stories. In the gap after the Erichthonios story the text picks up with fr. 346, 'may I but have a defence against cruel famine for my belly', then an unintelligible line, then a line which it is tempting to read as ἀλλ' Ἑκάλη λίπε λιτὸν ἔδος, then an unintelligible line, then 'and groats that dripped from the posset

---

[1] Cf. H. Lloyd-Jones, *C.R.* 65, 1961, 21; W. S. Barrett, *Gnomon* 32, 1960, 681. Cf. also *P. Oxy.* 2437.

[2] Pfeiffer puts fr. 756, 'the box of chaste-tree-wood', before this: perhaps also the account of evening in fr. 291 and fr. 340, 'sitting on a tree'; perhaps also four fragments about early Athens, fr. 266, 305, 520, 741.

[3] *Gnomon* 33, 1961, 342. I find this solution more convincing than that of V. Bartoletti, *S.I.F.C.* 33, 1961, 154.

upon the earth ... no one be brave enough (?) to go ... messenger of evil'. It looks as if, after the story of the crow's exclusion from the Acropolis for bringing the news about Erichthonios, the crow returned to the theme of Hekale's death before going on with the Koronis story. The sequence must be something like this: the crow needs food and now Hekale is dead, and the food is dripping on the ground; no one will be brave enough to tell Theseus. This means that the death of Hekale had already been told to the crow in the gap before the Erichthonios story, and it is at least possible that the owl had brought the news. The announcement must have been brief because this first twenty-two-line gap has also to include the end of the rejoicing over Theseus and the beginning of the crow's story.

Kallimachos' scholarly knowledge of early Attic legend and cult has burst out exuberantly for some ninety lines here. This is the poet of the *Aitia*, but he laughs at himself by putting his knowledge into the mouth of the crow, now aged about 250 years. The fourth *Iambos* is another instance of this technique: there Simos was warned to keep out of Kallimachos' circle by the story of the laurel and the olive, who stopped their quarrel to round on a bramble. The laurel praises itself but the olive puts its learned eulogy into the mouth of two birds chattering among its leaves. (The reference to the *Hekale* in l. 77 does not quite certainly put it later; it may merely show that Kallimachos was already thinking of *Hekale*. If it is later, the message of the fourth *Iambos* prepares for the first *Iambos*.)

After this excursion into scholarship, Kallimachos puts the birds to sleep with another reminiscence of Odysseus and Eumaios.[1] The dawn is frosty; the thieves have ceased to prowl; lamps are lit; the water-carrier sings; the waggon-axles squeak; the smiths start their deafening noise. Here sound is much more important than light; Apollonios on the other hand was more interested in light. But this is again a typical Hellenistic genre description.[2] The birds presumably did not tell the news to Theseus as he had to ask whom the neighbours were burying (fr. 262); fragments remain of the neighbours' lament (fr. 263) and of Theseus' lament (fr. 264). Then must have followed the establishment of the Deme and of the temenos of Zeus Hekaleios. Perhaps Aigeus himself was there, having come out

---

[1] Pfeiffer, *J.H.S.* 75, 1955, 71, Cf. above, p. 69.          [2] Cf. above, p. 70.

to meet Theseus as a result of the message sent after the capture of the bull.

The cause of the poem is the name and cult of an Attic deme. Kallimachos may have taken the story from his contemporary Philochoros (who was used by Plutarch). He is exposed then to two conflicting forces, the desire to tell a human story which reminds him of the meeting of Odysseus and Eumaios in the *Odyssey*, and the desire to put in the maximum of Attic legend and cult. The human story is told in more detail than by Homer: the descriptions of clothing and food are more elaborate; the storm is more realistic; midday and dawn awake a variety of pictures or sounds instead of a single formula; Hekale and Theseus are probably softer than Eurykleia and Telemachos. The atmosphere is conveyed by mellifluous verse, full of alliteration and assonance. Against the sweetness is the astringency of learned words and jokes: ἀμάζονες is not Amazons but men without bread, ποιήφαγον is not cattle but Hekale with her diet of vegetables. The greater difficulty is to find a place for the learning; and here Kallimachos uses two devices – the flashback when Aigeus tells of his instructions to Aithra and the flashback given by the crow's knowledge of Athens eight generations before the date of the story. This is a brilliant conception; how successful it was is hard to say without the whole of the poem.

The *Aitia* is a great outpouring of scholarship. The interesting question is how far the individual poems came alive. The question is difficult to answer, partly because the passion for aetiology, which was obviously present in the audiences of Apollonios and Kallimachos, is lost to us, partly because the poems are so fragmentary that we can only sometimes see how Kallimachos treated his subjects. The prologue is a late addition. The Dream (fr. 2) gives the framework: just as Hesiod was given the *Theogony* and the *Erga* by the Muses on Helikon, so Kallimachos dreamt in his youth that the Muses gave him the *Aitia*. The method was an interrogation of Kleio and Kalliope by Kallimachos. So the poems are written as questions by Kallimachos answered by the Muses.[1] But, although in the last poem of the *Aitia* Hesiod's conversation with the Muses is again recalled, Kallimachos seems to have changed the form after

[1] Cf. Pfeiffer, index s.v. *Musae loquentes*.

the second book; in the third and fourth books he tells the stories himself and sometimes quotes his human sources (fr. 75, 53; 92), but even in the *Akontios*, where he quotes Xenomedes as his authority, he ends 'whence the story hastened to my Kalliope' (fr. 75, 77), showing that he has not forgotten the fiction of the first two books.

Where we can see a longer passage, the poems have all the elegance, humour, learning, and variety which we expect from Kallimachos. In the Anaphe poem, in which the Muse tells the story of the Argonauts, probably as we have seen,[1] borrowing from Apollonios, the day of the sacrifice begins (fr. 21): 'Then Tito woke from the embraces of Laomedon's son to chafe the neck of the ox'. This is a learned variation on the Homeric dawn formula: 'Eos rose from the bed of noble Tithonos' (*Iliad* 11, 1, etc.). Tithonos is the son of Laomedon. Eos in Hesiod is the daughter of Hyperion and Theia, children of Ouranos, and so a Titan. Agricultural work starts at dawn, and Kallimachos here remembers Hesiod's advice to work early – 'Dawn, who appearing puts many men on the road and the yokes on many oxen' (*Op.* 581). Variation on a Homeric theme we have noticed already in the *Hymn to Artemis* as well as in the *Hekale*. Another very elegant instance is in the *Akontios*, where Apollo replies to Keyx (75, 22): 'My sister was not then harassing Lygdamis nor was she plaiting rushes in Amyklai nor washing off the dirt of the chase in the river Parthenios, but she was at Delos'. Here the scheme is given by Chryses' prayer to Apollo at his different addresses in the first book of the *Iliad* (37). But for simple addresses we here have allusions to history, cult and myth. The story of Theiodamas has the nice touch of the hungry young Hyllos tearing the hair on Herakles' chest, like the little Artemis with the Kyklops (fr. 24, *Hymn* 3, 76). A long recital of Sicilian cities starts with the scholarly sentiment 'the garlands on my head do not keep their scent, the food that I eat does not stay in my body. Only what I put in my ears remains in my possession' (fr. 43). A discussion of the worship of Peleus on Ikos starts at a dinner party given by an Athenian in Alexandria, at which Kallimachos sits next to a congenial Ikian (fr. 178), who satisfies his curiosity.

The poem of which we know most is the *Akontios* (fr. 67–75)

---

[1] See above, p. 67.

which ends with an abbreviated history of Keos from Xenomedes.
Till then Kallimachos narrates the story of the two lovers. They met
in Delos, he from Keos, she from Naxos. Then he describes their
beauty. 'No one came to the welling spring of shaggy old Seilenos
nor put delicate foot to the dance of sleeping Ariadne with a more
dawn-like face than she.' We think of the girls fetching water or
dancing on Greek vases; again the Homeric comparison of a beautiful woman to a goddess[1] is in the background and, nearer in date,
the lovely Theokritean 'Nycheia with spring in her eyes' (XIII, 45).
Kallimachos makes it a negative comparison with Naxian ladies
fetching water or dancing: Seilenos is a natural figure for an island
which worshipped Dionysos, and elsewhere Seilenos springs are
known; Kallimachos may have known sculptured Seilenoi as fountain figures. The dance must have been to wake Ariadne in her
capacity as an earth-goddess. After Akontios has been described and
then his passion, which hurt him as much as his beauty had hurt
others (fr. 70), the story continues with the ruse of the apple and then
the three attempts of Keyx to marry off Kydippe (fr. 75). In Naxos
the bride slept with a boy the night before her marriage. Kallimachos
stops himself from telling the origin of this rite in the pre-nuptials of
Zeus and Hera: 'Dog, dog, stop, wanton soul, you will sing what is
not holy. You are lucky that you have not seen the rites of the terrible goddess. You would even have poured out their story. Learnedness is a great danger for an unrestrained tongue: truly this boy has a
knife.' Then the lines quoted above about the oxen seeing the
sacrificial blade reflected in the water. Then the story runs swiftly
to the consultation of the oracle of Apollo and the marriage and the
naming of Xenomedes as source. The narrative is a simple story told
in elegantly decorative language. The learned man appears for a
moment in person but mockingly checks himself and goes on with
the tale; only when he has named his source does he go over to pure
information. The fascination of Kallimachos is this struggle between
the scholar and the poet, a struggle which with ironical humour
he makes no attempt to conceal.

[1] E.g. *Iliad* 24, 699; *Odyssey* 4, 14.

## CHAPTER VI

# Dramatists, Scholars, and Players

The great Alexandrians tell us little about the theatre. Two epigrams on masks by Asklepiades (*A.P.* VI, 308) and Kallimachos (*A.P.* VI, 310 = 48 Pf.) show that masks were dedicated to the Muses by schoolboys. Kallimachos is impressed by the gaping mouth of the Dionysos mask, and this may be why he gives tragic actors the voice of fish (fr. 192). Another by Kallimachos (VI, 311 = 49 Pf.) gives valuable evidence of a double-sided mask, half-white, half-brown, worn by a lover in comedy, who presumably like Sostratos in the *Dyskolos* worked on the land to win his girl. Hedylos (Ath. 176c) speaks of a flute-player who played for actors. Theokritos (*Ep.* 12) wrote the inscription for a choregos who had won a victory with a chorus of men; it was therefore a dithyramb. But success in Dionysiac contests eluded Kallimachos' friend Theaitetos, and though Kallimachos himself prays to Dionysos that he may be able to say that he was victorious, he implies in another epigram that the production of a single play lost him his friends (*Ep.* 7, 8, 59). But whatever happened to purists, Theokritos praises Ptolemy Philadelphos for his gifts to singers in the Dionysiac contests (XVII, 112).

In the description both of Philadelphos' banqueting-hall, erected to receive soldiers, Dionysiac artists, and visitors, and of his Procession (Ath. 196), the Dionysiac elements are numerous. The central columns of the hall were shaped like thyrsuses. In an upper storey there were grottoes showing symposia of tragic, comic and satyric figures in real clothing and with cups of gold beside them. Studniczka[1] suggests that these were characters from plays produced in the same year; for comedy the Dioskorides mosaic with the seated women gives an obvious parallel; satyrs drinking are easy to quote; characters from tragedy are more difficult to imagine. Perhaps rather in each grotto a single figure reclined, actor or poet, and masks were

---

[1] *Das Symposion Ptolemaios*, II, 93 f.

hung above as on the Paestan vase depicting the triumph of an actor.[1] The Dionysiac procession was led by Silens and Satyrs; there were more Silens and Satyrs in the body of the procession. 'After them marched Philikos the poet, who was priest of Dionysos, and all the Artists of Dionysos.' Then there were pageants on wheels, including Dionysos pouring a libation under a canopy decorated with ivy, vine, Dionysiac emblems, and masks; this was followed by women dressed as Maenads and then another float with Nysa, a figure so contrived that it rose and poured a libation of milk from a golden phiale. Further floats showed the bridal chamber of Semele, the infant Dionysos with Hermes and nymphs in a grotto, and Dionysos' return from India. The procession is a magnificent realization of elements in the story of Dionysos given in the Paian of Philodamos. The special jugs made in fayence with relief portraits of the Alexandrian queens (pl. XI) were also connected with the worship of Dionysos since they derive in shape from the Attic chous used at the Anthesteria and have masks of Papposilenos and Satyr at the attachments of the handle.[2]

Kallimachos attests tragedy and comedy in Alexandria; Theokritos attests the dithyramb and the hospitality of Ptolemy to lyric poets. The description of the banqueting-hall and procession confirms all this and adds 'Philikos and the Artists of Dionysos'. Inscriptions[3] of about 240 B.C. give something of the membership of the Guild of Artists at Ptolemais in Upper Egypt: a decree honouring a benefactor is signed by the priest (like Philikos), two tragic poets, two comic poets, three epic poets (one of whom is the clerk of the Guild), a kithara-singer, a kithara-player, a dancer, a tragic actor, six comic actors, four tragic *synagonistai* (these were presumably actors who played the second and third parts in tragedy), one tragic flute-player (we may remember here Hedylos' poem on Theon (Ath. 176c)), a trumpeter (perhaps we should remember Poseidippos' mention of the trumpeter Aglais here (Ath. 415b)), a *skeuopoios* (probably mask-maker), five representatives of other cities, and six

---

[1] Trendall, *Phlyax Vases*, no. 164; Bieber, *H.T.²*, fig. 538.

[2] E.g. Webster, *M.T.S.*, no. EV. 3. For pageant-cars, cf. *Annuario*, 39–40, 1961–2, 637.

[3] *O.G.I.S.*, nos. 50, 51. Pickard-Cambridge, *Festivals*, 289.

'friends of the Artists'. The signatories include epic poets, musicians, and a dancer, who are not dramatic in the strict sense; in mainland Greece (and, for all we know, in Alexandria itself by 240) they would take part in the *thymelikos agon* in the *orchestra*, as distinct from the *skenikos agon* on the high stage. Satyr-plays were probably acted by tragic actors, and this explains the absence of satyric actors. The absence of chorusmen may only mean that they were not specialized members of the guild and that in so far as they were needed for the interludes of tragedy and comedy and satyr-play they were chosen and trained for the particular performance, like the chorus of dithy-ramb mentioned by Theokritos (*Ep.* 12).[1]

Alexandria itself evidently had a chorus of *Ithyphalloi* like the Athenian chorus which met Demetrios Poliorketes and performed at the Great Dionysia: Athenaeus (497c) records a fragment of Theokles: 'We sacrificed today at the Soteria, all the Artists. With them I will drink the double horn and visit the very dear king.' The Soteria is the festival in honour of Ptolemy I and Berenike, and the double horn is the cornucopia which the queens are shown carrying on the fayence jugs. Theatre practice[2] as far as we can trace it from the surviving terracottas and vases in general agrees with Athenian practice – *onkos* masks for tragedy and the standard masks of New Comedy. They suggest that drama goes back to the earliest days of Alexandria, and the Athenian actor Gorgosthenes was there in the time of Ptolemy Soter. It may be possible to associate a new bearded satyr mask with the tragic poet Sositheos (see below). A young satyr mask with the inscription *Satyroi* appears on a silver cup which seems to go back to an early Hellenistic Alexandrian original; this mask also may be an Alexandrian innovation.

The dramatists came from abroad. Menander refused, but Phile-mon came when invited, and we have fragments of two or possibly three comedies that he wrote in Egypt. Plutarch tells the story that Magas, the king of Cyrene, had been publicly ridiculed by Philemon in the theatre: ' "letters are come from the king for you, Magas"; "unhappy Magas, you do not know letters" '; Philemon was then

[1] Cf. above, Ch. I, p. 18, on Soteria and on Athens.

[2] Webster, *M.T.S.*, nos. EV 3, NJ 1-2, JJ 2; *M.N.C.*, nos. ET 1-5, EV 1-3 are relevant for this period.

wrecked at Paraitonion and brought to Magas, who spared him (*Moralia* 458A = 144 K). Paraitonion is between Alexandria and Cyrene. Magas revolted against Philadelphos in 274, and this gives a top date for Philemon's play. Philemon's capture was presumably on his way back to Athens, and this was before his death in 264/3. Whether Magas was actually a character in the play or not, the ridicule is a return for a moment to the manner of Old Comedy. Philemon's *Panegyris* is fixed in Egypt by the lines: (58 K) 'Has the King made this street for you alone?' (59 K) 'An Egyptian has messed up my cloak.' The apparent echo of the women's difficulties in getting to the Adonis festival (Theokr. XV, 47, 52 ff., 87 f.) may be illusory: *himation* in the singular should be a man's cloak, and the remark about the street might well be made to or by a running slave. *Panegyris* as a title suggests that a boy and a girl fell in love at a festival. The third play,[1] which is certainly Egyptian, because of a reference to *Nomarchos*, an Egyptian official title, may be by Philemon, if fr. 189 K belongs; but the papyrus unfortunately only gives the first five letters of this line. The fragments are desperately corrupt. It is however clear that this is an intrigue play. A slave Strobilos confides his difficulties to a slave Daos. He has been told by his master to find a certain girl. She is in great trouble and is perhaps in the control of someone called Nikophemos. There is a considerable cook scene, which perhaps means that the young man's father Demeas has arranged a marriage for him. Strobilos discovers a great treasure apparently in a pyramid, which again fixes the play in Egypt. The study of the fragments promised by Professor Siegmann may bring out the story more clearly. One interesting and surprising element is a reference to comedy: 'when I see a comedy'; and then apparently the speaker goes on to say that in comedy cooks bring shame on all slaves by proclaiming their skill in stealing.[2] Such references to other comedies are well known in Plautus; it is worth noting that two of the instances are in plays adapted from Philemon (*Most.* 1149; *Capt.* 778). Now we must say that the trick was already known to

---

[1] Page, *G.L.P.*, no. 64 to which can now be added the new fragments P. Heidelberg 184. Cf. also M. Treu, *Philologus* 102, 1958, 215 f.

[2] P. Heidelberg 184, fr. 11. Treu., loc. cit., finds the model in Page, *G.L.P.*, no. 59b, which he places earlier in the same comedy.

Greek comic poets in the third century. Finally, and possibly also by Philemon, the comedy in which a man needs Philitas' dictionary to interpret his cook may have been written for Alexandria.

These are small remains of what, to judge by its influence, must have been an extremely popular form of art in Alexandria at this time. We have noticed its effect on the early epigrammatists, on Theokritos' mimes, on Herodas' *Mimiamboi*, and on the two last hymns of Kallimachos, but for direct evidence we can only point to these certain and possible fragments of Philemon, the statuettes of comic actors and small copies of their masks, and the few really early papyri of Menander.

Philemon was the contemporary of two writers who may be mentioned here because they were on the fringe of Comedy. Both Sotades and Sopatros worked in Alexandria in the time of Ptolemy Philadelphos.[1] The common term linking these two is *phlyakes*, and here we have to ask what there is in common between Sotades of Maroneia, Sopatros of Paphos, and the Western writers of *phlyakes* like Rhinthon: not dialect because Rhinthon wrote Doric. Metre unites Rhinthon with Sopatros but not with Sotades (but it may be that we possess no fragment of Sotades' *phlyakes*). All three are parodists: Rhinthon and Sopatros have mythological titles but their fragments are mostly descriptions of food; Sotades wrote an *Iliad* in loose Ionic metre (the point of this performance is completely unclear). Sopatros (like Rhinthon) seems to have written in the manner of Middle Comedy in the early third century, and Sotades may have done the same. In a nice fragment of Sopatros' *Galatai* (6 Kaibel) the speaker proposes to roast three philosophers and if they object to the process to sell them to 'the Zenonian master' for export. This may have been recited but can hardly have been acted, and though Hesychius calls Sopatros a comic poet, Athenaeus only calls him writer of *phlyakes* or parodist. The lines in metres other than the iambic trimeter perhaps imply recitative, if not singing.[2] Sotades' fragments are in the loose Ionic metre which is named after him and is also used for some short moral poems preserved by Stobaeus; they

---

[1] Ath. 71ab, 158d, 620ef. On *phlyakes* in general see Pickard-Cambridge, *Dithyramb etc.*[2], 138 ff.

[2] Fr. 2 Sotadean?, 5 Priapean, 24–5 anapaests (Kaibel).

have only the metre in common with Sotades. Outside the fragments of Sotades' *Iliad* only three fragments survive:[1] a line of the *Adonis*, and two obscene poems, one on a flute-player Theodoros and one on Ptolemy Philadelphos and Arsinoe, for which Sotades was apparently put to death.

Athenaeus (620e), before telling this story, includes Sotades with Alexander the Aetolian and others as a writer of poems called *Ionika* and then says that the reciter of such poems is also called *kinaidologos*. Strabo (XIV, 648) says that Sotades and Alexander wrote *kinaidic* poetry for recitation, but others wrote it for singing (including Lysis). Here at least we can hint at performers because the dancers in pointed caps who are known from many monuments are twice inscribed *kinaidoi*.[2] Glauke, who was sung by Theokritos' Korydon (IV, 31) and fluted by Hedylos' Theon (Ath. 176b), probably wrote this sort of poetry. This is the fringe of drama, the world of the music-hall, for which our one considerable piece of evidence is the Grenfell song, a lament of a female slave who has been shut out by her master whom she loves.[3] Alexander the Aetolian links the music-hall with tragedy and scholarship. Music-hall is perhaps a misnomer since these poems were recited and sung at the symposion, and Dionysos was the god of the symposion as well as the god of drama.

The Pleiad of tragic poets in Alexandria contains five certain names: Philikos of Corcyra, Homer son of Myro, Sositheos, Lykophron, Alexander. For the two other places in this list different sources give different names. The five certain names can all be dated to the reign of Philadelphos. Although they wrote large numbers of plays extraordinarily little has survived. Philikos was priest of

[1] Fragments are collected by J. U. Powell, op. cit., 238 f., Diehl, *Anth. Lyr.*, VI, 186.

[2] Cf. Binsfeld, *Grylloi*, 49.

[3] The Grenfell song (text in Powell, op. cit., 177) has been generally accepted as a *magodia*. The papyrus is dated second century B.C. How much earlier the poem is we do not know; Aristoxenos speaks of *magodia* in the fourth century, but this poem is unlikely to have survived very long. The *magodos* according to Athenaeus (621c) may impersonate women as adulteresses or procuresses as well as men drunk and proceeding in a *komos* to meet their mistresses. The girl of the Grenfell song repeatedly calls her lover *Kyrie* which implies that she is his slave.

Dionysos and led the Artists in the great procession. He was painted by Protogenes: Pliny describes him in the picture as *tragoediarum scriptorem meditantem* (*N.H.* 35, 106). The well-known Pompeian painting[1] of a poet (not an actor, because he is not wearing stage costume) contemplating a mask with high *onkos* and longish hair, probably female, has been supposed to be a copy of this picture; the peculiar position of the hand underneath the chin probably means rather more than meditation, something like a vision of what the female character experiences. The tragic poet, like the comic poet, writes the part with the mask before his eyes. Not even a title of Philikos' forty-two tragedies survives, unless we accept Meineke's conjecture that the *Themistokles* ascribed by the Suda to the comic poet Philikos belongs to the tragic poet. All we have is a *Hymn to Demeter* in choriambic hexameters.[2] It is in Attic dialect and the vocabulary is strongly indebted to tragedy. The Rape of Persephone was told in the early part of the hymn, then Demeter's search and the withering of all vegetation. Then a goddess (Tethys according to Latte, Dione according to Page) tries to persuade Demeter to relent and describes the honours which she will receive at Eleusis; the nymphs and women offer Demeter twigs. Iambe arrives and says that they should not give her goats' food: 'this is no good for a hungry god but ambrosia is the prop of her fine belly'. She offers her own cure. Here the papyrus breaks off, and the text for most of its length is too corrupt for any appreciation of the quality of the poem. Iambe's speech has a cumbrous humour and she belongs to the general class of Hellenistic realistic old men and women, like Kalli-machos' Hekale. The poem is also in an extremely difficult metre, which doubtless hampered the writer; Hephaistion[3] quotes the first line and also another line 'Grammarians, I bring you the gifts of the composition of inventive Philikos'. If this line belongs to the *Hymn to Demeter* (and it is unlikely that Philikos wrote two poems in this metre), it must belong to the epilogue, which is the traditional place for the poet to speak of himself. The hymn then, as we have sug-gested for Kallimachos' hymns, has nothing to do with cult but was

[1] Webster, *M.T.S.*, no. NP 36.
[2] *P.S.I.*, XII, 1282; Page, *G.L.P.*, no. 90; Latte, *Hermes* 11, 1954, 1 f.
[3] Diehl, *Anth. Lyr.*, VI, 296.

composed for a circle of intellectuals. Nevertheless Philikos had perhaps some real belief in the mysteries, since his epitaph (Page, *G.L.P.*, no. 106) promises that he 'shall see the fair places of the pious';[1] but that bliss may have been insured by his priesthood of Dionysos.

Of the other four certain tragedians of the Pleiad all except Sositheos are called by the Suda 'grammarians', the title which Philikos gives to his audience. They were then learned poets. Homer of Byzantium was the son of Myro of Byzantium, the authoress of a hexameter poem called *Mnemosyne*, two pretty dedicatory epigrams, and a hymn to Poseidon.[2] Of his fifty or so tragedies no title or fragment survives. Sositheos, whom the Suda describes as an 'antagonist' of Homer, i.e. as competing against him, has left three titles and five fragments. The title *Aethlios* presumably refers to the King of Elis who was father of Endymion: a pretty fragment compares a brave man among cowards to an eagle among birds (1 N). *Daphnis or Lityerses* was a play about Daphnis, who was in love with a nymph called Thaleia; she was carried off by pirates; Daphnis found her enslaved by Lityerses, a bastard son of Midas, who compelled foreigners to reap with him and then killed them. Herakles took pity on Daphnis, killed the king and threw him into the river. The two fragments give a description of Lityerses' behaviour to his visitors (2 N) and of Herakles throwing Lityerses into the river (3 N). The first fragment probably comes from the prologue and the second from a later messenger speech. Whether the contest between Daphnis and Menalkas judged by Pan was an incident or was simply narrated is unknown; the latter is more likely. Theokritos *Idyll* VIII is perhaps inspired by this but transposed into another key and magnified in scale. The story like the story of the *Aethlios* was a new one for tragedy. The versification is remarkable in having no long syllable resolved in the twenty-four surviving lines. This makes the conjecture that the play was a satyr-play extremely unlikely. On the other hand the line 'whom the folly of Kleanthes drives like oxen' (4 N) may come from a satyr-play because criticism of a contemporary is more likely in a satyr-play than a tragedy. Although the name of Kleanthes may have been known in Alexandria (as

---

[1] Cf. above, p. 58, on Poseidippos.    [2] Fragments in Powell, op. cit., 21.

Poseidippos' epigram suggests), only an Athenian audience would have applauded Kleanthes and driven Sositheos off the stage, which Diogenes Laertius says the audience did. The date should probably be later than the death of Zeno in 263. Sositheos, therefore, produced in Athens, and the tragic actor Sositheos, who in the mid-third century was honoured as an official of the Athenian guild, may have been a relation. Sositheos the poet was probably born in Alexandria in the Troad and died in Alexandria in Egypt. This is implied by the literary epitaph of Dioskorides (*A.P.* VII, 707),[1] who contrasts the satyr guarding the tomb of Sositheos with the satyr in Athens guarding the tomb of Sophokles. Dioskorides characterizes Sositheos' satyr as a return to the masculine, noisy, daring manner of Pratinas, the inventor of the satyr-play. Contemporary allusion may have been seen as part of this archaism; it is tempting to associate with Sositheos the new wild-haired satyr mask which appears in Alexandria on the Queen jugs of the time of Philadelphos.[2]

The other two certain members of the Pleiad, Alexander the Aetolian from Pleuron and Lykophron of Chalkis, were brought to Alexandria by Ptolemy Philadelphos to deal with the dramatic texts in the Library, Alexander with tragic and satyric texts, Lykophron with comic texts.[3] This probably took place in the late 270's as it seems to have been a parallel activity to Zenodotos' work on Homer. Here then scholarship and dramatic production were combined. Nothing is left of the tragedies of Alexander except the title of the *Astragalistai*, in which Patroklos killed the son of Amphidamas in the house of the schoolmaster Othnyoreus; all we can say is that this is an unusual subject. Other references to Alexander's treatment of mythology are not necessarily references to his tragedies, as he wrote a considerable range of poetry.[4] His *kinaidika* and *Ionika* have already been mentioned. A fragment (1 P) in hexameters from the *Halieus* tells how Glaukos, a favourite subject of Hellenistic writers, became immortal by eating the grass grown for his horses by the Sun: where Alexander

---

[1] On the details of this epigram see Gabathuler, op. cit., 86; Webster, *Studi Rostagni*, 218 ff.

[2] Cf. above, p. 123.

[3] Tzetzes ap. Kaibel, *C.G.F.*, 19, Pb I 19, 21, etc.

[4] Fragments in Powell, op. cit., 121 f.; a selection in Diehl, *Anth. Lyr.*, VI.

localized this is not clear. Two hexameters (2 P) from the *Kirka* tells of the *pompilos* fish guiding the raft of Odysseus. The other poems and fragments are in elegiacs.[1] The *Apollo* (3 P) is the story of Antheus and the wife of Phobios told as a prophecy in the mouth of Apollo; the vocabulary is rarefied, and a learned allusion to the expulsion of the Bakchiadai from Corinth is inserted merely to give a bottom date for Antheus. It is tempting to suppose that Alexander had found the *Antheus* of Agathon in the Library and retold the story as a Hellenistic short epic in this curious form. The *Muses* described how the people of Ephesos had a competition for hymns when they dedicated the temple of Artemis: the surviving lines (4 P) are a tortured description of Timotheos writing a hymn to Artemis. Another poem (5 P) praises the Syracusan parodist of Homer, Boiotos, who had been expelled by Agathokles, as superior to the earlier Parian parodist Euboios. The poem on Alkman (9 P)[2] is a literary inscription: 'Sardis, if I had been brought up in you, I should have been a Gallos; but now my name is Alkman, and I belong to Sparta of the many tripods, and I have learnt the Helikonian Muses, who have made me greater than Daskyles and Gyges'. Gabathuler suggests that this is a counterstatement to Sosibios' claim that Alkman was a native Spartan. Alexander hints also at the familiar Hellenistic contrast between the Gallos and the serious poet and expects his learned audience to remember Archilochos' Thasian carpenter who did not care for the wealth of Gyges (fr. 22D).

Lykophron for the Alexandrians was primarily the poet of the *Alexandra*, and on a silver cup which derives from an Early Hellenistic original he is shown contemplating her mask.[3] In fact the monologue cannot have been performed in the theatre. Some of Lykophron's many tragedies must have been performed in Alexandria as he was one of the Pleiad. The only play of which we know anything is the *Menedemos*; there Papposilenos bitterly complained to the satyrs of the quality of the food in Menedemos' home. We do not

---

[1] Fr. 7, Powell, Diehl in anapaestic tetrameters although attributed by Aulus Gellius can hardly be Alexander. Satyros in the third century B.C. attributes part of it to Aristophanes, part to Euripides. Presumably Aristophanes is the author.

[2] Cf. Gabathuler, op. cit., 66.

[3] *M.T.S..*, no. JJ 1.

know whether Menedemos of Eretria was himself brought on the stage; the description recalls Middle Comedy. As far as we can see it was a good-natured joke rather than satire, and Diogenes Laertius regarded it as an encomium of the simple life of the philosopher. It was presumably written while Lykophron was still in Eretria. Of the tragedies the *Kassandreis* must have had a modern subject as Kassandreia was only founded in 316 B.C. Most of the other preserved titles are mythological and many of them are stock subjects such as *Oidipous*, but *Orphan* and *Allies* may have had contemporary subjects. All that survives of the tragedies is four lines of the *Pelopidai* which show no resolved syllables, and the fifteen hundred lines of the *Alexandra* have only about twenty resolved syllables. In tragedy, as distinct from satyr-play (of which the surviving lines of the *Menedemos* give a specimen), Lykophron is as strict metrically as Sositheos.

The *Alexandra* is tragedy in the same sense that Isokrates' *Antidosis* is a speech. A slave, whom Priam has set to guard Kassandra, reports to him her prophecy in direct speech. This is a similar convention to the slightly dramatized narrator of Kallimachos' hymns. It anchors the prophecy in time, and the tragic form recalls the Kassandras of classical tragedy. The slave warns us that Kassandra will speak in riddles 'copying the voice of the dark sphinx'. But he is not much easier himself (10 ff.): 'Eos was flying above the sheer crag of Phegion on the swift wings of Pegasus, leaving Tithonos in his bed near Kerne, your brother by another mother' (this is perhaps not more tortuous than Kallimachos' 'Tito, lying by the son of Laomedon').[1] 'They loosed the sunny cables from the grooved rock and cut the ropes from the land' (every word here except 'sailors' and 'land' is a rarity). 'And the fair-faced many-footed stork-coloured Phalakraean girls' (Phalakra is a place in the Troad) 'struck maiden-slaying Thetis' (Thetis is the sea; the maiden is Helle) 'with their blades, over Kalydnae showing white feathers, stern ornaments, cloths held at arms length by northern blasts of raging wind, and she, splitting her inspired Bacchic lips on the high hill of Ate founded by the wandering cow' (Ate's hill was in Troy and Ilos founded his city where a cow stopped on this hill), 'Alexandra, began to speak'. All that this means is, that on the morning when Paris set sail, Kassandra

[1] Fr. 21, 3, cf. above, p. 120.

began to prophesy. The slave sets the style. This is not to be a modernization of a heroic figure like Apollonios' Medeia or Theokritos' Alkmene but an exercise in riddling style and difficult language, recondite synonyms, remote allusions. Kassandra prophesies what will happen and her prophecy moves through the Trojan story: Paris' voyage, the Trojan war, the Nostoi. The course is anything but straight. She remembers the earlier sack of Troy and therefore gives a life of Herakles. Paris' capture of Helen brings in the story of Helen and Theseus and their daughter Iphigeneia, and of Menelaos' earlier rescue of Paris in Troy. Then Paris returns to Troy, and she digresses on Neoptolemos, the sacrifice of Iphigeneia, and Telephos. Then the Greek invasion and the story up to the burial of Achilles. Then a series of lamentations for Trojans including Hektor and Hekabe. Then she moves from herself and the Palladion story to the disasters of the Greek returns from Troy caused by Nauplios, including an extremely obscure Odyssey set in the Western Mediterranean; Odysseus is finally to be buried in Etruria. Twice in her account of Odysseus she looks forward into recent history: the Siren Parthenope will be buried in Naples, and 'there one day for the first of the sister goddesses the lord of all Mopsops' navy will ordain a torch-race for his sailors in obedience to oracles' (732). The ancient commentator refers to Timaios for the identification of the admiral as Diotimos, who was *strategos* in 425. This aetiology goes back to a comparatively recent date. Secondly, Odysseus will be honoured in Epeiros 'where the Tympheian snake will at a banquet destroy Herakles, descended from the seed of Aiakos and Perseus and not far from the blood of Temenos' (801). This Herakles was a son of Alexander, murdered by Polyperchon in 309. Why Lykophron should have introduced this event here is unclear; the beneficiary was Kassander and possibly Lykophron had alluded to this in his *Kassandreis*, but that is pure conjecture. The wanderings of Menelaos permit further allusions to the West, including the aetiology of an Achilles cult in Kroton and oily pebbles on the beach in Sicily. Philoktetes and Podaleirios also wandered to the West. Kassandra returns again to Nauplios, the murder of Agamemnon, and her own murder. Agamemnon will be worshipped in Sparta and Kassandra herself in Italy. The Rape of Kassandra will be celebrated by the tribute of

Lokrian maidens sent to the temple of Athena in Troy (1141 ff.). Hekabe will have a cenotaph in Sicily, and Hektor will be honoured in Thebes. 'The glory of my ancestors' race shall be magnified by my descendants, having won by their spears the highest crown, taking sceptre and monarchy of land and sea. Nor, my unhappy fatherland, shall you hide a withered glory forgotten in darkness. Such a pair of young lions, a breed eminent in strength (*romei*), my kinsman will leave, the son of Aphrodite' (1226 ff.). Aeneas will go to Italy and be joined by Odysseus and two sons of Telephos: 'Therefore being adjudged even among his foes most pious he will build a country most praised in battles, a tower happy in late descendants' (1270 f.). Then a transition from the wanderings of the heroes to the history of Europe and Asia (1281 f.). This she pursues from the Rape of Io to the death of Agamemnon. 'With him I shall die and moving among the dead I shall hear of the rest, which I shall now tell' (1372). Orestes will ravage Aeolis, Neleus will occupy Ionia, the Dorians will settle in Asia, the Phrygians will invade Thrace, Xerxes will invade Greece, Alexander will conquer Asia. 'After six generations my kinsman, a great wrestler, will fight by land and sea and be reconciled; he will be praised as noblest among his friends, having won the first spoils of war' (1446 ff.). The problems of this passage are formidable, but it seems most likely that Professor Momigliano[1] is right in referring them to the struggle between Pyrrhos and Rome when Pyrrhos had lost Tarentum in 272 and the first Punic war had not yet begun; he also argues that the phrasing of the reference to the Lokrian maidens supports a date early in the third century.

This is an extraordinary poem. It is packed with knowledge of mythology, tradition, and cult. It is cruelly difficult in its riddling style and tortuous composition. But besides being immensely learned and ingenious it has a serious purpose, as Professor Momigliano has seen. We should remember not so much the Aeschylean Kassandra, who remains within the context of her story, as the Euripidean Kassandra, who perhaps in the *Alexandros* and certainly in the *Trojan Women*, when she speaks about offensive and defensive war, had an unbelieved message for fifth-century Athenians. In the *Alexandra*

---

[1] *J.R.S.* 32, 1942, 57 ff.; *C.Q.* 39, 1945, 49 ff.; E. Manni, *Kokalos* 7, 1961, 8 dates 285/2.

every chance of including Greek sites in the West is taken in the wanderings of the heroes after the siege of Troy, and this Western emphasis culminates in the praise of Rome founded by the descendants of 'the pious Aeneas' (1270 f.). This is taken up again at the end of the prophecy where Greek Pyrrhos is met and balanced by Asiatic Rome. In modern terms Lykophron states what Philadelphos had shown that he knew by sending an embassy to Rome, that Rome is a non-Greek state as dangerous to Hellenistic Greek kingdoms as Troy or Persia had been to heroic and classical Greece.

CHAPTER VII

# Later Alexandrian Poets

———◆———

The great works of Alexandrian poetry belong to the reign of Philadelphos; only the last poems of Kallimachos overlap into the reign of Euergetes. But the next hundred years, from the middle of the third to the middle of the second century, produced some interesting figures and shows the continuing interaction of scholarship and literature. Eratosthenes,[1] who was summoned from Athens by Euergetes to take over the Library from Apollonios Rhodios, had been a pupil of Kallimachos before he went to Athens. Besides extremely important work in geography and historical chronology and an interest in constellations, he wrote a large work on *Old Comedy*. This is the second generation of Alexandrian scholarship. Lykophron had already done the preliminary work on the manuscripts and Kallimachos had made the catalogue. Both were criticized by Eratosthenes: Lykophron for not understanding Kratinos (Ath. 501d) and Kallimachos for mixing up the first and second editions of Aristophanes' *Clouds* (Schol. *Nub.* 533).

The fragments of Eratosthenes' poems show his interests: the *Anterinys or Hesiod* was literary biography; the *Hermes* told of the god's youth and of how he became a star, and the poem includes a description of the Milky Way, the harmony of the spheres, and a view of earth from heaven, thus displaying the geographical and astronomical knowledge of its author.[2] The *Erigone* also ended with the placing of Erigone, Ikarios, and the faithful dog, Maira, among the stars. The story was that Ikarios, the king of Ikaria, was visited by Dionysos, who gave him the vine (fr. 23–4). A goat nibbled the vines and in punishment was sacrificed; the Ikarians danced on his inflated skin (fr. 22, 26–7); the Ikarians got drunk and killed Ikarios

---

[1] Fragments in Powell, *Collectanea Alexandrina*, 58; Diehl, *Anth. Lyr.* VI, 234. Cf. H. C. Baldry in *Entretiens Hardt*, VIII, 191.

[2] Solmsen, *T.A.P.A.* 73, 1942, 200 ff., works out the relation of this poem to Eratosthenes' *Platonikos*.

(fr. 25, 31, 36); his daughter Erigone hung herself and was put among the stars as Parthenos (it will be remembered that the Lock of Berenike was discovered among the stars in 246, but it is perhaps more interesting to note that Eratosthenes' explanation conflicts with Aratos). The questions which this poem raises are perhaps insoluble.[1] We know, however, that the third day of the Anthesteria with its Swing festival was connected with Erigone, the daughter of Ikarios, by Kallimachos in a poem written before 270/65 (fr. 178). The Swing festival itself is attested on Attic vases of the sixth century; but whether it belonged originally to Erigone, daughter of Ikarios, or Erigone, sister of Orestes, who provided the reason for the Choes on the second day of the Anthesteria, we do not know. We know however that Theophrastos (ap. Porph. de Abst. II, 10) said that goats were first sacrificed in Ikaria because they nibbled vine-leaves. We know also that dancing on the inflated goatskin was also an old Attic custom (it appears on early red-figure vases), and it is part of Herodas' dream (VIII) but in Herodas the custom is instituted by Dionysos himself and it is not localized in Ikaria. Latte[2] has suggested that Eratosthenes gave an origin in Ikaria for what was essentially a dance of Attic comedy, and that this was part of an Alexandrian theory of the origin of drama in Ikaria. The first proposition seems certain, the second depends on Virgil's adaptation in Georgics II, 380 ff. 'For no other reason (except that they damage young vegetation) the goat is sacrificed at every altar to Bacchus and the traditional shows enter the theatre, and prizes for talent at villages and crossroads were set by the sons of Theseus and happy in their cups they danced on the oiled skins in the soft meadows.' The connection between sacrifice of goat, drama, and dancing on the goatskin is here established, and presumably Virgil found it already in Eratosthenes. (Already in 264/3 the compiler of the Parian marble had said that Thespis' prize was a goat.) What Eratosthenes did, therefore, was to provide a mythical origin for drama in Ikaria. It is possible that this poem should be dated down to the time of the fourth Ptolemy Philopator (221/05 B.C.). Kallimachos speaks of the Anthesteria as

---

[1] See however Solmsen's very interesting reconstruction in T.A.P.A. 78, 1947, 252. On Aratos, cf. above, p. 35. On Herodas, cf. above, p. 96.
[2] Hermes 85, 1957, 385 f.

being celebrated by an Athenian in Alexandria; but Eratosthenes tells us (Ath. 276b) that Ptolemy IV founded a festival called Lagyno-phoria in which the Alexandrians used *lagynoi*[1] as the Athenians used *choes* on the second day of the Anthesteria; the *Erigone* may have been a new poem written for a new or remodelled Alexandrian festival, and the story was made more credible by finding Erigone in the stars.

A contemporary of Eratosthenes, Rhianos[2] of Crete, which had close connections with Alexandria all through the third century, made an edition of Homer. Homeric and Hesiodic echoes are very clear in the twenty-line fragment (1) on the follies of men and the action of Ate. He wrote a number of epics on Herakles, Achaea, Elis, Thessaly, and Messenia (the use of *poiai* 'grass' as a synonym for summer in fr. 54 is the one probable echo of Kallimachos (fr. 44), which can be found), and a number of epigrams, which fall into the usual types: dedications (66–8), epitaphs (69, 70, 76), symposion poetry (71–5).

Machon of Corinth or Sikyon, who lived the latter part of his life in Alexandria, brings us back to comedy. The chronology is not easy: the three indications that we have are: (1) Ath. 664a, he was a contemporary of Apollodoros of Karystos, who seems to have won his first victory at the City Dionysia about 280.[3] (2) He, like Sositheos, who was certainly writing after 263 (see above), was survived by Dioskorides, who wrote his epitaph. The Spartan poems of Dioskorides can be dated between 225 and 219.[4] (3) The Suda mentions him with Euphronios as the teacher of Aristophanes of Byzantium, to which Athenaeus adds that Aristophanes associated with him in his youth (664a) and learnt from him 'the parts relating to comedy' (241 f.). Euphronios was certainly alive in the reign of Philopator (221/05) and also taught Aristarchos, who was born

[1] Leroux, *Lagynos*, traces the shape back to the fourth century but its great popularity dates from the late third: cf. also Homer A. Thompson, *Hesperia* 3, 1934, Group C. For the dating to Philopator, cf. Studniczka, op. cit., 15.

[2] Fragments in Powell, op. cit., 9; Diehl, op. cit., 225. A new fragment of the *Herakleia*, *P. Oxy.* 27, 2463. On Aratos and Rhianos, cf. above, p. 30. On Rhianos and Hesiod, cf. K. J. McKay, *A.J.P.* 74, 1963, 22.

[3] *Studies in Later Greek Comedy*, 206.

[4] Cf. *C.A.H.* VII, 756, 762.

about 215. Aristophanes died about 180 and can hardly have been the pupil of Zenodotos, as the Suda says (unless Zenodotos lived on after Apollonios became librarian about 260); what this probably means is that he was the next great scholar after Zenodotos to edit Homer. He must have been born about 260, and his association with Machon cannot have been much earlier than 240. Machon's active life therefore would seem to have lasted roughly from 270 to 230.

Dioskorides (*A.P.* VII, 708) praises him as a writer of comedy, 'worthy of ancient art', who could claim that pungent Attic thyme sometimes grew beside the Nile. The two fragments of his comedies tell us nothing: in the *Agnoia* an Athenian praises the Macedonian dish, *mattye*, and in the *Epistole* a cook discusses flavouring (K. iii, 324). Gabathuler[1] quotes a papyrus fragment of Philodemos, which has been interpreted as saying that Machon quoted Aristotle's *Eudemos* in his *Auge*, making fun of Socratic dialogues; unfortunately the name of Machon is by no means certain, and the fragment cannot be used to show that Machon wrote Middle rather than New comedy. Probably therefore Dioskorides is not saying much more than that Machon is a true successor in Alexandria of the long line of Attic comic poets, but 'worthy of ancient art' suggests that he felt that Machon, like Sositheos, somehow revived an earlier and purer form of art. Rostagni[2] saw him as adding cantica and bawdy jokes to New Comedy and so advancing towards Plautus. But would Dioskorides have seen this as archaism? It is of course possible that the 'pungency' of the thyme means that Machon included contemporary allusions, just as Philemon did in his plays produced in Egypt. Machon's knowledge of earlier Attic comedy is shown in his *Chreiai*, a collection of anecdotes in iambics about hetairai, parasites, musicians and others, who range in date from Sophocles to Ptolemy Soter. A considerable amount of this unattractive work is preserved in Athenaeus. A possible connection with Aristophanes of Byzantium is given by the fact that Aristophanes wrote a work *On Hetairai* (who figure largely in Machon's *Chreiai*), but according to Athenaeus (241f) Machon taught Aristophanes 'the parts relating to comedy'. Meineke emended 'parts' to 'songs', and it would be attractive to connect this

---

[1] *Hellenistische Epigramme auf Dichter*, 88, quoting *Rh. Mus.* 83 (1934), 193 ff.
[2] *Scritti Minori* II, 1, 384–7; 2, 6 ff. On Philemon, cf. above, p. 124.

with White's[1] suggestion that Aristophanes of Byzantium in his text edition of the comic poet Aristophanes wrote the lyrics in cola; but we have no evidence for Machon's musical or metrical proficiency. 'Part' (*meros*) is used by Aristotle of prologue, parodos, etc. and at least once in papyri of an 'act';[2] then Machon would have taught Aristophanes the structure of comedy, but again we have no evidence. Perhaps, therefore, the 'parts' are rather 'parts' of Aristophanes' education. The range of comedy which Machon knew, if we can trust the quotations from the *Chreiai*, ran from the late fifth century to the early third.

Euphronios of the Chersonese, who is mentioned with Machon as a teacher of Aristophanes of Byzantium, wrote *Commentaries* on the comic poet Aristophanes.[3] Machon, according to Athenaeus (664a), was as good a poet as any after the Pleiad, but Euphronios was sometimes counted one of the Pleiad. This presumably means that he wrote tragedy, but nothing survives except three lines quoted by Hephaistion,[4] on which the ancient commentator says: 'the metre' (here choriambic dimeter B followed by Pherekratean) 'was called Priapeian because Euphronios the grammarian in the time of the Ptolemies wrote to Priapus in this metre'. The lines address the initiates of the new Dionysos and speak of a night procession. The new Dionysos is Ptolemy IV Philopator. Philopator, like his predecessors and probably even more than his predecessors, was interested in Dionysos, to whom he traced back his ancestry; he himself celebrated the mysteries in his palace and had a register made of all the initiated.[5] Priapos is associated with Dionysos as god of the mystics, presumably because he was a fertility god like Dionysos himself. Euphronios called him the god of Orneai, near Phlious, as he had a temple there.[6] But his association with Dionysos in Alexandria goes back at least to the time of Philadelphos, because he

---

[1] *Aristophanes Scholia on the Aves*, xix.

[2] *P. Oxy.* 17, 2086. 12 (cf. Körte, *Archiv*, x, 227) and perhaps *P. Antinoopolis*, 15, verso, 1.

[3] Cf. J. W. White, op. cit., xvii.   [4] Powell, op. cit., 176; Diehl, op. cit., 294.

[5] Nilsson, *G.G.R.*, ii, 152. G. Zuntz, however, regards this edict as issued by Ptolemy V to restrict the extravagances of the cult which had been encouraged by Ptolemy IV (*C.Q.* 44, 1950, 70).

[6] Strabo, VIII, 382.

appeared twice in the Procession, once by the side of Dionysos and once by the side of Alexander and Ptolemy.[1] Sotades also wrote a poem to him, and he is mentioned in the epigrams of Theokritos and Hedylos.[2] He is essentially a country god, and his association with Dionysos by the Alexandrians may be meant to emphasize this side of Dionysos, Dionysos as the god of wild nature as distinct from Dionysos as the god of the symposion and drama.

Dioskorides, the epigrammatist, is dated by his imaginary epitaphs on heroic Spartans to the end of Euergetes' reign and the early years of Philopator, when Kleomenes of Sparta was in favour in Egypt (225/19): they do not spare gory details in praising Spartan virtues.[3] A similar delight in physical detail marks some of his erotic poems.[4] His poems fall into the usual categories of epitaphs, real and imaginary, dedications, symposion poetry, erotic and literary. Many of them play with well-known themes.[5] The most interesting are those which reveal contemporary Alexandrian taste in literature and music.

The epigrams on poets all purport to be epitaphs. The Machon poem (*A.P.* VII, 708) may be a real epitaph. The poems on Archilochos, Sappho, Anakreon, Thespis, Aeschylus, Sophocles are obviously literary.[6] The other epitaph (*A.P.* VII, 707) on an older contemporary, Sositheos, is betrayed by its opening word 'I, *too*', as having been composed to pair with the literary epitaph on Sophocles. As we have seen, it praises Sositheos' satyr as a return to the masculine, noisy, daring manner of Pratinas – Dioskorides praises Sositheos' archaism just as he also praises Machon as 'worthy of archaic technique'. Sophocles' satyr (*A.P.* VII, 37) on the other hand is a degenerate; Sophocles transformed him into a golden (= useless) shape and dressed him in fine purple (like one of the satyrs on the fifth-century Pronomos vase). But he holds in his hand the mask of a mourning girl. It does not matter whether it is Antigone or Elektra,

[1] Ath. 201c, d.   [2] Theokr. *Ep.* 2, 3; Hedylos, *A.P.* V, 200; VI, 292.
[3] *A.P.* VII, 229, 430, 434.   [4] E.g. *A.P.* V, 54-6.
[5] E.g. Dedications: *A.P.* V, 52 is related to Kallimachos, *Ep.* 25; VI, 220 is perhaps the earliest of the group VI, 217-20 (cf. Gow, *J.H.S.* 80, 1960, 88 f.); Epitaphs: VII, 76 is related to 284 Asklepiades; 450 to 345; 456 to 455 Leonidas; Symposion poetry: V, 53 = 193 to 162 Asklepiades; XII, 37 with 38 Rhianos.
[6] For a full commentary on the epitaphs on dramatic poets see *Studi Rostagni*, 218 ff. I summarize this here.

L

because both are first-rate. Dioskorides says quite clearly that Sophocles' tragedies were first-rate, but his satyr-plays were feeble; it needed Sositheos to restore the early fire.

The other two epigrams on dramatists are also a pair: *A.P.* VII, 410, Thespis first made tragic song for his villagers, 'when Bacchos led on the chorus smeared with wine-lees (?), for which the goat was a prize and the basket of figs was a prize too' (or 'still'); there will be countless further developments. 'But mine is mine.' 411, 'This was Thespis' invention'; these rustic revels Aeschylus made sublime, not a careful craftsman but a mountain torrent; he also reorganized the stage; he was one of the archaic heroes. We cannot tell whether Eratosthenes had already published his *Erigone* when Dioskorides wrote; but in any case he was writing of a legendary period, whereas Dioskorides writes of Thespis. The Parian marble (in 264/3) recorded that at least thirty years before Thespis comedy was invented in Ikaria by Sousarion and the prize was a basket of figs. Dioskorides presumably alludes to this with his 'too' (or 'still'). But there was, he held, not a very clear distinction between tragedy and comedy. Aeschylus had to make the rustic revels of Thespis sublime. The picture of Aeschylus clearly draws on the contrast between him and Euripides in Aristophanes' *Frogs* – not the careful craftsman, but a mountain torrent. Dioskorides also knows something of the history of the theatre. But Aeschylus, like Pratinas, is an archaic hero – even if Sophocles' *Antigone* and *Electra* are first-rate. Aeschylus, after being practically ignored by Aristotle, has come into his own again in Alexandrian theory, if not in stage practice.

The other three poems[1] need only a brief mention. Dioskorides pictures the fierce Archilochos of Kallimachos rather than the mild Archilochos of Theokritos,[2] and does it by putting a passionate defence from the grave into the mouths of the daughters of Lykambes (*A.P.* VII, 351). The Sappho poem (*A.P.* VII, 407) is in hymn form – invocation. 'Sweetest support of their passion to young men in love', grounds: 'whether you are with the Muses' (an earlier epigram had made Sappho a tenth muse) 'or with Hymen' (an allusion to her marriage-songs) 'or with Aphrodite mourning Adonis' (cf. 140 L–P), prayer: 'all hail to you, goddess'. For

[1] Cf. Gabathuler, op. cit., 79 f.        [2] Cf. above, p. 60.

Anakreon (*A.P.* VII, 31) Dioskorides (much less brutal than Leonidas) remembers an earlier epigram (*A.P.* VII, 5), which invited a vine to grow over the poet's grave, and prays for wine, nektar, violets, and myrtle for Anakreon in the underworld: the names of Smerdys, Bathyllos, and Eurypyle come from Anakreon's poems, because Dioskorides' epigrams never forget their scholarship.[1]

Two much discussed poems describe contemporary entertainment in Alexandria. *A.P.* V, 138: 'Athenion sang the Horse, bad for me. All Troy was in flames, and I caught fire with it. I had no fear for the Greeks' ten years' toil. In that one blaze both Trojans and I perished.' Rostagni[2] suggested that Athenion played the part of Kassandra in the tragedy which Livius Andronicus adapted for his *Equus Trojanus*. Unfortunately we have no evidence for women playing in serious drama in the Hellenistic age. An epigram of approximately the same date by Alkaios of Messene (*A.P.* XVI, 7) praised the Theban flute-player Dorotheos for playing 'the mournful Dardanidai and the deeds of the horse'. It is perhaps most likely that the lovely Athenion sang a monody (or even a messenger speech) from tragedy at a symposion. The other poem is *A.P.* XI, 195:[3] 'Aristagoras danced Gallos. I told the story of the warlike Temenidai, the fruit of my great labours. He was sent off with high honour. One beat of the clappers drove unhappy Hyrnetho off. Into the fire with the stories of heroes. Among the unmusical a lark will sing more sweetly than a swan.' Kallimachos (fr. 193) had already complained that it was more profitable to be a Kybele dancer than a poet. Dioskorides repeats the complaint from his own experience. The contrast is between a serious poem on the Temenidai and a dance imitating a priest of Kybele. The occasion is unknown, but it is worth noting that the guild of Dionysiac artists at Ptolemais about this time included three epic poets and a dancer,[4] so that these performances may have been part of a public competition. Dioskorides stands out as a vivid and uninhibited personality, who felt strongly both in scholarship and in private life.

---

[1] Cf. also Stadtmueller's notes on *A.P.* IX, 340, Dioskorides on the flutes of Hyagnis. On Leonidas, cf. below, p. 219.

[2] *Scritti Minori* II, 2, 6.     [3] Cf. *Studi Rostagni*, 218 ff.

[4] *O.G.I.S.*, 50, dated by Dittenberger 240 B.C.

Ptolemy IV Philopator, who ruled from 221 to 205, was not only interested in Dionysos as god of the mysteries but also in Dionysos as god of drama. He himself wrote a tragedy called *Adonis*, in which he introduced Echo, like Euripides in his *Andromeda*.[1] Euphronios probably wrote tragedy, as we have seen, and the scholarship of comedy went on with Euphronios and Aristophanes of Byzantium, who besides editing the comic poet Aristophanes wrote a work *On Masks*[2] and *On Menander and his borrowings*: Aristophanes also asked 'whether Menander copied Life or Life copied Menander' – the same standard of realism which the women of Herodas and Theokritos applied in art criticism. But Aristophanes gave Menander the second place after Homer.[3] We do not know the date of Aristophanes' text of Homer; he became librarian at the end of the third century, but it is tempting to connect its publication with the Homereion of Ptolemy IV.

An epigram[4] celebrates the founding of the Homereion by Ptolemy after a dream, stresses Homer's immortality and congratulates the Euergetai (Ptolemy III and his wife) on a son as distinguished in war as in poetry. This dates the poem (and therefore the foundation) after 217, when Ptolemy IV defeated Antiochos III. (Körte's reading in the second line which makes Ptolemy found the shrine in obedience to a dream is likely to be right; a contemporary parallel is given by the pedestrian poem of Maiistas[5] recording the foundation and preservation of the Serapieion in Delos, in which Serapis twice appears to his priests in a dream.) Aelian (*V.H.* 13, 22) says that Ptolemy gave the Homereion a seated statue of Homer in the middle and round him statues of the cities which claimed him, and that the painter Galaton painted Homer vomiting and the other poets collecting his vomit in jugs. Pfuhl,[6] in his reasonable disgust at this subject, denies all connection with the Homereion. This seems difficult as the passage reads straight on in Aelian. Another possibility

---

[1] Schol. Ar. *Thesm.*, 1059.        [2] Ath. 659b.

[3] *Menander reliquiae*, Körte-Thierfelder, II, testimonia nos. 51, 32, 61.

[4] Page, *G.L.P.*, no. 105b with Körte's reading for the second line (no. 105a on the Ptolemaic fountain may rather belong to the time of Philadelphos, as the last line is very similar to 104b, 8).

[5] Powell, op. cit., 68.        [6] *Malerei und Zeichnung*, para. 885.

is surely that Aelian's description comes from a satirical epigram, which wilfully misinterpreted a not very happy conception of Homer as a river-god pouring water from his mouth for the other poets to collect. Wilamowitz saw the parallel between Galaton's picture and a poem,[1] probably Ptolemaic, in anapaestic dimeters, which says that all men in the Greek-speaking world glorify 'the immortal voice from the Muses, which you, Homer, having woven by your unwearying labours, like a sea, spewed forth upon the shore for other men'. Here and in Galaton's picture Homer is the source of all later poetry; here and in the epigram on the foundation of the Homereion Homer's immortality is stressed; here also the poet speaks of the wide spread of the Homeric epics – to Aetolia, Lokris, Delphi, Boeotia, and Athens (and wherever else was mentioned in the lost beginning of the poem).

These three ideas appear in another work closely connected with the Homereion, the second-century relief (pl. IV) by Archelaos of Priene.[2] Homer is seated with the *Iliad* and the *Odyssey* beside his throne and a frog and mouse (*Batrachomyomachia*) at his footstool. Time and the World put a wreath on his head. Their faces have been recognized as Ptolemy IV and Arsinoe II, his wife, and the seated Homer reproduces the statue in the Homereion.[3] The King and Queen have given him ubiquity and immortality. A sacrifice is being made to Homer by Myth and History (or is Historia here Research?), and he is greeted by Poetry, Tragedy, and Comedy. This group of personifications renders more elegantly the idea behind Galaton's picture, that all subsequent poetry derives from Homer. On the right a group, obviously inspired by earlier groups of a little boy carried off by three nymphs, contains a boy called Physis hanging on to and looking back at four women, Arete, Mneme, Pistis, and Sophia.

[1] Page, *G.L.P.*, no. 93, Powell, op. cit., 187; Diehl, op. cit., 310. After a gap the poem goes on with a very difficult monody of Kassandra (essentially clarified by Eitrem, *S.O.* 30, 1953, 109). Homer as the river-source of tributary writers occurs in *De Subl.* 13, 3; Manilius, 2, 8 ff., 58.

[2] British Museum 2191. *M.T.S.*, ES 1; Lippold, *Gr. Pl.*, 373; Bieber, *Hell. Sc.*, 127, fig. 497. See below, p. 175. On interpretation, cf. Leiva Petersen, *Zur Geschichte der Personifikation*, Würzburg 1939, 63 ff.

[3] Schefold, *Bildnisse*, 148, 219; cf. also below, p. 171. On seated statues of Homer, A. Sadurska, *B.C.H.* 86, 1962, 505.

This group is generally interpreted as showing the effect of Homer on the ordinary man. It would be easier to regard Excellence, Memory, Credibility, and Wisdom as elements of the genius (physis) of Homer. But the grouping of the whole should mean that Homer's influence spreads first to the poets and then to wider circles. Courage, memory (of the great Greek past), loyalty, and wisdom are the virtues which a knowledge of Homer brings to the young. All is easy here except Pistis, but whether it is to be found by reading Homer or not, it was naturally prized by the Ptolemies, as an iambic poem to a Ptolemaic officer of the late third century shows:[1] 'all the virtues are in him: good, noble, simple, loving the king, courageous, great in loyalty, modest, lover of Greeks, mild, affable, hating evil and revering truth'.

The relief (which was found at Bovillae in Italy) was presumably a dedication by the poet, who appears in the register above the Homer scene. He is represented as a statue on a base carrying a scroll, and a tripod stands behind him. Presumably he won the tripod at a competition in the Homereion and was awarded a statue by his fellow citizens. Presumably also, as he has no lyre, he wrote in hexameters or possibly iambics. The rest of the relief shows Zeus, Mnemosyne, and the Muses on a mountain – Olympos perhaps at the top because of Zeus, but Parnassos at the bottom, because Apollo stands in a cave between two of the Muses with the omphalos at his feet. It seems possible that the poet sang of Zeus, the Muses, and Apollo as the inspiration of Homer, who became ubiquitous and immortal, the source of all future poetry, and the educator of men. The bottom date for the poem is given by the date of the relief, which should probably be put in the second half of the second century B.C. The poem must have been written for the Homereion, but whether the poet was an Alexandrian honoured with a statue in Alexandria, or a visitor so honoured in his native town we cannot say. Adriani has claimed the style of the relief as Alexandrian, but Bieber stresses the fact that the artist signs himself as coming from Priene and that several of the Muses copy a group of Muses which was probably made in Asia Minor.[2] If the stylistic argument is valid,

---

[1] Page, *G.L.P.*, no. III.
[2] Adriani, *Coppa Paesistica*, 32; Bieber, *Hell. Sc.*, 127.

Archelaos may have come with his memories from Priene and worked himself into the Alexandrian style. Then the poet probably was an Alexandrian. The answer does not greatly matter, because in any case the poem must have been made for the Homereion, and poet and artist seem to have been in close contact.

The fascination of Homer and tragedy for the court of Philopator (or his immediate successor) is shown also by the so-called 'Homeric bowls'. In the latest survey of these hemispherical Boeotian cups U. Hausmann[1] dates them from 170 to 130 but derives them from Alexandrian silver cups of rather after 200. The bowls themselves fall into two classes: (1) those which derive from moulds taken from earlier originals and (2) those deriving from moulds into which stamps of individual figures taken from earlier originals were pressed. In class 2 (which overlaps with class 1 and runs roughly from 160 to 130) the combination of figures may be due to the Boeotian artist and it tells us nothing of the Alexandrian original. The Homeric bowls are part of the larger class of 'Megarian bowls', the earliest of which (dated about 250) have a very close parallel in an Alexandrian silver cup dated by coins of Ptolemy I and II.[2] Homeric bowls have sprightly small figures with plenty of space round them; Hausmann sees analogies in the Telephos frieze in Pergamon and the frieze of the Dionysion of Kos,[3] but something very like this style can be found in Alexandrian painting of the late third century.[4] It is therefore possible to regard the originals as a reflection of the spirit which created and maintained the Homereion. Among the sixty cups which survive are eleven replicas. Somehow a selection of moulds taken from rather over forty Alexandrian cups must have reached Boeotia and appealed to the literary tastes of the Boeotians in the second century.

[1] *Hellenistische Reliefbecher*, Stuttgart, 1960. Add a further example of no. 11 found in the Peiraeus, *A.J.A.* 64, 1960, 267. The inscriptions can be found in Robert, *Homerische Becher*; Courby, *Vases à Reliefs*; and later authors quoted by Hausmann. I have in general accepted their restorations. Hausmann has now published the *Antiope* bowl with a full commentary: the three scenes are Zeus raping Antiope in a cave; Amphion, Zethos, and shepherd; Bacchant (chorus), Dirke, Antiope (*A.M.* 73, 1958, 50).

[2] Hausmann, 20, pl. 1, 1.    [3] Op. cit., 41, 47.

[4] Brown, *Ptolemaic Paintings*, 31, 48 ff., pl. 11, 14–16.

The curious gaps in the coverage of subjects suggest that the Alexandrian originals were part of a much larger set or sets. The description of the Symposion and Procession of Philadelphos shows the kind of display that the Ptolemies liked: gold and silver cups and racks full of gold and silver cups are mentioned several times, and the description ends with four hundred waggon loads of silver vessels, twenty of gold vessels.[1] Thus Philopator could easily order a set of cups to illustrate Homer and the poets inspired by Homer. Such a set, to judge from the figures given for Philadelphos' festival,[2] would contain a large number of cups, and the work would therefore be given to a number of craftsmen. They were competent artists, who were accustomed to represent Greek mythology, so that they would not need any models (the assumption of illustrated texts as models is neither necessary nor probable: we know nothing of illustrated texts at this date; if they had illustrations every thirty lines, like the *Odyssey* bowls, they would have been of immense length; moreover, some of the explanations and some of the names on the bowls do not come from the texts). The artists were, however, either scholars themselves or had scholarly help, which is one reason for discussing them here.

The subjects are taken from the *Iliad* (books III, IV, VI, XI, XV, XVII, XVIII, XIX, XX, XXI, XXIII, XXIV), the *Odyssey* (books 5, 10, 12, 21, 22), the *Aithiopis*, the *Little Iliad*, the *Iliou Persis*, the *Nostoi*, a poem on the twelve labours of Herakles (perhaps we should remember that Theokritos wrote an epigram for Peisander), the *Thebais*, Aeschylus' *Phorkides*, Sophocles' *Athamas*, Euripides' *Antiope*, *Autolykos*, *Oedipus*, *Iphigenia in Aulis*, *Phoenissae*. Some bowls give the author and the poem (the number of the bowl in Hausmann's list is quoted in brackets): 'according to Homer from the *Iliad*' (6), 'according to the poet Lesches from the *Little Iliad*' (16, 17), 'according to the poet Agias from the *Nostoi of the Achaeans*' (13), 'Sophocles in the first *Athamas*' (1), 'Euripides' *Iphigeneia*' (10). Two bowls quote the texts that they illustrate between the illustrated scenes: no. 19 quotes eighteen lines between *Odyssey* 22, 161 and 234, and no. 18 quotes nine lines between *Odyssey* 22, 310 and 365. It is worth noting that in l. 234 the cup gives the vulgate form ἵστασο and not the form

---

[1] Ath. 197c, 199c, 202f.

[2] Studniczka, op. cit., 113, reckons 200 guests in the Symposion building.

ἵστao, which occurs in one manuscript and was recommended by Zenodotos and Aristarchos on *Iliad* X, 291; in date the original of the bowl (and indeed the bowl itself) falls between Zenodotos and Aristarchos.[1] The practice of quoting texts perhaps proved too time-wasting and difficult. But the drinkers could be helped with a bit of the story, as well as added names: one of the *Iliad* bowls (6) has easily recognizable scenes of the rescue of Aeneas by Poseidon (XX, 318 f.) and Achilles fighting Lykaon (XXI, 34 f.), but in addition two figures standing side by side, who are labelled Agamemnon and Achilles and have also the very necessary inscription 'Agamemnon swears to satisfy Achilles with a view to the battle'; the Greek is not elegant and Robert saw a reference to the proposal to feed the army (XIX, 155), but the reference must rather be to Agamemnon's oath that he has not touched Briseis (XIX, 257), after which the Myrmidons bring his gifts and Briseis to Achilles' hut. The four *Little Iliad* cups all have inscriptions of this kind (15, 16, 17, 14);[2] no. 17 makes it entirely clear that the source is Lesches and not Arktinos (who made Neoptolemos kill Priam at the altar), 'according to the poet Lesches from the *Little Iliad*. When Priam took refuge at the altar of Zeus, Neoptolemos dragged him from the altar and slaughtered him by the house.' One of the Herakles cups is inscribed 'the twelve labours of Herakles' (22); another (9) is inscribed 'the club of Herakles was made by Hephaistos. It was bronze. Athena gave it to him when he was going to Arcadia to deal with the Erymanthian boar. It is the fifth labour.' This, one feels, is a superfluity of explanation. The Sophocles cup (1) unfortunately survives only in a fragment. The relief showed Athamas receiving the child Dionysos, presumably from Hermes. To the right of Athamas was the title 'Sophocles in the *First Athamas*'. Above, a long inscription of which the certain words are 'Dionysos, whom brought up as a trust . . . of Hera'. The sense must be that Athamas received and brought up the child Dionysos and as a result incurred the wrath of Hera. Here the artist gave a considerable part of the argument of the play,

---

[1] Cf. Erbse, *Hermes* 81, 1953, 163 ff. for the rejection of Zenodotos by Apollonios, his successor in the Library.

[2] I assume that Theseus' rape of Helen (no. 14) was narrated when Aithra was restored to his sons.

but his picture showed an event, the handing over of Dionysos, which must have been narrated in the prologue; (so also the bowl (24), which Pottier convincingly connected with Euripides' *Oedipus*[1] shows Periboia, watched by Hermes and Euboia, discovering the infant Oidipous and Polybos accepting him (Hermes and Euboia were the father and mother of Polybos). These scenes cannot have been acted: they were part of a narrative, whether of Hermes in the prologue or of Periboia telling the story to Oidipous). Three bowls (2–4) give scenes from Euripides' *Phoenissae* and two (10–11) scenes from his *Iphigenia in Aulis*: one of each set has explanatory inscriptions of this type: on no. 4, which is unfortunately only a fragment, 'Oidipous gives orders that he shall be led to the body of his mother and wife and of his sons'. The phrasing again is not elegant, but it accurately recalls E. *Phoen.* 1693–7; on no. 11 one inscription identifies 'the letter-bearer to Klytaimnestra' (*I.A.* 155) and another 'the messenger about the presence of Iphigeneia' (*I.A.* 414).

This bowl (11) shows first Agamemnon handing the letter over to the old man (*I.A.* 155), then Menelaos seizing the letter (*I.A.* 303), then the messenger announcing the arrival of Iphigeneia (*I.A.* 414), then the arrival of Iphigeneia, then Menelaos' sympathy with Agamemnon's grief (*I.A.* 471). There are two curious points. In the play the arrival of Iphigeneia takes place after the second chorus of l. 590; the artist has misplaced the scene, perhaps to get it next to the messenger, but, as we shall see, such misplacings are not uncommon. Secondly, he has left out Klytaimnestra but included Elektra with Iphigeneia and Orestes. Elektra is not mentioned either in the messenger's description (415 f.) or in the scene of arrival (590 f.). Unfortunately the play has no scholia so that we cannot tell if any ancient scholar conjectured her presence.[2] There could be three reasons for introducing her: (1) she would not be left at home (Chrysothemis is forgotten after her brief reappearance in Sophocles' *Elektra* and Euripides' *Orestes*), (2) she could hold Orestes, which Klytaimnestra would be too proud to do herself (621 f.),[3] (3) good-will could con-

---

[1] Cf. Séchan, *Études sur la tragédie Grecque*, 438, fig. 124.

[2] Zuntz, *Political Plays of Euripides*, 138, notices this habit in hypotheses of Euripides' plays which he dates (perhaps too late) to the first century B.C.

[3] Cf. S. *Electra*, 1143–8.

strue *I.T.* 811–20 to mean that Elektra herself had been at Aulis. Whatever the reason, the artist intentionally embroiders here. The other bowl[1] (10) shows (1) Iphigeneia running ahead of Klytaimnestra and Orestes to greet Agamemnon (631), (2) Klytaimnestra and Achilles (819), (3) Klytaimnestra and the old man (855), (4) Klytaimnestra and Iphigeneia (with a bridal gesture) leave Achilles, (5) Iphigeneia and Orestes appeal to Agamemnon in the presence of Klytaimnestra. The fifth scene must be the appeal to Agamemnon (1211 f., particularly 1240 f.); the fourth scene is interpreted as illustrating Iphigeneia's attempt to get away when she sees Achilles coming (1338 f.). If so, the artist has misplaced the scene, as he misplaced Iphigeneia's arrival on the other cup. The sacrifice of Iphigeneia is omitted.

The picture of Oidipous at the end of the *Phoenissae* is only a fragment (4). Two other bowls are complete. On no. 2, (1) (pl. V*b*) Kreon appeals to Teiresias (834 f.). The artist has put in Teiresias' bird sanctuary and his tablets, illustrating ll. 838–40, and has given Teiresias' daughter the name Manto, which is not in the text but is given in the scholia on the authority of Peisander, the poet for whom Theokritos wrote a statue-epigram. (2) Polyneikes and Eteokles fight, Eteokles coming from a seated Thebe (cf. 1252). (3) The messenger summons Iokaste (1068), who in turn summons Antigone (1264). (4) Antigone makes supplication to Kreon (1643). On no. 3, Eteokles and Polyneikes have already fallen; the Argives are flying to Argos, pursued by the Thebans from Thebes. Antigone rushes towards her brothers (1435 f.) and Iokaste commits suicide (1455). To the left of the two dying men the artist has added one (and probably two) women leaving them; they are labelled *patroiai*[2] and the missing word in the gap was presumably *arai* 'curses': between the messenger's description of the brothers' deaths and the description of Iokaste and Antigone arriving on the scene the chorus say

---

[1] Séchan, op. cit., 369, fig. 107. Page, *Actor-Interpolations*, 202 (cf. also 167), interprets the third scene as 1532 ff.; but it is unjustifiable to reject the inscription 'Old Man'; the 'Messenger' is inscribed correctly on the *Phoenissae* bowl and on no. 11.

[2] Cf. Etruscan Ash-Chest in Copenhagen, National Museum, AB b 36, where two Furies spur the brothers on.

(1425): 'how greatly I bewail your woes, Oidipous. God seems to have fulfilled your curses.'

The whole of this bowl illustrates the messenger speech. Its long scene belongs therefore between the earlier messenger's summons to Iokaste and Antigone (scene 3 of no. 2) and Antigone's appeal to Kreon (scene 4 of no. 2). It is indeed arguable that the duel of the brothers (scene 2 of no. 2) belongs rather to this bowl since it is related in this messenger speech, and there is the further question of what scenes were included on the fragmentary bowl no. 4: there seems little more left at the end of the *Phoenissae*. Did the artist add earlier scenes or did he go on to another play? On the Euripidean bowls, therefore, the sequence of scenes may be varied on a single bowl or may jump from one bowl to another. The *Odyssey* bowls show the same phenomena. One of the inscribed bowls (19) starts with the seizure of Melanthios, goes on with Athena's encouragement to Odysseus, and then goes back to the tying up of Melanthios to the column, thus dislocating the sequence. The two inscribed bowls cover *Odyssey* 22, 161–361, but another bowl (21) gives scenes on either side of this passage: Penelope and the suitors from the beginning of Book 22 and Eurykleia and Odysseus from the end of Book 22. Finally, the bowl (5) which gives Priam appealing to Achilles in *Iliad* XXIV continues with Priam greeting Penthesileia before the tomb of Hektor and the death of Penthesileia, both scenes from the *Aithiopis*. All these bowls belong to the early series, which are direct reproductions of the presumed Alexandrian metal cups. A possible explanation of the dislocations is that the cups were ordered at short notice; the master artist planned out the scenes and captions and then distributed them to his craftsmen to work out on the bowls; they did not always bother about the exact order. If the bowls were to be used at a single great party it was not very serious if a scene from the end of the *Iliad* overlapped on to the *Aithiopis* cup, or that three drinkers had to compare notes to get the whole story of the *Phoenissae*.

The set was designed for a party interested in literature. The scenes have no particular artistic merit (even when allowance is made for the contrast between the unattractive Boeotian clay of the copies and the precious metal of the originals), nor do they give a particularly good rendering of the story; their purpose is to recall situations in epic and drama, and by adding names not in the text to comment on them (it would be interesting to know where the artists of nos. 26 and 27 went to find names of the comrades of Odysseus who were turned into animals by Kirke). This is scholarship for pleasure, like Dioskorides' epigrams on the poets. Two subjects, which apparently are out of harmony with high literature, the *kinaidoi* breaking up the peace of a corn miller's establishment (8, cf. 28) and *sympleg-mata* of men and women (36), are not perhaps so alien, if Alexander of Aetolia, scholar and tragic poet, also wrote *kinaidika* and *ionika*.[1]

The combination of poetry and scholarship lasted into the second century. The great librarian and scholar, Aristarchos, had a pupil, Moschos of Syracuse, who may have written on the Rhodian dialect (Ath. 485b). His *Europe*[2] is a charming hexameter poem describing how the Zeus-bull carried Europe off to Crete. It is light and pretty poetry with no deep emotions: even when Europe finds herself out of sight of land her distress lasts for less than a line (146). Dr Bühler has rightly noted the strong influence of the *Argonautika* of Apollonios Rhodios, but this is a much more light-hearted poem, and Moschos does not intrude his learning either in vocabulary or in references; the tone recalls the goddesses at the beginning of the third book of Apollonios much more than the Medeia scenes, although, like Medeia, Europe has a dream and goes out with her girls. The common source for both Hellenistic poets is Nausikaa's dream and journey to the sea-shore in *Odyssey* VI. Apollonios recalls the *Odyssey* to point the contrast between his hysterical girl and the calm princess. Moschos wants to emphasize the similarity.

Moschos' Europe is to be another Nausikaa; but, unlike Medeia and Nausikaa, she does not have a dream which calls for immediate action – to go and meet Jason or to wash the clothes. Like Atossa in Aeschylus' *Persae*, she dreams of a struggle between Asia and Greece.[3] Such a dream obviously demands interpretation, but because she has

[1] Cf. above, p. 127.
[2] Edited by W. Bühler, *Hermes*, Einzelschriften, 13, 1960, with full commentary, including references to literary and artistic sources.
[3] We have no evidence that Aeschylus also used this theme in his *Europe*.

to behave like Nausikaa she summons her girls and goes straight off to the meadow to pick flowers. They all carry baskets and Europe has a very special basket.

The Homeric Achilles has his shield, Apollonios' Jason has his cloak (1, 725); so Europe has her basket. The description occupies 26 lines of a poem 166 lines long. But if it is out of scale, the decoration is highly relevant, since it tells the parallel story of Zeus and Io of Argos, parallel not only because Io became a cow but also because Io's union with Zeus took place in another continent, Africa. (Europe, as daughter of Phoinix, lives in Asia, but Moschos does not tell us where.) On the basket the Io cow is gold and the sea is *kyanos* in the first scene; in the second the Nile is silver, the cow bronze, and Zeus is gold. This is the technique of Achilles' shield, and we need not look for parallels in Alexandrian art. Nor need we suppose that Moschos worried much about how the three scenes fitted the basket. He only becomes definite when he speaks of the peacock, which rose from the blood of Argos 'shading the rim of the basket with its feathers'; for this the cup from Herculaneum, possibly of Alexandrian origin, with Homer riding to heaven on an eagle provides a parallel.[1] What Moschos calls a *talaros*, we should call a *kalathos*; Europe already holds one on an Attic vase of the earliest fifth century,[2] and in Alexandria Demeter's *kalathos* was drawn by white horses through the city.[3]

The story goes on with the girls picking flowers, the arrival of the bull and its overtures to Europe. Europe leaps on its back and it makes off for the sea before her companions can scramble up. Then the procession across the sea with Poseidon leading, the Nereids riding monsters, and the Tritons blowing on shells; then Europe's lament, Zeus' declaration, and the arrival in Crete. Whether any of the later paintings which illustrate these events go back to originals which Moschos could have seen we cannot say.[4] But many of the elements can be dated before his time: Europe's helpless appeal to her

[1] Adriani, *Coppa Paesistica*, 33 n. 173, pl. 48, 139.

[2] Leningrad, St 1637; Beazley, *A.R.V.*, 161/3; *C.R.* 1866, pl. 5.

[3] Kallimachos, *Hymn* VI, 120.

[4] E.g. the original of the Pompeian painting, *R.P.*, 13/1, Curtius, *Wandmalerei Pompeiis*, pl. 4, which Lippold, *R.M.* 60/1, 1953/4, 126, refers to Antiphilos.

companions appears on an Attic vase[1] of about 450; the sea-procession on fourth-century vases from Attica and Apulia.[2] The Apulian vase only shows Nereids riding sea-monsters on either side of Europe riding the bull. The Attic vases add Zeus, Poseidon, and Triton. There are three differences between the Attic vases and Moschos' description: (1) they show Zeus seated in human form awaiting the arrival of the procession; this is unimportant – the seated Zeus tells us that he will resume human form when he reaches Crete. (2) Poseidon also is seated; the god of the sea watches the procession but does not lead it; here Moschos has changed the story. (3) Triton holds a staff instead of blowing a trumpet. The earliest evidence for Triton blowing on a shell, however, is contemporary with these vases, a mosaic from Olympia.[3] The fourth-century vases probably presuppose a popular literary source, perhaps a choral lyric. This may have been known to Moschos or he may have known paintings. The vases are rather serious: Moschos is joyous and playful: 'Why are you not afraid of the sea? The sea is the track for swift ships, bulls are afraid of the salt path' (136 f.), says Europe in her lament.

The other fragments attributed to Moschos – Aphrodite's proclamation that Eros has run away from her, the countryman and the fisherman, Pan and Echo, Arethousa, Eros ploughing – are on a smaller scale but show the same light, easy treatment. This light and charming play with traditional materials may truly be called Classicism.

[1] London, E 334, Beazley, *A.R.V.*, 653/4.

[2] Attic: e.g. Kertch and Leningrad, Metzger, *Représentations*, 306, nos. 17, 18. Apulian: Berlin F 3241, Neugebauer, *Führer*, pl. 82.

[3] Rumpf, *Malerei und Zeichnung*, 123, fig. 11, cf. *Meerwesen*, 105 f. Nearly contemporary with Moschos, the akroteria of the Altar of Zeus at Pergamon, Bieber, *Hell. Sc.*, fig. 469.

## CHAPTER VIII

# *Alexandrian Art and Alexandrian Poetry*

◆

Alexandria under the Ptolemies attracted artists as it attracted poets. The purpose of this chapter is not to give an account of Alexandrian art but to ask how far Alexandrian poets were conscious of Alexandrian art, whether they sometimes saw with the eye of contemporary artists, whether they sometimes reflected contemporary art in their poems, whether contemporary art can be used to illustrate their poems, and whether on their side the artists show the same interest in scholarship, in realism, and in landscape as the poets. Alexandrian poetry is a useful name for the work of a number of poets who came from all over the Greek world but worked for a longer or shorter period in Alexandria, being in some way connected with the court or the Mouseion or more loosely with other poets working under the Ptolemies. Alexandrian art will be used here in rather the same sense, as art which can reasonably be connected with the Ptolemies; it will not be necessary to raise the much debated question as to whether an Alexandrian art which is distinct from other Hellenistic art can be identified.

It is natural to start with the works of art actually mentioned by the poets. Some can be passed over quickly. Moschos may have been inspired by Antiphilos' painting of Europe when he described the arrival of the bull. Europe's golden basket owes more to Homer than contemporary art, and its decoration is due to Moschos' desire to give the Io story as a parallel to the Europe story: a decorated golden cup of this shape could certainly have been made, and the silver cup[1] from Herculaneum, which has this shape and affords a parallel for part of the decoration, may be a copy of an Alexandrian original. Jason's cloak in Apollonios is in the same literary tradition, but elaborate textiles are copied in contemporary tomb-paintings and mosaics[2] and the Symposion tent of Ptolemy Phila-

---

[1] Cf. above, p. 154.
[2] Cf. *Bulletin of the John Rylands Library* 45, 1962/3, 264.

delphos included 'very beautiful cloaks, some with portraits of the Kings, some with mythological stories woven in' (Ath. 196f); Theokritos (XV, 80 f.) speaks of a textile depicting Adonis in the royal palace. Kallimachos' description of the Hera of Samos (fr. 100–1), the Olympian Zeus (fr. 196), the Apollo of Delos (fr. 114) reflect the beginning of scholarship in the history of art. The poem on the Apollo of Delos is also interpretation, as Professor Pfeiffer has demonstrated:[1] 'in order to punish fools for their insolence, I have the bow, but to the good people I stretch out my hand with the Graces. I carry the bow in the left hand, because I am slower to chastise mortals, but the Graces in the right hand, as I am always disposed to distribute pleasant things.' In a further line something was said about the possibility of repentance. Thus Kallimachos was giving a modern ethical interpretation of an archaic statue.

In the same way (but much more simply because here the artist's meaning was explicit) Poseidippos interprets Lysippos' statue of Kairos (*A.P.* XVI, 275), and Lysippos' statue of Alexander has a ferocity which excuses the Persians, as cattle may be excused from fleeing before a lion (*A.P.* XVI, 119). Asklepiades (*A.P.* XVI, 120)[2] interprets Alexander's raised eyes as meaning that Alexander reserves the earth for himself, while leaving Olympos to Zeus. Rightly or wrongly we think of the bronze statuette in the Louvre for Poseidippos' epigram and the marble statuette from Gabii, also in the Louvre, for Asklepiades.[3] There is also a good marble head[4] of Alexander from Alexandria itself, which makes these judgments intelligible. Theokritos speaks of Alexander as a 'terrible god to the Persians' in the poem in praise of Ptolemy II (XVII, 16 f.). It is very possible that he knew two pictures or tapestries in the palace, one with Ptolemy I, Alexander, and Herakles feasting in the house of Zeus, and the other with Herakles returning home drunk, supported by Alexander and

[1] *J.W.C.I.* 15, 1952, 26, 30 ff.
[2] Plutarch, *Moralia*, 335b, quotes the Asklepiades epigram as inscribed on the statue when it was first made, but this is a fiction to account for Alexander's choice of Lysippos as his sculptor.
[3] Winter, *K.i.B.*, 334/3; 335/2; Lippold, *Gr. Pl.*, 268, 327.
[4] Cleveland Museum of Art, Bieber, *Hell. Sc.*, 90, figs. 334–5.

M

Ptolemy I, who carry his club, bow, and quiver. For the first, the artist had only to add Ptolemy and Alexander to a traditional symposion of the gods. The model for the other was the drunk Dionysos supported by Satyrs, known already in the fifth century and later in the Hellenistic age.[1] Herakles is shown with a large wreath on his head and a himation round his body in a terracotta statuette of the third century (pl. VI*a*) from Alexandria.[2]

Herodas in his fourth sketch makes Kynno and Kokale visit the temple of Asklepios at Kos.[3] The temple was built in the very early third century. In front of it stood a large altar, perhaps already at this date surrounded by columns; they formed a covered passage in front of the altar wall against which statues and reliefs could be set and on which votive offerings could be hung. We cannot say whether all the gods and heroes invoked by Kynno had statues. But the women certainly see a group of Asklepios and Hygieia by the sons of Praxiteles (20 f.). Kokale's prayer to Paion to be kind to the artists implies that they are still alive; as Pliny gives their floruit as 296, they may have been still alive in the 270's. Some fragments of sculpture[4] found near the altar are in the soft, sweet style associated with Praxiteles and his successors.

Then (27 f.) they see a girl looking up at an apple, an old man, a boy strangling a goose, and a statue of Batale daughter of Myttes. They are astounded at the passion in the gaze of the girl; the boy seems on the point of speaking; Batale's portrait is exactly like her. The standard is realism, a realism which makes interpretations, such as those we have already mentioned, possible. These four dedications (the first probably a relief, the old man and Batale portrait statues) show three important elements in Hellenistic art – interest in children (the girl and the boy), interest in nature (the apple tree), realism in portraiture (the old man and Batale). It is extremely useful to have this testimony to their existence early in the third century, and we

---

[1] Fifth century: e.g. Würzburg 491, Beazley, *A.R.V.*, 742; *J.H.S.* 59, 1939, 119. Hellenistic: e.g. 'Visit to Icarius', Bieber, *Hell. Sc.*, fig. 656 = *M.N.C.*, AS 3 (cf. below, p. 176).

[2] Alexandria 24160, Adriani, *Annuaire du Musée Gréco-Romain* 1935–9, 100, pl. C.

[3] Cf. above, p. 94. For the site, see R. Herzog and P. Schazmann, *Kos*, 1932.

[4] Bieber, *Hell. Sc.*, 20 f., n. 77, figs. 32–3, 43. Cf. also *Clara Rhodos*, IX, 17 ff.

shall return to them later. Lehmann[1] has quoted a Roman marble group in New York as a parallel for the girl looking up at the apple as it hangs on the tree, and a Hellenistic grave-relief in Ephesos is also relevant (pl. VIII*a*). The boy with the goose has naturally been brought into relation both with Pliny's account of a group by Boethos (*N.H.* 34, 84) and with the two very different Roman marble groups in Vienna and Munich; the group in Vienna, which comes from Ephesos, has been successfully connected with a base signed Boethos of Carthage; the child does seem about to speak, and the general scheme of the composition is attested for the third century by a terracotta from the Chatby cemetery in Alexandria.[2]

Svoronos[3] has interpreted all the sculpture (except Batale) as particularly relevant to Asklepios: he believes the girl to be Epione receiving the apple from her father Merops, the old man, and the boy with the goose to be the son of Asklepios, Iamiskos. He has produced good evidence for both children and geese represented on offerings to Asklepios in Athens and Epidauros. None of the evidence can be dated earlier than the third century, so that these offerings themselves show the Hellenistic interest in children. The interpretation of the girl with the apple and the old man as Epione and Merops is unlikely, because Kokale implies that the old man is as realistically represented as the girl, whereas Merops would be a stately figure. The two works are therefore better kept separate. All that can be said is that the dedicators of the girl and the boy may have intended them as a daughter and child of Asklepios, but Herodas' women completely fail to perceive this intention.

The women then go inside the temple. They disregard the sculpture but admire the painting, a naked boy with soft hot flesh, a silver fire-box so real that thieves might steal it, an ox with a fierce eye, a man leading it, a woman by the side, a man with a hooked nose, a

---

[1] Lehmann, *A.J.A.* 49, 1945, 430. Grave-relief from Ephesos: Vienna, I, 873; K.i.B., 371/5; Lippold, *Gr. Pl.*, 376.

[2] On the problem of Boethos and the difficulties see Rumpf, *J.D.Œ.A.I.* 39, 1952, 86 ff. Vienna 816, *K.i.B.*, 370/3; Lippold, *Gr. Pl.*, 308/1, pl. 117/1 (the inscription: see Rumpf); Bieber, *Hell. Sc.*, fig. 534. Munich 268, *K.i.B.*, 370/1–2; Lippold, *Gr. Pl.*, 329/3, pl. 117/2; Bieber, *Hell. Sc.*, fig. 285. Terracotta: Breccia, *Necropoli di Sciatbi*, pl. 73, 225.

[3] *A.E.* 1909, 137 ff.; 1917, 78 ff.

slave with a snub[1] nose, all wondrously alive; Apelles' work is life-like down to the smallest detail and his critics deserve whipping. The modern commentators convincingly take all these figures as components in a single scene of sacrifice, like the procession of the priest of Artemis of Ephesos, which Pliny (N.H. 35, 93) records among Apelles' works. The boy is lighting the fire on the altar; the woman carries on her head the tray of sacrificial offerings and implements; the man with the hooked nose is the dedicator of the picture.[2] Apelles, who painted Philip and Alexander, was still working in the early third century. His picture of Calumny was supposed to reflect his quarrel with the Alexandrian painter Antiphilos, who accused him of treachery against Ptolemy Soter. The echo of this quarrel is heard in Kynno's hatred of Apelles' critics.

The realistic silver fire-box has a parallel in the silver bowl painted on a hydria of Hadra ware.[3] On this Mrs Brown writes: 'in the painting of the silver bowl there seems even to be a glow of reflected light on the edge of the shadowed side'. This is perhaps the only third-century object which shows the painter's interest in light effects. But Pliny (N.H. 35, 138) tells us that Apelles' enemy Antiphilos painted a boy blowing up the fire so that the light was reflected on the walls and on the boy's own face. Alexandrian painting did, therefore, show the kind of light effects which interested Apollonios Rhodios: in the Argonautika Hylas' chest shines in the moonlight (1, 1231); at dawn 'the paths are bright and the dewy plains shine with a clear glow' (1, 1280); Medeia's heart ranges in her breast like a tinkerbell (3, 755); the fleece is like a cloud blushing in the rays of the rising sun (4, 125). Apollonios saw with the eye of the contemporary painter.

The last two descriptions of works of art which should be mentioned are the shepherd's cup and the Adonis bower in Theokritos. The shepherd's cup (I, 27 ff.) is made of wood; it is deep, has two

---

[1] I accept the original anasimos rather than the correction anasillos, because 'snub' is the right contrast for 'hooked'. Then anthropos is the ugly slave beside the aristocratic aquiline master.

[2] Cf. much earlier S. Eitrem, A.E. 1954, 26.

[3] New York 90.9.60. B. R. Brown, Ptolemaic Paintings and Mosaics 1957, 62–4, no. 45. On Apollonios, cf. above, Ch. III, pp. 70, 74.

handles; the lips are decorated with fruited ivy with a vine winding along it with yellow (gilded?) grape clusters;[1] 'within' a woman playing with two lovers, 'near them' an old man fishing; 'very near him' a vineyard with a little boy plaiting a locust trap, while one fox eats the grapes and another gets its nose into the boy's wallet; all round the cup is spread the pliant akanthos. Mr Gow, objecting to the three scenes on the outside of a cup with two handles, places them inside with the fisherman in the central tondo and the two three-figure scenes on the sides. Miss A. M. Dale[2] points out that a *kissybion* must be deep and this *kissybion* is called 'deep'; it cannot therefore be decorated on the inside. The fault lies with the poet, who, always imprecise, has a memory of at least two kinds of metal cup. He starts off with a two-handled skyphos (he uses the word in l. 143). The ivy and vine decoration round the lip is suitable for this. Then he puts a scene 'within' – *not* inside the cup, if it is deep, but within the frame-work of the ivy. Then he adds two more scenes, forgetting the handles. Finally he puts akanthos all round the cup; but this is impossible if it is a skyphos with a flat bottom; akanthos can rise from the stem of a cup over the bowl or can decorate a stemless bowl. In fact a bowl, like the contemporary 'Megarian' bowls, (pl. V*a*),[3] could accommodate the decorations very well, but it would not have two handles and it would not stand steadily enough to be used for milking (143). The scenes, however, are presumably scenes that occurred in contemporary art: the old fisherman is realistic art, and the third scene belongs both to child art and to country art; a parallel for the two predatory foxes can be found on the Augustan 'Ptolemy's cup'[4] with a kid leaping up to a bunch of grapes and a dog investigating an overturned amphora.

In the fifteenth idyll (117 f.) the Adonis singer describes the tableau at the Adonis festival. There are green bowers with soft dill, little

---

[1] Mr Gow, ad loc., takes the tendril however as the tendril of the ivy and the two fruits as identical. The intertwining of fruited ivy and vine is found on Gnathia vases, e.g. the oinochoe, British Museum F571, *C.V.*, pl. IV, Dc, 1, 4.

[2] *C.R.* 66, 1952, 129.

[3] Cf. Rostovtzeff, *S.E.H.*, I, 534, for the lay-out of the decoration.

[4] Paris, Bibliothèque Nationale, 368. Adriani, *Coppa Paesistica*, 23, fig. 8., pls. 30–1; Loewenthal and Harden, *J.R.S.* 39, 1949, 36.

Erotes flying from branch to branch, a couch of ebony, ivy, and gold with Ganymedes decorating the legs, on it Milesian and Samian rugs, and on them Aphrodite in the arms of Adonis. We have here a special kind of child art in the Erotes, and a special kind of country art, bowers with figures on couches. Not much more need be said about Alexandrian interest in children. The little Erotes of the Adonis bower have their counterparts in Asklepiades' 'little Eros, flown away from his mother, still easy to catch' (*A.P.* XII, 105). The child Eros is not new, but the child Eros with short wings is new and appears on Gnathia vases[1] in the last quarter of the fourth century. About 327 Aetion painted the Marriage of Alexander and Rhoxane and included two Erotes struggling to carry his spear; these were certainly children whether they had long wings or short. They may still have had long wings like the terracotta child Erotes in Attica of about 330.[2] Little Erotes are also found in the Early Chatby cemetery at Alexandria.[3] Apollonios' Eros is older and we have already quoted a Hellenistic group of Eros and Ganymede,[4] although we cannot claim it as specifically Alexandrian. But a Hadra hydria[5] shows Erotes hunting, and this may be claimed as an ancestor of Moschos' Eros ploughing. Except for Eros, who has wings, divine children are difficult to distinguish from human children; the boy with the goose and the girl looking at the apple may be divine children, but Herodas' women treat them as human children. Similarly the novelty of Kallimachos' Artemis is that, although she is divine and has divine power, she behaves as a human child, and we may think of her as like the charming terracotta statuettes[6] of little girls from the Chatby cemetery. Only an inscription can make it clear whether a child is human or divine; the pretty children of Theaitetos' epigram are labelled Nikanor and Phila (*A.P.* VI, 357) and this shows that they are human.

Theokritos' little Erotes fly from branch to branch of a green bower covering Adonis and Aphrodite. Such bowers are found also in the Procession of Philadelphos: both Nysa, the nurse of Dionysos,

[1] E.g. Naples 81007, *C.V.*, Naples, III, pl. IV E, 54. Cf. *J.H.S.* 71, 1951, 228.
[2] D. B. Thompson, *Hesperia* 21, 1952, 127, nos. 11 and 12.
[3] Breccia, *Necropoli di Sciatbi*, pl. 74, 227.      [4] Cf. above, p. 77.
[5] Berlin 3767, Pfuhl, *M.u.Z.*, fig. 759.
[6] Breccia, *Necropoli di Sciatbi*, pls. 70, 72, 73.

and Dionysos himself appear under bowers on the tableau-waggons (Ath. 198c–f). The more interesting is the bower over Dionysos: it was made of ivy, vine, and other fruits, and had attached to it wreaths, ribbons, thyrsoi, tambourines, fillets, and masks of tragedy, comedy, and satyr-play. Many of these things can be seen in the bowers on Ptolemy's cup in the Augustan period;[1] but such a bower appears already on a Paestan vase[2] of the third quarter of the fourth century: the branches of ivy and helichryse above the banqueters suspend three comic masks. Thus not only are the bowers traditional but also the representation of them in painting.

Bowers are artificial but grottoes are natural; the grottoes of the Procession and Banqueting tent[3] of Philadelphos reproduce supposedly natural caves. In the Procession (Ath. 200c) a cart carried a deep cave with ivy and yew, two fountains of milk and wine, and the Nymphs and Hermes about the infant Dionysos. This tableau also is in an artistic tradition.[4] Two earlier works are particularly relevant: on an Attic plastic[5] vase of the third quarter of the fourth century (pl. Ia) the infant Dionysos, with oinochoe and phiale, stands in a cave, around the face of which hang clusters of grapes; the Procession tableau is a greatly elaborated version of this. Secondly, a Corinthian mirror[6] of 350/25 shows a Nymph washing her hair in a cave while Pan looks on; wreaths and fillets hang in the entrance of the cave and plants grow from the floor; a lionhead spout pours water into a metal bowl (the fountains of milk and wine in the Procession cave probably had lionhead spouts). One of the pictures[7] in

---

[1] See above, p. 161.

[2] Vatican AD 1, Trendall, *Phlyax vases*, no. 164; Bieber, *History*[2], fig. 538. Cf. also the ivy and vines often hung with masks and scarves on Gnathia vases, e.g. *J.H.S.* 71, 1951, 225, fig. 1, etc.

[3] On the grottoes in the banqueting tent, see above, p. 122.

[4] Studniczka, op. cit., 93; *Bulletin of the John Rylands Library* 45, 1962/3, 248 f.

[5] Athens, Agora P 12822, D. B. Thompson, *Hesperia* 23, 1954, no. 13, pl. 19; cf. Higgins, *Cat. of Terracottas*, II, no. 1708. Cf. above, p. 2.

[6] Berlin 8148, Pfuhl, *M.u.Z.*, fig. 625; Züchner, *Klappspiegel*, no. 59; *Art and Literature in Fourth-century Athens*, pl. 13b.

[7] New York. Pfuhl, *M.u.Z.*, fig. 707; Rumpf, *M.u.Z.*, 158 ff., pl. 54/5. Mrs Brown, op. cit., 88, is unduly sceptical about Demetrios: Valerius Maximus calls him *pictor Alexandrinus*.

the cubiculum of the villa in Boscoreale combines the bower and the grotto: the bower, a kind of pergola covered with vines and grapes, surmounts an ivy-covered cave with a marble fountain inside it. This is probably a copy of an Alexandrian background for a satyr-play of the early second century, if Rumpf's very plausible connection with Demetrios the landscape painter may be accepted: here too the bower and grotto is connected with Dionysos. In fact there is just enough evidence to suggest that cave and vine as background for satyr-plays set in the country went back to the fifth century.[1]

Alexandrian country art, as illustrated by the bowers and grottoes, is an elaboration of a very old tradition, which embraces both the natural grotto of the Nymphs and the artificial bower of the symposion, and Dionysos with his train are naturally at home both in grottoes and bowers. Gow writes that Theokritos' *Epigrams* 1–3 would be suitable as inscriptions for works of art: 1, a landscape with browsing goats; 2, a still-life painting or a relief of rustic gear, perhaps with a statue or herm of Pan; 3, Daphnis stalked by Pan and Priapos. The third epigram fits easily into the tradition of the Corinthian mirror with Pan spying on the Nymph washing in her cave; Daphnis is asleep on a bed of leaves in a cave; Pan and Priapos, who has yellow ivy round his lovely head, stalk him. Priapos, as we have seen, appears in the tableaux of Philadelphos' procession.[2] (The fifth epigram is a variant of the same theme: Pan asleep in the cave, a flautist, a lyrist, and Daphnis with syrinx play outside.) The second epigram does not necessarily imply a work of art imaginary or real: it is a fictional dedication of Daphnis' gear. The first epigram runs: 'The dewy roses and the thick thyme (*herpyllos*) there are dedicated to the ladies of Helikon, and the black-leaved bays to you, Pythian Paian. . . . That horned goat, the white one eating the tips of the terebrinth branches, will shed his blood on the altar.' The demonstratives with the thyme and the goat suggest that the poet is (or imagines himself to be) looking at a picture, but he can only know that the goat is going to be sacrificed if a figure is seen approaching

[1] *Bulletin of the John Rylands Library* 45, 1962/3, 244, 248 f.
[2] Cf. above, p. 140. Cf. also terracotta from Ezbet el Makhlouf, *Annuaire du Musée Gréco-Romain*, 1935/9, 109.

the goat, as in a picture in the Casa degli Epigrammi at Pompeii[1] where a satyr drags a goat to sacrifice. The epigram allows us to claim for Alexandria in the early third century another kind of country art, a picture of a country shrine with figures of Apollo and the Muses and with wreaths dedicated to them, a goat nibbling a tree (as on the later Cup of the Ptolemies) and a figure coming to sacrifice him. The figure may be a satyr, and so this too would be mythical landscape rather than real landscape. It may perhaps be argued that these mythical landscapes have influenced the scenery of Theokritos' pastorals whether they are mythical or not: *Idyll* I, 21 f. has an elm, a statue of Priapos, fountains, a shepherds' seat, and oak-trees; III has a cave; V, 45 has oak-trees, galingale, two fountains, and a pine-tree; VII, 135 has poplars, elms, water from the cave of the nymphs, thorn bushes, pears, apples, and sloes; *Epigram* 4 has oak-trees, a wooden Priapos, a waterfall, bay, myrtle, cypress, and vine.

Only *Idyll* X is firmly contemporary; the other idylls are either mythical or fluctuate between contemporary and mythical.[2] If this scenery, as we have suggested, is traditionally connected with Dionysos, Nymphs, Satyrs, and Pan, we may ask two further questions; do the pastoral poets sometimes think of their mythical herdsmen as satyrs, and secondly is this the moment when landscape with ordinary humans was started alongside landscape with mythical figures (for which *Idyll* X provides an analogy in literature)? The equation of mythical herdsmen and satyrs is not impossible. The satyr Marsyas is called 'shepherd of Kelainai' by Dioskorides (*A.P.* IX, 340), and according to Alexander the Aetolian (fr. 15) he was taught by Daphnis. Was Daphnis the neatherd also a satyr or sometimes a satyr? In Sositheos' tragedy he defeated Menalkas with Pan as judge and married a nymph. In *Idyll* VIII (*not* by Theokritos) Daphnis competes with Menalkas before a goatherd (Pan?); both of them are red-haired like Sositheos' satyr, and Daphnis again is in love with a nymph, who lives in a cave, and in *Idyll* XXVII (*not* by Theokritos) he is called *satyriskos*. Tityros in *Idylls* III and VII has a satyr name; the goatherd in III describes himself as 'snub-nosed with

---

[1] Neutsch, *J.D.A.I.* 70, 1955, 155, fig. 7. Cf. also Bieber, *J.D.A.I.* 32, 1917, 31, fig. 8.

[2] Cf. above, p. 82.

a jutting beard' (8), which sounds like a satyr, and he too is in love with a nymph who lives in a cave. Thyrsis (*Idyll* I) would be a good name for a satyr, since it is derived from *thyrsos*.

Yet a further term to this equation is human initiates. The neat-herds (*boukoloi*) who were initiates in the mysteries of Dionysos at Pergamon may have been dressed as satyrs as early as the second century,[1] and similar figures may have existed in the Dionysiac mysteries in Alexandria; the triple equation, herdsmen = mystics = satyrs, may go back to archaic times in Attica and Ionia and have been recreated for their own countries by the Hellenistic kings. In the Hellenistic age there is a further complication: poets called them-selves 'herdsmen' and were Dionysiac initiates. The artist who alluded to these ideas could only represent satyrs or men with a satyr's fawn-skin or herdsman's crook.

The second question is whether in the time of Philadelphos we already have evidence for landscape with ordinary human figures. The Koans may have had a bronze relief of Philitas singing under a plane-tree as early as 290, and a case can be made for a third-century picture of Menander composing under a tree.[2] The girl looking up at the apple-tree in Herodas may be a daughter of Asklepios, and the little boy in the vineyard on Theokritos' cup (I, 47) might be a child satyr. But neither Herodas' women nor Theokritos' goatherd make the identification, and the natural assumption is that they are ordinary humans. It is unfortunate that we are so badly off for firmly dated archaeological material. But we must accept the evidence of the poets even if we cannot show contemporary parallels. The monuments usually quoted are an Alexandrian bronze cup[3] with a Marsyas, Athena, and Olympos between the trees and before a rustic shrine, a Roman relief[4] with a girl pulling a thorn out of a young man's foot

[1] Cf. R. Merkelbach, *Roman und Mysterium*, 205, 222; E. Simon, *J.D.A.I.* 76, 1961, 126. The great inscription, *Pergamon* VIII, 485, which gives 18 *boukoloi*, 2 *Seilenoi*, and 1 *Choregos*, dates from first century A.D. On *boukoloi* in Attica and Ionia, cf. Pickard-Cambridge, *Dithyramb etc.*[2], 153.

[2] Cf. above, p. 42, and below, p. 172.

[3] Alexandria Museum 25263. Adriani, *Coppa Paesistica*; rev. F. Matz, *Gnomon* 32, 1960, 290; J. M. C. Toynbee, *C.R.* 10, 1960, 268 (first century B.C. or A.D.).

[4] Naples. Adriani, loc. cit., 34, fig. 141; *K.i.B.*, 365/4.

(like the scene in Theokritos IV, 50 ff.), a painting from Herculaneum[1] with a tired satyr being lowered off a mule on to a stone beside a tree and a statue of Athena standing on a pillar, and a relief[2] from Tralles (pl. VIII*b*) with a youth tying up an animal under a plane-tree. The bronze cup and the relief from Tralles have been claimed as third-century originals; the dating depends on style alone and in the case of the bronze cup has been hotly disputed; the Roman relief and the painting are said to derive from early third-century originals, but as they are copies too much weight must not be placed on them. All show satyrs or mythical characters except the Tralles relief.

Two Alexandrian monuments, however, which are contemporary with the poets, give them some support: one is a fayence jug[3] with a picture of one of the early Ptolemaic Queens; she stands between a wreathed pillar on one side and an altar, from behind which a goat emerges, on the other. The other is the bronze plaque[4] from the Arsinoeion at Delos: Artemis (or perhaps rather Arsinoe as Artemis) walks between an altar tended by two men dressed as young satyrs and a statue of Artemis on a column. The country look of these two pieces is due to the wide-spacing of the design; both also have an altar with victim or attendants and a high column such as often occurs in later bucolic landscapes.

Outside the Alexandrian orbit the same wide-spacing and an undoubted country shrine is seen on a third-century kantharos (pl. II) from the Athenian agora.[5] The Telephos frieze (pl. XVIII*a*) of the Great Altar at Pergamon, carved between 197 and 160,[6] shows trees and rocks as the background for some of its mythical scenes; it is too

---

[1] Naples. Rumpf, *M.u.Z.*, 158, pl. 54/2; Pfuhl, *M.u.Z.*, 911, fig. 665; Reinach, *R.P.*, 121/5.

[2] Istanbul 547. Lippold, *Gr. Pl.*, 343; *K.i.B.*, 365/5. Mendel argues that the treatment of depth is earlier than on the Telephos frieze.

[3] Istanbul. Adriani, op. cit., 20, figs. 74–6. For the head, cf. the fragment in the Louvre, which Rostovtzeff, *S.E.H.W.*, 270, identifies with Arsinoe II.

[4] Delos. Bieber, *Hell. Sc.*, fig. 651; Lippold, *Gr. Pl.*, 318, pl. 115/1; Adriani, op. cit., 30, 54, pl. 50; Rostovtzeff, *S.E.H.W.*, II, 796.

[5] Cf. above, Ch. I, p. 4.

[6] Berlin. Bieber, *Hell. Sc.*, figs. 477–8; Lippold, *Gr. Pl.*, pl. 129, 1–2; *K.i.B.*, 354, 6–8, 10; 355, 7; Bruns, *der Grosse Altar*, 40, 41, 43, 50.

late for Herodas and Theokritos, but not too late for Moschos or perhaps for some of the pastorals included in the manuscripts of Theokritos. Rather earlier and still in the third century is the stele of Metrodoros from Chios (pl. XVa):[1] the dead man stands as an archer under a tree with a little boy behind him, and behind the little boy a pillar carrying an urn. The wide-spacing and lack of depth support the early dating of the Tralles relief. We can then reasonably suppose that country art, which began with grottoes and bowers, included country shrines in pictures with mythical characters and satyrs early in the third century, and fairly soon was extended further to include ordinary human beings.

The country art so far discussed emphasizes the pleasures rather than the pains of country life. The fisherman on Theokritos' cup (I, 39) is not idyllic; he is old; it is a mighty effort to gather up his net for a cast; the sinews stand out all along his neck; he is a sea-worn old man. The poverty of the fisherman's life had already been a subject for Philitas (fr. 17, 20, 24) and is echoed in the fishermen of the Theokritean collection (XXI). The surviving figures of old and sinewy fishermen are Roman copies;[2] the originals of some have been claimed for the third century; although this is uncertain, there are enough realistic terracottas of the late fourth and early third century to make the fisherman on the cup entirely credible. Apollonios' description of Phineus (2, 197 ff.) is a description of a starving man of great age: 'leaning on his stick, he went out on crooked feet, feeling the walls . . . his flesh was shrivelled and dry and squalid, only the skin held the bones together'. He is an extreme case, for which we shall not expect to find a close parallel in art. But it must be the signs of old age in the portrait statue in the temple of Asklepios which make Herodas' women cry out in amazement, and a number of Early Hellenistic terracottas are remarkably realistic portrayals of old men. Some of them are philosophers (pl. VIb), and some of them are

---

[1] Berlin 766a. Rumpf, *M.u.Z.*, 157, fig. 18; Pfuhl, *M.u.Z.*, fig. 746; Rostovtzeff, *R.M.* 26, 1911, 97 ff. The grave-reliefs with trees treated by Pfuhl, *J.D.A.I.* 20, 1905, 49 ff. are all later.

[2] E.g. Rome, Conservatori, *K.i.B.*, 345/7. British Museum 1765, Lippold, *Gr. Pl.*, 327 n. 4, third century; Rome, Vatican, Lippold, *Gr. Pl.*, 331 n. 10, pl. 119/1, third century.

teachers, shown instructing little boys with tablets; so we should imagine the Lampriskos of Herodas (III) like this. Some of the schoolmaster terracottas come from Alexandria; the old philosophers are Attic, but in terracottas especially the influence of Attica on Alexandria was very strong in the late fourth and early fifth century.[1]

There are also realistic portraits of women. Herodas' Kokale says that the statue of Batale is recognizable from her gait (IV, 35). She is presumably an old hetaira like the bibulous Gryllis of the first *Mimiambos*. Kallimachos in an epigram (38) speaks of a hetaira Simon dedicating her picture to Aphrodite. We naturally think of the well-known statue[2] of the old woman sitting drunkenly on the ground with a *lagynos* in her arms (pl. IX*b*). As, however, a statue which sounds like this is ascribed by Pliny to Myron and a Myron of Thebes worked in Pergamon in the early second century, this statue cannot be earlier than the late third century. Kallimachos also wrote an epigram on an old Phrygian nurse, called Aischre (ugly), whose statue one of her charges set up after her death; for this a good parallel can be found in an Early Hellenistic terracotta[3] from Tanagra, a hook-nosed old nurse with a baby on her lap. Hekale also, with her aged form, her shepherd's hat, her crook, and her staff (fr. 490, 292, 355), belongs to the same class of realistically conceived poor women, and the terracotta of the nurse shows that the much later shepherdess of the Conservatori Museum[4] could perfectly well have had a predecessor in the third century.

To one turning to Alexandrian poetry from New Comedy the bad treatment of slaves is surprising. In New Comedy slaves are sympathetically treated by the poets, and when they are punished their

[1] Old man. e.g. Boston 13. 155, D. B. Thompson, *Hesperia* 26, 1957, 118, pl. 35. Teachers: e.g. New York 23. 259, *Handbook*, pl. 109c; Bieber, *Hell. Sc.*, fig. 588. From Egypt, Rostovtzeff, *S.E.H.W.*, 416, 1. Cf. Rumpf, *Analecta Archaeologica*, Festschrift Fremersdorf, 95.

[2] Munich 437, Bieber, *Hell. Sc.*, 81, fig. 284; Lippold, *Gr. Pl.*, 322, pl. 112/2; *K.i.B.*, 345/8. The connection with Pergamon seems to me to necessitate this date; cf. however Lippold, loc. cit., and *R.E.*, s.v. Myron. Terracotta copy from S. Russia, Moscow, Pushkin Museum, Kobilina, pl. 24-5.

[3] British Museum 11. 74. 18. 10., etc., Winter, *T.K.*, ii, 465/12.

[4] Rome, Conservatori, Bieber, *Hell. Sc.*, fig. 591; *K.i.B.*, 345/6. Lippold, *Gr. Pl.*, 378, dates the corresponding figure of the fisherman 150/80 B.C.

masters have usually been provoked. It is true that in New Comedy, as distinct from Middle Comedy, there is a clear distinction in appearance between slaves and freemen, and that from the late third century the masks emphasize the arrogance, loquacity, and greed of slaves.[1] The slave of Herodas' fifth *Mimiambos* belongs to this class and certainly has given provocation. But the slaves in the other *Mimiamboi* (IV, VI, VII, VIII) seem entirely defenceless against the abuse of their masters, and it is tempting to equate them with the child-slaves of Hellenistic art: most of these are difficult to date, but a terracotta[2] of a negro-boy asleep (pl. IXa) was found at Ezbet el Makhlouf in a context which seems to be Early Hellenistic, and a bronze[3] of a boy, probably carrying an elephant's tusk, is judged Early Hellenistic on style; it is possible therefore that the scraggy running boy and the little boys asleep with their lanterns[4] repeat Early Hellenistic types and that it is these unfortunate children who get abused for their laziness and sleepiness by their masters and mistresses in Herodas and Theokritos. In accord with this realistic treatment of the poor is Pliny's note that Antiphilos, the Alexandrian painter who is said to have intrigued against Apelles, 'painted comic pictures of a man named Gryllus whose appearance was ridiculous, and after him this kind of painting is called *grylli*'.[5] Whether there was really a man called Gryllus does not matter; on this evidence caricature was known in Alexandria very early in the Hellenistic age, and the particular kind known as Grylli has been traced by Binsfeld in Pompeian paintings which show small people with very large heads.

Realism can naturally also be found in the pictures of performers. The *Kinaidoi* on a Homeric bowl have been quoted in the last chapter.[6] Terracotta statuettes of mime actors have also been found in

---

[1] Cf. *J.D.A.I.* 76, 1961, 102.

[2] Alexandria 24127, *Annaire du Musée Gréco-Romain*, 1935/9, 106, pl. E; *Ath. Mitt.* 77, 1962, 255.

[3] Paris, Bibl. Nat. 1009. Bieber, *Hell. Sc.*, fig. 381; Lippold, *Gr. Pl.*, 327, pl. 116/4; *K.i.B.*, 369/3.

[4] Bronze, running boy, New York, 18.145.10, Bieber, *Hell. Sc.*, 96, fig. 380. Boy with lantern, New York, Egyptian Dept., 23.160.82, Bieber, *Hell. Sc.*, 138, fig. 548.

[5] Pliny, *N.H.*, 35, 114. Binsfeld, *Grylloi*, 27 ff.; *R.E.*, Suppl. IX, 76. For Pompeii, cf. Rumpf, *M.u.Z.*, 169.

[6] See above, p. 153. And on this whole class of dancers, Binsfeld, *Grylloi*, 45.

Egypt, although none of them perhaps are certainly Early Hellen-istic.[1] Statuettes and masks of actors of tragedy, comedy, and satyric drama can be ascribed safely to the early third century; two dramatic portraits from Alexandria, Apelles' picture of the tragic actor Gor-gosthenes and Protogenes' picture of the tragic poet, Philikos, may survive in Pompeian copies – both are realistic in that the one shows the actor worn out after a successful performance and the other the poet seeing a vision of his character's situation.[2] The most attractive representation of an Alexandrian performer is a veiled, slippered dancer pirouetting, a bronze statuette (pl. X),[3] which Mrs Thompson has dated convincingly in the late third century; if the singer Athenion was half so attractive, Dioskorides' devastation is readily intelligible.

The representations of performers bring us near to the world of scholarship. We discussed in the last chapter the late third-century Homereion of Philopator with its seated statue of Homer surrounded by the cities which claimed him, and we connected with it the late second-century relief of Archelaos of Priene (pl. IV), probably illus-trating a poem which won a competition in the Homereion, and the rather earlier 'Homeric bowls', which may be copies of a set made for a festival attended by guests purporting to be interested in Homer and classical drama.[4] Apart from these bowls some other silver-ware and plaster casts from metal-ware have been connected with Alexandria in the Early Hellenistic period; here again the survivors may be from sets specially made for banquets like the banquets in Philadelphos' Symposion tent. The survivors which we have belong to the last century B.C. but in certain cases we can show or suggest that the designs are much earlier;[5] the connection with

[1] E.g. Alexandria 24012, *Annuaire du Musée Gréco-Romain*, 1935/9, pl. 69; Hildesheim, Pelizaeus-Museum, Bieber, *History*[2], fig. 826. Binsfeld, loc. cit., 42.

[2] See above, pp. 124, 128.

[3] W. C. Baker collection, New York. D. B. Thompson, *A.J.A.* 54, 1950, 371; Bieber, *Hell. Sc.*, figs. 378–9. Mrs Thompson is now inclined to see a dancer of the Dionysiac cult, Troy, *Supplementary Monograph*, 3, 104, n. 205.

[4] Cf. above, p. 147.

[5] Cf. G. M. A. Richter, *A.J.A.* 62, 1958, 369 ff.; *Record of the Art Museum, Princeton University* 18, 1959, 53; *Theoria* 1960, 179. (The Begram finds contain also objects of the late second and third century A.D., *Arch. Class.* 13, 1961, 168, Coarelli.)

Alexandria is well established for the Begram plasters[1] and can be suggested for the other cups which interest us because of their subject matter. Two plasters from Begram illustrate dramatic poets; one[2] has a tragic poet seated with a roll in his hand, on the left a youth listening, in the centre a woman with a lyre, on the right an actor with a club and a mask of Herakles pushed back on his head; on the other,[3] a comic poet seated under a tree with, before him, actor or muse holding a mask. The original of the plaster with the tragic poet can be dated between 330 and 150 because the actor wears an *onkos* mask but his *kothornoi* still have thin soles; it is tempting to see Euripides, as his *Herakles* was popular in the Hellenistic age. Mme Ghali-Kahil has suggested Menander for the comic poet, and there must be some relationship between the plaster and the well-known Menander relief:[4] the tree may perhaps be an allusion to the garden of the Peripatetics. If the plasters are a pair, the Menander should also be Early Hellenistic and so provides a parallel for the Koan relief of Philitas singing Bittis under a plane-tree.

Euripides and Menander appear again as skeletons holding masks on the two silver cups[5] from Boscoreale; the other skeletons are labelled Zeno, Epikouros, Sophokles, Moschion, Archilochos, Monimos, Krates, and Demetrios of Phaleron. The message is obvious: even the greatest poets and philosophers become skeletons; therefore drink. M. Picard has suggested that this assembly of worthies was created in Alexandria in the third century; it is a sign of scholarship to call Archilochos Myrinaios (he may have been born at Myrina in Paros) and to put in the hand of Menander's skeleton the mask of a rustic, because his *Agroikos* was a famous play. Two other cups[6] have figures which have been reasonably identified as Aratos,

---

[1] O. Kurz in Hackin, *Nouvelles recherches archéologiques à Begram*, 145; Adriani, *Coppa Paesistica*, 66, n.88.

[2] Kurz, op. cit., 134, fig. 450; *M.T.S.*, ET 15.

[3] Kurz, op. cit., 136; Adriani, op. cit., fig. 56; L. Ghali-Kahil, *Mon. Piot.* 51, 1960, 73, pl. 5.; *M.N.C.*, ET 65.

[4] *M.N.C.*, IS 10.

[5] Louvre, from Boscoreale, Schefold, *Bildnisse*, 166; Picard, *Mon. Piot.* 44, 1950, 53 f.; *M.N.C.*, NJ, 2.

[6] Paris, Cab. Med. From Berthouville. Schefold, op. cit., 47, 216; Picard, loc. cit.

Lykophron, Menedemos of Eretria, and Theokritos, all contemporaries of the early third century, whereas the pair of skeleton cups and the two Begram plasters, which are probably also a pair, combine recent with past worthies.

This sense of the continuity of literature and thought is seen again in the statues of the Serapieion (and on a tiny scale in the epigrams of Dioskorides on Thespis, Aeschylus, Sophocles, and Sositheos). In the Serapieion at Memphis[1] a semicircular building or exedra contained statues of poets and thinkers from Orpheus to Demetrios of Phaleron. The Serapieion in Alexandria had a similar group, if Professor Rees' conjecture on Kallimachos' *Iambos* I is right,[2] and there was at least one Early Hellenistic painting with a similar subject.[3] The exedra was a lecture room and the statues gave a sort of eternal parallel to the discussions of contemporary scholars. Professor Picard suggests that these worthies, who would be more naturally connected with the Muses, are here connected with Serapis because Serapis was identified with Dionysos. There is no hard boundary at this time between Dionysiac literature and Apolline literature: epic poets competed at the same festivals as dramatic poets, and at Syracuse the Artists of Dionysos deposited their decrees with the Muses in the Nymphaion.[4] The scholars of Alexandria (and their predecessors in stone) could meet as well in the Serapieion as in the Mouseion.

The statue of Serapis in the Serapieion at Alexandria is well known from descriptions and copies.[5] The god was seated with a sceptre in the left hand and the right hand caressing the heads of the Kerberos which sat beside the throne. If Kallimachos alludes to the statues of worthies in the Serapieion, it is possible that he also remembers the Serapis when he phrases the description of Iris in the *Hymn to Delos*, IV, 228: 'she sat beside the golden throne like a dog, a hunting dog which sits by the feet of Artemis, when she ceases from the chase, its

---

[1] Lauer and Picard, *Les statues ptolémaiques du Serapieion à Memphis*, 1955.

[2] Cf. above, p. 99.

[3] Cf. Lauer and Picard, op. cit., 158 ff.; G. M. A. Richter, *Collection Latomus* 44, 1960, 671.

[4] Bernabo Brea, *Musei e Monumenti*, 60.

[5] Cf. Charbonneaux, *Mon. Piot.* 52, 1962, 15. Most of the copies omit or have lost Kerberos, but it appears on Ince Blundell Hall, nos. 38 and 39 (Ashmole) and on a relief in Rome (Picard and Lauer, op. cit., 252, fig. 140).

ears erect, always ready to receive the goddess' orders. Even so the daughter of Thaumas sat beneath the throne.' This must be inspired by a statue, and Kerberos by Serapis' throne may have been the inspiration. Such visual description is rare in Kallimachos; even when he is thinking of a work of art, as in *Epigram* 51, he does not describe it. There the new statue of Berenike (probably the wife of Euergetes) is described as a fourth Grace 'still running with myrrh'. The words 'flowing with myrrh' intentionally recall another poem on the Graces: in his *Aitia* (fr. 7, 11) the Graces of Paros have lovely clothes and ointment always flowing from their locks. Berenike also must have been a clothed Grace, and it is possible that the statue is the origin of the Berenike with a double cornucopia who is shown on the Queen jugs (pl. XI).[1]

Two descriptions of gods suggest works of art. Apollonios' Apollo (2, 676) going from Lycia to the Hyperboreans, with bunches of golden hair beside his cheeks, a bow in his left hand, and a quiver on his back, suggests the Apollo Belvedere, but as we do not know where its original stood, we cannot say whether Apollonios could have seen it. Herodas' dream of Dionysos ordering the goatherds to compete in jumping on a wineskin must have some relation to the Roman mosaic[2] with Dionysos and Ariadne watching the jumping, but it is difficult to say what the relation is. He describes Dionysos (VIII, 28 f.) as wearing a saffron robe which comes down to the soft curve of his thighs; it is girded by a fawnskin; he has a kypassis on his shoulders; ivy on his head and kothornoi on his feet. The text is corrupt and the terminology is obscure, but Herodas seems to have a clear picture of Dionysos, and Herzog[3] has compared a Hellenistic terracotta from Eretria of a young standing Dionysos with short chiton, fawnskin, cloak, kothornoi, and ivy wreath. This is the type of work which Herodas remembers.

---

[1] E.g. Amsterdam 7582, *Algemeene Gids*, no. 1633; Rostovtzeff, *S.E.H.W.*, 270/2. Was the group of four clothed Graces the reason why Sosibios dedicated clothed Graces at Nemea? (Kallimachos, fr. 384/45).

[2] Cf. above, p. 97.

[3] Herzog-Crusius, *Mimiamben*, 1926, 179 f., fig. 19 = Winter, *TK*, 365/2. *Kypassis* is normally a chiton, cf. D. L. Page, *Sappho and Alcaeus*, 221, but, as it is round his shoulders, it must be a cloak here.

When the Argo set sail,[1] all the gods watched from heaven; the nymphs of Pelion on their highest peaks were amazed at the sight; and Cheiron came down with his wife from the mountain. The great moment is enhanced by the divine spectators. Apollonios is working in an old tradition here, which goes back to Homer and is echoed on the East frieze of the Parthenon; nearer to Apollonios' time are the big Apulian vases of the last third of the fourth century which habitually have a register of gods above the human scene. Thus on a volute krater in Leningrad,[2] when Amphiaraos sets out in his chariot to war, commending vengeance to the young Alkmaion, Apollo, Athena, and Hermes watch from above, but there is also a Fury to point the end of the story; so in Apollonios (4, 475), when Jason and Medeia murder Apsyrtos 'the powerful Fury marked with eyes askance the cruel crime they pitilessly committed'. In one point the description of the Argo's departure is Hellenistic rather than classical: the nymphs of Pelion are not entirely identified with their mountain but they sit on the highest peak. So also in Kallimachos' *Hymn to Delos* (IV, 159) the islands run away from Leto, or rather the nymphs of the islands run away from their islands. In art the new conception can be seen in the *Odyssey* pictures from the Esquiline (pl. XII),[3] which probably derive from second-century originals, the personifications of winds, mountains, pastures, and coasts are quite small and are shown within or on the elements or places that they personify: the wind gods are in the winds and the mountain god lies on his mountain; at this stage the landscape dominates the figures. The Early Hellenistic poets are between this stage, where the personifications hardly matter any more, and classical art, where the personifications are a substitute for landscape and Nemea looks on while Herakles slays the lion.

We have been chiefly concerned with the common strands which unite art and poetry in the period of Philadelphos, but owing to the difficulties of dating we have been forced sometimes to look at later things in art. The theatre scenes from Boscoreale and the *Odyssey* pictures derive from originals which cannot be far in date from

[1] Apollonios Rhodios, 1, 547. For other instances, cf. above, p. 80.
[2] Leningrad, Hermitage 406. *Bull. Nap.*, n.s., 3, pl. 6.
[3] Vatican, Rumpf, *M.u.Z.*, 160, pl. 55/1, 2; Pfuhl, *M.u.Z.*, figs. 721–2.

Moschos' *Europe* and the relief with the Apotheosis of Homer. Classicism, the term which we applied to the *Europe* of Moschos, is a vague word but it implies first of all a dependence on earlier models, secondly a prevailing impression of grace and charm whatever the subject. The fearsome battles of the Laistrygones in the *Odyssey* pictures (pl. XII) are only part of a large scene which is dominated by the lighter and darker patches of landscape and sea; the realistic peasants of the later bucolic reliefs[1] are only single figures of a composition in which their animals and the architectural setting are more important. The reminiscences may be reminiscences of classical works or may be reminiscences of earlier Hellenistic works. The poets had their library and the artists could see the royal collections, which started at least with Euergetes. Moschos remembers Apollonios Rhodios as well as Homer, and a first-century mosaic[2] from Alexandria (pl. VII), which might reasonably be put beside Moschos' Eros ploughing, has a group of Erotes killing a deer, which is strongly reminiscent of the Early Hellenistic Pella mosaic. The relief[3] with the Apotheosis of Homer (pl. IV) puts a group of Hellenistic Muses into a new setting. The later so-called 'Visit to Ikarios' (really 'Dionysos visits a comic poet'), which is known in many slightly differing versions,[4] has a famous fourth-century figure of Dionysos in an elaborate architectural setting. The main group of Dionysos, satyrs, and maenads is already found on a Neo-Attic krater of about 100 B.C., but in a different context.[5] In the British Museum 'Visit to Ikarios' the slave-masks on the table beneath the poet's couch are unlikely to be earlier than the first century B.C., and may be as late as the middle of the first century A.D., and the palm-tree in the background may localize the scene in Alexandria. The Begram plasters probably give a bottom date in the late first century B.C. for this whole group of classicistic works but, as we have seen,[6] some of the plasters derive

[1] E.g. Vatican, Sala degli Animali 157; Bieber, *Hell. Sc.*, 155, fig. 658; *K.i.B.*, 366/2, Munich 455; Bieber, *Hell. Sc.*, fig. 659; Adriani, op. cit., fig. 22.

[2] Alexandria Museum, Room XIX, Brown, op. cit., no. 50, pl. 44/1.

[3] Cf. above, p. 145.

[4] British Museum 2190. *M.N.C.*, no. AS 3; Bieber, *Hell. Sc.*, 154, fig. 656; Watzinger, *J.D.A.I.* 61–2, 1946/7, 78 dates Neronian–Flavian. Cf. *K.i.B.*, 366, 1. Cf. below, p. 308.

[5] Cf. below, p. 248.    [6] Cf. above, p. 172.

directly or indirectly from much earlier originals. The Apotheosis of Homer (pl. IV) shows that the style had started in the second half of the second century B.C. This relief and the British Museum version of the 'Visit to Ikarios' may be Alexandrian; the Begram plasters are certainly Alexandrian; but Alexandria did not have a closed style of its own in the Late Hellenistic period any more than in the Early Hellenistic period, and we shall have to consider as we survey the art of Asia Minor, the Islands, and Mainland Greece the other components of this style. The Apotheosis of Homer was found at Bovillae, the Alexandrian landscape painter Demetrios lived in Rome, and most of the close parallels for the Begram plasters are found in Italy. This classicistic art was then the kind of Hellenistic art which was also practised in Italy in the last century of the Republic and the Early Imperial period.

## CHAPTER IX

# The Greek Cities in Asia

The Greek cities of Asia during the Hellenistic period came under the shadow of the great Hellenistic rulers, first Lysimachos in the northern area and then from a few years before his death in 281 Philetairos and his successors the Attalid kings of Pergamon; in the South Seleukos established his capital at Antioch on the Orontes in 300. The Attalid and Seleucid kingdoms shielded the old Greek cities from the westward incursions of the Gauls, but they might always fight each other for the overlordship of Greek Asia Minor. Both at the same time set themselves up as centres of Greek civilization. The islands off the coast of Asia Minor, Samothrace, Lesbos, Chios, Samos, Kos, Rhodes were themselves disputed ground between the Antigonid kings of Macedonia and the Ptolemies. From the time of Attalos I the power of Rome was growing in Asia. Attalos III willed his kingdom to Rome in 133, and the whole of Asia west of a line drawn from Kyzikos on the Sea of Marmara to Knidos in the South was organized as a Roman province in 129. The invasions of Mithridates were a temporary setback to Roman rule, but a year after his death in 63 Bithynia in the North and Cilicia and Syria in the South were also organized as provinces.

The disputes of kings seem to have hindered the movements of artists and poets remarkably little. Artists from the Greek mainland worked for Seleukos I at Antioch and with Rhodian artists for the Attalids at Pergamon, just as they worked for the Ptolemies. Euphorion of Chalkis was summoned by Antiochos III to take over the library at Antioch, just as Eratosthenes was summoned by Ptolemy III to take over the library in Alexandria. From the late second century the move westwards to Italy becomes visible.

The local division of poets and artists is to some extent unreal and the account given of Alexandrian poetry and art in the preceding chapters justifiably included poets from Ionia, Greece, and Sicily and artists from Athens, Rhodes, and Ionia, who worked in Kos as well as

Alexandria. The justification for calling their work Alexandrian was the close ties of various sorts which connected them with Alexandria: poets who worked in the library or produced plays in Alexandria or contributed to early Alexandrian anthologies or praised the Ptolemies, artists whose works have been found in Alexandria or in the sphere of influence of the Ptolemies or whose works illustrate Alexandrian poetry or can reasonably be traced back to Alexandria. But whereas it is true that Philitas and his successors in poetry and scholarship were first in the field and that therefore learned poetry in this sense originated in Alexandria, Philitas came from Kos and of the early Alexandrian poets only Apollonios Rhodios was himself an Alexandrian; and various tendencies which are claimed for Alexandrian art, such as interest in nature, interest in children, interest in old age, are also visible in the art of Greek Asia, wherever they in fact originated.

The centre of this chapter must be an account of Pergamon and its influence in the great period which lasted from approximately 225 to 150. Before that a few disconnected points may be briefly noticed. Alexander set the style for the appearance of his successors as we know them from their portraits on coins. They keep the youthful leonine hair, even when it disagrees with their middle-aged worn faces, but it is bound with the royal fillet.[1] It was probably Abdalonymos, appointed King of Sidon by Alexander, who in the late fourth century ordered for himself the extraordinarily rich marble sarcophagus (pl. XIII)[2] which, better than anything else preserved, shows us how lovely coloured sculpture of the Early Hellenistic age was. One pediment has a battle of Greeks and Persians; one a Greek being killed. Under the pediments runs a very beautiful frieze of vine leaves in low relief. The four sides have battle of Greeks and Persians, battle of Alexander with Persians, panther-hunt, lion-hunt. From the style of the Greek heads the artist would seem to be an Athenian of the post-Praxitelean school. Even if, as is probable, he derives some of his figures from major paintings, like the original of the Pompeian

---

[1] E.g. coins of Ptolemy I, Seleukos I, Demetrios Poliorketes, Lysimachos, Philetairos: Winter, *K.i.B.*, 338/4, 6, 8, 10, 12; 339/3; Bieber, *Hell. Sc.*, figs. 304, 140, 147, 415, 416.

[2] Istanbul 68. Winter, *K.i.B.*, 335/4, 336-7; Lippold, *Gr. Pl.*, 288, pl. 82/2; Bieber, *Hell. Sc.*, 72, figs. 250-1; Lullies and Hirmer², *Greek Sculpture*, pls. VIII-IX.

mosaic,[1] he has achieved an amount of vigour and violence which far surpasses the Amazonomachies of the Mausoleum.

Seleukos may have been responsible for setting up the group of Niobids (pl. XIV),[2] which is known from many copies and was subsequently removed from Seleukeia in Cilicia to Rome. It is not known how the grandiose group of Niobe, her children in various positions of flight and collapse, the pedagogue, and perhaps also Artemis and Apollo, was set up. They may have occupied the spaces between the columns of a long colonnade. Certainly they recalled the Niobid group with which Pheidias decorated the throne of Zeus at Olympia, but his classical art has been transposed into grandeur and pathos. The emphasis seems to have been on Niobe's suffering rather than her pride. Perhaps the story had a local rather than a literary interest for Seleukos, as he claimed Niobe's mountain in his kingdom. Ancient scholars disputed whether the artist was Praxiteles or Skopas; we have violence in the post-Praxitelean Alexander sarcophagus but the heads of the Niobid group have a pathos which is alien to him, and the group is too late for either sculptor.

The other work which can certainly be associated with Seleukos is the statue or rather group (pl. XIV*b*)[3] made by Eutychidas of Sikyon, a pupil of the great Sikyonian sculptor Lysippos, to celebrate the founding of Antioch in 300. A female, wearing a turreted crown and holding palm-fronds in her right hand, sits on a rock and puts her right foot on the shoulder of the young river god, Orontes, who swims by. The group is extremely successful both in conception and in composition. The figure is not just Tyche, the personification of Chance which seemed to rule the Hellenistic world and has been termed the *idée maîtresse* of Menander's comedy, but the success of Victory which gained the new city, whose future is forecast in the goddess' gaze. The Orontes has swum past the rock from the begin-

[1] Naples 10020. Webster, *A.L.A.*, 82, pl. 12; Pfuhl, *M.u.Z.*, fig. 648; Rumpf, *M.u.Z.*, 148.

[2] Rome, Vatican; Florence, etc. Winter, *K.i.B.*, 307, 372/6; Lippold, *Gr. Pl.*, 309, pl. 111; Bieber, *Hell. Sc.*, 74, fig. 253/65. The group was dedicated in Rome by Sosianus who had been *legatus* in Syria (Pliny, *N.H.*, 36, 28).

[3] Rome, Vatican, etc. Winter, *K.i.B.*, 340/1; Lippold, *Gr. Pl.*, 296, pl. 106/2; Bieber, *Hell. Sc.*, 40, fig. 102; T. Dohrn, *die Tyche von Antiochia*. Cf. above, Ch. I, p. 5.

ning of time but now looks back at the new and imposing figure enthroned on its banks. In both figures we see the Early Hellenistic
form of local personification: human figures and local element are
both given, but the figures still dominate the element.[1] The composition is a construction of triangles set in different planes: the main
lines are given by the arms and head of Orontes, the right leg and
left hand of the goddess, the right forearm, crown, and left arm of
the goddess. The spectator is forced to think three-dimensionally, as
he also is by the projecting left arm of Lysippos' Apoxyomenos. The
triangular group became popular: it was used for the boy pulling a
thorn out of his foot which we know in several versions,[2] and for the
nymph seated, tying on her shoe.[3] This last figure was completed by
a young satyr beating a foot-clapper; the group seems to have stood
in Kyzikos and may have been by an artist in the following of
Lysippos (nearer or more remote).

A very popular work by a follower of Lysippos was the Aphrodite
bathing which is attributed to Doidalsas of Bithynia.[4] The copies are
cold, and the scheme which the sculptor followed is ancient; we have
already quoted the fourth-century bathing nymph on a Corinthian
mirror, but before that the crouching figure appears on an Attic
squat lekythos from the circle of Meidias, and before that on the
Chalkidian Phineus cup.[5] It was evidently regarded as a charming
subject.

Another pupil of Lysippos brings us back to the old Greek cities.
At the end of the fourth century Chares of Lindos was responsible

---

[1] Cf. above, p. 175.

[2] British Museum 1755, Winter, *K.i.B.*, 369/1; Lippold, *Gr. Pl.*, 331, pl. 113/4;
Bieber, *Hell. Sc.*, 138, fig. 550. Berlin, terracotta, from Priene, Winter, *K.i.B.*,
369/2; Winter, *TK*, 448/1. Rome, Capitoline Museum, Winter, *K.i.B.*, 235/3;
Lippold, *Gr. Pl.*, 387 (an archaizing combination of the Hellenistic body with an
early fifth-century head, perhaps first century B.C.).

[3] Florence, etc. Winter, *K.i.B.*, 368/5–7; Lippold, *Gr. Pl.*, 320, pl. 113/3; Bieber,
*Hell. Sc.*, 139, figs. 562–6.

[4] Paris, Louvre. Winter, *K.i.B.*, 346/3; Lippold, *Gr. Pl.*, 319, pl. 112/1; Bieber,
*Hell. Sc.*, 82, figs. 290–3. Copied by terracottas from Myrina; Bieber, *Hell. Sc.*,
fig. 603; Winter, *TK*, 205/1.

[5] Corinthian mirror, cf. above, Ch. VIII, p. 163. Attic squat lekythos, Embirikos
collection. Phineus cup, Würzburg 354, Pfuhl, *M.u.Z.*, fig. 164.

for converting the bronze from Demetrios Poliorketes' siege-train into a colossal statue of Helios over 100 feet high to tower above the harbour.[1] The technical feat was incredible and the grandiose conception suggests how tremendous the Rhodians had felt the danger to have been.

We could wish for more information about the art and literature of Rhodes in the early third century. We know that the Peripatetic philosopher Praxiphanes settled there after leaving Athens, and it is possible that with his very different idea of poetic aesthetics he welcomed Apollonios Rhodios and made war on Kallimachos.[2] Otherwise we have only the fragments of Simias of Rhodes[3] (the little that we have of Antagoras seems to have been written in Greece). Like the early Alexandrian poets he wrote a number of 'hymns' in different metres (fr. 9, 13-17), and his choriambic experiment is said by Hephaistion to have been earlier than Philikos' poem. The curious poem (fr. 1-5) about Kleinis, who visited the Hyperboreans (on an eagle?) and tried to introduce the sacrifice of asses into his own country with disastrous results, obviously owes much to Herodotos' account of Aristeas and was apparently in its turn used by Kallimachos: Marsyas, Phaethon, and Niobe were also included (if these fragments are rightly attributed to the *Apollo*). His elegiac epigrams fall into the usual types. Three poems have lines of different lengths so that when they are written out (in two cases the odd lines have to be written from the top and the even lines from the bottom) they form the shape of an object: one is a pseudo-inscription for the wings of an Orphic Eros, the second for the axe of Epeios, and the third for the egg of a nightingale stolen by Hermes. Presumably such poems were originally inspired by the real need to shape an inscription to the inscribed object; a simple and pleasing example is given by Kallimachos' dedication epigram for a quiver (*Ep.* 38).

Phoinix of Kolophon is said to have lamented the capture of

---

[1] M. A. Gabriel, *B.C.H.* 76 (1932), 331; H. Maryon, *J.H.S.* 76 (1956), 68; D. E. L. Haynes, *J.H.S.* 77 (1957), 311.

[2] Cf. above, pp. 104.

[3] The fragments are collected by J. U. Powell, *Collect. Alex.*, 109 (whom I follow in excluding *A.P.* VII, 19, 22, 60); Diehl, *Anth. Lyr.*, VI, 140; A. S. F. Gow, *Bucolici Graeci*, 172. Commentary in H. Fränkel, *de Simia Rhodio*.

Kolophon in 286;[1] his choliambic poems are therefore certainly earlier than Kallimachos' *Iamboi* and probably than Herodas' *Mimiamboi*. The long and rather slow moving fragment about Ninos (1 P) who only ate, drank, and made love, and left an epitaph that he possessed what he ate but his belongings are plundered by his foes, is typical of the psychology of the comic parasite. The man who ate up his portion and therefore had to dig (Ath. 304b) could also come from comedy. So could the moral fragment addressed to Poseidippos (who might even be the comic poet) about the rich who spend their money on buildings and starve their souls (6 P). Nor is it impossible that the attractive crow song (2 P), which may be in origin a popular song like the Rhodian swallow song, reached him through comedy. If these flat poems are based on comedy, they may have suggested to Herodas the use of the choliambic metre for his own brilliant comic sketches.

Nikainetos of Samos[2] was probably rather younger. A pretty dedication to the Heroissai of Libya (*A.P.* VI, 225) recalls the description of them in Apollonios Rhodios (4, 1309 ff.). Another symposion epigram describes a feast in the country, apparently in the precinct of Hera (Ath. XV, 673b); he may be remembering the rather similar poem of Anakreon which Athenaeus quotes in the same passage, but as he is a Samian it seems more likely that the custom of wearing withy wreaths in honour of Hera survived in Samos. A pseudo-epitaph on Kratinos in alternate hexameters and iambic trimeters (*A.P.* XIII, 29) is like the epigrams on poets by Theokritos in recalling the metres used by the poets who are the subjects of the epigrams: Kratinos used hexameters in the *Odysses*, and it is possible that the first two lines are, as they purport to be, direct quotations of Kratinos, presumably his *Pytine* (199 K); the authorship of the epigram is disputed but it is certainly Early Hellenistic.

Considerable poetic effort must have gone into drama, but we can very rarely say what the plays were or how many of them were

---

[1] Pausanias I, ix, 7. Fragments in J. U. Powell, op. cit., 231; Diehl, *Anth. Lyr.*[3], III, 124; A. D. Knox, Loeb Classical Library with *Theophrastus Characters*. The Strasbourg papyrus (Knox, fr. 4) may be by Phoinix but is desperately obscure: an appeal by a parasite for a cloak to the comic poet, Lynkeus of Samos?

[2] Fragments in Powell, op. cit., 1; cf. Gabathuler, op. cit., 65 on *A.P.* XIII, 29.

revivals. (Menander's contemporary, Lynkeus of Samos, seems to have produced in Athens.) At Samos in 306 the famous actor Polos of Aegina acted at a festival in honour of Antigonos and Demetrios; he was thanked for taking no fee beyond the theatre-takings; the inscribed stone which records this is decorated with a beardless head and a club; one of the plays, therefore, was probably about Theseus. At the same time we have evidence for tragedy at the Dionysia in Samos. Later in the third century an actor called Nikophon from Miletos played three dramas in three days at Samos and was duly honoured. Rhodes in the third century had a guild with the unusual title of 'the artists who served the Muses of Dionysos'.[1]

Certainly by 237 and probably before the middle of the century the actors were organized in a guild, which was called the Association of Artists of Dionysos of Ionia and the Hellespont. The headquarters was at first at Teos, and the members included at least tragic poets, actors, and assistant actors, comic actors, dithyrambic poets, flute-players, lyre-players, and singers to the lyre.[2] Early Hellenistic theatres with a straight *proskenion* have been excavated at Assos, Priene, Ephesos, and Sardis (Pergamon is a special case because the stage-building there was always a temporary wooden structure built when necessary in the roadway).[3] The theatre with a straight *proskenion* front seems to have been as characteristic of this area as the theatre with ramps leading on to the high stage is of the area where the Isthmian-Nemean guild functioned.[4]

The magnificent terracotta statuettes of Myrina (midway between Teos and Pergamon) give an idea of the appearance of actors in comedy; the procurer in his magnificent mantle, a pair of young men dancing with tambourine and clappers, a parasite in skimpy cloak with strigil and oil-bottle, an old slave hurrying with news, a

---

[1] Polos: *S.E.G.*, I, 362. Dionysia: *Clara Rhodos*, X, 27. Nikophon: *I.G.*, XII, 7, 226. Rhodes: *Annuario 2*, 1915/16, 139.

[2] Cf. Poland, *R.E.*, V, A 2, s.v. *technitai*, 2486 f. summarized Pickard-Cambridge, *Festivals*, Ch. VII.

[3] Cf. Bieber, *History*[2], 108 f., figs. 416 Priene, 440 Assos, 441 Ephesos.

[4] Cf. Bieber, *History*[2], 118 f., figs. 271 Epidauros, 285 Eretria, 455 Sikyon, 460 Corinth.

wreathed slave gesticulating in triumph, a soldier slave on his travels with hat, bedding, flask, and sword. The main group with the best of these actors is dated by two which have inscriptions late in the second century, but the style of the slave-beards and the occurrence of identical young men with tambourine and clappers on a mosaic by the Samian artist Dioskorides, which seems to be a copy of an early third-century original, suggest that these figures go back to the early third century, possibly to a set of paintings in the temple of Dionysos or in the Council house of the Guild, either in Teos or in Pergamon.[1] If the mosaic with the young men dancing is evidence of the practice of this guild, so also presumably is the mosaic[2] by the same artist with the two young women and the old woman, which has been reasonably claimed as an illustration of the opening scene of Menander's *Synaristosai* or *Women at breakfast*, translated by Plautus as the *Cistellaria*. It is a slender piece of evidence for what is in any case likely, that Menander was played in the Greek theatres of Asia. The mosaics are copies of paintings, and there is no difficulty in supposing that the Myrina terracottas also were sometimes inspired by paintings. Pottier[3] suggested this long ago for the flying Erotes, and a terracotta group of Dionysos and Ariadne from Myrina is repeated in the paintings of the Villa of the Mysteries, which have themselves been regarded as deriving from Pergamene originals.[4] The comic actors, particularly the slaves, have something of the violence and vigour of Pergamene sculpture, which we have now to review; but these are also the qualities which distinguish the slaves of Plautus from the slaves of Menander, as far as we know them. There may be a real parallel if Plautus at the end of the third century was translating actors' texts, in which the slave parts had been developed to suit contemporary taste.[5]

The great period of Pergamon is the century from 240 to 140, the

---

[1] Webster, *M.N.C.*, 78, particularly *M.T.*, 1, 2, 9, 15, 19, 27, 28 = Bieber, *History*[2], figs. 341, 153, 386, 342, 372, 396, 399. Dioskorides mosaic: *M.N.C.*, NM 2 = Bieber, *History*[2], fig. 346.

[2] Bieber, *History*[2], fig. 347 = *M.N.C.*, NM 1.       [3] *Diphilos*, 102.

[4] Terracotta, Pottier, *Diphilos*, no. 471; Winter, *TK*, 366/5; E. Simon, *J.D.A.I.* 76, 1961, 131 f. See also below, pp. 196.

[5] Cf. below, Ch. XI, p. 273.

reigns of Attalos I and his sons, Eumenes II, and Attalos II. Attalos I saw his victory over the Gauls as an achievement of the same kind as the Persian wars, and conceived of his capital as a great centre of culture; Eumenes II (when he had defeated the Gauls) built the great altar of Zeus to be the Parthenon of this capital, and his use of parchment successfully defeated Ptolemy V's attempt to wreck the library by an embargo on the export of papyrus. Attalos I had dedicated on the Athenian Acropolis a reduced copy of the monument which he set up on the Acropolis of Pergamon to celebrate his victory over the Gauls; Attalos II gave Athens the great Stoa which bounds the East side of the Agora. The connection with Athens was further emphasized by a marble copy of the Athena Parthenos erected with the statues of the poets in the Library, probably by Eumenes II.[1] (Besides the copy of the Parthenos Pergamon had original sculptures from Greek cities given to Attalos I by Rome, including the Graces of Boupalos and the Apollo of Onatas, and Attalos II had Polygnotos' paintings in Delphi copied.) Eumenes II built the propylaion, which gave a slanting view of the fourth-century temple of Athena, like the view of the Parthenon from the Athenian propylaion, and the whole ensemble was completed by the Stoai erected by Attalos II. Eumenes II was probably responsible also for the theatre as we see it and for arrangements with the Guild of Artists of Dionysos.

The Library, unlike the Library of Alexandria, was the work and home of scholars rather than poets, and therefore only concerns us as evidence for the high value which this dynasty set on learning, a disposition which justifies us in looking for learning also in their works of art. Their artists came from various places,[2] but achieved a unity of style which justifies the name Pergamene. The monument

[1] Varro ap. Plin. N.H., 13, 70 on parchment and papyrus. Statues in the library: copy of Parthenos, Berlin, Winter, K.i.B., 372/1; Bieber, Hell. Sc., 157; Lippold, Gr. Pl., 359; Richter, Three Periods, 34, fig. 62. Bases of statues of poets: Alkaios, Sappho, Timotheos, Homer found in the library, Pergamon, VIII, 198–203. Early originals: Pergamon, VIII, 46–50. Copies made in Delphi: S.I.G.³, no. 682, the restoration 'some of the paintings in the Lesche' seems probable, and the famous paintings in the Lesche were by Polygnotos.

[2] Epigonos of Pergamon; Phyromachos of Athens; Stratonikos of Kyzikos; Antigonos of Karystos (?); Menekrates of Rhodes; also from Tralles and Ephesos. Cf. particularly Richter, Three Critical Periods, 27 ff.; Bieber, Hell. Sc., 107 ff.

on the Acropolis of Pergamon[1] which Attalos I erected to celebrate his victories consisted of a central group (pl. XVI*a*) of a Gallic chief killing himself after killing his wife, surrounded by figures of dying Gauls, of which the most famous is the dying Gaul of the Capitoline Museum. In the dedication at Athens[2] at any rate, the parallel seems to have been drawn between this victory and the earlier Greek victory over the Persians and the mythical Greek victory over the Amazons. The parallel between Amazonomachies and Persian wars had already been drawn in the fifth century. The fifth-century pictures had however always shown Greeks and Persians, Greeks and Amazons; here in the chief monument at any rate, unless the reconstruction is gravely at fault, one only saw the defeated. The measure of the victory is the physical strength and the fierce independence of these adversaries, who preferred death to life in captivity. The categories of *Hybris* and *Sophrosyne* under which the Greeks of the fifth century saw the Persian war are not applicable to this battle. Perhaps we should remember that the sophists had asserted that Greeks and barbarians shared the same nature (*physis*) and that Alexander had married noble Greeks to noble Persians: Gauls are different from Greeks, unlearned perhaps but in no way despicable, because they are strong and brave and proud. The memorial testifies to the qualities of the victor by exalting the strength of the vanquished.

The central group carries further the kind of composition already seen in the Tyche of Antioch (pl. XIV*b*), the group which has to be seen in the round because it has no satisfactory single view. But the style has nothing to do with Lysippos; these passionate heads develop the tendencies associated with Skopas in the fourth century. Composition and style have suggested that other works should be attributed to Pergamene sculptors of the late third century. The theme of standing figure supporting drooping figure, which forms the centre of the monument, is repeated in a group of Menelaos carrying the

[1] Rome, Terme, etc. Winter, *K.i.B.*, 348–9; Lippold, *Gr. Pl.*, 341 f., pl. 122/1, 3; Bieber, *Hell. Sc.*, 109, figs. 281–3, 424–7.

[2] Naples, etc. Winter, *K.i.B.*, 350–1; Lippold, *Gr. Pl.*, 353, pl. 127; Bieber, *Hell. Sc.*, 109, figs. 430–7. The only evidence that victors were represented in this dedication is the story in Plut. *Ant.* 60 that a bronze Dionysos was blown off the wall of the Acropolis, which may have belonged to this group.

dead body of Patroklos,[1] of Achilles with the body of Penthesileia,[2] of Artemis with the body of Iphigeneia, for which she is substituting a deer (pl. XVI*b*).[3] If they are Pergamene, they show Pergamene interest in the mythology of the Trojan war, and Pergamene learning has been seen in the fact that the decoration of Menelaos' helmet can be interpreted as symbolic of his wanderings to Libya and Aethiopia.

Style rather than composition has suggested three other attributions worthy of note. The first is the group of Marsyas, the Scythian, and Apollo.[4] Marsyas is hanging from a tree; the Scythian is crouching, whetting his knife, ready to flay him; Apollo sits quietly by with his lyre, his right arm over his head as he awaits inspiration. The physique of Marsyas and the Scythian, the professional appraisal of the Scythian, and the tortured face of Marsyas suggest Pergamon. It is a strange cruel group which emphasizes the absolute unconcern of the god and the agonized apprehension of his victim. The other two works presumably belonged to groups but the key is lost; one is a young sleeping satyr[5] and the other the sleeping female head[6] which used to be interpreted as Medusa but may be a Maenad or a Fury.

A collection of largely mythological reliefs set on supports adorned the sanctuary at Kyzikos which Eumenes II and Attalos II built in honour of their mother, Apollonis of Kyzikos, who had herself dedicated the Demeter temple in Pergamon. The reliefs are described in epigrams which are collected in the third book of the *Anthology*. The common theme is naturally mothers and sons. It is unfortunate that so many mythological mothers had unsatisfactory husbands, so

[1] Florence, Loggia dei Lanzi, etc. Winter, *K.i.B.*, 306/3; Lippold, *Gr. Pl.*, 362, pl. 122/2; Bieber, *Hell. Sc.*, 78, figs. 272–7; Schweitzer, *Abh. Sächs. Ak.* 43, 1936, 104 ff., on Pergamene learning.

[2] Geneva, etc. Lippold, *Gr. Pl.*, 362; Bieber, *Hell. Sc.*, 79, figs. 278–80.

[3] Copenhagen, Ny Carlsberg 1048–9; Lippold, *Gr. Pl.*, 363; Bieber, *Hell. Sc.*, 76, figs. 268–9; Studniczka, *Abh. Sächs. Ak.* 37, 1926.

[4] Rome, Conservatori, etc. Winter, *K.i.B.*, 347/1–4; 376/6, 8; Lippold, *Gr. Pl.*, 321, pl. 112/3–4; Bieber, *Hell. Sc.*, 110, figs. 438–45.

[5] Munich 218. Winter, *K.i.B.*, 346/1; Lippold, *Gr. Pl.*, 330, pl. 118/2; Bieber, *Hell. Sc.*, 112, figs. 450–1.

[6] Rome, Terme. Winter, *K.i.B.*, 347/5; Lippold, *Gr. Pl.*, 363; Bieber, *Hell. Sc.*, 112, figs. 452–3.

that the relevance of the stories is confined to the sons' love for their mothers. The idea of illustrating a modern event by a number of vaguely relevant mythological parallels is reminiscent of Euphorion's *Thrax*. The sequence starts relevantly enough with Dionysos and Semele, Telephos and Auge. Alkimede and Phoinix, Kleopatra and the sons of Phineus, Merope and Kresphontes, Antiope and her sons, Tyro and her sons, Hypsipyle and her sons, Danae and Perseus, Bellerophon, Melanippe and her sons, all recall tragedy. Odysseus and Antikleia in the underworld is a memorable epic scene of son and mother. Ixion taking vengeance for the murder of Megara, and Alkmene wedded to Rhadamanthys by Herakles are more récherché. Leto, Artemis, and Apollo are repeated: they appear first with Pytho and then with Tityos; invention seems to have run low here. The last three reliefs are interesting: two brothers saving their mother from the eruption of Etna, Kleobis and Biton (from Herodotos), and finally Romulus, Remus, and Servilia. The nineteen reliefs on their inscribed supports were set between twenty columns of the sanctuary. The visitor was invited to consider first the god Dionysos, who was held in peculiar honour by the Attalids, then their mythical predecessor Telephos, then a whole series of mythological examples, many of them from tragedy, then two historical examples which now rated with the heroes of the past, and finally an example from the great power in the West, with which Eumenes II made common cause against Antiochos III in 191 and to whom his nephew Attalos III was to bequeath his kingdom.[1]

The great altar of Zeus shows no such awareness of the future. It celebrates the past and present. It is below the temple of Athena on the South, just as the theatre is below the temple of Athena on the North-West. The three, although the temple of Athena and the theatre were earlier, were conceived as an architectural unity by Eumenes II. He gave Athena her title of Nikephoros, as having made the Attalids victorious over the Gauls, and built the propylaion, and his brother Attalos II dedicated to Zeus and Athena the stoai which completed Athena's precinct. The great altar, like the temple, was

---

[1] The meaning of *Stylopinakia* and therefore the kind of reliefs and their arrangement has been explained by A. Rumpf, *B.J.* 158, 1958, 260. On the Sicilian story, cf. Ar. *de Mundo*, 400 b 1. On Euphorion's *Thrax*, see below, p. 226.

o

approached by a propylaion, which also gave a slanting view. The slanting view of the Athenian Parthenon is thus twice repeated in Pergamon, once for the temple of Athena and once for the altar of Zeus. The Athenian had to look high to pediments and metopes and through the column shafts to the frieze if he wanted to read Pheidias' message. The Pergamene frieze was only about seven feet off the ground and the Telephos frieze was at eye-level for walkers in the colonnade. The Athenian had to guess what was represented; the Pergamene had every figure inscribed to tell him. If he followed the direction which was given him by the line of the propylaion, he would start at the North end of the East frieze and would see as he walked southwards Ares and his horses, then Nike and Athena tearing Alkyoneus from his mother Ge (pl. XVII*b*), then a group round Zeus (pl. XVII*a*) and Herakles, and Hera with the chariot of Zeus, then Apollo, Artemis, and Leto, and finally Hekate, who seems to be driving a snaky giant round the corner on to the South side. There he will find an earlier generation of gods doing battle, Phoibe, Hyperion, Selene, Helios, Eos, and Rhea; then round the South-West corner the short side to the right of the steps is occupied by Nysa and Dionysos, who cannot be missed as he strides magnificently into battle; round the corner and up the steps his Maenads were playing their part. Presumably the visitor would then climb the steps and inspect the Telephos frieze in the colonnade at the top. As he came out again he found himself among sea-gods and sea-goddesses and they carried him on round the North-West corner to where Poseidon was fighting at the end of the North frieze, then the Moirai, Nyx, and finally Dione, Eros, and Aphrodite at the corner, back to back, as it were, with Ares.[1]

The use of the Gigantomachy as a symbol of Eumenes' victory over the Gauls is also a reminiscence of the Parthenon, of the Gigantomachies on the Eastern Metopes and inside the shield of the Parthenos herself. Much learning went to establishing the combatants, and probably far more than we can hope to understand could be read

---

[1] Berlin. Winter, *K.i.B.*, 352–5; Lippold, *Gr. Pl.*, 354, pl. 124/3, 128; Richter, *Three Critical Periods*, 27 ff.; Bieber, *Hell. Sc.*, 113 ff., figs. 458–70; G. Bruns, *der Grosse Altar von Pergamon*, 12 ff.; E. Schmidt, *The Great Altar of Pergamon*, figs. 4–59.

from the details of giants with lion heads, giants with wings made of leaves, and giants with a watery transition to their snaky limbs. We ourselves, however, know the text (*Odyssey* XI, 305 ff.) for Otos and Ephialtes, who had just grown to youthful human beauty when they were killed by Apollo. Like the Gauls, the giants may be uncouth by Greek standards but they are tremendous adversaries and the gods have to deploy all their equipment of winged horses, lions, eagles, snakes and thunderbolts to win. There is no doubt about the hard-ness and reality of the battle, but there is also no doubt as to who is winning. It is one of the triumphs of the frieze to have made the battle seem so equally poised although no god is a casualty, no god or goddess shows a trace of emotion, no curl of hair and no fold of elaborate chiton or himation is out of place, while the giants writhe in agony and their faces are distorted with pain. Sometimes certainly it is tempting to see conscious reminiscence of earlier figures, not only in the comparatively unimportant Helios and Selene but in the Artemis, who recalls the Artemis of Versailles, in the Apollo, who recalls the Apollo Belvedere, and in the Athena and Nike (pl. XVII*b*), who recall the East Pediment of the Parthenon.[1] If these reminiscences are true and if, as I believe, the visitor was meant to observe them, these gods had the whole classical Greek tradition behind them, and Eumenes II was claiming that his dynasty had fought for classical Greece against a superbly strong and dangerous adversary.

Both the glory and the agony of the Gigantomachy are echoed in other works, which clearly bear some relation to the artists of the frieze. The Nike of Samothrace (pl. XV*b*)[2] lands dramatically in a swirl of draperies on the prow of a ship projecting into a pool with an ornamental fountain; it is certainly an original of the earliest second century and, whatever its occasion, the dramatic conception is in tune with the frieze. The agonized faces of the bearded giants have often been compared with the blind head of Homer,[3] which may

---

[1] Cf. particularly M. Bieber, loc. cit. Apollo Belvedere and Artemis of Versailles, ibid., figs. 200–1.

[2] Paris, Louvre 2369. Winter, *K.i.B.*, 342/1–2; Lippold, *Gr. Pl.*, 360, pl. 126/4; Bieber, *Hell. Sc.*, 125, figs. 493–6.

[3] Naples, etc. Winter, *K.i.B.*, 345/5; Lippold, *Gr. Pl.*, 385, pl. 133/3; Bieber, *Hell. Sc.*, 143, figs. 598–9.

have been sculpted for the library at Pergamon, and with the head of Laokoon:[1] the whole group conveys the same certainty of tortured annihilation, as the best parts of the frieze, and the latest discoveries seem to allow a date in the second century. A similar violence and a similar boldness in building a complicated group (although we only know it in an elaborated copy) is shown in the punishment of Dirke, a vivid illustration of the messenger speech from Euripides' *Antiope*, which is also illustrated on a Homeric bowl and on the Kyzikos relief[2] commemorating the mother of Eumenes II and Attalos II.

I know no close parallel in contemporary poetry for this delight in muscle and pain: earlier it can be found in Theokritos' description of the boxing-match (XXII) and later in Roman epic. But it is perhaps a variation of the same kind of realism as appears in the descriptions of old people in Alexandrian poetry and their representations in Alexandrian art,[3] which is also well represented in the rustics and slaves among the Myrina terracottas[4] and with again a slightly different slant in the figures of mime-actors with exaggeratedly hooked noses, enormous ears, and distorted bodies, found in several Asia Minor sites:[5] for them the drunkard mime[6] provides a text but presumably an Alexandrian text. This realism however was international. Nearer to the realism of the tortured giants of the Pergamene frieze are the gory details of Spartan heroism in the nearly contemporary epigrams of Dioskorides.[7] They are in their turn copied by Nikander of

---

[1] Rome, Vatican 74. Winter, *K.i.B.*, 383/1–2; Lippold, *Gr. Pl.*, 384, pl. 135/2; Bieber, *Hell. Sc.*, 135, figs. 530–3; Richter, *Three Critical Periods*, 66 ff.; Magi, *Atti della Pont. Acc.*, Memorie 9, 1960, with a new reconstruction, which brings Laokoon's right forearm down towards his head and the right forearm of the son on the left also down towards his head. Cf. *Archaeology* 66, 1963, 124.

[2] Naples 260. Winter, *K.i.B.*, 357/1; Lippold, *Gr. Pl.*, 383, pl. 135/1; Bieber, *Hell. Sc.*, 133, fig. 520. The Homeric bowl, cf. above, p. 147.

[3] Cf. above, p. 168.

[4] E.g. Winter, *TK*, 441/9 = Rostovtzeff, *S.E.H.W.*, 246/3; 451/8 = *S.E.H.W.*, 239/1; 452/5 = *S.E.H.W.*, 238/1; from Priene, *TK*, 443/5 = *S.E.H.W.*, 246/1. The distinction between rustic and rustic in mime is hard to draw.

[5] Myrina, *TK*, 437/5 = Rostovtzeff, *S.E.H.W.*, 239/4. Pergamon, *TK*, 443/1 = *S.E.H.W.*, 239/3. Asia Minor, *TK*, 437/1–3. Cf. from Egypt, Bieber, *History*[2], figs. 825–6, and in general W. Binsfeld, *Grylloi* 1956, 42.

[6] Page, *G.L.P.*, no. 74. Cf. above, p. 171.

[7] Cf. above, p. 141.

Kolophon,[1] who wrote a hymn to Attalos III and found plenty of scope for unpleasant and realistic physical details in his lengthy descriptions of the bites of snakes and spiders in learned vocabulary interwoven with remote mythological allusions.

This digression into further examples of ugly realism has led away from the altar of Zeus at Pergamon. There it is a necessary component of the Gigantomachy: the gods cannot suffer, the giants must. It hardly appears in the surviving slabs of the Telephos frieze.[2] The difference of style between the Gigantomachy frieze and the Telephos frieze is often mentioned; it is due to its different position and its different purpose. To say that the Gigantomachy corresponds to the pediments and metopes of the Parthenon and the Telephos frieze to the Parthenon frieze probably reflects the creator's intention in part, and the Gigantomachy frieze is carved to be seen from some little distance; but it could also be seen from close at hand and the Telephos frieze could only be seen close at hand. The Gigantomachy gives a complete view of the battle at one moment; the Telephos frieze tells the whole life of Telephos. The serial story made up of scenes in which the hero is seen again and again had been known in art since at least the Theseids of late sixth-century vase-painting. At this time serials were popular on the Homeric bowls, but unfortunately no Homeric bowl survives with illustrations of Euripides' *Telephos*. Telephos had a triple interest for Attalids: he was a former Greek ruler of Mysia, the area of Pergamon; he was a son of Herakles, whom they claimed as an ancestor;[3] and he was involved with Dionysos, who was particularly their god. The preserved slabs show first perhaps Aleos of Arcadia consulting the oracle; then his wife and a servant (or son) receiving Herakles; then certainly Herakles entering the grove where he raped Auge (this Herakles is not obviously drunk like the Herakles of the Pompeian painting, which has been

---

[1] Edited A. S. F. Gow and A. F. Scholfield, 1953. Spartan epigrams fr. 105–6 = *A.P.* VII, 435, 526. Hymn to Attalos III, fr. 104.

[2] Berlin. Winter, *K.i.B.*, 354/5–10, 355/5–9; Lippold, *Gr. Pl.*, 357, pl. 129/1–2; Bieber, *Hell. Sc.*, 120, figs. 477–8; Bruns, *der Grosse Altar von Pergamon*, 55 ff.; Schmidt, *Great Altar of Pergamon*, figs. 60–7.

[3] Nikander's hymn to Attalos III (fr. 104) calls him both descendant of Teuthras and descendant of Herakles.

referred to a Pergamene original; there the inspiration may have been Euripides' *Auge*, in which Herakles pleaded his drunkenness).[1] The next scene shows the preparation of the ark in which Auge is to be cast adrift. When the ark arrives in Mysia, it is met by the king, Teuthras, who moves towards the shore with something of the splendour of the Nike of Samothrace. Then a scene which has been recently interpreted by Dr Erika Simon[2] as a maenad heating water to bathe the infant Telephos under the eyes of Arkadia, who is seated above on a rock, a figure reminiscent of the city goddesses on Homeric bowls and more remotely of the Tyche of Antioch. If this attractive interpretation is right, Dionysos, as patron of the maenads, was responsible for the salvation of Telephos. The next scene is certain: Herakles under a plane-tree watches Telephos being suckled by a lioness which lies outside its cave (pl. XVIII*a*). (The landscape elements in this and in the Auge scene we have noticed already in connection with Alexandrian art).[3]

The Herakles in this scene and the Arkadia of the preceding scene recur in a magnificent painting from Herculaneum (pl. XVIII*b*,)[4] which must therefore go back to a Pergamene original of this date. There Arkadia's vision of the royal future of Pergamon is super-imposed on the discovery of Telephos; eagle and lion symbolize the future; the child is suckled by a hind instead of a lioness as in the literary versions. Herakles has been led there by Parthenos, Arkadian mountain and star (in this identification the Pergamenes seem to have followed Aratos rather than Eratosthenes). Behind Arkadia stands a young satyr with crook and Panpipes to represent Dionysos. One other parallel should be noticed here: the Herakles of the picture immediately recalls the bronze statue of a Hellenistic prince in the Terme Museum:[5] this should therefore be an original by a Pergamene artist of the mid-second century, whether it represents Demetrios I of Syria or another, whether it was made in Asia Minor or in Rome.

---

[1] Simon, *J.D.A.I.* 76, 1961, 141, fig. 22. Euripides fr. 265 N.

[2] Simon, *J.D.A.I.* 76, 1961, 160.    [3] Cf. above, p. 167.

[4] Naples, N. M. Pfuhl, *M.u.Z.*, fig. 659; Simon, op. cit., 138, 140, 144, figs. 20, 28. Cf. below, p. 196.

[5] Rome, Terme 544. Winter, *K.i.B.*, 339/1; Lippold, *Gr. Pl.*, 298, pl. 105/4; Bieber, *Hell. Sc.*, 160, figs. 682-3, 685.

In the next preserved scenes of the frieze Telephos arrives in Mysia, and Teuthras presents him with Auge as a bride. The next scene showed the recognition of mother and son in the marriage chamber after she had tried to kill him: the end of the bed just appears on the edge of the slab, and the next slab shows the snake which prevented her. This version is apparently based on Sophocles' *Mysians*. Then the battles against the Greeks, where one of the slabs shows the same violence as the Gigantomachy. Dionysos intervenes to entangle Telephos in a vine so that Achilles can wound him. Then Telephos goes to Greece to get his wound healed. We see him snatch the child Orestes and take refuge on the altar. As in Euripides' play,[1] someone, perhaps Odysseus, had accused Telephos of being a spy. Then he is seated showing his wound to four Greek chiefs, one possibly Odysseus; Achilles, who seems, as in Euripides, to have just arrived, stands behind with the spear which will heal the wound.

The story continues with the transference of the cult of Dionysos from Arkadia to Mysia; this is Telephos' reconciliation with Dionysos after his healing and the establishment of the royal cult in Pergamon: his title Kathegemon may well have been interpreted as the god who brought Telephos home.[2] On the slabs we see a man looking left, perhaps Telephos, at the entrance of a cave (?), a maenad dancing with two torches, a column with an animal on the top, a rocky landscape with a goddess seated in the background, a satyr holding a thyrsos and seated facing right, then a woman, then another seated satyr who looks over his shoulder right, then another woman who shakes hands with the first woman. The two women are making an agreement, and as satyrs and rocks are involved, it is an agreement to transfer a Dionysos cult from Arkadia to Pergamon. The man, the maenad, and the column are the left side of an earlier scene; perhaps more of it is preserved on another slab on which women institute a cult to Athena under a plane-tree. If this slab belongs here, the plane-tree and the cave establish the place as the mountain Parthenion where Telephos was suckled and close to which

[1] Cf. E. W. Handley, *Telephos of Euripides* (B.I.C.S. London, Supplt. no. 5), 33, 35 f. On Sophocles' *Mysians*, see Pearson.

[2] Simon, op. cit., 140; Pausanias VIII, 54, 5–6.

Dionysos Mystes had a shrine.[1] Telephos establishes or at least recognizes the cults (of Athena and Dionysos) in Arkadia and transfers them to Mysia. Another slab perhaps shows the death of Telephos.

Apart from its obvious artistic interest as an extremely competent piece of narrative and the importance of the story of Telephos as the Greek background claimed by the Attalids, the frieze (and the Pompeian picture) give evidence of how the Pergamenes conceived satyrs, a problem which met us before in discussing Alexandrian satyrs and pastoral poetry.[2] It may not be irrelevant to remember that Ptolemy Philopator, who came to the throne in the latter part of the reign of Attalos I, was extremely interested in Dionysiac mysteries and celebrated them in his palace.[3] In Pergamon Dionysos Kathegemon was a god of mysteries, and his devotees were called *Boukoloi*, 'neatherds':[4] the young satyr in the picture from Herculaneum (pl. XVIII*b*) has his crook, and he is therefore the mythical counterpart of the mystics. In the palace the kings had a private chapel of Dionysos Kathegemon; it is not impossible that its decoration was repeated by the paintings in the Pompeian Villa of the Mysteries, since the central picture of Dionysos and Ariadne there is so like a terracotta from Myrina that a Pergamene original for the painting may be assumed.[5]

Dionysos Kathegemon was also the god of drama in Pergamon. In inscriptions of the middle of the second century the 'Artists who serve Dionysos Kathegemon' are coupled with the 'Artists of the Hellespont and Ionia', and Eumenes II intervened on behalf of the Hellespontine-Ionian Guild when they were quarrelling with the

[1] The order of the slabs is uncertain and many arrangements have been proposed: the sequence in the text seems likely to me. The following events may be regarded as certain: Herakles and Auge; Auge and the ark; Herakles and the infant Telephos; recognition of Telephos and Auge; wounding of Telephos; Telephos and Orestes; Telephos and the Greek chiefs. On Aratos and Eratosthenes, cf. above, p. 137.

[2] Cf. above, p. 165.        [3] Cf. above, p. 140.

[4] For the cult in second century B.C., cf. *Pergamon*, VIII, 248. The *Boukoloi* are not attested till the first century A.D. (*Pergamon*, VIII, 484–6) but the title should go back to the time when the cult was founded.

[5] Cf. above p. 184 and Simon, op. cit., 131, 166. The altar-room: *Pergamon*, V, 1; its mosaic, ibid., pl. 12. Cf. below, pp. 300–01.

city authorities of Teos, a quarrel which subsequently caused the removal of their headquarters to Lebedos.[1] The exact relation between the two Guilds is unclear, but presumably the 'Artists who served Dionysos Kathegemon' were responsible for performances in the theatre of Pergamon, which was partly remodelled under Eumenes II: the marble gateway which led into the orchestra from the North had a frieze decorated with alternate masks of papposilenos and wild-haired satyr attached to ivy-swags and bore the inscription: 'Apollodoros, son of Artemon, clerk of the people, dedicated to Dionysos Kathegemon and to the people this gateway and the curtain in it'.[2] (The date is approximately the same as the dedication of *thyromata* in Oropos and it is tempting to suppose that here too, as probably also in Priene, the new stage-building had large realistic paintings of the type we know from Vitruvius and from the cubiculum of Boscoreale.)[3] Similar friezes of comic and tragic masks of approximately the same date were found in the Upper Marketplace, which was near the temple of Dionysos Kathegemon, and a very fine mosaic with a mask of a hetaira wreathed with ivy was found in the private chapel of the royal palace: the magnificent tragic masks in the Casa del Fauno at Pompeii have also been thought to be copies of Pergamene originals.[4]

The masks found at Pergamon or attributed to Pergamon follow standard Hellenistic practice, but one revolutionary and strangely successful innovation in tragic costume may be due to Pergamon. The theatre was extremely steep and the orchestra level was more than 180 feet below the highest of the eighty rows of seats. Even with the gain of 12 feet or so given by the high stage, the desirability of giving extra elevation to tragic actors must have been obvious. It may not therefore be chance that the earliest figure with an extra-thick sole is the figure of Tragedy (pl. XIXa), a draped woman with

[1] Poland, op. cit., 2509; Pickard-Cambridge, *Festivals*, 301, 309, 315; *I.G.*, XI, 4, 1061; *Pergamon*, VIII, 163. For the theatre, cf. Bieber, *History*[2], figs. 243–7, 461–2.
[2] Istanbul 287. *Pergamon*, IV, 1, 13; VIII, no. 236; Lippold, *Gr. Pl.*, 372.
[3] Cf. above, p. 163; below, p. 243.
[4] Frieze: Webster, *M.T.S.*, ZS 2; *M.N.C.*, ZS 2; Winter, *K.i.B.*, 362/1–2; Lippold, *Gr. Pl.*, 358; Bieber, *History*[2], figs. 311–13, 380. Mosaic mask: *M.T.S.*, ZM 1; Rumpf, *M.u.Z.*, pl. 56/4. Masks from Casa del Fauno: Naples 9994, *M.T.S.*, NM 4; Rumpf, *M.u.Z.*, 152; Bieber, *History*[2], fig. 574. Cf. below, p. 300.

a sword, found on the Acropolis of Pergamon[1] and dated stylistically to the end of the third century. The soles of Tragedy on the relief with the Apotheosis of Homer (pl. IV) are three times as thick, and on a terracotta statuette of a tragic actor from Amisos five times as thick, in proportion to the height of the whole figure; the only other earlyish original with thick soles is the seated tragic Muse on the marble basis from Halikarnassos, but comparative measurement on a seated figure is difficult.[2] There are no other Greek originals with high soles dating from the second century B.C. Amisos is in Pontus on the South shore of the Black Sea, and Halikarnassos is on the mainland opposite Kos, so that both could well be within the sphere of influence of the Ionian-Hellespontine Guild; the sculptor of the Apotheosis of Homer came from Priene and, as we have seen, the Muses which he adapted for the upper part of the relief seem to have been created in the neighbourhood of Kos. It is therefore possible that the strange practice of mounting tragic actors on thick soles was invented for the unusually steep theatre at Pergamon and spread rapidly to the Ionian-Hellespontine Guild and from them to the other Greek guilds. The movement of tragic actors could be thus frozen without too much loss. Luckily comedy could not give up its running slaves, and the chief actor took the slave's part.

We have a few more facts about dramatic activity in the East during the second and first century.[3] Professor Bieber[4] suggested that the relief of a tragic actor in Dresden may be a memorial to an actor who was the priest of Dionysos in the Ionian-Hellespontine Guild. The suggestion is attractive. The actor is shown seated, in Dionysiac costume with fawnskin and crook; the boots have soles of about the same thickness as the Pergamene figure of Tragedy, which would

[1] Berlin. Winter, *K.i.B.*, 359/3; Lippold, *Gr. Pl.*, 358, pl. 126/3; Bieber, *Hell. Sc.*, 119, fig. 473.

[2] Apotheosis of Homer, cf. above, p. 145. Terracotta statuette from Amisos, Louvre CA 1784, *M.T.S.*, ZT 1; Bieber, *History*[2], fig. 290. Halikarnassos base, British Museum 1106, *M.T.S.*, ZS 1; Winter, *K.i.B.*, 363/1-4.

[3] Except where otherwise indicated references will be found in Poland, op. cit., 2507 ff.; Pickard-Cambridge, *Festivals*, 299 ff.; *Theatre*, 242; Webster, *Griechische Bühnenalterthümer*, 44 ff.

[4] M. Bieber, *das Dresdner Schauspielerrelief*, 83, 88; *History*[2], 84, fig. 307; *M.T.S.*, US 1.

give a date early in the second century; probably a lost figure on the right held his mask. He had according to this theory a parallel position to that of Philikos in the Alexandrian Guild, and one is reminded of the epitaph promising Philikos the rewards awaiting the mystic.[1] Here the crook and the fawnskin suggest the mystic and it seems possible that the actor was shown both in tragic costume and as a mystic of the cult of Dionysos Kathegemon.

In the second century the Guild sent two tragic, two comic actors, one kitharode, and one kitharistes to help the people of Iasos maintain their festivals. At Samothrace, where the new temple was completed in the mid-second century with a pediment representing Dike and the child gods (Harmonia, Dardanos, and Aetion) of the Mysteries,[2] Dymas, a tragic poet who was also honoured at Iasos, produced at about the same time a play about Dardanos. In the first century delegates from the Guild were sent to Samothrace. At Teos a new temple of Dionysos was built in the middle of the second century, and an inscription records poets and actors of satyr-plays including a play called *Persai*, an inexplicable title for a satyr-play. In Samos a second-century record of the festival of Hera (?) records an old tragedy, a new satyr-play by Hermias of Rhodes, a new tragedy by Sosistratos, and a new comedy by Ariston of Athens. At Priene the theatre was rebuilt, and some excellent terracotta masks found in a private house testify to interest in comedy.[3] The temple of Athena, built in the mid-second century had a coffered ceiling[4] with a Gigantomachy in the violent style of the Pergamene frieze. The same style is seen in the frieze of the temple of Artemis Leukophryene inland at Magnesia;[5] there the Guild was invited to send performers in the second century, and for the festival of Rome in the first century we have titles of new tragedies, including *Hermione* and *Klytaimestra*, of

[1] Cf. above, p. 129.

[2] Vienna. Winter, *K.i.B.*, 342/4; Lippold, *Gr. Pl.*, 318, pl. 115/2 and 4; P. Lehmann, *Pedimental Sculptures of the Hieron at Samothrace*, 1962 (cf. for dating *J.H.S.* 71, 1951, 246 f.). Cf. also F. Salviat, *B.C.H.* 80, 1956, 148.

[3] Webster, *M.N.C.*, ZT 20–4; Bieber, *History²*, fig. 387.

[4] British Museum 1165–76 and Berlin. Winter, *K.i.B.*, 356/3–5; Lippold, *Gr. Pl.*, 373; Bieber, *Hell. Sc.*, 105.

[5] Paris, Louvre, etc. Winter, *K.i.B.*, 356/1; Lippold, *Gr. Pl.*, 374; Bieber, *Hell. Sc.*, 164, figs. 702–3.

new satyr-plays, including *Thytes*, *Aias*, *Protesilaos*, and *Palamedes*, and new comedies, including *Homoioi* and *Milesia*.

Fragmentary and unsatisfactory as the evidence is, it testifies to a lively theatrical practice over the whole region from the late fourth century to the first. Many new plays were written, and the use of the word 'new' in these records implies that there were also performances of classical tragedy, satyr-play, and comedy. On the fringe of Greek Asia in Armenia Tigranes had collected Greek artists for the dedication of his theatre at Tigranocerta when he was captured by Lucullus in 69, and in Parthia in 53 Jason of Tralles was playing Agave in the *Bacchae*, with a chorus, for Hyrodes, when Crassus' head was brought in and used for Pentheus' head in Agave's great scene.

Roman interest was considerable. Early in the second century L. Scipio Asiagenus, after defeating Antiochos III, brought Artists of Dionysos from Asia to Rome. There is no reason to doubt that the performances continued when Asia was a Roman province, and some of them must have been seen by the Roman Governor and his staff and by other Romans who visited the province. (The number of Romans and Italians in Asia was very considerable if 80,000 were massacred on the orders of Mithradates.)[1] In the first century we have further evidence of Roman interest: Sulla[2] gave privileges to the Guild; Pompey was so impressed by the theatre at Mitylene that he made his stone theatre in Rome on a similar plan. According to Plutarch Antony in 32 compelled 'all the Artists' to assemble in Samos and choruses competed before crowded audiences; he also gave Priene as a 'dwelling-place' to the Guild.

Terracotta statuettes,[3] particularly the great series found at Myrina, give a good idea of the tastes of the ordinary Greek of the second and

[1] The group of Prometheus and Herakles from Pergamon has been held to symbolize Mithradates' liberation of Asia: Berlin. Winter, *K.i.B.*, 364/1–2; Lippold, *Gr. Pl.*, 372, pl. 131/2; Bieber, *Hell. Sc.*, 122, figs. 485–7. It is, however, difficult to reconcile the allegorical interpretation with the attribution of a group of Leda and the Swan to the same monument (Lippold, loc. cit., Winter, *K.i.B.*, 372/4).

[2] Scipio: cf. below, p. 279. Sulla: M. Segré, *R.I.F.C.* 66, 1938, 253 (I owe this reference to Mr D. M. Lewis). Pompey: Plut. *Pomp.* 42. Antony: Plut. *Ant.* 56, 57.

[3] Pottier, *Diphilos*, 96 ff.; Pottier and Reinach, *La Nécropole de Myrina*; D. Burr, *Terracottas from Myrina in the Museum of Fine Arts*, Boston, 1934.

first century. At Myrina and elsewhere they have been found in private houses as well as in tombs so that they were made to please the living, and what pleased the living was expected also to please the dead. Many of them reproduce large sculptures and paintings; we have already mentioned figures and groups derived from Hellenistic paintings; some of the original sculptures reproduced in terracotta date from the fourth century or even the fifth. Here the terracottas perform the function of modern reproductions and show the ordinary man's interest in great art. Others cover the world of entertainment: tragedy occasionally, comedy brilliantly, and mime often. Military life enters in only rarely, but a war elephant once tramples a resistant Gaul. The two worlds which concern us now, the world of bucolic poetry and the world of elegiac epigram are well represented: the former by scenes of rustic life, by laughing young satyrs, by a group of Pan and Eros, the latter by Erotes flying, walking, naked or clothed, by groups of Eros and Psyche, by countless statuettes of beautiful women.

Arcadia on the Telephos frieze (pl. XVIIIa) consists of rocks and caves and plane-trees and is inhabited by the satyrs and nymphs of Dionysos, satyrs who are herdsmen. Arcadia had always been the home of Pan, as Theokritos remembers in *Idyll* VII (106) and elsewhere. But the great popularity of Arcadia as the scene of later pastoral poetry may derive from its being the mythical ancestral country of the Pergamene mystics. Into the initiation scenes of the Villa of the Mysteries, which were probably painted about 60 and have been plausibly traced back to a Pergamene original of the early second century, is inserted a bucolic landscape,[1] a satyr-boy with syrinx and crook and a satyr-girl sitting on a rock among their goats. This is the life for which the mystic hopes. Dr Simon, interpreting the scene, notes the very pretty love duet in the Theokritean corpus (*Idyll* XXVII)[2] in which the girl calls Daphnis 'Little Satyr'. The poem could well belong to this area and time, and the pretty group of young satyr and nymph from Kyzikos, which has already been quoted,[3] gives us an idea what they looked like. Trees, rocks, altars, and animals also invade grave-reliefs of the second to first century

[1] Simon, op. cit., 126 ff., fig. 11; Pfuhl, *M.u.Z.*, fig. 713.
[2] Cf. above, p. 165.      [3] Cf. above, p. 181.

and again one may ask whether the countryside belongs to this world, to a mythical world, or to a hoped-for next world. The relief from Tralles (pl. VIIIb)[1] with a man apparently tying up an animal under a plane-tree is probably a dedication after a sacrifice, and there is no reason to refer it outside the present world. But a grave-relief[2] (pl. VIIIa) from Ephesos with a girl picking fruit from a tree behind a wall might well be a forecast of mystic bliss such as that proposed for Philikos, the head of the Alexandrian Guild.

A link between the pastoral of Asia Minor and the pastoral of South Italy is perhaps provided by Bion of Smyrna.[3] In the *Epitaphios* (70 f.) Bion is said to have been born in Smyrna but to have drunk the Syracusan water of Arethusa. The funeral song is sung by an Italian singer, who is a pupil of Bion (94). It is a pastoral lament: the nightingales are to tell Arethusa that Bion the neatherd is dead. He is mourned by Apollo, Satyrs, Priapoi, Pans, and Nymphs (26). Bion therefore was not a neatherd in any literal sense but rather an initiated poet whose death can be mourned by his kin whom he will join, just as in life he sang beside the nymph Galateia. Who, asks the poet (111), could be so cruel as to poison you? But Justice visits all. Bion must really have been poisoned, whether intentionally or accident-ally. The statement of the crime and the appeal to Justice recalls Euphorion's *Thrax*, but this need not have been a near ancestor. The poem is ascribed to Moschos presumably because of the appeal to Sicilian Muses, but this is impossible because the writer says that he is an Italian and Moschos came from Syracuse. Besides, Moschos was a pupil of Aristarchos in Alexandria, whereas this Italian poet was a pupil of Bion in Smyrna or in Sicily.

Bion himself is said to have sung to Galateia on the shore, which need not mean more than that he wrote Sicilian pastoral (cf. XVI). It seems to be generally assumed that the reference to the Sicilian

---

[1] Cf. above, p. 167. Istanbul 547. Winter, *K.i.B.*, 365/5; Lippold, *Gr. Pl.*, 343. On Hellenistic grave-reliefs from Ionia, cf. E. Pfuhl, *J.D.A.I.* 20, 1905, 47, 133; Winter, *K.i.B.*, 370/5; Bieber, *Hell. Sc.*, 137, 153, figs. 538–9, 646–7.

[2] Vienna, I, 873. Winter, *K.i.B.*, 371/5; Lippold, *Gr. Pl.*, 376; Noll, *Gr. u. Lat. Inschr. der Wiener Antikensammlung*, 1962, no. 48, Iomede, daughter of Diphilos.

[3] The *Adonis*, the fragments of Bion, and the *Epitaphios* can be found in Gow, *Bucolici Graeci*, 153 ff.

Muses is to Moschos, and that therefore Bion must be considerably later than Moschos, but why should not the reference be to Theokritos, who is also the latest poet mentioned in the *Epitaphios*? We should therefore accept Theokritos rather than Moschos as giving a top date for Bion. In Bion's own poems the pretty fragment in which Eros is taken to a music-teacher (X) clearly belongs to the same genre as Moschos' *Runaway Love* (I) and *Love ploughing* (VIII). Rumpf[1] compares the so-called 'Diotima' bronze relief from Pompeii, which he interprets not as Sokrates and Diotima but much more convincingly as Aphrodite bringing Eros to a schoolmaster, as he is brought to a music-teacher in Bion's poem. This would suit a date in the second half of the second century for Bion.

Bion's *Adonis* (I) is the lament itself; the parallel is not the song at the festival which the Argive woman sings in Theokritos (XV, 100) but the song which made Dioskorides (*A.P.* V, 53) wish that he were Adonis so that he could die in the arms of the singer. Bion's song is presumably not the actual lament, but like the song in Theokritos, a translation into hexameters. The lament technique is very clear in the repetitions and near-repetitions; and the ancient form of leader and chorus, as we know it already in the laments for Patroklos and Hektor in the *Iliad*, is echoed in the refrain lines (which recur with variations through the poem): 'I mourn Adonis: "Dead is fair Adonis", "Dead is fair Adonis", the Erotes mourn thereto' (1). Further on Aphrodite herself plays the Adonis 'singer' and mourns her love (42–63), Aphrodite's tears turn into anemones, and the blood from Adonis' wound turns into roses. At the end the Erotes with shorn heads mourn Adonis. There is a luxury of lamentation here which exceeds Theokritos' lament for Daphnis (I), but then there is a new luxury of physical pain in the dying giants of Pergamon, and the phenomenon may be Hellenistic rather than Oriental.

'The Pastoral Muses were once scattered. Now they are all together in one fold, in one herd' (*A.P.* IX, 205). This two-line epigram is by Artemidoros of Tarsos. The conceit that the poem about neatherds is first called a Muse and then the Muse is identified

---

[1] *Festschrift Premersdorf*, 95. 'Diotima' relief: Bieber, *Hell. Sc.*[2], fig. 124; Schefold, *Bildnisse*, 162 f.

with the animals looked after by the neatherds is possible any time after Kallimachos' 'nightingales' or his 'large woman' or Theokritos' 'Graces'. The suggestion therefore that Artemidoros of Tarsos, who was not included in his anthology by Meleager, nevertheless lived early in the first century B.C. may be right, and this gives a date for a collection of bucolic poetry and a bottom date for Bion.[1]

The other Eastern epigrammatists who need consideration belong partly to the second and partly to the first century. Dionysios of Kyzikos can be dated between the death of Eratosthenes in 194 and the publication of Meleager's *Garland* about 70 (*A.P.* VII, 462 and XII, 108 seem from their position in the *Palatine Anthology* to have been included in the *Garland*). 'Gentle old age and not weakening disease quenched you, and you sleep the allotted sleep after climbing the heights of thought, Eratosthenes. Nor did nurse Kyrene receive you in an ancestral grave, son of Aglaos, but you are a friend buried in foreign soil here by the edge of the beach of Proteus' (*A.P.* VII, 78). The language is simple and expressive, and the demonstrative in the last line suggests that Dionysios himself was in Alexandria when he wrote the poem; it may even be a genuine epitaph. It is certainly far more distinguished than the Kyzikene epigrams from the precinct of Apollonis, the mother of Eumenes II and Attalos II, and one would be unwilling to ascribe those to Dionysios.

Antipater of Sidon was a far more prolific author. Meleager (*A.P.* IV, 1) calls him 'the new henna from Phoenicia', which suggests that he should not be pushed further back than necessary. He was known in Rome before 91 as a poet extremely skilful in improvisation. Certain dates are the epitaph (*A.P.* VII, 241) on the young Ptolemy who died in 150 and the poem on Mummius' sack of Corinth (*A.P.* IX, 151) in 146. Possibly the poem on Philip V (*A.P.* VI, 115) was written soon after Philip's death in 179. As Antipater died old, his life may well have spanned most of the second century.[2]

---

[1] Cf. Wilamowitz, *Bucolici Graeci*, iii; Gow, *Theocritus*, lx, lxi, 549.

[2] On dating, cf. Gow, *C.R.* 4, 1954, 1; Mackail, *Select Epigrams*, 320, quoting Cic. *Or.* 3, 194; Pliny, *N.H.* VII, 172. There is confusion between Antipater of Sidon and Antipater of Thessalonica. I hope that in the following selection all the epigrams quoted belong to Antipater of Sidon. On Antipater in Rome, cf. below, p. 303.

The practice of capping epigrams which we have noted from the beginning of the Hellenistic period[1] has now changed into the practice of remodelling already published epigrams. At least by the Early Hellenistic poets the illusion was preserved that this was part of symposion practice, although in fact anthologies were made very early. Now it has become a literary exercise: a new poem is made by remodelling an old poem and at a rough assessment more than a quarter of Antipater's epigrams are formed on Early Hellenistic models. His chief favourite was Leonidas of Tarentum, whose style strongly influenced him particularly in the use of anaphora and compound adjectives.[2]

A typical instance of this echoing is *A.P.* VII, 146, which is very closely modelled on *A.P.* VII, 145 by Asklepiades, an imaginary epitaph for Ajax: Arete sits by his tomb mourning because Apate (deceit) has more influence with the Greeks than she. Antipater repeats the four lines of Asklepiades in different words, jazzed up with compound adjectives in asyndeton and adds two more: 'the arms of Achilles would say: "Manly prowess, not crooked words, is *our* desire" '. A similar expansion turns a four-line epigram of Leonidas (*A.P.* VI, 110) dedicating a deer's antlers into a six-line epigram (*A.P.* VI, 111), but here Antipater has adapted the earlier poem to a contemporary event, the slaying of a deer by Lykormas, son of Thearidas who belongs to a known Arcadian family, as Gow has shown. This would suggest that Antipater was in Greece in the middle of the century. It may therefore have been personal knowledge which puts the very genuine emotion into the two epigrams on Mummius' sack of Corinth in 146: one an epitaph on a mother who killed her daughter to avoid Roman slavery, like the Gaul and his wife in the Attalos monument (*A.P.* VII, 493), the other a lament for the utter destruction of Corinth (*A.P.* IX, 151): 'everything war has seized and devoured. We alone remain unsacked, Nereids, daughters of Ocean, halcyons of your woes.' Rome is synonymous with war for Antipater, and in a very pretty poem on Antiodemis, the Cyprian

---

[1] Cf. above, p. 48 ff.

[2] Other authors whom Antipater echoes are Anyte, Asklepiades, Kallimachos, Theodoridas, Alkaios, Damagetos, Dioskorides, Herakleitos, Plato, Xenophanes. On Leonidas, see below, p. 217 ff.

P

*lysiodos*[1] 'with melting eyes softer than sleep' (here he remembers Alkman (3, 62 P), 'with arms as fluid as water, with a boneless body like cream-cheese' (here the reminiscence is Theokritos' Galateia (XI, 20)), he says that she has gone to Italy 'that she may stop Rome from war and from the sword by her soft charm' (*A.P.* IX, 567). Another poem with a historical reference is the lament for the young Ptolemy Eupator, the son of Ptolemy Philometor, who died about 150 from plague at the age of eighteen (*A.P.* VII, 241): 'great Egypt tore her hair, and the wide house of Europe (Sidon) groaned'. This must have been written in Sidon at the time when Alexander Balas was relying on Egyptian support.

There are a number of poems on poets.[2] Most of them are re-handlings of familiar themes. Homer is the 'unageing mouth of the whole world' (*A.P.* VII, 6), which is exactly what Archelaos of Priene meant when he showed Homer crowned by Time and the World.[3] The two-line epigram on Sappho (*A.P.* VII, 15) has also been found inscribed on the base of a statue of Sappho in the Library of Pergamon.[4] There is no reason why it should not have been commissioned by the Attalids, and many of these epigrams on writers may have been designed either for statue bases or for manu-scripts of the poets. This distich was presumably designed for a statue of Sappho which was to be placed not far from a statue of Homer: 'I surpassed all women in song as much as Homer surpassed all men'. Stesichoros (*A.P.* VII, 75) is a new subject, and Antipater quotes Pythagoras' view that he was a reincarnation of Homer. The epitaph on Pindar (*A.P.* VII, 34) recalls the Pindaric metaphor of the bee but also names him a trumpet and a heavy smith of pure songs. The 'pure' songs remind us of Kallimachos' ideal and conflict with the 'heavy smith', but the conflict is present in Pindar. The same con-flict appears in the Antimachos poem (VII, 409):[5] 'Praise the strong verse of timeless Antimachos, worthy of the frown of ancient heroes'

---

[1] Cf. above, p. 127. *Lysiodos* is a Lysis singer. Lysis wrote *kinaidic* poetry for singing.

[2] See Gabathuler, op. cit., 95 f.    [3] Cf. above, p. 145.

[4] *Pergamon*, VIII, no. 199. Cf. above, p. 186.

[5] Del Corno, *ACME* 15, 1962, 63, with good commentary, ascribes to Antipater of Thessalonica.

(here he remembers Dioskorides on Aeschylus), 'beaten out on the anvils of the Muses, if you have a clear ear, if you admire the un-laughing voice, if you want the path untrodden and unwalked by others'; if Homer is a Zeus among singers, Antimachos is a Poseidon – in fact, if you want to be a Kallimachos, copy Antimachos. The quotation of the prologue to the *Aitia* and of the condemnation of the *Lyde* is unmistakable, but Antipater replies that a criterion of pure poetry which excludes the massive verse of Antimachos, whom he rates very high, is too narrow.

Another kind of pseudo-epitaph which Antipater develops is the interpretation of the grave-relief. *A.P.* VII, 425: 'Do not be sur-prised at seeing on Myro's tomb a whip, an owl, a bow, a blue goose, a swift bitch'. He transfers to the epitaph a type of description used previously in poems interpreting works of art, for instance Kallimachos on the Apollo of Delos (fr. 114). The elaborate grave-relief has come into favour again; we have quoted[1] above second-century examples from Ionia, and these could well have provided Antipater's inspiration.

A number of epigrams describe well-known works of art and again it is worth remembering that the time of wholesale copying is just beginning: a free copy of Pheidias' Athena Parthenos stood in the Library at Pergamon. The Pergamene kings were also great col-lectors, and it was the price that Attalos II was prepared to pay for a picture by a fourth-century painter that persuaded Mummius that there must be something in painting.

Antipater describes (I omit epigrams where he merely follows earlier epigrammatists) Nikias' Nekyia in Athens (*A.P.* IX, 792), Praxiteles' Aphrodite in Knidos and Himeros in Thespiai (*A.P.* XVI, 167), Apelles' Aphrodite Anadyomene at Kos (*A.P.* XVI, 178). There is no reason why Antipater should not have seen all these, but he may have known them from some history of art. The group of three Muses, one by Aristokles with a lyre, one by Ageladas with a *barbiton* (a special kind of lyre), one by Kanachos with a flute, is only known from Antipater (*A.P.* XVI, 220): the sculptors were con-temporaries, who lived at the turn of the sixth to fifth century, Ageladas from Argos and the other two from Sikyon. Kanachos

[1] Cf. above, p. 202.

made the Apollo for Branchidai, but otherwise these artists are not recorded outside mainland Greece. Antipater may have seen the Muses in Greece; or if they were in Aigina they may have been brought to Pergamon. It is interesting that Antipater shows such interest in an archaic group; like Kallimachos on the Apollo of Delos, he adds a modern interpretation: one Muse is concerned with tone, one with colour, and one with harmony. Another group (*A.P.* IX, 603) of five dancing maenads, one with a lion, one with a deer, one with a bird, one with a tympanon, and one with a cymbal, have been thought to be the Thespiades of Praxiteles, but the Thespiades are more likely to have been Muses.[1] The maenads are called servants of Dionysos Saotes, a title recorded by Pausanias for Lerna and Troizen (II, 31; 37). Antipater's description makes the modern reader think of the Neo-Attic maenad reliefs;[2] this may not be a false trail as the Neo-Attic maenads derive from Attic works of the very late fifth century in the style of the Nike balustrade. Between the original and the copies is the wonderful free copy of a single maenad on a round base from Pergamon (pl. XIX*b*),[3] which brings us into the time and area of Antipater. So Antipater is evidence of interest in and knowledge of great works of art from the late sixth century to the early third.

A curious and almost total omission from his repertoire is the love epigram: for that Meleager of Gadara makes full amends. Meleager interests us both as anthologist and as epigrammatist. He is said to have flourished in the time of Seleukos VI Epiphanes, who reigned 95/3, and published his anthology about 70. The other facts come from three similar epigrams about himself (*A.P.* VII, 417–19): he was son of Eukrates, born at Gadara, brought up in Tyre, he lived to old age in Kos, he wrote *Charites*, which were inspired by his earlier fellow-townsman Menippos; he 'joined sweet-tearful love and the Muses with the cheerful *Charites*'.

The anthology is introduced by the *Garland* (*A.P.* IV, 1): 'Dear Muse, to whom do you bring this fruited song or who is the maker of the garland of singers? It was completed by Meleager and he

---

[1] Roscher II, 3248.        [2] See below, p. 248.

[3] Istanbul 575. Winter, *K.i.B.*, 372/3; Lippold, *Gr. Pl.*, 371; Bieber, *Hell. Sc.*, 120, fig. 479, Fuchs, *Vorbilder der neuattischen Reliefs*, 153.

toiled over this grace as a memorial for noble Diokles, weaving in many lilies of Anyte, many daffodils of Moiro, and of Sappho a few but roses.' This gives us author and dedication and the principle of equating poets with flowers. Some of these equations tell us a little about the poets as Meleager saw them: 'myrrh-scented, fair-flowered iris of Nossis, for whose tablets Eros melted the wax . . . sweet myrtle of Kallimachos full of sour honey . . . and from the pasture the flower of the crooked-leaved akanthos of Archilochos, small drops from the Ocean . . . and he threw in Aratos, wise in the stars, cutting the first shoots of a palm tall as heaven . . . and with them also the early violets of his own Muse'. At the end of the poem he says that the garland is a grace or thank-offering (*charis*) to his friends, but can be shared by all the Mystics. The Mystics here are lovers of poetry. The transference of the term is natural enough. We have seen that Philikos, Poseidippos, and the dramatic poets and actors at Pergamon were Mystics, and Dionysos the god both of mysteries and drama was closely associated with the Muses in Rhodes and elsewhere. Mixed garlands are frequently represented in art, and Meleager's garland was not much earlier than the wonderful mixed floral decoration of the silver cups in the British Museum (pl. XX*b*),[1] which Professor Corbett and Mr Strong ascribe to a decorative tradition which leads back to Attalid Pergamon.

The garland theme is picked up in various epigrams (including the lovely Heliodora poem: *A.P.* V, 147) and Professor Wifstrand,[2] whose excellent study has done much to make the original shape of Meleager's anthology intelligible, thinks that a poem which describes a garland of Tyrian boys may have ended the anthology: *A.P.* XII, 256. 'A fruited soul-stealing garland Eros made for you, Kypris, gathering with his hand the flower of boys; for he wove in the scented lily Diodoros and Asklepiades the sweet violet . . . Happiest of islands Tyre which has the myrrh-scented grove bearing the

---

[1] *B.M.Q.* 23, 1962, 81.

[2] *Lund Universitetet Årskrift* 23, 1927, 75. Cf. also A. S. F. Gow, *Hellenic Society Supplementary Paper*, no. 9, 1958; D. Page, *Studi Rostagni*, 544. The largest sections of the *Garland* preserved in the *Anthology* are V, 134–215; VI, 109–57; VII, 406–529; XII, 36–171; but V and XII have been artificially separated from each other and the epigrams of Meleager and earlier poets in IX belong to those in VI.

flower of boys to Kypris.' The echo in the early lines of the early lines in the garland of poets suggests that this is a corresponding conclusion, a wreath of boys, matching the wreath of poets. Finally, after this balancing conclusion, the collection is ended by the *Koronis* poem, which is interesting as being the first of its kind, *A.P.* XII, 257: 'The *Koronis* which announces the end of the race, most faithful guardian of the written pages, I say that Meleager completed the task of collecting from all the poets into one and rolled them up into this book, and plaited with flowers this poetic wreath for Diokles, to keep memory alive for ever; and I, twisted in curls like a snake's back, sit enthroned by the end of his learning.' Catullus and his successors took over from Meleager this new idea, that the actual physical appearance of the book is a subject for poetry.

Within these boundaries Meleager seems to have divided the poems by subjects (the love poems have later been divided between the fifth and twelfth books of our Anthology) and within the subjects it is generally an association of ideas which leads from one poem to the next. It follows that his own poems are largely literary remodellings of earlier themes, written for insertion at suitable places in the garland. He is an extremely accomplished poet, and though his sources are very often clear he uses them with great dexterity to make a poem which rings sincere. Much more than Antipater he has caught the spirit of Early Alexandrian symposion poetry, and he therefore models his poems most often on Asklepiades, Poseidippos, and Kallimachos, but Antipater, Alkaios of Messene, Anakreon, Erinna, Hedylos, Moschos, Rhianos, Theodoridas, Leonidas, and other poets whose names we may not know but whose poems he preserved in the Garland also moved him to imitation. Outside the anthology, the group of poems in which Meleager threatens to take vengeance on the child Eros (*A.P.* V, 177–9) recall Bion's Aphrodite taking Eros to the music-master as well as Moschos' runaway love (*A.P.* IX, 440), and Wifstrand has very interestingly found two reminiscences (*A.P.* V, 191; XII, 83) of that lugubrious composition generally known as the Grenfell song in which a woman bewails her lover's desertion:[1] it is perhaps the only link between Meleager and the world of drama and popular entertainment.

[1] Wifstrand, 62–3. Cf. above, p. 127.

A few examples will give some idea of his technique.[1] *A.P.* V, 8: 'Holy night and lamp, we both chose no other witnesses but you to our oaths; and he swore that he would love me and I swore that I would never leave him. You listened to both. Now he says those oaths are written in water, and you see him in the embrace of others.' This follows in our Anthology, as presumably in Meleager's Garland, a poem by Kallimachos on the worthlessness of a lover's oath and a poem by Asklepiades to a lamp which witnessed a faithless girl's oath that she would come. Meleager combines the two themes into a new poem. *A.P.* V, 136: 'Pour, and again say, again, again say "For Heliodora", mix the sweet name with the unmixed wine. And yesterday's myrrh-drenched wreath tie on my head in memory of her. The rose likes lovers, it is weeping because it sees that she is elsewhere and not in my arms.' The sources are not so near here, whether they were in Meleager's anthology or not; the beginning comes from Kallimachos (*Ep.* 29 = *A.P.* XII, 51): 'Pour and again say "For Diokles",' and the weeping rose is a variation on Asklepiades (*A.P.* V, 145). Again he combines the two themes into a new whole. An epigram by either Asklepiades or Poseidippos (*A.P.* XII, 77) has the conceit that a boy is so lovely that Kypris could not distinguish him from Eros: Meleager uses it twice for Antiochos (78, and 54), and develops the idea further (on lines indicated by Kallimachos' poem on Berenike as the fourth Grace (*Ep.* 51 = *A.P.* V, 146) and by the epigrams on Praxiteles' Eros (*A.P.* XVI, 167, 204)) by introducing a boy called Praxiteles so that Praxiteles the boy, Eros, and Praxiteles the sculptor form the terms of two equations: in the first poem (*A.P.* XII, 56) Praxiteles the sculptor made a statue of Eros, but now Eros has made a living statue of himself, Praxiteles; the second poem is more subtle (*A.P.* XII, 57): 'Praxiteles, the ancient sculptor, made a dainty statue, soulless, dumb impression of beauty, informing the stone. Today's Praxiteles, bewitching living things, modelled the villain Eros in my heart. Or perhaps he only has the same name and his deeds are greater, changing the shape not of stone but of the

---

[1] Many more are given by Wifstrand, op. cit., 40 ff. My few examples are deliberately chosen to show how Meleager takes off from Early Hellenistic epigrams which have been discussed above in their context; cf. pp. 51, 174. On the lamp epigrams, cf. now W. Ludwig, *M.H.* 19, 1962, 156 f.

spirit in my breast. May he kindly mould my ways, that having formed my soul within me he may occupy it as a temple of Eros.' In our Anthology Kallimachos' epitaph on himself (*Ep.* 35 = *A.P.* VII, 415) is immediately followed by a two-line epitaph: 'Stranger, I hold Meleager, son of Eukrates, who mixed sweet-speaking Graces with the Muses'. Although the poem is anonymous it is surely Meleager's own response to Kallimachos, from which he developed the three longer autobiographical epigrams which we have discussed already. Finally, Antipater's riddling epitaphs (*A.P.* VII, 423-7) inspired Meleager to flank them with two more, one on himself (421) and one on Antipater (428), whom he, probably wrongly, interprets as a poet of love, who died because he fell when he was drunk: this must presumably be regarded as a compliment; truthfully or not, Antipater is depicted as a new Anacreon.

The term classicism was used to describe Moschos' *Europe* and contemporary Alexandrian art. The same term is not inept for the sophisticated and charming use which the second- and first-century Asiatic epigrammatists make of traditional material. The vast majority of the poems so far discussed have drawn on material within the Anthology. Meleager's lament for Heliodora uses the traditional technique of lament, as we see it for instance, in Bion's lament for Adonis, which may be nearly contemporary, but here there is no doubt of his sincerity (*A.P.* VII, 476): 'Tears to you below the earth, Heliodora, I give, relic of love, in Hades, tears, cruel tears. On your much-wept tomb I pour the memory of desires, the memory of friendship. Piteously, piteously you, my dear one, even among the dead, I lament, Meleager, an empty grace to Acheron, Alas, where is the flower of my desire? Hades snatched it, snatched it. Dust dirties the fresh blossom. But I beseech you, Earth, who nurture all, gently her, whom all bewail, enfold, mother, in your embrace.' The effect is attained very largely by repetitions and near-repetitions, by the spondaic opening of the first three pentameters, by the repetition of long vowels, by alliteration, and by the five-syllable words ending the second and fourth pentameters. Meleager presumably expected his audience to know their *Odyssey*, and the reminiscence of Odysseus' mother (XI, 202 f.) in the *philophrosyne* of the second pentameter and of Nausikaa (V I, 157) in the *thalos* of the fourth hexameter is intentional: his grief is of the same kind as the grief which killed Odysseus' mother and Heliodora's beauty was like the beauty of the young Nausikaa.

The *Palatine Anthology* (IX, 363) ascribes to Meleager a poem of twenty-three lines in hexameters, describing the country in spring. Stadtmüller in his edition proposes to give it to Nikander, but it has none of the learned vocabulary which Nikander employs even in his descriptions of the country (e.g. *Ther.* 21 f.), and the traditional ascription to Meleager should be upheld. Winter is gone, the grass and flowers are growing, the herdsman is piping in the mountains, the sailors have taken to the sea, the ivy-wreathed dancers worship Dionysos, the bees are making honey, and the birds are singing: 'if there is joy in the leaves and flowers and the earth teems, if the shepherd pipes, and the woolly flocks are happy, and the sailors sail, if Dionysos dances and the birds sing and the bees travail, how should the singer fail to sing a fair song in spring?' It is a pretty poem which recalls on the one hand the pastoral reliefs of contemporary art (and here undoubtedly the countrymen are real contemporaries) and on the other the long tradition of country scenes in Greek poetry, particularly the *parodos* of Euripides' *Phaethon* (773 N) and the dawn descriptions of Early Alexandrian poetry. In that sense it is Neo-classical.[1]

Philodemos of Gadara would surely have had some of his poems in Meleager's Garland if his work had been known to his fellow-townsman. This is one argument for putting the Garland as early as possible and supposing that Philodemos' epigrams may not have been published until he reached Italy. He was a pupil of Zeno of Sidon in Athens in the early years of the first century and came to Italy between 80 and 70, where he became the friend of Piso. His epigrams are on traditional lines and he lacks the passion of Meleager. He has instead a light realistic touch, which somewhat recalls Kallimachos: the unfaithful wife complains that her lover only wants to sit about doing nothing (*A.P.* V, 120), a girl complains of the contrast between her lover's words and behaviour (*A.P.* V, 306), a man succeeds or fails in picking up a girl (*A.P.* V, 46, 308).[2]

---

[1] Cf. above, p. 70.

[2] This irony seems to me to be shown in the last two lines of IX, 570, which should not be cut out.

So he charmingly puns on his own name (*A.P.* V, 115): because he is called Philodemos, he has been in love with five different ladies called Demo. In another poem (*A.P.* XII, 173) he chooses Demo the virgin in preference to the hetaira Thermion, because, like Kallimachos, he despises what is ready to hand. Another twist is given to this idea in *A.P.* XI, 34, where he rejects a drinking party with a hetaira for a virgin who will keep her nest.

Very few of his poems give an indication of place or date. But a pretty prayer to sea-gods and Thracian Zephyr asks for his safe-conduct to Athens, presumably on his way from Asia (*A.P.* VI, 349). One of his ladies, whom he describes with a detail worthy of Dioskorides, is an Italian called Flora: she cannot sing Sappho, but then even Perseus loved the Indian Andromeda (*A.P.* V, 132). It is Celtic snow which chills him when he prays to Kypris to waft him into the haven of Naias (*A.P.* X, 21), a lady who had saved him from a more exigent lover (*A.P.* V, 107). At the age of thirty-seven (*A.P.* XI, 41) white hair announces the approach of wisdom, but he still likes music, talk, and love: only he prays that Xanthippe may be the *Koronis* of his madness. He quotes 'white hair announces the approach of wisdom' in another poem (*A.P.* V, 112): 'when it was the right time to play, I played. Now that it is no longer, I will seize on better thoughts.' Where in this sequence, the poem to Piso (*A.P.* XI, 44) should be put is not clear: he invites Piso to celebrate Epikouros' birthday simply with him, abandoning rich living for talk better than the *Odyssey*: 'but if you turn your eyes on us, Piso, our feast will be rich instead of simple'.

How much of the love-life of this distinguished Epicurean philo-sopher was real and how much literary fiction inspired by the irony of Kallimachos' epigrams, we cannot know. He portrays himself very much as Horace portrays himself in the Odes.

If Philodemos looks forward to Horace, Erykios of Kyzikos looks forward to Virgil in one poem. The epitaph (*A.P.* VII, 368) on an Athenian woman, captured by Sulla in 86 and sold into captivity in Rome, who then died in Kyzikos, could have been written about the middle of the century. The scathing pseudo-epitaph (*A.P.* VII, 377) on Parthenios as a bad poet and a foolish critic of Homer gives a rather earlier date.[1] Why Parthenios was so violently attacked, we do not know. For us he is a figure of great interest because he was taken to Italy and his influence can be traced on Roman poets. Perhaps his elegies on his friends seemed too original. Most of Erykios' poems are on traditional themes: one (*A.P.* VI, 96) on the well-worn theme of the dedication of an animal's horns to Pan begins 'Glaukon and Korydon, who herd cattle in the mountains, Arkadians both'. Virgil must have remembered this when he wrote *Arcades ambo* in an *Eclogue* (VII, 4) in which one of the goatherds is called Corydon and they sing of offering the horns of a stag to Diana. For Erykios, living at Kyzikos in the orbit of Pergamon, Arcadia is the country from which Telephos brought the cult of Dionysos, whose satyrs were *boukoloi*, neatherds, the prototypes of human mystics. His Glaukon and Korydon belonged to that world. How did Virgil interpret them?

---

[1] On Parthenios, see below, p. 305. Pfeiffer, *C.Q.* 37, 1943, 30 dates his transference to Italy 65 B.C. Erykios' dialogue epigram on a rustic Herakles (IX, 237) has been interpreted by Roux, *R. Phil.* 37, 1963, 87.

## CHAPTER X

# *Mainland Greece*

◆

The strong moral flavour which appears in the *Phainomena* of Aratos can be seen also in other poets of the third century, particularly those who have some relation to Stoic or Cynic philosophers. Kleanthes[1] was in fact head of the Stoic school from Zeno's death in 263 to his own death in 232; his inclusion here as a poet is due chiefly to his hymn to Zeus. One other fragment (fr. 4) is worth quoting, because it shows a kind of ethical pride equal to and perhaps influenced by the literary pride of Kallimachos: 'Do not look at reputation if you want to be wise nor fear the uncritical and shameless speech of the many. The multitude has no intelligent judgment, nor just nor honourable; only among few men would you find this.' The hexameter hymn to Zeus is in traditional hymn form with invocation (1–6), ground (7–31), and prayer (32–9). Much of the language is traditional, but it is a Stoic god who is clothed in this traditional form. In the second line Zeus steers everything by law (*nomos*). In the third line Kleanthes quotes Aratos: 'For from thee we come by race', and whatever the exact text of the end of the line may be it certainly contained the sentiment expressed by Tennyson as 'we are but broken lights of Thee'. The ground starts 'All this universe circling round the earth obeys thee and willingly accepts thy rule', and we remember the sad story that Kleanthes said that the Greeks ought to prosecute Aristarchos of Samos for impiety, because he assumed that the heavens stood still and the earth went round, revolving on its own axis. But appreciation of modern science was not to be expected from a Stoic.[2] The traditional thunderbolt of Zeus becomes for Kleanthes the Stoic fire which makes the universe take shape according to a common formula permeating the whole. In the world of human affairs Zeus makes a unity of good and evil

---

[1] Texts in Powell, op. cit., 227 f.; Commentary: Wilamowitz, *Hell. Dicht.*, 257; Zuntz, *Rh. Mus.* 94, 1951, 337; *H.S.C.P.* 63, 1958, 289; Stark, *Maia*, 15, 1963, 263.

[2] Von Arnim, *Stoicorum Veterum Fragmenta*, no. 500.

(the Stoic reconciliation of opposites). Men do not see the common law of god but pursue reputation or gain or pleasure, unaware that they are really pursuing the reverse of these things. (The colouring here comes partly from Zeus' speech in the first book of the *Odyssey* and partly from Solon's elegy.) 'But Zeus, giver of all, dark-clouded, lord of the thunderbolt, save men from the sorrows of ignorance, which, father, scatter from their souls and grant that they may attain judgment, trusting to which thou steerest all things with justice, that being honoured we may requite thee with honour, praising thy works continually, as a mortal should, for there is no greater privilege for men or gods than to praise in justice the common law.' In this last passage, as in Aratos' poem, the reminiscence of Hesiod is clear, and this is a traditional Greek ethic given a new Stoic setting. It is good hymn-writing by a competent poet with real religious feeling.

Not unnaturally his solemnity aroused the mockery of comic poets. Arkesilaos,[1] who was head of the Academy, excluded Baton from his school because he had mocked Kleanthes in a comedy; a reconciliation followed. We have a little more evidence that comedy was occasionally still satirical: Euphron (fr. 11 K) put a cook on the stage, who claimed to be the pupil of a cook who had deceived Nikomedes of Bithynia, and later in the third century Epinikos (fr. 1 K), who was probably an actor as well as a poet, brought on Mnesimachos, the historian of Antiochos III the Great, to give a parody of his artificial and affected style. Sositheos,[2] the tragic poet of the Alexandrian Pleiad, also caused displeasure by the line: 'whom the folly of Kleanthes drives like oxen' (4 N). Presumably this came in a satyr-play produced in Athens.

Kleanthes was a professional philosopher. The three other poets who seem to me to show something of the same moralizing temperament are in no sense professionals, and their inclination is perhaps more to the Cynics than to the Stoics. They are Leonidas of Tarentum, Euphorion of Chalkis, and Kerkidas of Megalopolis. Leonidas was one of the most prolific and popular writers of epigrams as the many imitations of his style show. The case for mentioning him here is that, as far as they can be localized, his poems show an acquaintance

---

[1] Plut. *Mor.* 55c.  [2] On Sositheos, cf. above, p. 129.

with mainland Greece and even with the East Aegean; it seems likely therefore that he left his Western birthplace early. His style and his general outlook seem to me to owe something to Timon of Phleious. Mr Gow[1] has destroyed the normal early dating by removing the Pyrrhos poem (*A.P.* VI, 130) from Leonidas and suggests that he was a contemporary of Dioskorides. He lived at any rate for some considerable time. *A.P.* VII, 715: 'I lie far from Italy and from Taras my home. This is more bitter to me than death. Such is the life of wanderers, no life. But the Muses love me; in return for miseries I have honey sweet. The name of Leonidas does not sink. The very gifts of the Muses herald me to every sun.' As Gabathuler says, the poem is probably meant for the end of a collection of poems like the similar pseudo-epitaphs of Kallimachos and Poseidippos.[2] There is something of the Cynic in Leonidas' insistence on his poverty: VII, 736, 'Be not destroyed, O man, as you drag out your vagrant life, rolling from land to land; be not destroyed, even if a hut is your shelter, which a little fire warms with its kindling . . .'; VI, 302, 'Away from my hut, darkling mice; in no wise can Leonidas' poor bin feed mice. The old man is independent if he has salt and two buns . . .'; VI, 300, 'Laphria, welcome this thank-offering from wandering, poor, small-binned Leonidas, rich cakes and well-treasured olive and this green off-bough fig, and have the five-berried fragment of a well-wined cluster and this cup-bottom libation. And if, as you saved me from sickness, so you rescue me also from hateful poverty, welcome a goat-sacrificer.' The literal translation of this last poem is designed to show Leonidas' love of strange compounds, which are amusing in Timon of Phleious but harsh and violent in this kind of poetry. If the emendation Laphria is right, this poem is localized in Central Greece by the worship of Artemis Laphria.[3]

He wandered far from Tarentum and he reached Central Greece. We can be a little more precise. Thebes is indicated by the musical daughters of Antigeneidas (V, 206); Sikyon by the dedication to

---

[1] *C.Q.* 8, 1958, 113. My debt to this article will be obvious all through.

[2] Gabathuler, op. cit., 68. Cf. above, pp. 58, 107.

[3] Wilamowitz, *Hell. Dicht.*, ii, 109; Nilsson, *G.G.R.*, i, 454 f. But note that it was already corrupted by the time of Gaetulicus (VI, 190).

Pan of Akroria;[1] Arcadia by a dedication to Pan on the Arcadian cliffs (VI, 188); Messenia by a dedication to Athene Koryphasia (VI, 129). References to the river Maeander (VI, 110) and to the Aphrodite Anadyomene in Kos (XVI, 182) suggest that he reached the eastern side of the Aegean (the phraseology of the epigram on the Aphrodite also recalls Theokritos, XV, 83). Any sort of precise dating is more difficult. The following seem to me the more valuable indications: Mr Gow places the poem on Myron's cow, which was in Athens, (IX, 719) as the earliest of the series and therefore earlier than Dioskorides' poem, and the poem on Aratos' *Phainomena* (IX, 25) well after the publication of Aratos; it must indeed be later than Kallimachos' epigram (27 Pf.) since the first line is modelled on Kallimachos; it is certainly not earlier than 270. Several other echoes of Kallimachos have been seen. Single word echoes are unsafe,[2] but it is tempting to suppose that the picture of the attractive old lady Platthis (VII, 726) owes something to the *Hekale*, which was probably not written before 265.[3] The relation of the poems about Hipponax (VII, 408) and Anakreon (XVI, 306–7) to Kallimachos is a little complicated: Hipponax is a wasp, who criticized even his parents and can wound even in Hades. This pseudo-epitaph is unaffected by the kindlier picture of Hipponax in Theokritos and late Kallimachos,[4] and it is unnecessary to suppose that the image of the wasp was borrowed from Kallimachos' *Grapheion* (fr. 380), where it is used of Archilochos; the wasp as a symbol of anger is as old as Homer; this poem is perhaps unlikely to be later than 260. On the other hand the Anakreon poem (XVI, 306) seems to have borrowed *methyplex* from another poem of Kallimachos (fr. 544), which mentioned Archilochos (it is unlikely that both poets independently distilled Archilochos' 'thunderbolted with wine' into the same word and Kallimachos used the new word of Archilochos himself, so that Kallimachos is likely to have been the earlier). The *dinotos* of the Anakreon poem may come from Apollonios Rhodios (3, 44) rather than direct from Homer; and the coupling of *adrania* with Old Age in VI, 296, also shows acquaintance with Apollonios Rhodios

---

[1] *P. Oxy.* 662; Page, *G.L.P.*, no. 107, 3; Gow, op. cit., 123.
[2] E.g. VII, 448 with Kall. *Ep.* 24/4; 295 with Kall. fr. 1, 6.
[3] Cf. above, p. 99.      [4] Cf. above, pp. 60, 100.

(2, 200). Finally the pseudo-epitaphs on a broken tomb (VII, 478, 480) seem to have been the inspiration of Theodoridas' epitaph on Herakleitos (VII, 479),[1] which would date them before rather than after 250. Gow's contention that Leonidas is not one of the earliest Hellenistic epigrammatists is probably right, but I should be inclined to put his time range about 270/20. He seems to have known the work of Apollonios Rhodios and Kallimachos, and his poems are certainly in the tradition of Early Hellenistic epigram, including dedications, epitaphs, pastorals, poems on poets, and poems on works of art. The most obvious exclusion is the world of the symposion, which only enters his work incidentally and the one love poem is almost certainly wrongly attributed.[2]

His own contribution is partly what I have termed roughly a Cynic outlook, partly (and connected with this) an interest in poor men, which also chimes in with the realistic old figures of Hellenistic art,[3] and partly style, particularly the freely coined compound adjectives, which are used among other things to describe the dedications of poor men. Lesky[4] describes this style as elevated into baroque, and there is perhaps an analogy with the violent style in Hellenistic art, which culminates in the Pergamene gigantomachy. What I have called the Cynic outlook appears not only in the autobiographical poems and in the well-disposed pseudo-epitaph on Diogenes (VII, 67) but also in the epitaph (or more probably pseudo-epitaph) on Gorgos, VII, 731: ' "Like a vine by its stake, I am now only held up by my stick. Death calls me to Hades. Don't be deaf, Gorgos. What more joy in three or four harvests under the sun?" So speaking without arrogance the old man shoved life away and came to the dwelling place of the majority.'[5] Leonidas may have remembered the story of Epicharmos and his old friends, which is preserved by Aelian (*V.H.* ii, 34) and derives from the late fourth-century literature about Epicharmos; they discussed whether they would like to live three, four, or five years more, but Epicharmos asked

---

[1] Cf. also VII, 731 (below) with 732, Theodoridas.

[2] V, 188; cf. Wilamowitz, *Hell. Dicht.*, I, 141. I also exclude VI, 154, 293 (see below), VII, 13, 19 (cf. Carrington, *Mnem.* 15, 1962, 173).

[3] Cf. above, p. 168.    [4] *Geschichte*[2], 791.

[5] On the word for harvests see Kall. fr. 44.

them why they squabbled about a few days when they were all in the sunset of life. Leonidas was no professional philosopher and can mock a Cynic when it suits him; the pseudo-epitaph on Sochares (VI, 298)[1] will serve as an example also of his method of describing poor craftsmen: 'Wallet and untanned goatskin gone hard and this stick for walking and scraperless flask and copperless purse and hat, covering of an impious head – these, when he died, Famine hung on a tamarisk bush as spoils from Sochares.'

The poem on Anakreon (XVI, 306) seems to describe a Hellenistic statue of an old derelict – loaded full with wine, twisted above the decorated base, a swimming look in his lecherous eyes, his himation trailing down to his ankles, one shoe lost in his drunken stumbling, lyre in hand and singing of Bathyllos or Megisteus: 'But father Dionysos, guard him. For it is not right that Bacchos should make a Bacchic servant fall.' Certainly Leonidas is thinking of a statue of some kind, and Schefold[2] has plausibly suggested that he has re-thought the well-known heroic fifth-century statue of Anakreon into the shape of a drunk old man. Not all Leonidas' poems have this acerbity, and in contrast one pretty pastoral dedication may be quoted, IX, 326: 'Cold water leaping from the double rock, hail; and pastoral images of the Nymphs and drinking places of the fountains and your countless dolls, maidens, wetted in the water, hail. Aristoklees, the wayfarer here, I give this present with which I dipped and thrust away my thirst.' Leonidas' poems were quickly disseminated and had a considerable influence, particularly on Antipater of Sidon.[3]

Euphorion[4] was born at Chalkis in Euboea in 276/5; he went to be head of the library at Antioch during the reign of Antiochos III the Great (222/187). As he must therefore have been at least fifty-three when he went to Antioch, his poetry may be regarded as Greek rather than Asiatic, and some of it was certainly written in Greece. He is said to have studied philosophy with Lakydes

---

[1] The other poem on Sochares (VI, 293) I suspect to have been moulded on this poem by another poet, who gave it a new twist at the end.

[2] *Bildnisse*, 204.     [3] Cf. p. 205.

[4] Texts in J. U. Powell, op. cit., 28; Page, *G.L.P.*, no. 121; P. *Oxy.* 2219–20; *P.S.I.* 1390.

Q

and Prytanis and poetry with Archeboulos. Lakydes succeeded Arkesilaos as head of the Academy in 241/40, but Euphorion's studies need not necessarily be put as late as this. Archeboulos (probably from Thebes rather than Thera) gave his name to a long Aeolic metre which was used by Kallimachos in 270 (fr. 228); he was therefore presumably an Early Hellenistic poet. Euphorion was a favourite of Nikaia, the wife of Alexander, king of Euboea. If the royal title can be used for dating, this would have been after 250, when Alexander declared his independence of Antigonos, and before 247 when he died.[1] This Alexander was probably the addressee of the poem called after him. The *Apollodoros*, *Demosthenes*, *Hippomedon*, *Lament for Protagoras*, and *Polychares* may also have been named after contemporaries.[2] The *Alexander*, at least, is likely to have been written in Greece about 250.

The echoes of Alexandrian poetry in some cases certainly show that texts had reached Greece by the time that Euphorion was writing. The ancient commentator says that Euphorion (fr. 145) knew from Apollonios Rhodios that the statue of the mother of the gods was made of vine-wood, and Apollonios (2, 735) placed a cave of Hades on the Black Sea, where Euphorion made Herakles bring Kerberos to earth (fr. 37); it must however be admitted that where Euphorion's version of the Argonaut story survives (e.g. fr. 4, 76, 79), he differs from Apollonios, although this may be conscious divergence.[3] A number of agreements in subject matter have been noted with Kallimachos[4] in the *Arai*, the *Dionysos*, the *Hippomedon*, and other poems. It is more difficult to find certain echoes of language: Euphorion (fr. 9, 11) uses *empelateira* in its root sense of 'visitor', Kallimachos uses it in the derived sense of 'hetaira' (fr. 527), here we may hesitate whether to say conscious divergence or no connection. That both should call Boreas the son-in-law of Erech-

---

[1] *C.A.H.* VII, 221 f.

[2] The *Theoridas* (fr. 3) seems to have been a work of criticism like the *Hypomnemata* (Ath. 495c; Schol. Ar. *Av.* 1377). It is unjustifiable to emend to Theodoridas in order to identify him with the author of *A.P.* VII, 406.

[3] The verbal echo of Apollonios Rhodios 1, 389, in fr. 139 is too slight to build on.

[4] See Pfeiffer's index.

theus[1] (in a slightly different form) is hardly significant. But that both should use *ear* or *eiar*[2] in the sense of blood, and the rare verb *olopsato* with the noun *korse* is hardly due to chance.[3] A strange use of *charon* as a substantive for a lion (fr. 84) is shared with Kallimachos (fr. 339) and Lykophron (*Al.* 455). Euphorion agrees on various points of mythology with Lykophron or Alexander of Aetolia or both: Hektor is the son of Apollo (fr. 56), Odysseus has a dolphin on his shield (fr. 67), Iphigeneia is the daughter of Helen and Theseus (fr. 90), Amphilochos and Mopsos had a contest in Cilicia (fr. 98). In the description of Mounitos, son of Laodike and Akamas, Euphorion (fr. 58) seems to remember the language of Lykophron (*Al.* 495), and therefore even where we are told that the Alexandrian poets were borrowing from Stesichoros or Ibykos, it is likely that Euphorion was using the later poets rather than their originals. Both Lykophron and Alexander of Aetolia had crossed to Alexandria while Euphorion was a child, if not before he was born, and the *Alexandra* at least was written in Alexandria and would only have been known to him from texts. But Lykophron like Euphorion was a native of Chalkis, and was one of the circle of Menedemos of Eretria. Euphorion therefore grew up into a mainland tradition of learned poetry; an obvious link with Alexandria was his exact contemporary Eratosthenes, the pupil of Kallimachos, who studied with Arkesilaos and Ariston of Chios and only left Athens when Ptolemy III Euergetes summoned him in 246 to take over the library. Both Euphorion (fr. 22)[4] and Eratosthenes (fr. 17) wrote on the death of Hesiod, but the relation between the two poems is unknown.

Even now that longer stretches of Euphorion are known from papyrus, it is difficult to form any idea of his poetry. Certainly it was learned poetry in difficult language, which often dealt with obscure

[1] Euphorion, *P. Oxy.* 2220; Kallimachos fr. 321.

[2] Euphorion fr. 40; Kallimachos fr. 177/22.

[3] Euphorion, Page, no. 121b 31; Kallimachos, *Hymn* III, 77–8. Cf. perhaps also Euphorion, fr. 134, with Kallimachos, fr. 43/41.

[4] To fr. 22, 22b have been added fr. 87–9. Fr. 87 about the Graces of Orchomenos may belong; fr. 88 about people whose faces were white (or whitened) like corpses is a wild guess; fr. 89 about a crow croaking is possible; cf. Pausanias IX, 38, 3. On Eratosthenes, cf. above, p. 136.

legends. When he wants to say a silver cup he calls it an 'Alybeid kelebe' (fr. 8) and the reader must remember that Homer (*Il.* 2, 857) called Alybe the source of silver. A typical fragment (fr. 94) describes the pursuit of Orestes: 'Forth frightful on his fated path to the white hill the granddaughters of Phorkys drove him, the Eumenides, their tresses wreathed with narcissus'. Probably the poet's precise purpose cannot be solved without the context: perhaps he simply wants to awaken a memory both of the prologue of Aeschylus' *Eumenides* and of the Kolonos chorus of Sophocles' *Oedipus Coloneus* (670 f.) The adjective 'frightful' is the Homeric adjective for Furies, so the first line is a traditional description of Orestes. 'White' translates the adjective *arges* which is only used of a place in Sophocles' *Oedipus Coloneus*, so that indubitably Orestes is going to Kolonos. But the Furies are 'granddaughters of Phorkys', and this recalls the prologue of the *Eumenides*, because there the priestess thinks that the Furies are Gorgons and the Gorgons are daughters of Phorkys in Hesiod; why Euphorion makes the Furies 'granddaughters' rather than 'daughters' is not clear, unless he simply wants to avoid identifying them with the Graiai and the Gorgons. Finally, the 'white hill' is firmly marked as Kolonos because in the last line the Furies become 'Eumenides wreathed with narcissus'; in Sophocles they are worshipped as Eumenides at Kolonos and narcissus is the ancient crown of the great goddesses (*O.C.* 683). Euphorion is not identifying the Eumenides with the two great goddesses; the Eumenides who live near them wear their flower. Without the context we cannot say whether his only purpose is to call up memories of two great passages of tragedy or whether he is suggesting that the Furies of Klytaimnestra became the kindly goddesses of Kolonos who received Oidipous. Probably the simpler explanation is right; as he has two incompatible accounts of the death of Orion (fr. 101, 103), he was probably not interested in systematizing theology.

This is certainly learned poetry. He lacks the lightness of touch which makes Kallimachos so attractive, and he lacks the vision which makes Apollonios' scenes clear and alive. On the other hand, B. A. van Groningen[1] has praised his euphony, and tricky though such judgments are, a number of fragments show alliteration, asson-

---

[1] *La Poésie verbale grecque*, 1953.

ance, internal rhyme and the like to a degree which can hardly be fortuitous.[1] Professor van Groningen has also given figures for his metrical technique, which show a marked preference for certain types of line, particularly lines with spondaic endings and lines composed of a small number of long words. Certain effects of sound seem therefore to have been consciously sought.

Only three poems give any hint of his composition. *Curses or the cup-thief* (fr. 8–9, Page, no. 121a) seems to consist of a series of curses on the man who stole his 'Alybeid kelebe'. May he (or she) suffer like Hersa when she opened the box with Erichthonios in it, like the wanderers who were dashed to pieces by Skeiron, like women (or men) killed suddenly by the bow of Artemis, like Askalaphos carrying his boulder for ever in Hell. If, as seems likely, Hersa and Skeiron are meant to recall Kallimachos' *Hekale*, it is probable that each curse is meant to recall a passage of poetry; the reference to Artemis may simply be meant to recall Homer; who told the story of Askalaphos we do not know.

The *Dionysos* remains desperately unclear in spite of the papyrus fragments (*P. Oxy.* 2219–20): the book fragments show that Hera drove Dionysos mad (fr. 14), that the action took place partly in Attica (fr. 16–17), partly in Argos (fr. 18), and perhaps also in Lydia (fr. 15).[2] The papyrus fragments show that the poem contained more than a hundred lines. The first papyrus fragment (*P. Oxy.* 2220 with remains of over twenty lines) seems to be set in Attica, as they mention Oreithyia, Aphidna, Herakles and a lion, which is probably the lion of Kithairon.[3] What all this has to do with Dionysos is not clear, but then the transition to Dionysos comes: the sense here seems to be 'But of Dionysos, who gave Melainai to the Athenians ... the priests of Dodona will tell'. Then after about eight lines the text resumes (*P. Oxy.* 2219) with the Maenads of Nemea and the sack of Argos because of the resistance of Perseus to Dionysos (thus combining the old fragments 18 and 86; possibly also 176 belonged here). As can be seen from this summary, the

---

[1] E.g. fr. 2, 9, 75, 87, 94, 112, 122. Page, no. 121.

[2] There is no valid reason for connecting fr. 13 on the sparagmos in Delphi with this poem.

[3] So Lobel, comparing Apollodoros, ii, 4, 9.

connections are completely unclear and each story seems to be cut quite short. The mention of Oreithyia may, as we have seen, recall the *Hekale* (fr. 321); the madness inflicted on Dionysos by Hera is known to Euripides. Melainai must be connected with Melanthos; the Melanthos story is first attested here but must be an old story told to explain the cult of Dionysos Melanaigis. Perseus attacking the Maenads has been recognized in art of the fifth century and earlier.[1] This poem too seems to be a sequence of short sections recalling earlier poems.

The *Thrax*[2] ends with the belief that a murderer will suffer in Hell and his victim will receive the immortality of fame. The allusion seems to be contemporary, and it is suggested that the poem is a series of imprecations on the murderer of a friend. The final section begins with a prayer to Ares to send Peace, Themis, and Justice to men (this may be described as a Hellenistic variation on a well-known Hesiodic theme, just as the contemporary Cretan poet Rhianos (fr. 1 Powell) writes in much simpler language a variation on the Homeric theme of human folly and Ate). Justice is inescapable, and Euphorion illustrates this by two mythological examples very allusively told in the nine lines before his statement that the murderer will suffer in Hell. It is a reasonable suggestion that the prayer to Ares implies a state of war, and may carry an allusion to Nikaia's troubles after the death of Alexander in 247, but primarily the passage marks a transition from private to public crime. Before this came the story of Apriate, a Lesbian girl who refused the advances of Trambelos, the son of Telamon, and wished him an evil marriage for which she quoted mythological examples; she then leapt into the sea and was apparently saved by dolphins, but Trambelos was killed by Achilles. Earlier still Euphorion had at least alluded to Krisa, Tereus, and the daughters of Pelias; and before that he told the story of Klymenos' incest with his daughter Harpalyke, her murder of his son, her transformation into an owl, and his suicide. The book fragments add the death of Amphiaraos (fr. 23), Kerberos (fr. 24), the giants killed by Herakles and buried in

---

[1] Madness of Dionysos: E. *Cycl.* 3. Dionysos Melanaigis, cf. Pickard-Cambridge, *Dithyramb etc.*[2], 120. Perseus and Maenads, cf. *Lustrum* 1956, 104; Beazley, *A.B.V.*, 373, no. 174; K. Schauenburg, *Perseus in der Kunst* 1960, 93, 139.

[2] *P.S.I.* 1390 with full bibliography; Page, *G.L.P.*, no. 121b; Powell fr. 23-9.

Mykonos (fr. 25), and the revenge taken by Herakles on the Hippo-koontids for the murder of Oionos (fr. 29). These stories too fit into the general scheme of punishment of sinners: Euphorion may have adopted a version in which the arrival of Kerberos was a punish-ment for Eurystheus: two other fragments describe Kerberos, one is ascribed to the *Xenios* (fr. 37) but the other (fr. 51) may belong here. If, as Körte suggests, the poem was only one hundred and fifty lines long it must have been packed with mythological allusion, strung on the thread – sinners are punished, therefore this murderer will suffer. (It was perhaps a reflection of Euphorion's taste for concentrated mythological examples which caused Eumenes II and Attalos II to celebrate their love for their mother by nineteen sculptured illustrations of mythical and historical dutiful sons).

The central thread of this poem and of the *Curses* is a belief in justice, and this Hesiodic outlook is shared by Euphorion with Rhianos, with Aratos, with Kleanthes, and to some extent with Leonidas. This was not what made Euphorion survive; his sur-vival depended rather on his exotic learning and the euphonic characteristics of his poetry.

Euphorion is the subject of an epitaph by Theodoridas of Syracuse, *A.P.* VII, 406: 'Euphorion, master of excessive poetry, lies by these Peiraean legs. But do you pay the mystic an offering of pome-granate or apple or myrtle. For when he was alive he loved.' Diametrically opposed interpretations have been given of this poem:[1] either it is a genuine epitaph, praising Euphorion as a poet, attesting his grave by the Long Walls, and speaking of him as a mystic in the same terms as Philikos and others,[2] or it is satirical – 'excessive' means not 'finely wrought' but 'extravagant', Peiraean is a pun on *peira* in its sense of seduction, the fruits are sexual symbols and the addressee is his elderly mistress, Nikaia, the wife of Alexan-der of Euboea. The Suda is clear that Euphorion died in the East, whether at Apameia or Antioch, and we have no evidence that he returned to Greece. The tradition of satirical pseudo-epitaphs on poets had already been started by Aratos' epitaph on Diotimos.[3]

On the other hand it must be admitted that the satire is much less

---

[1] Cf. Gabathuler, op. cit., 92; Geffcken, *R.E.*, 15, 2247; Maas, *R.E.*, 5a, 1804.
[2] Cf. above, p. 129.      [3] Cf. above, p. 27.

obvious than in Theodoridas' poem in mixed iambic metre on Mnasalkas of Sikyon (*A.P.* XIII, 21): 'The tomb of Mnasalkas of Plataiai, the writer of elegy. His Muse was a fragment of the modelling of Simonides, and empty in noise and an inflated dithyramb-crucible. He is dead; let us not shoot. If he were alive, he would be blowing it up to drum size.' The translation includes Mr Quincey's[1] convincing interpretation of κἀπιλακυθίστρια διθυραμβόχανα, which incidentally shows that Theodoridas knew Kallimachos' 'lekythising tragic muse' (fr. 215 Pf.), probably from the late *Iambus* XIII. But if Mnasalkas was melting down and blowing up a fragment, we do not want a fragment of a shoulder-blade (Quincey) or a fragment of papyrus (LSJ) but a fragment of a statue, which is in fact what the manuscript πλάθας means with a minimum change of accent. It is a pity that Theodoridas did not turn such admirable literary invective on Euphorion instead of attacking his private life, and we do not know how Mnasalkas incurred it. Did he perhaps forsake elegiac for lyric poetry and win a victory over Theodoridas, who was himself a dithyrambic poet (Ath. 699 f.)?

Theodoridas not only wrote a dithyramb called *Centaurs* and a song to Eros (Ath. 475 f.) but was also listed by the Suda among the *Ionikologoi*, the writers of light verse.[2] He came from the West, from Syracuse. The majority of his poems are simple and beautiful dedications and epitaphs in the Early Hellenistic manner. The poem on the skolopendra is located in Italy (VI, 222) and the poem on the shell in Sicily (VI, 224). He may have come to Greece early, and the two poems which pick up Leonidas may be a compliment to an earlier wanderer from the West. Neither of them copy the peculiarities of Leonidas' style; the open coffin by the roadside (VII, 479) is made more pointed because for Theodoridas it is the coffin of Herakleitos 'the divine dog who barked at the people'. The other (VII, 732) answers much more simply Leonidas' poem about the old man with a stick who committed suicide (VII, 731): 'You are gone, still unstaved, Kinesias, son of Hermolaos (?), to pay the debt you owe to Hades, still in old age completely perfect. Finding you a just debtor all-subduing Acheron will love you.' Here we have the normal practice of copying literary epigrams, but most of Theo-

---

[1] C.Q. 43, 1949, 42.     [2] Cf. above, p. 127.

doridas' poems read like true inscriptions: VII, 439, an epitaph for a young Aeolian, perhaps a Thessalian, 528 for Phainarete of Larissa, 529 for Dorotheos of Phthia. IX, 743 is also for Phthia: 'These cows are Thessalian. They stand by the porch of Athena Itonias, a fair gift. All bronze, twelve, the work of Phradmon, and all spoil from the stripped Illyrians.' Phradmon is known as a fifth-century sculptor and this may be a literary epigram on a classical work of art; but it may rather have been a real inscription for Phradmon's cows in their new position. All these poems are localized in Northern Greece, and Theodoridas must have lived there.

Mnasalkas of Sikyon, who was so roughly handled by Theodoridas to Wilamowitz' delight,[1] is perhaps known from an inscription at Oropos,[2] but this only tells us that he was made a proxenos for that city. He is a competent writer in the tradition of Anyte,[3] and he also knew Asklepiades and Kallimachos. He covers the usual range of dedications and epitaphs with, in addition, a single love poem. The love poem (XII, 138) appeals to a vine to wait to shed its leaves on Antileon when he goes to sleep under it; the idea comes from Asklepiades' appeal (V, 145) to a wreath, hanging over his beloved's door, to shed his tears on the young man's head.[4] A reference to Kallimachos is apparent in the pseudo-epitaph on Hesiod (VII, 54) 'whose glory is the greatest among men when men are judged by the touchstone of wisdom'.[5] Athenaeus (163a) preserves a poem which parodies Asklepiades' literary epitaph on Ajax (VII, 145), the same poem which was later elaborated by Antipater: in Asklepiades Virtue sits by the tomb of Ajax, mourning if the Achaeans prefer Deceit to her; Mnasalkas makes Virtue sit beside Pleasure, mourning if everybody prefers Enjoyment to her. The purpose of the poem is not clear, but presumably Mnasalkas has simply taken a poem on a particular heroic situation and converted it into general morality of Stoic flavour with a criticism of the Epicureans as allowing Virtue and Pleasure to sit together. The one poem which

---

[1] *Hell. Dicht.*, I, 138. Contrast Gow, *C.R.* 6, 1956, 91.

[2] *I.G.*, VII, 395.

[3] E.g. the shield dedications *A.P.* VI, 125, 128, 264; the locust poems, VII, 192, 194; and IX, 333, for which see Gow, loc. cit.

[4] Cf. above, p. 51.     [5] VI, 9 also recalls Kall. *Ep.* 37 Pf.

has reasonably been thought to have a political reference is the epitaph on fallen patriots written in a manner which goes back to Simonides (VII, 242): 'These, saving their country as it had the tearful yoke on its neck, were clothed in dark dust. They win the great praise of valour. Seeing them, let each citizen endure death for his country.' The occasion may have been the liberation of his native city in 251 by Aratos of Sikyon.

The intricacies of Aratos' politics, of his relations with the Achaean League, with Antigonos Gonatas, Antigonos Doson, and Philip V, with Alexander of Euboea, with Kleomenes of Sparta, and with the Ptolemies do not concern us. He stands out as a great and cultivated man, who was very much responsible for stability in the Peloponnese. He impinges on our subject in two ways, as a connoisseur of painting and as a friend of Kerkidas of Megalopolis. According to Plutarch (*Arat.* 12) 'Aratos found Ptolemy well-disposed towards him, because Aratos, who was a good judge of painting and collected works of the best artists, particularly Pamphilos and Melanthos, had sent a number of them to him'. The period is the reign of Euergetes and Aratos therefore appears as a collector half a century before the Attalids. Pamphilos and Melanthos were Old Masters since Pamphilos was painting before 388 and Melanthos in the reign of Philip of Macedon, i.e. about 350.[1] And the story establishes not only Aratos in Sikyon but also Ptolemy III as a collector of classical painting.

Aratos brought Sikyon into the Achaean League; his friendship with Kerkidas[2] was well established by the time of the complicated negotiations which brought Antigonos Doson (who succeeded the successor of Antigonos Gonatas in Macedonia) in on the side of the Achaeans with Aratos against Kleomenes and led to the defeat of Kleomenes at Sellasia in 221. In all this and in the subsequent political

---

[1] On the influence of Sikyonian painting in the Early Hellenistic age, cf. above, p. 22.

[2] Texts, J. U. Powell, op. cit., 201; Diehl, *Anth. Lyr.*[3], III, 141; A. D. Knox in the Loeb volume, *Theophrastus Characters*, 189; Commentary, D. R. Dudley, *History of Cynicism*, 74; F. W. Walbank, *C.Q.* 37, 1943, 10. It is impossible to believe that the flat and boring Choliambics 17-18 P, Knox 228, Diehl, *Anth. Lyr.*[3], III, 131 belong to Kerkidas.

settlement of Megalopolis Kerkidas played a leading part. He is said to have had the first two books of the *Iliad* buried with him and to have made a law that boys should learn the second book by heart. His poems are called *Meliamboi*, which presumably means satire in lyric metre; the metre consists of alternate blunt and pendant kola, and these kola can have either double or single-short rhythm, so that the whole makes a very free kind of dactylo-epitrite.[1] Timon had shown the comic use of compound adjectives in this kind of poetry, and Kerkidas follows him; in high poetry they belonged particularly to choral lyric, so that Kerkidas is parodying style as well as metre. Diogenes (fr. 1 P) is 'stick-carrying double-cloaked aithereater'; this fragment appears to be the end of a poem in which Diogenes' suicide ('For he was truly son of Zeus and heavenly dog') was contrasted with something else – presumably the disgusting adherence to life of an elderly hedonist.[2] He acclaims the Cynic here, and he shows Cynic realism in his poem on Love (fr. 5 P): there are said to be two winds which Eros can blow on us; if he blows from his right cheek, the ship of love can be steered by the modest rudder of Persuasion; but if he blows from his left cheek the whirlwinds and withering storms of Desire, the whole voyage is wave-tossed; 'Euripides[3] was right'; then after a break of some twelve lines, he goes on 'But Aphrodite from the Agora and caring for nothing, whenever you wish, whenever you want, there is neither fear nor confusion. Lay her for an obol and think you are the son-in-law of Tyndaros.' It is part of the style to use persuasive personifications like Modesty, Desires, Persuasion. The tradition also of quoting high literature (here Euripides) goes back to Simonides' quotation of Pittakos. But Kerkidas was genuinely interested in Homer, as we know, and he evidently prized his own poetry (fr. 7): 'Your heart in your breast is undaunted and unstirred by all the anxieties of the fat-flesh-eaters. Therefore no beauty ever escaped you, but all the tender cubs of the Muses were in your entrails, and you, my Soul, were a most excellent fisher and hunter of the Pierides.' This is a

---

[1] P. Maas, *Greek Metre*, 68.

[2] The very difficult and corrupt fr. 6 seems to describe such people 'shade-nurtured tribes' and 'pleasure-struck men'.

[3] Fr. 929a Snell.

difficult expression: it must somehow explain 'no beauty ever escaped you'; 'beauty' is therefore the object of the fishing and hunting, and the Muses are the patrons of his sport as Artemis is the patron of the chase; perhaps then the tender cubs of the Muses are not the quarry but the hounds. This is a poem written in old age and so parallel to the late poems of Leonidas and Poseidippos.[1] It breaks off when he seems to be promising himself a last successful hunt perhaps beyond the grave; was it from the end of this poem that Aelian (*V.H.* XIII, 20) derived the story that Kerkidas hoped to meet Pythagoras, Hekataios, Olympos, and Homer?

At least it is clear that he set great store by his poetry and presumably he hoped that his startling memorable verse would have the same sort of effect on the Megalopolitans as Solon had had on the Athenians. The very unclear fragments (fr. 8, 9) about the Stoics are certainly critical; they certainly attribute logic-chopping to the Stoics and 'Zenonian love' seems to be homosexual desire; Sphairos is mentioned, and Sphairos was a pupil of Zeno and Kleanthes, and helped Kleomenes to train the Spartan youth; Kerkidas could reasonably accuse the Stoics of Spartan vices as well as their own and would sharply distinguish the philosophy which was in the pay of the hated Spartans from his own Cynicism. Undoubtedly political is the long fragment (fr. 4); here the parallel to Solon's social poems is close, and Kerkidas also is dealing with a social crisis, sometime in the period of distress which preceded or succeeded the destruction of the city by Kleomenes of Sparta.[2] The poem is an appeal for human aid for human problems. Why does god give all the money to the wrong people? 'Has the eye of Justice a cast, and does Phaethon squint with a single pupil, and is bright Themis bedimmed?' (Hesiod's Dike and Themis are in his mind; to them he adds the sun (here Phaethon) as traditionally a recording angel). 'How are they still gods, who have neither sight nor hearing?' (this echoes the complaint of the Athenians who welcomed Demetrios Poliorketes; but deification of a Hellenistic king is not Kerkidas' solution). 'Yet the solemn lightning-gatherer in the midst of Olympos holds the scales aloft and never nods. And Homer said this in the *Iliad*: "He

---

[1] Cf. above, pp. 58, 218.

[2] See Walbank, loc. cit., on the various interpretations and datings.

inclines them, whenever the fated day is there for valiant men".'
(We have seen his technique of free quotation before in the poem
on Love.) 'Why then does the upright weighman never incline them
towards me? . . . To what gods or what sons of heaven should one
go to find one's deserts, when the son of Kronos, who begat us all,
shows himself the stepfather of some and the father of others? It is
better to leave this to the heaven-beaters. I expect they find it easy.'
(The 'heaven-beaters' are presumably the Stoics, and the whole
reference to Zeus is a criticism of Kleanthes' hymn, where a Zeus
clad in Homeric trappings can fit bad and good together to make a
world.) 'But let us care for Paian and Metados, for she is a goddess,
and Nemesis on Earth.' Here again Kerkidas is using the Hesiodic
technique of persuasive personification and the reader is meant to
remember that Aidos and Nemesis left the earth in Hesiod's Iron
Age (*Op.* 197). Kerkidas thinks rather of his trinity as forces which
are in men's own hands to apply, not as divine figures, daughters of
Zeus, as Hesiod said, or as stars in the sky, set there by Zeus, to remind and warn men, as Aratos said of Justice. Nemesis for Kerkidas
is not retribution but distribution; Metados is sharing, and Paian is
healing not in the literal medical sense but in the metaphorical sense
of helping people in distress. This is the noblest expression of Cynic
realism – the cure for human ills is in man's own hands – urged with
all the force of literary reminiscence, lyric metre, and violent style.

Professor Walbank has argued that Alkaios of Messene[1] was in
the same political tradition as Kerkidas and may even have met him
when Kerkidas was in exile after the destruction of Megalopolis.
Achaean and Messenian were bound together by a common hatred
of Sparta. To others Kleomenes seemed admirable; Dioskorides'
poems in praise of Spartan virtues have been connected with the
temporary friendship between Egypt and Kleomenes. Admiration
for Sparta is very clear in the epigrams of Damagetos and this is seen
not only in the praise of the Spartan Gyllis, who fell at Thyrea
(VII, 432) but also in the poem on the Spartan wrestler (XVI, 1).
'Sparta is my country glorious in her men. The others are technicians.
I, as Lacedaemonian boys should, win by strength.' Friedländer

---

[1] Loc. cit.; cf. also *C.Q.* 36, 1942, 134 ff., and A. Momigliano, *J.R.S.* 32, 1942,
53. On Damagetos see P. Friedländer, *A.J.P.* 63, 1942, 78.

has shown that an epigram preserved on stone has echoes in this and other poems by Damagetos and must almost certainly be his; it is written all through in the old heroic manner: 'Stranger, dust glorious in men covers here in its bosom Timokritos honoured by the Muses. Striving for his country with the Aetolians, the brave man was ready either to conquer or to die. He fell in the front line leaving to his father endless grief. He did not conceal the ideals of his education, but preserving in his heart the Spartan command of Tyrtaios, he chose valour in preference to life.' It is a conscious statement of how a contemporary can and did behave like a hero of old. But where Kerkidas preaches Cynic realism, Damagetos goes back to Tyrtaios.

Alkaios of Messene wrote iambics as well as elegiacs but nothing of his satyric iambics survives. His non-political epigrams are of the usual type and many of them may have been actual inscriptions. In one Homer is connected primarily with Ios, and this may have been designed for a statue there (VII, 1). Hesiod, who has tasted the pure fountains (this is the Kallimachean tradition), has a tomb raised by the Nymphs, and the shepherds tend it with milk and honey (VII, 55); but Hipponax' tomb is covered with brambles and wild pears (VII, 536); these two poems might therefore well be a pair composed for two statues near together. The epitaph on Phidis (VII, 429) is one of the earliest riddling epigrams, a type much developed by Antipater. The only love poems are three to young men (XII, 29, 30, 64), the last a young athlete, whom Alkaios fears that Zeus may take as his cupbearer like Ganymede. Of the poems on works of art the Marsyas might be inspired by the Pergamene group[1] (XVI, 8): 'for now your hands are tight in inescapable fetters, because you a mortal met Phoibos in a contest with the gods, and the flutes which shrilled a note as honeyed as the lyre won from the contest not a crown but death'.

There are also two interesting poems on mortal musicians: one is the dedication of a flute by the Theban flute-player Dorotheos son of Sosikles (XVI, 7). The dedication was probably in Thebes, because Lyaios, in whose temple the flute was dedicated, is simply a poetic variant for the Theban Dionysos Lysios. 'Alone among the

[1] Cf. above, p. 188.

holy prophets of Dionysos he escaped the swift wings of Blame.'
This presumably means that Dorotheos was extremely successful in
Dionysiac competitions. The first four lines give his repertoire:
'Blending the voice' (of the singer) 'harmoniously with his soft
flutes, Dorotheos blew the lamenting Dardanids and Semele's
thunderstruck travail and the deeds of the Horse'. The songs for
which he provided a flute accompaniment are the Sack of Troy, the
Birth of Dionysos (probably by Timotheos), and the Trojan Horse.
The Trojan Horse may be the same song with which the lovely
Athenion captured Dioskorides.[1] The Birth of Dionysos recalls a
slightly later inscription on a statue base in Delphi[2] according to
which a famous Samian flute-player Satyros gave a special performance in the Stadion described as 'a song with chorus "Dionysos"
and a lyre-piece from the *Bacchae* of Euripides'; presumably he performed as a flautist and therefore accompanied both the chorus and
the lyre-piece; what the lyre-piece was we cannot say but it is interesting to know that Euripides was so performed.

Alkaios' other epigram on a performer leads us to another performance of Timotheos (VII, 412). This is an epitaph for Pylades,
who was a famous kitharode, and praises him extravagantly. All
Hellas is in mourning; Apollo has taken the laurels off his hair; the
Muses weep; Asopos stops its streams; the halls of Dionysos cease
from dancing. Praise of a Hellenistic musician is nearly as extravagant as praise for a Hellenistic ruler. Pylades, when Philopoimen
entered the theatre at the Nemean games in 205 after his victory over
the Spartans at Mantineia, was beginning to sing Timotheos'
*Persai*: 'Making a great and glorious crown of freedom for Greece';
the whole theatre looked at Philopoimen and clapped.[3] Alkaios'
appreciation of Pylades may therefore have been political as well as
aesthetic. Pylades was apparently singing Timotheos' nome as a solo;
the hexameter beginning which is quoted may have been his own
composition.

The complications of Alkaios' relationship with Philip V of

---

[1] Cf. above, p. 143.     [2] *S.I.G.*[3], no. 648.
[3] Plut. *Philopoemen*, 11. For appreciative epigrams on Philopoimen's later
destruction of Sparta, cf. *A.P.* VII, 723, of which Page, *G.L.P.*, no. 107, 2 is a
variant, and Paus. VIII, 52, 6.

Macedon have been plausibly explained by Professor Walbank. True to the political tradition which he inherited from Kerkidas, Alkaios supported the Macedonians as a counterpoise to the Spartans. So an epigram on a statue of Philip set up about 220 in Epidauros praised him as having defended the Peloponnese from both Aetolia and Sparta. Alkaios, probably after Philip's naval successes in 201, wrote (IX, 518): 'Heighten, Zeus, your Olympian walls. Philip can climb everywhere. Shut the brazen gates of the blessed. Earth and sea are tamed beneath Philip's sceptre. The road to Olympos remains.' The inspiration here comes from the epigrams on Alexander, and Alkaios deliberately overbids Asklepiades, whose Alexander allows Zeus to keep heaven for himself.[1] Philip was used to such praise; he claimed descent from Herakles, as Samos' epigram[2] on the bull of Orbelos proves; Alkaios knew this, and his Philip, like Herakles, will go to Olympos but, unlike Herakles, will capture Olympos. So in another epigram of unknown authorship (XVI, 6), which Walbank also dates to 201, Philip is 'sovereign of Europe, on land and sea as much Lord of Mortals as Zeus is Lord of Immortals – Philip's glory has again come near the thrones of the gods'.

Alkaios, however, completely changes his tune in three bitter poems. Two accuse Philip of murder; the victims are unknown but were presumably friends of Alkaios. Both use the literary epigram with its literary associations for a violent attack. The first (IX, 519) is in form a drinking song: 'I will drink more than the Cyclops when he had filled his belly with human flesh. I will drink. Would I had smashed Philip's skull and drunk out the brains' (like Tydeus), 'Philip, who tasted a friend's blood by the mixing bowl, pouring poison into the wine.' The second (XI, 12) starts with a Homeric reminiscence already used by Kallimachos in a literary epitaph (*Ep.* 61 Pf.): 'Wine killed the Centaur, not only you. Such a wine-bibber is One-eye, to whom may you very swiftly send the same cup from Hades.' Philip, who prided himself on his descent from Antigonos the one-eyed, is equated with the cannibal Cyclops of

---

[1] Epidauros: *I.G.*, IV², 1, 590. Alexander epigrams, cf. above, p. 51. I do not feel certain that Alkaios alludes to *A.P.* VI, 171, as Professor Walbank thinks. Cf. also on these epigrams A. Momigliano, *J.R.S.* 32, 1942, 53.

[2] *A.P.* VI, 116 copied by 114, 115.

*Odyssey* IX. These literary curses have the violence of Kerkidas and are quite unlike the diffuse *Thrax* of Euphorion, which essentially has a similar theme. The third poem (VII, 247) is the epitaph on the Thessalians who were killed when Titus Flamininus defeated Philip at Kynoskephalai in 197: 'unwept and unburied, wayfarer, on this ridge we lie, thirty thousand Thessalians, a great woe to Emathia. That bold spirit of Philip was gone more lightly than swift deer.' Philip answered in a parody (XVI, 26b): 'Barkless and leafless, wayfarer, on this ridge a high stake is planted for Alkaios'.

Alkaios later added two lines in the middle of his poem:[1] the Thessalians were 'overcome by the Ares of the Aetolians and of the Latins, whom Titos brought from broad Italy'. Thus he had transferred his allegiance to the Romans, and now writes (XVI, 5): 'Xerxes brought a Persian host to Greece and Titos brought his from broad Italy. But the one came to set the yoke of slavery on the neck of Europe and the other to relieve Greece from slavery.' Not the Spartan (as a few years before after Philopoimen's victory) but Philip is compared to Xerxes; Rome is the liberator. There may be also a reminiscence of Lykophron's *Alexandra*, where Rome appears as the latest of the Asiatic powers who have fought with Greece.[2]

Descent from the Trojans was accepted by Flamininus himself, as in one of the epigrams written on his dedications at Delphi he is called Aineadas and in the other 'leader of the Aineadai'.[3] In one of these poems he is called 'divine Titos', an adjective used, of course, for his heroes by Homer and later commonly used of Homer himself. More was to come. In Chalkis, which Flamininus had saved when its government was compromised by loyalty to Antiochos III Epiphanes, buildings were dedicated to 'Titos and Herakles' and to 'Titos and Apollo', and Plutarch[4] has preserved the end of a paian in dactylo-epitrites, which was sung in Flamininus' honour when his priest had been appointed: 'Sing, maidens, of great Zeus and Rome and Titos and the Faith of the Romans. Hail Paian. O Titos Saviour.'

One other poem should be mentioned here, although we have no external evidence for place or date, Melinno's *Hymn to Rome*.[5] Sir

---

[1] Plut. *Flam.* 9.       [2] Cf. above, p. 135.       [3] Plut. *Flam.* 12.
[4] *Flam.* 16; J. U. Powell, op. cit., 173.
[5] Diehl, op. cit., VI, 315; C. M. Bowra, *J.R.S.* 47, 1957, 21.

R

Maurice Bowra in his excellent commentary puts the date between our earliest evidence for the worship of Rome in the Greek world (particularly the celebration of a festival of Rome at Delphi in 189) and the sack of Corinth by Mummius in 146. The phraseology continually recalls the poems which we have been examining. Rome is addressed as a daughter of Ares, which Sir Maurice interprets as meaning an Amazon; naturally she appears as a great warrior. She 'dwells on earth in a holy Olympos always unassailable'. We remember the threat that Philip would attack and capture Olympos (*A.P.* IX, 518); Rome has brought Olympos to earth; I suppose that Melinno is thinking of the Capitoline Hill and the gods who live on it. Fate has given Rome alone unbreakable rule 'that having sovereign power you may rule'. 'Sovereign' (*koiranos*) is not a very common word and Melinno has coined the adjective; she seems to remember the address to Philip as 'Sovereign of Europe' (*A.P.* XVI, 6). 'Beneath the fetter of your strong yoke the breasts of earth and grey sea are constricted; you safely steer the towns of men.' 'The towns of men' is an Odyssean echo; 'steering' was the function of Kleanthes' Zeus; the old phrase 'breasts of earth' has been changed so that earth and sea become horses in Rome's victorious chariot. This is a new twist of the rule over 'land and sea' which had been attributed to Philip by Alkaios and to Rome by Lykophron.[1] Everything else is changed by time, but Rome has always a 'sail-filling breeze of rule'. Kerkidas (fr. 4) had exhorted his fellows to use the breeze while they had it, but Melinno's Rome has it all the time. For Rome alone gives birth to warriors as regularly as the fields of Demeter send up corn. The reading at the end is uncertain, but the allusion to the Spartoi of Thebes is clear. Melinno uses her Sapphic stanzas for a solemn hymn; the basis of her poetic language is Homeric, like the language of Kerkidas and Alkaios, but on this is set the third-century description of Hellenistic rulers, to which she gives a new turn to express the reality of Roman rule.

Rome has now taken her place beside the Hellenistic kings as a powerful force influencing Greek affairs and she will supersede the

---

[1] *Alexandra*, 1447 f. Cf. above, p. 134. Does the use of πρέσβιστος there and πρέσβιστα four lines before in Melinno show that she was thinking of the *Alexandra*?

Hellenistic kings one by one and gradually turn the Greek world into Roman provinces. The damages and rewards that came from contact with these powerful personages are illustrated by the behaviour of the Attalid kings towards mainland Greece at the end of the third and in the first half of the second century. When Rome sacked Aigina, it was bought by Attalos I and its art treasures were carried off to enrich his royal collection.[1] But five years later he dedicated on the Athenian Acropolis copies of the sculpture which celebrated his defeat of the Gauls; his son Eumenes II gave the Athenians the great Stoa which extended to the West of the theatre of Dionysos under the Acropolis; in the sanctuary of Dionysos just under the theatre is a beautiful round base with a decoration of garlands and masks, which are closely paralleled by similar decorative sculpture in Pergamon.[2] Eumenes II also financed the reconstruction of the theatre in Delphi about 160 B.C.[3] His brother Attalos II built the magnificent Stoa which bounded the East side of the Athenian Agora and has now been reconstructed by the Americans.[4] Attalos II also, with his brother-in-law Ariarathes, King of Cappadocia, dedicated in the Stoa a seated portrait of Karneades, who was head of the Academy.[5] The two kings merely give their names and the Attic deme in which they were enrolled as honorary citizens; the statue is a tribute to Athens and to the philosopher under whom they sat in their youth.

The base in the Agora shows that this was a seated bronze statue; the bust[6] is known, a lined elderly face with orderly hair and beard, and well-draped himation and chiton, as befitted an Academic who went on a state mission to Rome and educated princes from the East. This portrait is a breakaway from the tradition of the derelict philosopher, which still appears very clearly in the portrait of the Stoic Chrysippos[7] executed by the Athenian Euboulides late in the

[1] Cf. above, p. 186.

[2] M.T.S., AS 12; Bieber, History[2], fig. 752; Kraus, Ranken der Ara Pacis, pl. 23. Cf. the relief with masks, above Ch. IX, p. 197.

[3] S.I.G.[3], 671, B 12.    [4] I.G., II[2], 1371 and Agora I 6135.    [5] I.G., II[2], 3781.

[6] Cast in Copenhagen; Lippold, Gr. Pl., 350, pl. 123/2; Schefold, Bildnisse, 140 (the torso by Zeuxis is dissociated as a poet by G. M. A. Richter, Catalogue, no. 190).

[7] Body: Louvre 80. Head: British Museum 1846. Lippold, Gr. Pl., 338, pl. 123/1; Bieber, Hell. Sc., 69, figs. 234–42; Winter, K.i.B., 344/6, 8; Schefold, Bildnisse, 126; Richter, Three Critical Periods, fig. 45.

third century; a little man with a bald head and a large nose, no chiton and a rather untidy, scanty himation, seated also but emphasizing his points by counting them off on his fingers. What little we know of mainland and island art in the second century suggests that not only was realistic portraiture out of fashion but that here in spite of Attalos' dedication the violent style of the Pergamene Gauls and Giants was rejected in favour of a solemn classical style reminiscent of Pheidias and Alkamenes.

Three sculptors can be named: Damophon of Messene, Eukleides of Athens, and Euboulides of Athens, the grandson of the Euboulides who made the portrait of Chrysippos. The New Classical style puts the three together; Damophon's restoration of the Zeus of Olympia can probably be dated by the earthquake of 183 (this restored Zeus deeply impressed Aemilius Paulus in 167); Euboulides belonged to the second half of the second century, if his grandfather was working late in the third century. Damophon executed a number of commissions in temples of Messenia and Achaea, including the great group for the temple of Despoina at Lykosoura in Arcadia, of which parts have been discovered.[1] Despoina and Demeter were seated; Despoina was the Arcadian Persephone; Artemis, who was here regarded as the daughter of Demeter, stood on one side, on the other side stood Anytos in armour, a Titan who in local legend had brought up Despoina. The Anytos head (pl. XXI*a*) clearly owes something to Hellenistic satyr masks but retains a classical breadth and calm; the two female heads seem to be of fifth-century inspiration with fourth-century hair styles. Despoina had a remarkable robe decorated in low relief with Nereids, Victories, and Women-dancers wearing animal masks (this was presumably a local rite). Eukleides' head of Zeus (pl. XXI*b*)[2] is in the same style as the Anytos, wild hair and beard round a solemn classical face: this was a

---

[1] Athens, N. M. 1734–7, 2171–5. Winter, *K.i.B.*, 373/1–4; Lippold, *Gr. Pl.*, 350, pl. 124, 1–2; Bieber, *Hell. Sc.*, 158, figs. 665–8, 670; Pausanias VIII, 37, 3. On Aemilius Paulus see below, p. 278.

[2] Athens, N. M. 3377, 3481. Winter, *K.i.B.*, 373/7; Lippold, *Gr. Pl.*, 274, pl. 95, 4; Bieber, *Hell. Sc.*, 158, figs. 671–2; Pausanias VII, 26, 4; Walter, *J.D.Œ.A.I.* 27, 1932, 146, adds an arm with a sceptre (the date is disputed; Walter proposed the mid-fourth century).

seated statue at Aigeira in Achaea. In Athens a head of Athena, which is little more than a free copy of a late fifth-century type, and a female torso, which may belong to a Muse, have been associated with a recorded group of Athena Paionia, Zeus, Mnemosyne, and the Muses and Apollo.[1] The find spot is right and a block with Euboulides' signature was also found there. It is not quite clear from Pausanias whether Euboulides made the whole group or only the Apollo or alternatively whether the Apollo alone was dedicated by him (i.e. was his gift) but all the rest were also made by him. The evidence is however good enough to connect him with this New Classical style.

Euboulides was also a favourite portraitist of the time: his solemn style matched the solemn claims of his patrons, as the poem on the base of one of his statues shows:[2] 'Pallas, Leader of the Erechtheids, in your temple is this Philtera the priestess set up, of the true blood of the Boutadai; her father was five times leader of the army, Pausimachos; her ancestors flourished among the Aegeids – Lykourgos and Diogenes honoured in Attic land; of them one was satisfied with the word of the orator, by the other's deeds the country saw its ancient freedom'. This noble lady, who traced her descent back to the fourth-century finance-minister Lykourgos (who rebuilt the theatre, setting up statues to the three great fifth-century tragedians and at the same time having their texts preserved), was the daughter of a Pergamene, Pausimachos, and granddaughter of the Macedonian Diogenes, who commanded the garrison in the Peiraieus until he handed over to the Athenians in 229 after the death of Demetrios II. However the Athenian aristocracy was none the worse for being mixed, and Diogenes' act inaugurated a period of prosperity for the city. We know two epigrammatists of the late third to early second century who wrote for wealthy Athenians. Phaidimos wrote a pretty traditional epigram for Leon, son of Kichesias, when he dedicated sandals to Artemis on the birth of a son, whom we know in public life in 187/6 (*A.P.* VI, 271). He also wrote a poem in iambics

[1] Athens, N. M. 233, 234. Winter, *K.i.B.*, 373/5–6; Lippold, *Gr. Pl.*, 366; Bieber, *Hell. Sc.*, fig. 669; Richter, *Three Critical Periods*, 35, fig. 65. Signature, *I.G.*, II/III², 4298. Pausanias I, 2, 5; Wycherley, *The Athenian Agora*, III, 20, no. 2.

[2] *I.G.*, II/III², 3474. Ferguson, *Hellenistic Athens*, 425, cf. 201.

for Kallistratos, son of Apollodoros, who dedicated a relief of Hermes: 'Kallistratos to you, messenger of Zeus, set a relief, which shared his youthful form. The boy is from Kephisia. Rejoicing in it, Lord, save the son of Apollodoros and his country' (*A.P.* XIII, 2). The Homeric echoes are obvious. The curious phrase 'relief which shared his youthful form' equates Kallistratos with Hermes; the equation of an ordinary young man with a god is something new, a debasing of the equation of Hellenistic rulers with gods. More startlingly Artemon writes a poem equating a young Athenian, Echedemos, with Apollo (*A.P.* XII, 55): 'Son of Leto, you hold the sea-girt neck of Delos, son of great Zeus, speaking oracles to all. Echedemos holds Kekropia, a second Phoibos in Attica, in whom soft-haired Eros has lit a lovely flower. Athene of his fathers, who rules on the wave and the land, has now enslaved Hellas to beauty.' Echedemos is probably one of the Athenians of that name from Kydathenai who are recorded in the second century. Presumably the recovery of Delos justified the boast 'ruling over land and sea', the formula applied to Philip V and Rome, and for the same reason Apollo is specifically the Delian god in the first line. It is quite a pretty poem with its progression of slave-owners: Apollo, Echedemos, Athene, and after all why should not a love poem (cf. XII, 124) use the same terminology of flattery as a poem to a Hellenistic prince or musician?

   Euboulides' group of Apollo and other gods was set up in a house which was devoted to the cult of Dionysos Melpomenos. As the priest of this Dionysos was chosen from the Artists of Dionysos, and as we know they had a precinct early in the first century (Ath. 212c) this house was probably theirs. The continuance of dramatic performances is another element of stability in the Greek world, and we have various interesting records and dramatic monuments from this period and this area, particularly in Delphi, Boeotia, and Delos. At Delphi the Soteria seem to have become quadrennial instead of annual soon after the middle of the century.[1] About 228 Delphi was asked to guarantee the travel of Artists from the Isthmian-Nemean Guild to the triennial festival of Dionysos Kadmeios in

---

[1] *S.E.G.*, II, 260. In 224 Aristomachos son of Philonides (cf. above, p. 17) was one of the performers, *S.I.G.*[3], no. 509.

Thebes,[1] and we have evidence for theatre-building and festivals in various places in Boeotia during the Hellenistic age.[2] Another sign of interest in classical Greek literature are the 'Homeric' bowls, which have been discovered in quantity in Boeotia.[3] Someone in the early second century must have imported silver cups from Alexandria with scenes from Homer and Tragedy and reproduced them in clay, and they were evidently popular. The most interesting information about drama comes from Oropos and Tanagra. In Oropos, where drama was performed at the festival of Amphiaraos, an inscription records the dedication of the *skene* and the *thyromata* about 150. *Thyromata* is the word for wide panels enclosing the practicable doors and capable of taking illusionistic painting of the kind that we know from the cubiculum of Boscoreale.[4] If it is right to connect this fashion with Alexandria, this is another instance like the 'Homeric' bowls of Alexandrian influence in Boeotia. The Tanagra records[5] of the first century not only give the names of winners of first and second prizes but also give the budget of the festival (Serapieia); there was both a musical and a dramatic contest; the winners were a satyric poet from Tanagra, a tragic poet from Thebes, a tragic actor from Thebes, a comic poet from Athens, a comic actor from Athens, an actor of old tragedy and an actor of old comedy from Thebes. Some of the winners of the second prizes are interesting; the satyric poet came from Anthedon, the tragic poet is called Poplios Popliou Romaios, the Athenian who won the first prize for acting new comedy also won the second prize for acting old comedy. The musical contest included competitors from Aigeira, Kyme in Aiolis, Smyrna, and Tarentum. Thus this small town had an international festival of considerable scope including both old and new plays.

Among the many rich houses discovered in Delos and decorated with floor mosaics is the House of the Masks,[6] dated by the

[1] *S.E.G.*, XIX, 379; *B.C.H.* 85, 1961, 78.
[2] Cf. *Griechische Bühnenalterthümer*, 38 f.     [3] Cf. above, p. 147.
[4] Cf. above, p. 163. The inscription, *I.G.*, VII, 423.
[5] Chrestos, *A.E.* 1956, 34; *S.E.G.*, XIX, 335.
[6] *Délos XIV.* Dionysos, *M.T.S.*, DM 1, Rumpf, *M.u.Z.*, pl. 56/5; Simon, *Gnomon* 34, 1962, 193. Masks, *M.N.C.*, DM 1. Dancing slave, DM 2. On Delian

excavators to the early second century and reasonably supposed to be a place where visiting performers at the Delian festivals were entertained. Three mosaics make this connection with the theatre likely. One is a Dionysos wreathed and in full tragic costume riding a leopard. The leopard belongs to the Indian story of Dionysos, but the red-shoes, the long chiton, and the himation belong to the theatre. The rather formal folds of the chiton and the cold regularity of the features justify the attribution to the New Classical style. The second mosaic is a chessboard pattern with at each end a band of five masks hanging from an ivy branch, a type of decoration which goes back to the middle of the fourth century at least;[1] here the slave-masks have the deep beard of third-century slaves and not the semicircular beard which was well-established by the time that the mosaic was made; this may therefore be a copy rather than a New Classical original. The third mosaic has a wreathed comic slave dancing before a naked flute-player seated on a rock. Imagination and representation have met here; the slave belongs to the theatre, but the nudity of the flute-player and the presence of the rock show that the scene is imagined to be in the country, a country comedy like Menander's *Dyskolos*. This rich second-century Delos (which received an Athenian cleruchy in 166) had its echo in Athenian comedy. The comic poet Kriton,[2] whom we know from Athenian theatre records of the early second century, describes a parasite who thought that Delos alone had three things that were good for him: an agora rich in food, an enormous crowd of worshippers, and the fact that the Delians themselves were parasites of the god.

In spite of his savagery in destroying Corinth Mummius seems to have confirmed the diplomatic privileges of the Isthmian-Nemean Guild, and the rivalry between the Isthmian-Nemean Guild and the Athenian Guild was adjudicated on more than one occasion by the Romans.[3] Of peculiar interest is the Pythais of 128/7, which the Athenian Guild presented to the Delphians,

---

houses see A. Rumpf, *J.D.A.I.* 50, 1935, 1 ff. The newly discovered House of the Comedian will also be relevant, *B.C.H.* 87, 1963, 869.

[1] Cf. above, p. 163.     [2] *I.G.*, II², 2323; Kock, *C.A.F.*, III, 354/3.

[3] Pickard-Cambridge, *Festivals*, 294 ff.

sending forty singers for the paian with a trainer, 'and musicians to make the holy days festive', two flute-players, seven kithara-players, an aulode, a kitharode, tragic and comic actors and trainers of choruses.[1] As Limenios is one of the kithara-players, it is a reasonable assumption that the paian by him which was inscribed at Delphi with its musical notation was sung on this occasion.[2] What the considerable dramatic forces performed we do not know. The first of the two inscribed hymns is in cretic-paeonic metre all the way through, the second, which is by Limenios, changes to aeolic for the last fifteen lines. The first was probably called a song with lyre, and the second was called 'Paian and Prosodion' (presumably the aeolic section is the prosodion). Both are remarkably alike in subject matter and use traditional language: both summon the Helikonian Muses to sing Apollo in Delphi; Apollo is being celebrated by the Athenian Artists of Dionysos, Apollo who slew the snake and disposed of the Gauls. The transitions are clearer in Limenios' song, and the first hymn may have been a shorter version modelled on it. In Limenios' paian Apollo is born in Delos; the heaven rejoiced, the aither held the winds quiet, the waves of Nereus and great Okeanos were still (this silence is traditional in epiphanies of a god but is not found after the birth of Apollo either in the Homeric hymn or in Kallimachos' hymn). From Delos the god came to Athens. 'The Libyan lotos sang its honeyed song, mixing its sweet voice with the brilliant songs of the lyre, and rock-dwelling Echo cried, Paian, iê, Paian. And he rejoiced because he recognized and welcomed the immortal design of Zeus. Wherefore from that beginning we call him Paieon, all the autochthonous people and Bakchos' great thyrsos-smitten holy swarm of Artists dwelling in the Kekropian city.' This is a new version in so far as Athens is made the connecting link between Delos and Delphi, a version attuned to the present political situation. And the cry iê, Paian, which was firmly connected with Delphi in the Homeric hymn (III, 500), in Kallimachos' hymn (II, 102), and by Apollonios Rhodios (II, 711), if, as seems certain, it is rightly inserted here, is here the rock-echo of a duet given by Athena and Apollo, if we may suppose that it was Athena who played

[1] S.I.G.³, 698; cf. later 711, 728.
[2] J. U. Powell, op. cit., 141; Diehl, *Anth. Lyr.*², VI, 303.

the flute when Apollo brought his lyre to Athens. The death of Pytho and the flight of the Gauls follows. In traditional hymn form, after the narrative of the god's doings comes the prayer: 'But, Phoibos, protect the divinely founded city of Pallas and its famous people; join him, goddess, mistress of Cretan bows and hounds, Artemis, and you, most glorious Leto. Preserve the dwellers of Delphi with their children, mates, and homes unstumbling; and visit with favour the holy servants of Bakchos, and give increase to the spear-protected rule of the Romans that it may flourish victoriously in ageless might.' So the paian ends with a prayer for the great Western power which at the moment had made Athens safe and prosperous.

What we have called the New Classical style in literature and art is a genuine attempt to create in the spirit of the classical past. The same aim can be seen in two famous statues from Melos, the Aphrodite in the Louvre[1] and the Poseidon in the National Museum at Athens.[2] It is difficult to speak of the Aphrodite when the reconstruction is completely uncertain: somehow a balance must have been achieved on the right-hand side, but whether she held a shield like the earlier Aphrodite of Capua or rested her left arm on a high pillar or how the composition was arranged is quite uncertain. The treatment of the marble for body and drapery is modern and exciting; so is the rotation of axes through the figure. The main outline of the composition is probably classical and the head is certainly a hardened and simplified version of Praxiteles' Aphrodite of Knidos. The Poseidon also seems to repeat the general outlines of a fourth-century statue, and the head has been compared with the fourth-century Asklepios from Melos: it is a grand dramatic representation of the god.

We have noticed already Attalos' enthusiasm for earlier sculpture and the uses made of it by the Pergamene sculptors;[3] we have noticed also the reflection of this interest in the epigrams of Anti-

---

[1] Paris, Louvre 399. Winter, *K.i.B.*, 378/1–2; Lippold, *Gr. Pl.*, 370, pl. 130/3; Bieber, *Hell. Sc.*, 159, figs. 673–7; Toynbee, *J.H.S.* 76, 1956, 131.

[2] Athens, N. M. 235. Winter, *K.i.B.*, 374/8; Lippold, *Gr. Pl.*, 370, pl. 130/4; Bieber, *Hell. Sc.*, 160, fig. 684.

[3] Cf. above, p. 186 ff.

pater of Sidon.[1] The desire to re-create the majestic deities of the past is very clear in the mainland and island sculpture of the second century which we have just been discussing. From now onwards the academic character of mainland art becomes increasingly apparent. Without trying to draw the lines too clearly or to give too detailed an account, it is possible to distinguish copies, adaptations, and, much more rarely, new creations. Free copying, as we have seen, was already known in Pergamon. Mechanical copying seems to have started early in the first century, since one of the earliest examples we possess is the Diadoumenos from Delos, which is unlikely to be later than the devastation of Delos in 69.[2] The two copies of the herm of Alkamenes, which were found with earlier bronze originals waiting shipment presumably to Italy from the Peiraieus, can probably be dated to 86 when Sulla set fire to the town.[3] A curious side-line which shows the enthusiasm of the Romans for Greek art is the equipping of portrait heads with heroic Greek bodies: again Delos provides two early examples probably dating before the end of the second century; both are heroic nude statues copied from late fourth-century statues of Hermes: one has the name of C. Ofellius with the artists' names, Dionysios and Timarchides,[4] inscribed on its base, the other has a middle-aged, bald, and unprepossessing portrait head (pl. XXIIa).[5]

A form of adapting earlier models which was extremely popular was the so-called Neo-Attic relief: these can be traced in many examples from the late second century B.C. to the Hadrianic period and later. These and their models have been studied in great detail by Dr W. Fuchs,[6] who makes a good case for an early period when Neo-Attic works were made in Athens, followed by a migration of Attic artists to Rome after Sulla's sack in 86 (although production in Athens continued much later and much of it was exported). The

[1] Cf. above, p. 207.    [2] Richter, *Three Critical Periods*, 42.
[3] *Archaeology in Greece*, 1958, 23.
[4] Delos. Bieber, *Hell. Sc.*, 173, fig. 727; Richter, op. cit., 54, fig. 111. Cf. below, p. 294.
[5] Athens, N. M. 1828. Bieber, *Hell. Sc.*, 172, figs. 728–9.
[6] Die Vorbilder der neuattischen Reliefs, *J.D.A.I.*, Ergänzungsheft, 20, 1959; cf. review by M. Bieber, *A.J.A.* 64, 1960, 392.

dating of the works is difficult and so also is the detection of their originals. Here we are concerned only with the early period and that primarily as an indication of taste in the Greek and Roman world – Roman as well as Greek, as the finds in a ship wrecked at Mahdia show that early Neo-Attic products were exported. The Mahdia wreck is well dated by pottery to the late second or early first century[1] and shows two different trends in contemporary Neo-Attic work. Two fragmentary marble kraters, of which the Borghese krater in the Louvre[2] is a later copy, have a superb thiasos of Dionysos, Ariadne, satyrs and maenads. Here we have a last link (followed by mechanical reproduction on the Borghese krater) of a long chain of Bacchic scenes going back to the archaic period with obvious nearer ancestors in the thiasoi of the late fifth century by the Dinos painter and the thiasos on the late fourth-century bronze krater from the Macedonian tomb at Dherveni;[3] but the group of the young satyr supporting a fallen satyr (pl. XXIII*a*) shows the inspiration of the Pergamene Gaul supporting his dead wife (pl. XVI*a*),[4] and similarly the maenad in back view with the tympanon has something of the elegance and contortion of the Baker dancer (pl. X).[5] The style is in fact Late Hellenistic and more specifically Pergamene; a contemporary import into Athens from Pergamon itself is a terracotta krater in the Athenian Agora[6] with a thiasos not unworthy to be compared with this. The Attic artist of these two fragmentary kraters from Mahdia did not look far back for his originals and may have followed a single original. The artist of the two other fragmentary kraters[7] (and he may, for all we know, have been the same man) did not follow a single original, and the ancestry of his kraters is much more complicated. His Dionysos and satyrs including the group of papposilenos supporting maenad, recur in

[1] Fuchs, op. cit., 183 ff. Cf. also *Bilderhefte D.A.I.(R.)*, 2.

[2] Tunis, Musée Alaoui, C1202–3, Fuchs, pls. 22, 24, 25, 26; Richter, op. cit., fig. 106. Louvre, Bieber, *Hell. Sc.*, 166, 184, fig. 795.

[3] Cf. above, p. 23.        [4] Cf. above, p. 187.        [5] Cf. above, p. 171.

[6] Agora P 3155, Homer A. Thompson, *Hesperia* 3, 1934, 311 ff., E 153.

[7] Tunis, Musée Alaoui, C1204–5, Fuchs, pl. 15. Copies. The maenads, Fuchs, pls. 15–20; Bieber, *Hell. Sc.*, figs. 793–4; Richter, op. cit., figs. 104–5 (copies), fig. 107 (Tunis). The satyrs and Dionysos; Merlin-Poinssot, *Cratères de Mahdia*, pls. 1–22, 24, 28–9, 33–4; cf. Watzinger, *J.D.A.I.* 61–2, 1946/7, 76 ff. on ancestry.

the scene of Dionysos visiting a comic poet,[1] where the little satyr untying Dionysos' shoe makes more sense, because Dionysos is entering a house; the Dionysos copies a late fourth-century statue,[2] the satyrs and the drooping maenad are not earlier than Hellenistic, but the dancing maenad is, as far as we can see, an accurate copy from a great late fifth-century set of reliefs in the style of the Nike balustrade, possibly the work of the sculptor Kallimachos.

The rich decorative style of the late fifth and early fourth century particularly caught the taste of the Neo-Attic artists; the Nike balustrade, the girl dancers with basket crowns, and the mantle-dancers all appear, and it is the other figures of the Mahdia kraters which are the exception to the prevailing taste. Sometimes, as with the mantle-dancers, a sequence of detailed variations and stylistic changes can be traced between the Attic original and the Neo-Attic examples: once the type of mantle-dancer was invented it was used again and again for votive reliefs of nymphs.[3] Here clearly the needs of cult caused the repetition with slight variations of a successful type.

Cult also sometimes caused the repetition of archaistic figures of gods, whereas normally the Greeks represented their gods in the latest fashions and poses of the day. The Alkamenes herm repeats a hairdressing style of a hundred years earlier, and surprisingly two Attic oinochoai[4] of very special shape painted about 410/400 show a Hermes and an Athena wearing clothes of the Persian war period; these confirm the dating in the early fourth century of the archaistic base with four gods in the Acropolis Museum[5] (Zeus, Athena, Hermes, Hephaistos) and that was the inspiration of some Neo-Attic reliefs in the late second century (pl. XXIIIb). The original was presumably an attempt to catch a lost religious fervour; the Neo-Attic artists saw in it another pleasing piece of mannerism. An

---

[1] Cf. above, p. 176.

[2] London, British Museum 1606. Winter, K.i.B., 293/4; Lippold, Gr. Pl., 242. Picard, Manuel, IV, i, 322 notes the connection.

[3] Athens, Small Acropolis Museum 176, 177, 177a is dated by Fuchs about 300. Studniczka, Kalamis, 26 ff.

[4] J. R. Green, Hesperia 31, 1962, 92.

[5] Fuchs, op. cit., 45 f, pls. 8, 10. Athens, Acr. 610. C. Mitchell, H.S.C.P. 61, 1953, 73, Athens, Agora S 7327.

ill-defined line separates the Neo-Attic artists from what we have called the New Classical style. In the latter Greek artists were working for Greeks, who were conscious of their heritage and were trying to live up to the old standards in a new world. Neo-Attic reliefs were essentially decorative and were to a large extent made for Romans, who were fascinated with the beauty rather than the meaning of Greek art.

One of the few original creations of the late second century is the group[1] of Aphrodite, Eros, and Pan from one of the most magnificent houses in Delos, the club house of the Poseidoniastai of Beirut; one of these merchants, Dionysios, son of Zenon, son of Theodoros, dedicated this group to the gods of his native country. The technical skill is great: the ugly Pan lays his hands on Aphrodite, inspired by the little winged Eros, who is suspended between them with his feet on Aphrodite's shoulder and left hand on Pan's horns. She raises her slipper to spank Pan. It is a pretty and frivolous group; it is surprising to find it as a religious dedication, but Greek gods were always expected to take pleasure in what pleased their worshippers.

The two last epigrammatists who belong to this period and area, Phanias and Alpheios of Mytilene, fit into this picture of accomplished imitative art. Phanias[2] has one epigram about buying fish, which descends ultimately from the marketing scenes of comedy (A.P. VI, 304) and another about a boy growing old, which is an expansion of the preceding epigram by Alkaios (A.P. XII, 30). Some of his epigrams, however, revive the dedicatory epigrams of Leonidas: the best takes the catalogue of the poor man's tools (which are normally dedicated) and gives a new twist at the end (A.P. VI, 307): 'Eugathes of Lapithe (in Elis) spat out mirror, hair-towel etc. etc.; left his barber's shop and leapt into Epikouros' house as a horticulturalist, where he was a donkey listening to the lyre; he would have died of hunger if he had not been content to relapse'. The theme of the unsuccessful late-learner is, of course, traditional; but this is pleasantly done; he wants to be a horticulturalist because Epikouros taught in the garden; 'he is content with *palindromia*'

---

[1] Athens, N. M. 3335. Lippold, *Gr. Pl.*, 369, pl. 135/3; Bieber, *Hell. Sc.*, 147, figs. 629–30; J. M. Cook, *Greeks in Ionia*, pl. 52.

[2] Gow, *C.Q.* 6, 1956, 231.

means, I think, not only that he ran back to his shop but also that he 'relapsed', which is the medical sense of the word.

Alpheios of Mytilene, as one would expect, recalls rather the manner of Antipater and his successors. He copies Antipater in a dedication (*A.P.* VI, 187) and expands Diodoros in an epitaph on Themistokles (VII, 237). He has a pretty conceit on a hen which shamed Prokne and Medeia in dying to save its chicks (IX, 95). There is a little group of tourist epigrams (IX, 100, 101, 104): Delos may be destroyed but it is still the birth-place of Apollo and Artemis; Mycenae is only a goatherd's tale; Mycenae and Argos are now less than Roman Troy. A poem to Rome[1] (IX, 526) warns Zeus to close his gates; 'for already sea and land are yoked beneath the spear of Rome, but the path to heaven is still untrodden'. This is a direct imitation of Alkaios on Philip V of Macedon (IX, 518) and shows that that poem was already in the anthologies. The theme of the beloved who appears kindly and unkindly to his lover in a dream (Artemon, XII, 124) is taken up and given a new twist (XVI, 212): 'I will snatch the fiery pine from your hand, Eros, and steal the quiver hanging about your shoulders, if you are really asleep, son of fire, and we mortals for a little while live in good order – without your arrows. But even so I fear you, weaver of wiles, lest you conceal one against me and see an unpleasant dream in your sleep.' The 'weaver of wiles' is, of course, a quotation of Sappho, and in another poem Alpheios remembers Archilochos (IX, 110). These urbane, cultured trifles are a literary parallel to the Neo-Attic reliefs.

---

[1] Walbank, C.Q. 36, 1942, 135 wants to date *A.P.* IX, 526 to Claudius' conquest of Britain, but a real event is not needed to justify a literary answer to an earlier epigram. On the other hand IX, 100 should be not too long after the destruction of Delos in 69 B.C.

## CHAPTER XI

# Italian Epilogue

◆

With the defeat of Pyrrhus at Beneventum in 275 and the capture of Tarentum in 272, the establishment of a colony in Paestum in 273 and at Brundisium in 296 and the conquest of Sicily after the First Punic war in 241, Greek South Italy and Sicily gradually lost their independence to the Romans. The Campanians had already become Roman allies in 338, and their art, known to us best from Campanian vases of this date, must have been well known to the Romans. Through the medium of Etruscan art (and to a smaller degree through imports of Corinthian, Laconian, and Attic pottery) the inhabitants of Rome itself gained some knowledge of Greek forms and Greek stories from the seventh century onwards; the magnificently decorated temple of Jupiter Optimus Maximus on the Capitoline was dedicated in 509,[1] and in the early fourth century the cult statues of Juno from Veii and of Jupiter from Praeneste were brought to Rome. The power of this reflected Greek art at its best can be seen in two well-known works: one is a cylindrical bronze box[2] made by Novios Plautios in Rome in the third century. Whatever the nationality of the artist, he was working in traditional Etruscan technique, and his subject, the boxing-match of Polydeukes and Amykos, was taken from a famous Greek picture of the early fourth century, of which other reflections survive on Etruscan red-figure vases. Besides being an extremely competent and interesting work, it attests the knowledge of Greek art and Greek legend in Etruria and Rome. The other work[3] is the magnificent terracotta seated Apollo

---

[1] For the earliest period and its works of art see Einar Gjerstad, *Early Rome*, particularly II, 124, etc., and III, 484 on imports; III, 168 f., on the temple of Jupiter Optimus Maximus.

[2] Rome, Villa Giulia. Bieber, *Hell. Sc.*, 169, fig. 718; Rumpf, *M.u.Z.*, 128, fig. 13; Beazley, *Etruscan Vase-Painting*, 5, etc.

[3] Rome, Villa Giulia. Bieber, *Hell. Sc.*, 168, fig. 713; P. J. Riis, *Etruskiske Kunst*, 198, fig. 113.

from the pediment of the temple at Falerii, which must be earlier than the Roman sack of 241 and challenges comparison with, for instance, the Apollo Belvedere. The Romans were not therefore ignorant of Greek art or of art influenced by the Greeks when the plunder from Greek cities started pouring in after the capture of Tarentum in 272.[1]

Vases and terracottas give some idea of the artistic and literary life of the Greeks in South Italy and Sicily in the Early Hellenistic period. It is curious that after Zeuxis in the late fifth century we scarcely know the name of an artist from this area, and most of the poets, Alexis of Thourioi, Philemon of Syracuse, Apollodoros of Gela, Theokritos of Syracuse, Leonidas of Tarentum (as later Theodoridas and Moschos of Syracuse), migrated to Athens, Alexandria, or elsewhere. Plays seem to have been imported from Athens: this is the easiest explanation of the scenes from Euripides depicted before a stage background and with some of the characters in stage costume on Apulian vases of the last third of the fourth century.[2] The scenes from comedy on Apulian, Paestan, Campanian, and Sicilian vases from 400 to 330 can always be paralleled from Attic comedy, just as the costumes and masks can be paralleled on Attic terracottas, and sometimes the cross-reference is completely clear.[3] Apulian vase-painters did not only paint in red-figure: they also painted in applied colour on the black glaze (this group is called Gnathia, and the best of them were certainly made in Tarentum). The two styles run parallel from the middle of the fourth century and share the beautifully painted and elaborate floral ornament, which we have already compared with the floral ornament of the Pella mosaics and derived from Sikyonian painting.[4] There may be some connection between this suggested activity of Sikyonian painters in Tarentum and the fact that the city possessed two colossal bronzes by Lysippos of Sikyon,[5] a Zeus in the Agora and a Herakles on the Akropolis (which was

---

[1] The literary texts for Roman art and works of art brought to Rome are very conveniently assembled and discussed by O. Vessberg, *Studien zur Kunstgeschichte der Römischen Republik*, Act. Inst. Romani Regni Sueciae, VIII, 1941, 5–114.

[2] Cf. *M.T.S.*, 73.                    [3] Cf. *M.M.C.*, 3.

[4] See above, p. 22.

[5] Strabo VI, 278; Pliny, *N.H.*, 34, 40; L. Forti, *Klearchos*, 1963, 18.

s

removed to the Roman Capitol by Q. Fabius Maximus in 209). The style is reflected in Tarentine limestone reliefs.[1]

The Gnathia vases[2] continued well into the third century, probably until the end of the first quarter, and together with a very fine silver cup[3] and a number of dramatic terracottas[4] they establish the fact that Tarentum quickly followed Athens in adopting the onkos mask for tragedy and the new masks and costumes which accompanied the introduction of New Comedy. The same story is told for the Aeolian islands by the very interesting series of dramatic terracottas from Lipari,[5] and Campania provides a good set of comic statuettes and masks from Nola, Naples, and Capua.[6] It is important to establish this identity of practice between South Italy and Athens, since it is from this area that the early Roman dramatists come, Livius Andronicus from Tarentum, Naevius from Capua, Pacuvius from Brundisium, Ennius from Rudiae not very far from Tarentum.

The Gnathia vases and Tarentine terracottas show that New Comedy was being played in Tarentum by the end of the fourth century. But there was also a continuation of mythological travesty in the manner of Middle Comedy. The facts are obscure, and we know little of the three poets Rhinthon, Blaisos, and Skiras, who are named together.[7] Rhinthon is dated by the Suda to the first Ptolemy, the latest fourth or earliest third century. He is called 'originator of the *hilarotragoidia* (cheerful tragedy), which is *phlyakographia*'. His titles are the titles of Euripidean plays, and the few fragments seem to be parodies in broad Doric iambics. Phlyakes was probably the Italian name for padded dancers, who went back to the archaic period and became successively the chorus and actors of Epicharmos and later of Middle Comedy in South Italy and Sicily.[8] The fourth-century vases show that mythological comedy, probably Attic, was popular in South Italy and it is difficult to see what was original in

---

[1] Cf. Lippold, *Gr. Pl.*, 262; Bieber, *Hell. Sc.*, 170.

[2] *M.T.S.*, GV 8–10.      [3] *M.T.S.*, TJ 1.      [4] *M.N.C.*, TT 1–2, TV 1.

[5] L. Bernabo Brea, *Meligounis-Lipari II*; Webster, *Griechische Bühnenaltertümer*, 52 f.

[6] *M.N.C.*, NT 1–21.

[7] Testimonia and fragments in Kaibel, *Comicorum Graecorum Fragmenta*, 183 ff.

[8] Cf. Pickard-Cambridge, *Dithyramb etc.*[2], 138 f.

Rhinthon. Perhaps the novelty was the Doric dialect, or perhaps these were symposion sketches for recitation rather than acting, like the phlyakes of the Alexandrians Sopatros and Sotades.[1] Rhinthon was known in Syracuse as well as Tarentum, since the Locrian poetess Nossis calls him a Syracusan (*A.P.* VII, 414).

The poem is interesting and Nossis herself is the only Early Hellenistic poet working in Italy of whom anything survives. 'Pass by with a clear laugh and a kindly word for me. I am Rhinthon of Syracuse, a minor nightingale of the Muses, but I picked an ivy-wreath all my own from tragic phlyakes.' The 'clear laugh' (*kapyron*) recalls the claim of Theokritos that he was a 'clear mouth of the Muses' (VII, 37); and the claim to minor originality recalls Dios-korides' poem on Thespis (*A.P.* VII, 410). The date of Rhinthon gives a top date for Nossis;[2] if she really knew Dioskorides' poem, she cannot have lived before the late third century. So many of her poems are for real occasions that it seems natural to put her in the third century rather than later. The reminiscence of Theokritos gives a top date of 270 and the form, pseudo-epitaph on a poet, is unlikely to be much earlier. The dedication of shields won by the Lokrians from the Bryttians (*A.P.* VI, 132) is surely a real inscription, but the last lines 'whose valour (the Locrians) they praise as they hang in the temple nor do they grieve for the arms of the cowards whom they left' reads like a conscious variation of an epigram by Leonidas (*A.P.* VI, 131) on Lucanian shields which 'grieve both for the horses and the men'; this again would give a top date of 270.[3] The pseudo-epitaph on herself (*A.P.* VII, 718) has naturally been compared with the similar pseudo-epitaph of Kallimachos (35 Pf.) and probably like the corresponding poems of Leonidas and Poseidippos was meant to conclude a book of her poems:[4] probably therefore she wrote in the second half of the third century.

In the pseudo-epitaph on herself she compares herself to Sappho: 'Stranger, if you sail to Mytilene with its lovely dancers, which inspired the flower of Sappho's graces, say that I was dear to the Muses and the Locrian land bore me. Knowing that my name is Nossis, go.' The text is difficult, but the rare word for 'inspired'

---

[1] Cf. above, p. 126.      [2] Cf. Wilamowitz, *Hell. Dicht.*, I, 135.
[3] Cf. above, p. 220.      [4] Cf. above, p. 218.

(ἐνανσαμέναν) probably recalls Kallimachos' poem on the writers of choliambics (*Iambos* XIII, 14). The comparison with Sappho is not unjustified; Nossis was a woman who usually wrote for women, and the pretty poem *A.P.* V, 170 is full of reminiscences of Sappho:[1] ' "Nothing is sweeter than love, all things that men prize are second. I spit even honey out of my mouth." This says Nossis. Whom Kypris does not love, she does not know what flowers are roses.' Formally this is a symposion poem and presumably, like some of Sappho's songs, it could be sung or recited at women's parties.[2] The other poems are dedications, and an interesting small group are inscriptions for portraits dedicated in the temple of Aphrodite. The standard is realism, as for the women of Theokritos and Herodas. 'Kallo dedicated the picture in the house of fair-haired Aphrodite, having had the portrait painted exactly like herself. How charmingly she stands. See what a flowering of grace. Bless her. She has no fault in her life' (IX, 605).[3] The charming and slightly tart poem *A.P.* IX, 332 is only in form an inscription. 'Let us go to the temple of Aphrodite and see the statue, how cunningly wrought in gold it is. Polyarchis had it erected, enjoying many possessions from the beauty of her own body.' The first line recalls the rhythm of a marching song, and contrasts sharply with the end. Nossis is a charming and sophisticated poet; it is sad that so little survives.

The Sicily which the Romans learned to know and ultimately conquered was the Sicily of Hiero II, who rose to power in 275/4, became their ally in 263 and remained loyal to them until his death in 215:[4] after revolutions and counter revolutions Marcellus succeeded in defeating both Syracusans and Carthaginians and captured Syracuse in 212. Hiero II was a considerable patron of the arts and his city was already rich in the culture of preceding centuries. We know for instance of two important late fourth-century sculptures there, an Apollo by Leochares and the Sappho of Silanion.[5] The temple of Athena on the island of Ortygia, which was built by the first Gelo at the beginning of the fifth century, was according to Cicero[6] full of

---

[1] Cf. Sappho 16 L-P, 55 L-P.     [2] Cf. *Greek Art and Literature, 700–530*, 36 f.
[3] Cf. VI, 353–4, IX, 604.     [4] On dating, cf. Gow, *Theocritus*, II, 305.
[5] Plato, *Ep.* 13, 361a; Cic. *In Verr.* II, iv, 125.
[6] Cic. *In Verr.* II, iv, 122–3.

pictures which were spared by Marcellus in 212 and removed by Verres in 73/70: they included twenty-seven pictures of Sicilian tyrants and kings – a series which presumably started with Gelo I and ended with the family of Hiero II – and an equestrian battle of Agathokles (late fourth to early third century). They were dedications to Athena by her beneficiaries; but Cicero's contemporaries regarded the temple as an art gallery: they were charmed by the skill of the artists, by the fact that these men were commemorated and that they could see what they looked like. Hiero himself built the great theatre, which has obliterated the traces of all previous theatres.[1] If the inscriptions naming blocks of seats after Gelo II and his wife Nereis are contemporary, the theatre was built between 238 and 217, and the statue of Epicharmos for which Theokritos composed an inscription[2] will have belonged to an earlier theatre. From the beginning Hiero's theatre seems to have had a proskenion and raised stage, and this plan is confirmed by the little theatre at Akrai[3] which is contemporary. At the back above the Syracusan theatre is a grotto with a fountain fed by an aqueduct; here were found statues of the Muses[4] and inscriptions[5] which mention the Council of the Technitai and a statue in the Mouseion. Both the inscriptions and the statues are dated to the second century. It is natural that such a theatre should have a local Guild of Artists of Dionysos and interesting that they should be associated also with the Muses: this is part of the overlap between Apollo and Dionysos which we have noticed elsewhere.[6] But this Mouseion had already received from Dionysios I the lyre, writing-tablet, and pen of Euripides, for which he had paid a talent.[7]

Hiero II also built a monster ship[8] and rewarded the Athenian poet Archimelos, who celebrated it in nine elegant elegiac couplets, with 1,000 bushels of wheat. The officers' quarters had a mosaic floor which represented 'the entire story of the *Iliad*'. This is interesting as a

[1] L. Bernabo Brea, *Musei e Monumenti in Sicilia*, 1958, 54.
[2] Cf. above, p. 81.
[3] Cf. L. Bernabo Brea, *Akrai*, 1956; *Musei etc.*, 65.
[4] Syracuse 695, 711, 5072. L. Bernabo Brea, *Musei etc.*, 60; Lippold, 346 n. 4.
[5] *I.G.*, XIV, 12–13; Rizzo, *Teatro Greco di Siracusa*, 123.
[6] Cf. above, pp. 173, 184.  [7] *Vita Euripidis*, 5.  [8] Athenaeus V, 206d.

kind of parallel to the Homeric bowls, which are believed to derive from Alexandrian originals of the end of the third century. It is even possible that Ptolemy IV got the idea, if indeed it was his, from Hiero, because, when Hiero found that no Sicilian harbours could take the ship, he renamed it 'Alexandris' and sent it as a present to Ptolemy.

Sicilian painting is best represented by the vases found at Centuripe, which lies inland behind Catania. The origins of this style can now be traced back to a pyxis[1] with Seilenos among the nymphs, which was found near Tyndaris, and the pyxis[2] by the Lipari painter with Aphrodite and the Little Eros on her lap. These belong to the latest fourth century: the figures stand out large and gracious against the black ground and blue, red, yellow, mauve, and green are freely applied to their drapery. Whatever the origin of the big painting that inspired these vase-painters and their successors in Centuripe, it had nothing to do with the Sikyonian style, which flourished at Tarentum and is seen in Syracuse itself in the elaborate floral patterns on the ceiling of a naiskos.[3] The colour range and elegance of the Centuripe figures suggest rather Tanagra figurines and their Attic predecessors. The main group of Centuripe vases[4] are dated in the third century; those with a black background like the Lipari vases are probably rather earlier than those with a mauve background. The large figures are set against a plain background and the foreground is reduced to a narrow shelf. Scale and treatment of space correspond to the Pella mosaics and the Boscoreale pictures,[5] which are, as Professor Rumpf says, hereby confirmed as copies of Early Hellenistic paintings. Professor Robertson rightly sees a reminiscence of mid-fifth-century art in these large quiet figures; the painters have moved a little away from the elegance of the figures on the rather earlier Lipari vases. The pictures show women in their quarters, sacrificing

---

[1] B. Pace, *Arte e Civilta della Sicilia Antica*, 1938, 472, pl. VII; Trendall, *Atti del Settimo Congresso di Archeologia Classica*, 1961, II, 140.

[2] L. Bernabo Brea, *Musei etc.*, 81.        [3] Syracuse, Museo Nazionale 30285.

[4] B. Pace, op. cit., 171 ff., A. D. Trendall, *B.M.M.* 1955, 161 ff.; L. Bernabo Brea, op. cit., 58; Pfuhl, *M.u.Z.*, fig. 761; Rumpf, *M.u.Z.*, 153, pl. 52/2-3; M. Robertson, *Greek Painting*, 173.

[5] Cf. above, p. 24.

or attended by flying Erotes; one wonderful fragment in Syracuse has a standing woman, a seated youth with a wreath, and a little Eros by his head; this must be a marriage scene whether the pair are mortal or divine. Occasionally a portrait head or portrait bust takes the place of the picture and reminds us of the life-like portraits of women celebrated by Nossis. The vases themselves, bell krater or lekanis, provide a large cylindrical body or high conical lid for the figures, and these flat surfaces covered by the polychrome painting are admirably set off by the rather heavy floral or architectural mouldings of knob, rim, or stem, which are coloured yellow. They make a final and wonderful epilogue to the long history of Greek vase-painting.

The rest of this chapter will describe the reception in Rome of the double current of Greek art and Greek literature. The report of Florus (*Epit.* 1, 13 (18)) that the triumph of M. Curius Dentatus over Pyrrhus in 275 was the first time that Romans had seen rich textiles, statues, and paintings in a triumphal procession may well be true and marks the beginning of Greek plunder coming to Rome. In 240 they had their first taste of Greek literature in translation. The brute fact that Livius Andronicus translated and produced Greek tragedy and comedy and translated the *Odyssey* is far more important than the little that can be said about the few surviving fragments. This was the beginning of Roman literature, and Roman literature began as translation from the Greek. The dates and facts about Andronicus' life are disputed.[1] The most likely view is that he grew up in Tarentum and came to Rome, possibly when he was about thirty, not very long before 240. As he is said to have acted in his own plays, he may well have been a member of the Tarentine guild, and the guild will have included rhapsodes as well as actors, so that he could have got his *Odyssey* as well as his plays there. Nothing can be said of his comedies; he took some of his tragedies from Sophocles and Euripides; we do not know who wrote the originals of the *Aegisthus* and *Equos Trojanus*; perhaps the latter was a famous Hellenistic tragedy, which also provided songs for Athenion in Alexandria and Dorotheos in Thebes.[2]

Two of Andronicus' titles, *Danae* and *Equos Trojanus*, were

---

[1] Beare, *Roman Stage*[2], 15 ff.; *C.Q.* 34, 1940, 11 ff.; E. Fraenkel, *Elementi Plautini in Plauto*, 439; F. Leo, *Geschichte der römischen Literatur*, 55 ff.

[2] Cf. above, pp. 143, 235.

repeated by Naevius,[1] who started to produce in 235. He was born in Capua and therefore is likely to have been acquainted with Greek drama in Campania from his earliest youth. He may have learnt more in Southern Italy and Sicily, if he went there in the course of the First Punic war. The *Andromeda* and *Iphigenia*[2] were derived from Euripides; the *Lycurgus* perhaps from Aeschylus (the vase evidence suggests that, till the late fourth century at any rate, Aeschylus was more popular in South Italy than in Athens).[3] The *Hector Proficiscens* may derive from the *Hektor* of the fourth-century poet Astydamas, which certainly gave Hektor's departure from Troy (2 N). Fraenkel lays great stress on two lines from the *Danae*, Ribbeck VI, *desubito famam tollunt si quam solam videre in via*, an iambic tetrameter, and Ribbeck IV, *eam nunc esse inventam probris compotem scis*, a bacchaic tetrameter. The first sounds like a complaint of Danae, the second like a report of Danae's guilt to Acrisius; both would naturally be spoken trimeters in Euripides, and Fraenkel claims them as early evidence that the Romans, on the analogy of the actor monodies in late Euripidean tragedy, translated spoken scenes into sung scenes and then transferred the technique from tragedy into comedy. (The problem will engage us later in connection with Ennius and Plautus.)

For the originals of the comedies of Naevius the only evidence is the titles: Menander, Philemon, Diphilos, Alexis, Dionysios, and Euboulos have been plausibly suggested as authors. All these poets were still writing in the third century except Euboulos; a good case[4] can be made for combining the fragments of Naevius' *Corollaria* with those of Euboulos' *Stephanopolides*, which was probably produced 350/20 B.C.; this Middle Comedy, which with its intrigue already had a strong flavour of New Comedy, may well have survived in revivals. The metres used are iambic senarii, iambic and trochaic septenarii and octonarii; one doubtful line is explained as

[1] Fraenkel, *R.E.*, s.v.; Beare, *Roman Stage*,[2] 23 ff.; Leo, op. cit., 76 ff.

[2] The surviving fragment sounds like a prayer of Orestes in the *I.T.* but is not found in the text.

[3] Cf. *Hermes* 82, 1954, 295 (on the *Hektor*, 305). Séchan, *Études sur la Tragédie Grecque*, 66 n. 3 thinks the story recoverable in the fragments is too long for Aeschylus and must have been rehandled by a Hellenistic tragedian. This is not clear.

[4] *L.G.C.*, 61 f.

cretics (25 R) and another as anapaests (58 R). The fragments show that Naevius enlivened his translation by introducing Roman food (65 R) and the names of Italian towns (21 R). According to Varro Naevius was imprisoned for 'continuously reviling and abusing high officers of state in the manner of Greek poets'; how much of the biography woven out of this is true we cannot say; but isolated instances of personal abuse in New Comedy[1] are known, and Naevius' attack on the Metelli and their answer is not unlike the contemporary give and take in epigrams between Alkaios and Philip V of Macedon.[2]

Naevius' epic of the Punic war does not concern us because we have too little of the corresponding campaign epics of the Hellenistic kings to compare. The scanty fragments[3] are for the most part terse and dry. He must have used a Greek source for that part of the narrative which brought the story from the Sack of Troy down to the foundation of Rome. We have seen Lykophron's interest in this story, and Eratosthenes, who was an exact contemporary of Naevius, said, like him, that Romulus was the grandson of Aeneas.[4] Two fragments clearly show a Greek poetic source: the description of Rhoikos and Porphyrion (19 M) from the first book comes from a work of art, *inerant signa expressa*, and Fraenkel[5] suggests that it was a Gigantomachy on a shield; other suggestions have been made and we have lost the clue; what is more important is that Naevius borrowed, and the Romans were already prepared to hear, the same kind of description as, for instance, Apollonios Rhodios gave of Jason's cloak.[6] In the second book 'then powerful with arrows, famous bow-holder, holy son of Jupiter, Pythian Apollo' (30 M) is a word for word translation of a Greek description of Apollo. Naevius must have known a Greek *Sack of Troy* and perhaps the connection of Aeneas with Romulus suggests that it was a contemporary or nearly contemporary poem.

Marcellus' capture of Syracuse in 212[7] marks for Livy and Plutarch the beginning of the age of plunder and the beginning of Roman

[1] Cf. above, pp. 12ff., 217. On Naevius' attack see O. Skutsch, *C.R.* 1, 1951, 175.
[2] Cf. above, p. 236 f.    [3] See Morel, *Fragmenta poetarum Latinorum*, 17 ff.
[4] See above, p. 134.    [5] *J.R.S.* 44, 1954, 14.
[6] See above, p. 156.    [7] Vessberg, op. cit., 26 ff.

admiration for Greek art. Undoubtedly they exaggerate both cause and effect, but it is true that Marcellus' triumph, which was accompanied by the dedication of Syracusan statues and paintings in the temple of Honos and Virtus,[1] foreshadowed the second-century triumphs over mainland Greece. Marcellus also dedicated spoils from Syracuse in Lindos and Samothrace.[2] In 209 Fabius Maximus captured Tarentum and removed the colossal bronze Herakles of Lysippos and many other statues and paintings to Rome. Thus Roman interest in Greek art was increasing all the time, and it was into this atmosphere that Ennius, who was born at Rudiae, some sixty miles East of Tarentum, came when he arrived at Rome in 204. Like Andronicus and Naevius, he wrote comedy as well as tragedy, but practically nothing of his comedy survives. Of the tragedies we have considerable fragments, including fragments of plays which have survived entire in Greek. His *Andromache* perhaps derives from the fourth-century poet Antiphon,[3] his *Achilles* from Aristarchos, who may be the poet named in the Suda as a contemporary of Euripides, his *Alcumeo* perhaps from Theodektes. Aeschylus' *Eumenides* was a favourite play in South Italy in the fourth century: the four surviving fragments of Ennius translate iambics of the original; in one of them he uses trochaic septenarii instead of iambic senarii. The *Ajax* may be a translation of Sophocles.

Of the eleven plays claimed as Euripidean the *Cresphontes* cannot be the Euripidean *Cresphontes*, since that play has no place for Merope's father (III R); the *Medea* may be the Euripidean *Aigeus*. The *Alexander* (of which the original was probably known in Lipari in the fourth century)[4] also shows a change from the iambics of the original to trochaic septenarii (VI R), since enough remains of the Kassandra scene in Greek to show that it began and ended in iambics; Kassandra's monody however was presumably in lyric metre in the original, like her marriage song in the *Troades* (308). It is possible that a trochaic septenarius (VII R) in the *Telephus* represents a choral aeolic line of the original.[5] In the *Hecuba* again iambic trimeters are

---

[1] Platner and Ashby, 258.      [2] Plut. *Marc.* 30.      [3] Cf. *Hermes* 82, 1954, 299.

[4] Cf. *Griechische Bühnenaltertümer*, 53. Snell has incorporated the Ennius fragments in his reconstruction, *Hermes*, Einzelschriften, 5, 1 ff.

[5] Cf. E. W. Handley and J. Rea, *B.I.C.S.* Supplt. 5, 1957, 40.

rendered into trochaic septenarii (IV R.) The lyric anapaests of Hekabe's monody (68 f.) are turned into an iambic octonarius (II R), but her later lyric anapaests which run into an iambic close (165 f.) are rendered very freely into anapaests (V R).

The *Medea Exul* raises interesting questions. Again iambic trimeters are rendered by trochaic septenarii (once alternating with octonarii, V R).[1] In the only lyric passage dochmiacs (1251) become trochaic septenarii (XIV R).[2] There are two places where Ennius differs interestingly from our text. Ennius says: 'Would that the pine had not been felled in the grove of Pelion nor had the beginning of commencing the ship been begun, which is now called Argo'. Euripides started: 'Would that the Argo had not passed the Symplegades and the pine had not been felled'. Timachidas criticized Euripides for the *hysteron-proteron* and is in his turn criticized for ignorance of poetic use by our scholiast. Ennius cannot have known Timachidas, and it is unlikely that the change had been made in an actor's text; this must be free translation. The other passage is the beginning of Medea's speech to the chorus; Professor Skutsch[3] has won back from Cicero something like *ne mihi vitio vos vortatis, exul a patria quod absum*, and suggests that Ennius is thinking of his own situation as a foreigner in Rome. Miss A. M. Dale's suggestion that he had the reading of L, μή μοί τι μέμψησθ', and interpreted ἐξῆλθον δόμων as 'I left my home' seems to me very likely; the actors liked a resounding first line with no overlap, just as in 85 they changed τίς δ' οὐχὶ θνητῶν; ἄρτι γιγνώσκεις τόδε and said τίς δ' οὐχὶ θνητῶν τοῦτο γιγνώσκει σαφῶς. Here Ennius may have used a Hellenistic actor's text.

In the *Iphigenia* (in Aulis) Ennius keeps the anapaests of the opening dialogue and the trochaics of the discussion between Agamemnon and Menelaos, but changes Achilles' iambics (953 f.) into trochaic

---

[1] XIII R, translating E. *Med.* 1069, is perhaps lyric dactyls.

[2] Cf. O. Skutsch, *Rh. Mus.* 96, 1953, 197. XVI R is difficult; I am not convinced that it translates E. *Med.* 431, and suggest that it comes from a monologue of Medea in the *Aegeus* (it is quoted from *Medea*, not from *Medea Exul*, but this is not a certain criterion; however, 241 R also quoted from *Medea* certainly derives from the *Aegeus*).

[3] *Navicula Chiloniensis*, 1956, 107 ff., vindicating a proposal of Elmsley.

septenarii with a very free translation. Much more startling, however, is the insertion of a male chorus, singing in trochaic septenarii
what Professor Skutsch[1] plausibly explains as a translation of a
chorus in Sophocles' *Iphigeneia*, which either itself echoed or was
echoed by the surviving iambic line (308 P): 'nothing good is produced by purposeless leisure'. There seems to be no escape from this
conclusion, and the older suggestion that the chorus was transferred
from the *Telephos* becomes less likely the more we know of the
*Telephos*. This seems to be a certain case of transference, and the only
question is whether Ennius made it himself or whether it had
already been made in the text that he used. Euripides seems to have
introduced a subsidiary chorus of Argive men to welcome Klytaimnestra (590), and this may have been a hint for an actor-producer to
abandon the lengthy and not very relevant songs of the Chalkidian
women and introduce a chorus of men singing a song or songs from
another play: considerable liberties were taken by actor-producers –
the *Rhesos* (perhaps first produced in the early fourth century) was
produced with a new iambic prologue before 300 and produced
again with a different iambic prologue in dialogue form before 200.[2]

We can summarize briefly the certainties and uncertainties. It is
certain that Ennius translated iambic trimeters into longer iambic and
trochaic metres used stichically and did not restrict himself to iambic
senarii; once (235 R) he seems to have used lyric dactyls. The analogy
for the use of long metres in tragic dialogue was given by the
trochaic tetrameter scenes of late Euripidean tragedy, which were
presumably accompanied by the flute and may well have had successors in Hellenistic tragedy, although we have no evidence for this.
It is extremely unlikely that any Hellenistic actor-producer rewrote
existing iambic trimeters as trochaic or iambic tetrameters, but it is
perhaps not unthinkable that a flute accompaniment should have
been occasionally introduced for iambic trimeters: the Soteria[3] inscriptions of the mid-third century give each tragic troupe a flautist,

[1] *Rh. Mus.* 96, 1953, 193 ff.
[2] First argument cf. Nauck,[3] 660a. The phrasing of the description of the dialogue
– prologue of Hera and Athena (itself obviously modelled on the *Trojan Women*) –
recalls Aristophanes of Byzantium and therefore gives a date.
[3] Cf. above, p. 16.

who presumably accompanied monodies and tetrameters, and an Oslo papyrus seems to give a musical accompaniment to tragic trimeters, but it may, of course, have been a musician's text rather than an actor's text.[1] Probably, however, the rewriting was a purely Roman development. It is certain also that Ennius rendered actors' monodies into elaborate metres, which may recall the metre of the original (*Alexander, Hecuba, Medea Exul*). This may also account for the single bacchaic line of Naevius' *Danae* (IV R) and the possibly anapaestic line of Ennius' *Medea* (XVI R); both may be monodies in which the chief character addresses himself or herself. Very few lines survive from choruses: trochaic septenarii in the *Telephus*, *Medea Exul*, and *Iphigenia*. The Greek evidence suggests that choruses still performed for satyr-play and tragedy,[2] but we have no evidence what they sang; we know that the practice of singing *embolima* (interludes) started with Agathon, and papyrus fragments of fourth-century and Hellenistic tragedy, like the papyri of comedy, have simply the word *XOPOY* and no text for the song.[3] A chorus from another play or a paian to a relevant god may have been sung in these gaps; the Ennian practice of substituting recitative for lyric metres (if it was his normal practice) is unlikely to have been Greek. Finally one passage in the *Medea Exul* suggests that Ennius was using an actor's text which differed from our book texts.

The reason for placing Ennius, whose other works will be briefly considered later, before Plautus is that Ennius like his predecessors wrote tragedy as well as comedy, whereas Plautus confined himself to comedy. The earliest Roman dramatists wrote both, and therefore may very well have borrowed tragic technique for comedy. Production dates for Ennius and Plautus are nearly identical: Ennius came to Rome in 204 and produced the *Thyestes* in 178; Plautus produced the *Stichus* in 199, the *Pseudolus* in 190, and died in 183; the probable date for the *Miles*, 203, puts it within a year of Ennius' arrival in Rome.[4] Ennius was certainly acquainted from youth with

[1] S. Eitrem, L. Amundsen, and R. P. Winnington-Ingram, *S.O.* 31, 1955, 1 ff., particularly 20 ff.
[2] Cf. G. Sifakis, *B.I.C.S.* 10, 1963.
[3] Cf. E. W. Handley, *C.Q.* 3, 1953, 58 n.3.
[4] Leo, *Pl. F.*, 69.

Greek South Italy. The case for Plautus is not quite so clear:[1] he came from Sarsina in Umbria and probably reached Rome very young; later, he returned to Rome penniless, after he had lost in trade all the money that he had gained *in operis artificum scaenicorum*. This must mean that he had been a successful actor. His name Maccus points to Atellane farces, but *artifices scaenici* is Gellius' normal translation of the Greek *technitai*. In any case Atellane farces point to South Italy and seem to have been a degenerate Oscan form of Greek comedy.[2] It is therefore at least possible that Plautus learnt his Greek and his Greek comedy by acting in Greek comedy in South Italy. In assessing his work, therefore, what we know about the development of comedy and about theatre practice in the third century has to be remembered as well as what we know of the particular originals which he adapted.

His originals included plays by Menander, Philemon, and Diphilos; Demophilos, who wrote the original of the *Asinaria*, is unknown and may have been a contemporary. The original of the *Menaechmi* may have been the *Adelphoi* of Alexis which was produced soon after 342; the original of the *Persa* was first given earlier than 338; the original of the *Amphitruo* was produced not long after 331.[3] As revivals of comedy at the Great Dionysia in Athens started in 340, these plays may well have been in the repertoire of Greek actors in South Italy in the third century. That Plautus was a genius who was very free in adapting his originals is obvious; but as all his originals are lost it is not easy to be precise about his methods. Roman allusions are clearly his own, and Naevius had shown the way there. He also had more actors at his disposal than the Greek poets. No passage of Menander needs more than three actors[4] (except for the rare use of a mute figure to speak a single line or half line) and for the middle of the third century the inscription recording the Soteria at Delphi gives the canonical number of three comic actors in each troupe.[5] A rough count gives at least thirty scenes in Plautus in which more than three

---

[1] Cf. Leo, *Pl. F.*, 65.

[2] For a connection with Paestum and therefore with Greek comedy, cf. P. Zancani-Montuoro, *A.S.M.G.* 1958, 1.

[3] *L.G.C.*, 72, 78, 91.    [4] Körte, *R.E.*, s.v. Menandros, 755.

[5] Cf. above, p. 18.

actors are needed, but in the *Aulularia, Cistellaria, Menaechmi, Mercator*, and *Stichus* he preserves the Greek convention and never uses more than three. In the scenes with more than three speakers the excess is due either to making mute characters speak or to telescoping two scenes into one (or indeed to both causes). Greek drama never minded a mute character, a mute Pylades accompanying Orestes without a word through the whole play, or a flute-girl as part of the revelry (Habrotonon in the *Perikeiromene* or Parthenis in the *Dyskolos*). But in the *Poenulus* (207, 1174, 1280) and the *Bacchides* (1120) Plautus gives both sisters speaking parts; in the *Miles* (1137, 1216) the servant Milphidippa is given a part as well as her mistress Acroteleutium, and later the slave is given a part as well as his master (*Miles* 1311, cf. *Bacch.* 1120). The same explanation probably accounts for Delphium in the symposion scenes of the *Mostellaria* (313, 348); in the original she would have been a mute character.[1] In the *Asinaria* (890), where as in the *Bacchides* (830) a drinking party is viewed through the door, the hidden drinkers are given speaking parts. The telescoped scenes cannot be analysed with great certainty in the absence of the originals: a very likely instance is *Rudens* 1045: Daemones enters with the two girls and they both speak (1048); then the scene goes forward with the arbitration between Trachalio and Gripus, until Trachalio says that the box contains the girls' recognition tokens; Daemones then makes the girl describe the tokens, which establish her as his daughter and she is congratulated by Trachalio. How Diphilos managed this we do not know; there is no need for either of the girls to be present during the arbitration; perhaps Gripus went off when he had given the box to Daemones (1127) and Palaestra (with Ampelisca mute) was fetched out at that point for the recognition; Plautus, however, wanted a single long scene with five speaking characters.[2]

The plays of Plautus also exhibit a far greater variety of metre than any Greek New Comedy that we know. Fraenkel[3] puts great weight

---

[1] Further examples: *Cas.* 353, Cleustrata; 815, Chalinus and Cleustrata; *Capt.* 998, Stalagmus.

[2] Further examples: *As.* 590; *Cas.* 963; *Curc.* 599, 679; *Epidicus* 607; *Persa* 549, 711, 777.

[3] *Plautinisches*, 340, 346 ff. = *Elementi* 323, 349 with new note on 439.

on the parallel here with Ennius' procedure in tragedy and argues that Livius Andronicus first wrote cantica for comedy on the model of the cantica in tragedy and that Naevius and Plautus followed his example, but that when Plautus introduced dances, as in the *Stichus*, *Pseudolus*, and *Persa*, he was drawing on his knowledge of solo performances of Greek *technitai*. Marx[1] lists the examples of lyric metre in Greek comedy of the fourth and third centuries and decides that there is no need to seek any precedents outside Greek comedy. Rostagni,[2] in discussing Dioskorides' epigram on Machon, makes the very interesting suggestion that Machon adapted New Comedy to Alexandrian taste in the late third century by adding cantica and polymetry and that actors' texts thus adapted were the texts which the earliest Roman comic poets used.

Fraenkel's case that Plautus and his predecessors were influenced by Roman tragedy is very strong: until Plautus Roman comedy was written by poets who also wrote tragedy; the Romans expected more music with their tragedy than the Greeks; and close parallels with tragedy both in metre and in style can be shown, particularly between Plautus and Ennius. In two cases where we can check a Greek original against a Latin adaptation, a polymetric canticum has been substituted for spoken iambics. One is Caecilius' adaptation of the old man's speech in Menander's *Plokion*, for which we have to trust Aulus Gellius.[3] The other is the beginning of Plautus' *Cistellaria*: here we have the first line of the Greek original,[4] Menander's *Synaristosai*, two and a half lines (385 Kö.) corresponding very freely to l. 19, and three and a half lines (382 Kö.) corresponding closely to l. 89. All are in iambic trimeters, and all Greek analogy suggests that the opening dialogue ran through in iambic trimeters; Plautus has built an elaborate canticum of mixed metres for the first thirty-seven lines, followed by twenty lines of iambic septenarii and sixty lines of trochaic septenarii. On Rostagni's theory, of course, an actor's text of the *Synaristosai* would have been considerably remodelled before it

---

[1] *Plautus: Rudens*, 254 ff.          [2] *Scritti Minori*, II, 1, 384–7; II, 2, 26 ff.

[3] *N.A.*, II, 23 = Caecilius, *Plocium*, I R.

[4] A. Thierfelder, *Studi Urbinati* 25, 1961, 113. Note that the trochaic fragment 389 Kö. cannot be the original of *Cist.* 49 because of the masculine subject, but belongs rather to the neighbourhood of *Cist.* 402.

reached Plautus; such violent metrical remodelling of a Greek text by a Greek actor seems extremely unlikely, but the theory raises the more general question whether Plautus (as we suspected for Ennius) did use remodelled actors' texts. On Marx' theory Plautus would have found his metrical models in other Greek comedies rather than in earlier Roman comedy or tragedy; this again seems unlikely, but the list of Greek precedents which he gives prompts the question whether the lyric element in the Greek comedy available to Plautus was not larger than we normally suppose and whether he may not have also found models there.

Marx' Middle Comedy instances cannot be excluded since some Middle Comedy plays came into the Roman repertoire. (I quote only a few examples, not all of them in Marx.) Euboulos' *Stephanopolides*, adapted by Naevius, had a dactylic chorus about hetairai, probably the opening chorus (K, ii, 199/104-5), and it is tempting to think that a rather similar chorus may have been the inspiration of Ballio's hetaira-parade in the *Pseudolus* (173 ff.). A master in Mnesimachos' *Hippotrophos* (K, ii, 437/4) gives instructions to his slave about his guests in anapaestic dimeters. In Axionikos' *Phileuripides* (413/4) a discussion of fish is conducted by one character in anapaests and by the other in lyric metre. In Antiphanes' *Homoioi* (82/174) a description of a feast in trochaic tetrameters is interspersed with Diphileians. In his *Aleiptria* (19/25) a woman-slave abuses her fellow-workers in catalectic iambic tetrameters. Nikostratos' *Antyllos* (221/7) has three aeolic lines sung by someone who is frightened of eating cuttle fish. Nothing in lyric metre survives from Philemon, but Diphilos is said to have used Eupolideans as well as the dactylic metre called after him, and his *Anasozomenoi* (544/12) contained an Archilochian line: 'old woman, my jug is empty but my bag is full', which may be an appeal by a reveller to a procuress. Menander's scenes in trochaic tetrameters were known before the discovery of the *Dyskolos*: Knemon's serious speech in that metre was unexpected (708), as was the final scene in iambic tetrameters, in which Getas and Sikon rag the old man. Anapaestic dimeters survive from the *Leukadia*, which was adapted by Turpilius; they seem to have been sung by a temple servant of Apollo (258 Kö.), and appealed for silence before a sacrifice; a cross influence from this through Diphilos to the *Rudens* is

T

certainly possible. A list of fish, borrowed from Mnesimachos in the *Kolax* (fr. 7 Kö.) is doubly interesting: it shows both that Menander borrowed from an earlier poet and that he described food in anapaestic dimeters. The ancient metricians speak of Menander using ithyphallics in the *Phasma* and Eupolideans elsewhere. In the *Theophoroumene* papyrus the men expect the girl to 'leap out here' in ecstasy and they hear the sound of a flute; there the fragment breaks off, but the ancient commentator on Euripides' *Andromache* 103 speaks of 'the song in the *Theophoroumene*'; it sounds as if Menander was parodying or echoing here Kassandra's song in the *Trojan Women* (308). Finally Persius' (V, 161 ff.) description of the beginning of the *Eunuch*: *dum Chrysidis uvas ebrius ante fores extincta cum face canto* perhaps suggests that the play opened with an unsuccessful serenade by Chairestratos (Phaidria in Terence). For the continuation of music into the late third century we have two kinds of evidence: first representations of comic actors dancing (to which we shall return) and secondly the Soteria inscriptions,[1] which allot a flute-player to each of the comic troupes, whether the plays produced were new or old; as the troupes shared the services of a comic chorus and the chorus presumably sang traditional songs, the separate flute-player was probably chiefly concerned with providing music for the actors.

This Greek evidence suggests that within the mass of Plautine cantica certain classes can be distinguished where Plautus could have been touched off by a Greek passage which was either recited or sung to the flute. All the cantica in long metres used stichically may have been based on Greek scenes in trochaic or iambic tetrameters; this is very clear for the cook scene of the *Aulularia* (406–74), where the basis was surely a trochaic tetrameter scene but Plautus has made it more exciting by elaboration and metrical variation. Similarly the iambic tetrameters of the jubilant slave and cook at the end of the *Dyskolos* (880 ff.) suggest that Plautus may have found a germ in some scene like this for the immensely expanded canticum of Chrysalus in the *Bacchides* (925 ff.), to which we shall return. In general, apart from special cases like Knemon's apology, the temple servant in the *Leukadia*, the inspired girl in the *Theophoroumene*, most of the Greek excursions into recitative (as distinct from spoken) or

[1] Cf. above, p. 18.

sung metres belong to the context of the symposion: marketing, inviting guests, feasting, drinking, komos, and serenades. Thus a Greek original (recitative or song) can easily be imagined for the serenade of the *Curculio* (147 ff.), for the komos of the *Mostellaria* (313 ff.) but without a part for Delphium, or for the symposia at the end of the *Stichus*, *Persa*, and *Pseudolus*, although these last have special features which need consideration. The battle-narrative of the *Amphitruo* (203) may well have been in trochaic tetrameters in the original. For the frightened entry of Palaestra in the *Rudens* (664) and the pretendedly frightened entry of Pardalisca in the *Casina* (621) it is doubtful whether Plautus is imitating Roman tragedy or whether Diphilos had already imitated Greek tragedy.

There is, however, no doubt that in those cantica which we know or have every reason to believe were based on iambic scenes in the Greek, the metrical form and the accompaniment is entirely due to Plautus and may have been influenced by Roman tragedy. We know this for the beginning of the *Cistellaria* and strongly suspect it for other scenes such as the plan-making of the two young men in the *Captivi* (215), the monologue on love in the *Trinummus* (223), and Eunomia's persuasion of her brother in the *Aulularia*: the only possible parallel for these is the scene in recitative trochaic tetrameters in which Knemon makes his final dispositions in the *Dyskolos*, but even if any of the Greek originals for these scenes were in this metre Plautus has stepped it up into complicated polymetry.

The symposion scenes of the *Persa*, *Stichus*, and *Pseudolus* need a moment's consideration because in them Plautus mentions *ionica* or *cinaedica* or both (*Pers.* 804, *Stich.* 769, *Pseud.* 1273), and Fraenkel suggests that in these dance scenes Plautus was drawing on his knowledge of Hellenistic virtuosi of his own time. The question is whether we need suppose that Plautus went straight to Hellenistic virtuosi or whether the scenes were not already in the texts which he adapted. The evidence for characters dancing in New Comedy is considerable: Getas and Sikon force Knemon to dance a pace or two at the end of the *Dyskolos*; third-century terracottas of comic actors from Tarentum and Cyprus show slaves and young men dancing,[1] on one of the

[1] Tarentum, *M.N.C.*, no. TT 27; Cyprus, V. Karageorghis, *B.C.H.* 85, 1961, 270, fig. 23. Cf. also *Annuaire du Musée Gréco-Romain (Alexandria)*, 1935–9, 100, pl. 44/5.

Dioskorides mosaics[1] two young men are dancing with tympanon and clappers to a flute-girl, and on a mosaic of the early second century in Delos a slave with a wreath on his head is pirouetting to a flute-player in an open-air scene.[2] The only question is whether the references to *kinaidoi* and Ionic songs, which we know chiefly from third-century Alexandria,[3] are too late for the originals of Plautus' plays; if so, they may yet have been introduced into the text by an actor before Plautus' time.

This possibility that the actors' texts which Plautus adapted were already different from the original texts of the poets concerned must also be considered in connection with the glorification of the slave. No one believes that the slave of Menander's *Dis Exapaton* (to take the most obvious example, since we know something about the slaves of Menander) behaved like Chrysalus in the *Bacchides*: Plautus' fourth act (640) starts with a long canticum in which Chrysalus asserts his superiority to all ordinary slaves, who only trick two or three *minae* out of their masters; in 709 Chrysalus uses an elaborate military image to describe his operations. At 925 in another long canticum Chrysalus compares his trick to the Trojan Horse. The comparison is continued in 1053, 1069. 'The unity of the act has been masked by the insertion of two great cantica, the first largely and the second entirely the work of Plautus.' [4] In writing this I was thinking rather of Plautus in relation to Menander than of Plautus in relation to a later acting version of Menander. But in any case the interesting question is not whether this particular canticum (925) was developed from a text which already had an elaborate aside by 'Chrysalus' as he went into the house but whether there is other evidence both for this elaboration of slave parts between Menander and Plautus and for actors' texts of revived comedy which differed from the original texts.

A study of the dramatic monuments of the late fourth and third centuries shows that the glorification of the slave was Greek as well as Roman. In the course of time slave-masks become more and more common in comparison with other masks, and in the first century B.C. an Athenian actor had a slave-mask on his gravestone,[5] which

---

[1] Cf. above, p. 185.     [2] Cf. above, p. 244.     [3] Cf. above, p. 127.
[4] S.M., 131; cf. Fraenkel, *Pl.Pl.*, 61 ff., 237 ff.          [5] M.N.C., AS 4, pl. 3b.

shows the importance of the slave's part then. The very fine and ebullient slaves among the Myrina terracottas remind us much more of Plautus than of Menander, and, as has been said above, they seem to reflect third-century practice in the Ionian-Hellespontine Guild.[1] By the end of the third century there was a change in slave-masks which spread fairly quickly over the Greek world: the beards of the two leading slaves, which had hitherto been either deep and rounded or triangular became shallow and semicircular. Thus the slave's mouth was strongly emphasized, and he was branded from the moment he appeared as a braggart and a glutton, the two most obvious characteristics of the Plautine slave.[2]

It is therefore probable that such passages in Menander as Sikon's triumphant speech in the *Dyskolos* (639), Daos' scorn of the slave who cheats a lazy and unexacting master (*Perinthia*, fr. 1), and another Daos' rapid fire of tragic quotation to carry off an intrigue (*Com. Flor.* 55) are the beginnings of the glorification of the slave. The fragments of later comedy help us very little except to show that the cook[3] becomes more and more boastful and exotic in his language, but it is at least a possibility that the glorification of the slave proceeded side by side with the glorification of the cook. For actual expansion of existing parts, presumably by actors, there is one good piece of evidence from comedy (besides the evidence from tragedy already quoted to illustrate Ennius): a papyrus[4] of the late third century gives a shorter version of a cook's speech preserved by Athenaeus (382c): in Athenaeus the papyrus version has been expanded by about a quarter of its original length. Athenaeus attributes his version to Straton but elsewhere quotes the first three lines as by Philemon (659b). Straton may therefore have taken over a speech by Philemon and expanded it, just as Menander borrowed lines from Mnesimachos. It does not very much matter whether Straton expanded Philemon or whether, as others think, an actor expanded Straton. If it was an actor expanding Straton, he was poet enough to write twelve quite decent comic iambics, just as the actors who wrote

[1] Cf. above, p. 184. Cf. also D. B. Thompson, *Hesperia*, 32, 1963, 285.
[2] Cf. *M.N.C.*, 5 f., 26 f.; *J.D.A.I.* 76, 1961, 102.
[3] Cf. A. Giannini, *ACME* 13, 1960, 135 ff.
[4] Page, *G.L.P.*, no. 57; *L.G.C.*, 145; Treu, *Philologus*, 102, 1958, 235.

successive prologues for the *Rhesos* were competent composers of tragic iambics. In fact it may be more useful to speak of actor-poets than of actor-interpolations.

Actor-poets are a known class, and when they revived old plays they are very likely to have become actor-interpolators. Philemon himself acted for Anaxandrides; the younger Philemon may very well be the Philemon recorded as a comic actor on the choregic monument of Thasos; Antiphanes who acted in Athens in 299/8 may have been the poet who wrote a comedy datable to 290; Demetrios, Philostephanos, and Epinikos are other probable cases; and Kephisodoros, who appears in the Soteria lists twice as a *didaskalos*, i.e. comic poet, also appears as a member of the comic chorus.[1] Revivals, as the terminology[2] shows, were produced by actors, who had the chance of making alterations. If both Livius Andronicus and Plautus were themselves actors, the probability is that they used actors' texts; they were themselves a special kind of actor-poet, special because they not only expanded but translated. The monuments show that Greek comedy in South Italy was running parallel to comedy elsewhere, and it was on this living tradition of comedy that Plautus drew, even if he far outstripped his models in devising a kind of play which appealed to the Roman audience.

Caecilius, who came from Milan as a young captive about 222, had almost certainly started producing before Plautus died, and he died himself in 168.[3] The three places where Gellius[4] gives us Caecilius' Latin and Menander's Greek side by side show Caecilius as a very free translator: in the Greek all three are in iambic trimeters; in Caecilius the first is a polymetric canticum in the Plautine manner, which goes far away from the Greek; the second and the third are in iambic senarii, but the second introduces the physical unpleasantness of the rich wife, which is not mentioned in the Greek, and the third cuts a gnomic passage in the Greek from nine to four lines. If we

---

[1] The elder Philemon as actor, Ar. *Rhet.* 1413b 25; Aeschines I, 115. The younger Philemon, cf. above, p. 19. Demetrios etc., cf. Wilhelm, *Urkunden*, 154, 156. Kephisodoros, cf. above, p. 18.

[2] The phrase in *I.G.*, II², 2318 is παρεδίδαξαν οἱ τραγῳδοί or οἱ κωμῳδοί: i.e. the actors produced the old play alongside the new plays.

[3] Leo, *Geschichte*, 223.     [4] *N.A.*, II, 23 = Caecilius, *Plocium*, I, II, VIII, R.

assume, as we must, that Gellius is quoting the right passages and that his text was not substantially different from the text used by Caecilius (the only possible doubt here is whether Gellius was quoting an expanded actor's text of the last passage since the last four lines could well be an actor's addition), then Caecilius was writing a Roman play on a Greek theme rather than translating a Greek play and we should probably assume the same sort of licence in Plautus. Against this must be set the considerable number of other surviving lines[1] which read like direct translation from the Greek, and the judgment of Varro that Caecilius was the best constructor of plots, while Plautus wrote the best dialogue.[2] It is possible that the *Plocium*, which Gellius quotes, was an early adaptation made when Caecilius was strongly influenced by Plautus, and that he gradually moved away from free adaptation towards translation; Varros' praise of his plots may suggest that the majority of the large number of plays by Menander which he used (perhaps sixteen out of a total of forty) were translated late in his career. Caecilius may be a bridge between the very free adaptation of Plautus and the much more accurate translation of Terence. One reason for such a change would be the growth of a public which knew the Greek originals and expected to be reminded of them. Evidence for knowledge of Greek literature in Roman readers can be found in the non-dramatic works of Ennius to which we can now turn.

They only concern us in so far as he can be shown to be using Greek sources. The *Epicharmus* seems to have translated a forged poem of Epicharmus on the nature of the world; this was presumably circulating in Tarentum. The *Hedyphagetica* was translated from another Western poet, Archestratos of Gela. *Euhemerus* is called after the writer of the late fourth century, who was known to Cassander and had a statue in Alexandria.[3] Ennius, therefore, had every reason to call himself *dicti studiosus* in the Alexandrian sense of *philologos* and with an allusion to Alexandrian philology.[4] That the *Annals* should reproduce Greek epic particularly in the earlier part, which took the story from the fall of Troy to the foundation of Rome (he follows

[1] E.g. 20, 47, 76, 78, 82, 94, 136, 216, 224, 259, R.
[2] *Sat. Men.*, 399.          [3] Cf. above, p. 100.
[4] O. Skutsch, *The Annals of Quintus Ennius*, 1953, 8.

Naevius in making Romulus the grandson of Aeneas) is expected; he also used his knowledge of Euripides to colour particular speeches and descriptions;[1] but what is entirely new is the demand that his audience must know Greek poetry in order to understand him or at least in order to enjoy him to the full. He calls his work *poema* instead of *carmen*; he writes in hexameters instead of Saturnians; and he addresses his poem to the Muses of Olympus instead of to the Camenae. More important still he puts himself into the tradition of Greek poets who professed to have been called to poetry by a strange experience, Hesiod and Archilochos but more recently Kallimachos and Herodas,[2] and his experience can only be understood fully by those who knew Kallimachos' *Aitia*. Like Kallimachos, he claimed to have had a dream. In his dream he met Homer, who seems to have told him that he was a reincarnation of Homer; the doctrine of trans-migration of souls was well-known in Southern Italy, and this application of it provided a very skilful answer to Kallimachos' scorn for those who tried to imitate Homer.[3] But the flavour is lost to the reader who does not know of the Alexandrian quarrel and its echoes in later Greek poetry. Translation gave the Romans a modern and to some extent modernized version of the Greek classics. Creative Roman poetry, as conceived by Ennius, must be read against its Greek background just as much as the Pergamene altar needs a knowledge of the Parthenon for its full understanding. The poem may have concluded with the triumph of M. Fulvius Nobilior in 187 after his Ambracian campaign, on which Ennius accompanied him: on his return Fulvius erected a temple of Hercules and the Muses.[4] Here we see very clearly the new spirit of the second century.

Thus Greek Muses were firmly planted in Rome, although a small shrine containing the ancient Camenae was imported into the temple. The statues of the Muses were brought from Ambracia, presum-ably from the palace of Pyrrhos, which provided Fulvius with many bronze and marble statues and paintings to adorn his triumph.[5] The Hercules was apparently an addition to the group. The statues have

---

[1] E.g. 174–6 Warmington with E. *Tro.* 1158; 227 ff. with E. *Or.* 917 ff.
[2] Cf. above, p. 95.      [3] Cf. O. Skutsch, op. cit., 9 f.; *C.Q.* 38, 1944, 79 ff.
[4] O. Skutsch, *C.Q.* 13, 1963, 89 f.
[5] Texts: Polybius 21, 30, 9; Livy 38, 9, 13; 39, 5, 13; Pliny, *N.H.*, 35, 66.

been identified with a lyre-playing Hercules and nine Muses on the coins of Pomponius Musa, minted in 67.[1] In the next year, 186, Fulvius gave the games which he had vowed to give after the Aetolian war. Livy (39, 22) notes as something new that many *artifices* (Artists of Dionysos) came to Rome to do him honour; in the same chapter Livy tells us that L. Scipio Asiagenus collected Artists of Dionysos in Asia after his war with Antiochus III for the games which he now gave. Thus the Romans now had the chance of seeing Greek performances given by Greeks. Scipio[2] two years before had brought for his triumph a large number of embossed gold and silver vases and over a hundred *oppidorum simulacra*. Vases of precious metal became extremely popular in Rome, and we shall meet them again. Whether the *oppidorum simulacra* were figures like the Tyche of Antioch or paintings of the capture of the town, which was a very old Eastern tradition and passed from the Orient to the Greeks, is unknown. Scipio[3] also had a statue of himself erected on the Capitol in Greek dress: the artist was presumably a Greek. Flamininus, who had brought bronzes, marbles, and silver vases for his triumph over Philip V of Macedon in 194, had a bronze statue in Rome with a Greek inscription, also therefore the work of a Greek.[4]

The next triumph which is of considerable interest is the triumph of L. Aemilius Paulus in 167.[5] Aemilius Paulus had conquered Perseus, the King of Macedon, at Pydna. He then went to see the sights of Greece; at Delphi he sacrificed to Apollo, and finding an unfinished four-sided pillar which was to hold a statue of Perseus he used it as a base for a statue of himself. The reliefs from these survive; they illustrate cavalry engagements at the battle of Pydna; the scenes are vigorously realistic and closely paralleled in a South Italian

---

[1] Sydenham, *Roman Republican Coinage*, nos. 810–23; Grube, *B.M. Coins of the Roman Republic*, i, 441; iii, pl. 45, 13–22; Lippold, *Gr. Pl.*, 305; Roscher, I, 2189, 2190. The Hercules looks later than the Muses, but it is difficult to judge from reproductions on coins; Lippold dates the Muses about 280. On the temple, see Platner and Ashby, *Topographical Dictionary*, 255. The cycle of Herakles and Muses on Augustan Arretine ware is not connected (Dragendorff-Watzinger, 84).

[2] Livy 37, 59.     [3] Cic. *Rab. Post.* 10, 27.

[4] Plut. *Titus* 1. His triumph, Livy 34, 52.

[5] Livy 45, 27; 28; 32; 39. Plut. *Aemilius*, partic. 27, 28; Pliny *N.H.*, 34, 54; 35, 135.

relief in Lecce.[1] In Olympia Aemilius Paulus was deeply moved by
the Pheidian Zeus and said that Pheidias had sculpted the Zeus of
Homer; somewhere he managed to get hold of an Athena by
Pheidias and dedicated it in Rome, presumably the first Pheidias in
Rome. In Athens he asked for a philosopher to educate his sons and a
painter to paint his triumph, and the Athenians chose Metrodoros to
fulfil both roles: again a Greek artist came to Rome, and what is
perhaps new, a Greek tutor for young Romans. Equally important
perhaps was the fact that he allowed his sons to take over Perseus'
library, and thereby secured a considerable amount of Greek literature for the Romans. Before he returned to Rome he held games at
Amphipolis and every kind of performing Artist gathered to take
part. In his triumph he had 250 waggon-loads of statues and paintings,
and great numbers of silver and gold cups (described as Antigonids,
Seleukids, and Therikleia – the last perhaps here meaning Corinthian
cups).[2] We do not hear more of Metrodoros' educational or artistic
powers; in Rome a far more important influence on the sons of
Aemilius Paulus, Fabius and Scipio Aemilianus, was the Greek politician, soldier, philosopher, and historian, Polybios, who was one of
the thousand Achaeans sent to Italy after Pydna and captivated the
young Scipio at the age of eighteen.[3]

It is probable that Pacuvius, Ennius' nephew from Brundisium,
wrote his tragedy *Paulus* in celebration of Pydna and possible that
Aemilius Paulus commissioned him to paint a picture in the temple
of Hercules;[4] in any case Pacuvius, quite apart from his tragedies, is
interesting as a painter from Greek South Italy who migrated to
Rome. The other painter (besides Metrodoros from Athens) whom
we know to have been in Rome at this time was the Alexandrian
Demetrios, who received Ptolemy VII in Rome when he was driven
out of Alexandria in 164. He was called *topographos* and may have
been drawn to Rome by the opportunity of painting sieges for

[1] Delphi. Lippold, *Gr. Pl.*, 351, pl. 125/2; Bieber, *Hell. Sc.*, 171, fig. 723; D.
Strong, *Roman Imperial Sculpture*, 8, fig. 13 (with the relief in Lecce, fig. 14).

[2] On Therikleia, cf. S. S. Weinberg, *Hesperia* 23, 1954, 109.

[3] Cf. Leo, *Gesch.*, 316 f.

[4] Pliny, *N.H.*, 35, 19. Leo, op. cit., 226 (this depends on an emendation to
Festus making the temple *Aemiliana*).

triumphs. But he has also been connected with the realistic tragic, comic, and satyric *scaenae frontes* described by Vitruvius and illustrated in the cubiculum of the villa at Boscoreale.[1] We do not know very much about scenery for Roman stage productions at this time. In 179 Aemilius gave a contract for the construction of *theatrum et proscaenium ad Apollinis*;[2] *theatrum* means auditorium, but it is difficult to know what we should understand by *proscaenium*. Plautus uses the word for stage in three passages, but once he seems to contrast it with *scaena* in the sense of the part of the auditorium near the stage.[3] To a Greek it naturally meant not only the *proskenion* proper but the area on the top of it, the stage. Greek theatres of the *proskenion* type had been built in Sicily and South Italy; Livius Andronicus, Naevius, Ennius, and probably Plautus, all knew the Greek theatre with the high stage, and the Greek Artists who performed for Fulvius Nobilior and Scipio Asiagenus in 186 were all used to performing on the Greek high stage. On the other hand at this time all Roman stage buildings were temporary, and the Romans may therefore have used the low stage from the first. Polybios,[4] who was also used to the *proskenion* theatre in his native country, has a very difficult description of the games at the triumph of Anicius over the Illyrians, a triumph celebrated in the same year as the triumph of Aemilius Paulus, 167; the essential words are these: 'He summoned the most distinguished artists from Greece and erected a very large *skene* in the Circus . . . he put the four flute-players on the *proskenion* with the chorus and told them to play altogether . . . a lictor told them to turn it into a battle . . . the choruses invading the *skene*[5] attacked their antagonists and then retired again . . . one energetic member of the chorus raised his fist against the flute-player coming towards him, and brought the house down. . . . While they were still contending, two dancers were brought into the *orchestra* . . . and four boxers went up on to the *skene* with trumpeters and horn-players. . . . As for the

---

[1] Cf. Rumpf, *M.u.Z.*, 158 ff., and above, p. 164.
[2] Livy 40, 51; J. A. Hanson, *Roman Theater-Temples*, 18.
[3] *Proscaenium* and *scaena* contrasted: *Poen.* 17, 20; *proscaenium*: *Truc.* 10, *Amph.* 91, *Poen.* 57; *scaena*: *Capt.* 60, *Pseud.* 568.
[4] Polybius, 30, 14 = Athenaeus 615b.
[5] There is no need to emend here.

tragic actors, whatever I say will be thought to be a caricature of the truth.' *Skene* is evidently used in the first sentence for the background, and the fact that it was a 'very large *skene*' suggests that it may have carried the sort of illusionistic painting which we know from Boscoreale and associate with Demetrios; the association of great size with a scenery-painter occurs again with Serapion,[1] who in the early first century painted a very large picture and was also an excellent scene painter. In the next sentence of Polybios *proskenion* clearly means stage; it is perhaps used because *skene* has just been used for background; after this Polybios twice uses *skene* in the sense of stage. The fact that the chorus can invade the *skene* and that a member of the chorus can raise his fists against a flute-player coming towards him shows that it must have been a low stage with steps communicating with the *orchestra*, like the stage of the later Roman stone theatres. We may therefore think of the plays of Terence and Pacuvius, at any rate, as acted on a low stage with sometimes a painted background not unlike the paintings in the cubiculum at Boscoreale.

The inability of the audience to appreciate Greek choruses and tragedians need not be attributed to their lack of knowledge of Greek, as Terence's *Hecyra* was unsuccessful for the same sort of reasons in 168 and again on its second production. The prologue which was written for the second performance attributes the failure of the first to popular interest in a tight-rope walker (the second prologue says 'well-known boxers'); the second production failed because the people were fighting for seats for a gladiatorial show, which was to come immediately afterwards. The third and successful performance was at the funeral games of Aemilius Paulus in 160. Terence,[2] unlike Plautus, is not connected with actors or acting by any ancient authority, and when he died on his return journey from Greece he was said to have had with him new translations from Menander. He therefore seems to have used book texts rather than acting texts. Whether his noble friends were Scipio and Laelius we do not know, but he wrote for an audience which had Greek culture and

[1] Pliny, *N.H.*, 35, 113. The name occurs in Athens: B. C. Merritt, *Hesperia* 32, 1963, 54, no. 102.
[2] See Leo, *Gesch.*, 232 ff; Beare, *Roman Stage*, 81.

appreciated Greek comedy, and the fact that such plays could be produced at all in Rome is the measure of the advance of Roman knowledge in the twenty years or so which separates Terence from Plautus. He does of course enliven his plots by inserting scenes from other plays, as he says in his prologues:[1] a scene from the *Synapoth-neskontes* of Diphilos is introduced into the *Adelphoi* of Menander, Charinus and Byrrhia come into the *Andria* from the *Perinthia*, stretches of the *Eunuch* are made more exciting by inserting a livelier soldier and flatterer from the *Kolax*. Like Plautus, he gives speaking parts to mute characters of the original, because he can command more actors than Menander:[2] the recognition scene in the *Andria* (904 f.) seems to be a telescoping together of two scenes in the original; in the *Heautontimoroumenos* (614) Sostrata speaks back into the house as she leaves, but Terence with his extra actor makes the nurse answer her; in the *Eunuch* Antipho is introduced so as to convert Chaerea's monologue into dialogue. The suppression of Menander's prologue speeches by a god or a personified abstract is a more important change because this leaves the audience without the knowledge on which Menander plays for his effects:[3] Terence prefers the effect of surprise, and if he had translated the *Perikeiromene* he would not have warned the audience of the identity of Moschion and Glykera. Metrically, he is much simpler than Plautus: the vast majority of his lines are in iambic senarii or in the ordinary recitative metres; he only twice approaches the more elaborate Plautine cantica and both passages are quite short – Charinus in distress (*Andria* 625–38) and Aeschinus in distress (*Ad.* 610–24): but these are short and simple compared with the monologue on love in the *Trinummus* (223). Viewed fresh from Plautus, Terence seems much more like the Menander known from papyrus and, where original and copy can be compared, he only seems to take the normal liberties of a translator, generalizing particularities which would appeal to a Greek more than to a Roman audience and restylizing in terms of his own rhetoric.[4] He restricted himself to the kind of comedy which he liked

---

[1] Cf. *S.M.*, 67, 77 f., 87.    [2] Cf. *S.M.*, 69, 70, 81, 89 f.

[3] Cf. *S.M.*, 77, 84; *L.G.C.*, 207. On the larger aspects of Terence's originality see H. Haffter, *M.H.* 10, 1953, 1 ff., 73 ff.

[4] Cf. Juliane Straus, *Terenz und Menander*, Zurich, 1955.

best: the six plays only represent two authors, Menander and Apollodoros, and the plays which he was bringing back on his last journey were plays by Menander. His major divagations from his originals were noted in the prologues, and his critics evidently demanded faithfulness. In terms of art history Terence would rank somewhere near his contemporaries who made free adaptations of classical masterpieces and are clearly distinguished from the mechanical copyists of the end of the second century. Turpilius,[1] as far as can be seen from the fragments, carried on this tradition of Terence for another fifty years.

Pacuvius,[2] the nephew of Ennius from Brundisium, was born in 220 and competed with Accius in 140, after which he seems to have retired to Tarentum. The play on Pydna can be dated to 168. Otherwise his tragedies cannot be dated, although it has been suggested that Plautus already echoed the *Antiopa* in 191.[3] Like Ennius he seems to have used recitative metres, where the original used iambic trimeters.[4] The only monody (or rather lyric dialogue) is in anapaestic dimeters and may repeat the metre of the original:[5] nothing survives in the least like the great monodies of Ennius. Pacuvius had both the chorus of old men and the chorus of bacchanals in the *Antiopa*, but the only fragment which is probably choral is too short to show the metre (XII).[6] As far as we can see, the *Antiopa* and the *Periboea* (on the Oeneus story) followed Euripides fairly closely and the *Niptra* and *Teucer* followed Sophocles. The *Hermione* also probably followed Sophocles but we know too little about Sophocles' play to say anything useful.

The fact that Pacuvius grew up in South Italy suggests that he may have learned his tragedy as well as his painting there and that he may have used actors' copies of comparatively recent tragedies. The *Armorum Judicium, Atalanta, Chryses, Dulorestes, Iliona, Medus* seem to belong to the sort of exciting play full of incident which was

[1] Cf. Beare, op. cit., 105.
[2] Leo, *Gesch.*, 226 ff.; Beare, op. cit., 69 f., Frassinetti in *Antidoron H. H. Paoli*, 96.
[3] Thierfelder, *Hermes* 74, 1939, 155 f.
[4] *Niptra* X certainly, probably also *Niptra* I.
[5] *Niptra* IX, cf. S. *Trach.* 974 ff.
[6] *Inc.* IV probably belongs and is dactylic.

already popular about the middle of the fourth century.[1] The *Armorum Judicium* not only dealt with the contest for Achilles' arms in which Ajax and Odysseus stated their case and were apparently judged by the Trojan captives,[2] but continued far enough with the story to include the debate over Ajax' body. In Aeschylus' *Judgment of Arms* the Nereids formed the jury and the suicide of Ajax belonged to another play,[3] the *Thracian Women*. Aeschylus therefore cannot be the source. Plato in the *Republic* (469D–E)[4] says that people who strip corpses and prevent their burial are like dogs which get angry with the stone that hits them instead of the people who throw the stone. Pacuvius quotes the image in the scene in which presumably Odysseus demands burial for Ajax (XIV). The Greek poet whom he is translating must have known his *Republic* and it is tempting to think of Theodektes, who came over from Isocrates to Plato and wrote an *Ajax* including the scene of judgment.[5]

We have no direct evidence that Theodektes was produced in South Italy, but another fourth-century play, Chairemon's *Achilles Thersitoktonos*, is illustrated on an Apulian vase of the late fourth century.[6] Euripides' *Antiope* was also in the South Italian repertoire. But a more interesting, if tenuous, link with Pacuvius is given by the Apulian vase with Medea.[7] This *Medea* at least mentioned Hippotes, the brother of Kreousa, since on the vase he rushes with Merope to help his sister. Other divergences from Euripides are the saving of one of Medea's children, the appearance of the ghost of Aietes, and the introduction of Oistros on a snaky chariot. Hippotes reappears in Pacuvius' *Medus*, which is summarized in Hyginus (*Fab.* 27). This is an extraordinary story: Medus was the son of Medea and Aegeus; in pursuit of his mother he arrived at Aea (fr. I, II) to find Perses reigning and afraid of an oracle, which warned him against the descendants of Aeetes; Medus pretended to be Hippotes but was caught and imprisoned (fr. X); Medea arrived on her snaky chariot

---

[1] *Periboea* and *Pentheus* yield nothing: on the latter see Frassinetti, loc. cit.
[2] Frassinetti, op. cit., 105 on fr. VIII.     [3] Aesch. fr. 174; 83 N.
[4] Cf. Bielinski, *Acc. Pol. Rome* 16, 1962, 47.
[5] Cf. *A.A.L.*, 61; Nauck, p. 801. Does Nauck³ fr. 438b refer to this play?
[6] Boston, 03.804; *A.A.L.*, 67, pl. 9.
[7] Munich 810 (Jahn). See Regenbogen, *Eranos* 48, 1950, 34 ff.

(fr. XI)¹, and pretended to be a priestess of Diana. When she heard that Hippotes was in prison, she told the king that he was Medus and asked to have him to kill; when she found that he really was Medus, she gave him a sword to kill Perses, and he thus secured the kingdom. Euripides' *Cresphontes* was clearly known to the poet of this play; but the curious emphasis on Hippotes shows that he too was known and his name, the snaky chariot, and the fact that Aeetes is already dead suggest that the *Medea* illustrated on the Apulian vase was also known to the poet whom Pacuvius translated. At least we can say with some probability that both this *Medea* and the Greek *Medos* were performed in Tarentum.

A still more tenuous link connects the original of the *Chryses* with South Italy. Again Hyginus has summarized the story (*Fab.* 121);² when Agamemnon restored Chryseis to Chryses I, she was pregnant and in due course gave birth to Chryses II, whom she said was the son of Apollo. Iphigeneia and Orestes arrived at Chryse (or Sminthe), chased by Thoas, and Chryses II proposed to give them up to him. But Chryseis told Chryses that in truth he was the son of Agamemnon and Orestes was his brother. The brothers then killed Thoas and brought the statue of Artemis safely back to Mycenae. The Pacuvius fragments give: I, calm after a storm, which presumably had driven Orestes to Chryse; II–IV, a king who has inherited from his father, consulting his citizens about a portent (this fits admirably with Chryses II as the adopted son of Chryses I); V, a criticism of augury and exstipicy, perhaps slightly Romanized but very much in the spirit of Orestes in Euripides' *I.T.* 570 ff.; VI–VII, curious fragments on sky and earth, which Frassinetti rightly points out do *not* derive from Euripides' *Chrysippus* (839 N); VIII, IX, someone has climbed a mountain which gives a view of the Hellespont; presumably Pylades or another reports the arrival of Thoas' ship; XII, description of a cave on the shore: here on the analogy of *I.T.* 106, 260, one would expect Orestes, Pylades and Iphigeneia to have been discovered by the inhabitants; XIV, someone has discovered which of the two is Orestes (cf. XVIII, XIX). It may have been in this play by Pacuvius

---

¹ Perhaps also inc. XXXVI, XXXVII.

² I have put down the simple story which emerges from Hyginus' difficult and partly corrupt text (see Rose, ad loc.; Nauck³ fr. 279c).

that Pylades claimed to be Orestes (*Inc.* XII–XIII), and this will belong to the moment when the three are first brought to Chryses. XXI, someone prays that the gods may 'remove thy madness', so that presumably Orestes still sees Furies. The story becomes clearer from the illustration on a silver cup (pl. XX*a*)[1] of the late second or early first century B.C.: there Orestes, Pylades, and Iphigeneia with the statue of Artemis are gathered at the shrine of Apollo; Orestes' gesture shows that he is seeing a vision and presumably therefore he sees Furies (cf. fr. XXI). Chryseis is telling Chryses that Orestes is his brother at the moment when Chryses is parleying with Thoas and an attendant.

There is little to indicate the date of the play from which the scene on the silver cup is derived, but it may be pointed out that the figure of Chryseis is very like the female figures[2] on the large Apulian vases with dramatic scenes which were painted between 330 and 300. This would give a bottom date for the original. The top date must surely be Euripides' *Iphigenia in Tauris*, since the play is obviously designed as a sequel to it and the arguments that Euripides first introduced Orestes into the story of the return of the Tauric Artemis appear well-founded. Sophocles' *Chryses*, which was produced before 414, is therefore excluded, and no shred of evidence connects the fragments of that play with this story.[3] I cannot suggest a convincing title or author, but the play certainly belongs among the plays which exploited Euripidean themes, a tradition which started in the fourth century.

Yet another play which exploited Euripides, this time the *Hecuba*, was the *Iliona*. Polydoros was given to Iliona, wife of Polymestor, to bring up: she gave out that he was her own son and that Polymestor's son was Polydoros. When Polymestor was bribed by Agamemnon to kill Polydoros, he in fact killed his own son. Pacuvius' play started with the ghost of this boy demanding burial of his mother; the real Polydoros came home and was told the truth by Iliona, who

[1] British Museum 1960. 2—1.1. P. E. Corbett and D. E. Strong, *B.M.Q.* 23, 1961, 68 ff.

[2] Cf. e.g. the Medea vase quoted above.

[3] For earlier discussions, cf. Zielinski, *Tragodoumenon*, 316; Jebb-Pearson, *Sophocles Fragments*, II, 327; Platnauer, *Iphigenia in Tauris*, XII.

U

incited him to blind Polymestor. The mistaken identities of this play recall the deceptions of the *Medus* and again suggest an original of the fourth century or later. Two other plays may derive from the same kind of late and exciting original, although the details are obscure: in the *Dulorestes* Orestes returned home as or disguised as a slave (of Pylades?) and in carrying out the murder of Clytemnestra seems to have become involved with Oeax (Oeax aiding Aegisthus against Orestes is already mentioned in Euripides' *Orestes*). The *Atalanta* is also obscure but perhaps treats Atalanta's discovery of Parthenopaeus, whom she had exposed, when he had grown up. The very strangeness of these plays makes it probable that Pacuvius was not so much translating book editions of the classics as Romanizing plays which were being performed in South Italy.

Accius[1] was born in 170 at Pisaurum in Umbria and was still living about 90. He competed with Pacuvius in 140 and visited him in Tarentum on his way to Asia. He wrote over forty tragedies. To start with the known authors, Aeschylus is represented by the *Myrmidones* and the *Prometheus* (unbound). Of the latter only two lines survive; the fragments of the former fit well with what we know of Aeschylus' *Myrmidones* and very possibly the *Achilles* is an alternative title.[2] We then have from the scene of the Embassy to Achilles fr. II, III, V, VIII and fr. II and III of the *Achilles*; from the ensuing scene with Antilochos fr. I and VII, and from a later scene when Patroclus has already gone out and is too successful for Achilles' liking fr. IV and IX: Achilles' reproach to Patroclus in IV does not imply his presence; in IX Patroclus is defended probably by Antilochus. Here, as far as our meagre evidence allows us to judge, Accius follows his model closely. The second play of the Aeschylean trilogy, the *Nereides*, took the story from the arming of Achilles to the death of Hektor; perhaps this was the source of Accius' *Epinausimache*, in which a Greek hero claims to have dyed the Scamander with blood

---

[1] Leo, *Gesch.*, 384 ff.; Beare, op. cit., 109.

[2] See most recently G. Barabino, *Antidoron H. H. Paoli*, 57 ff. On Aeschylus *Myrmidons*, W. Schadewaldt, *Hermes* 71, 1936, 25. The newer fragments in *P. Oxy.* 2163, 2253, 2255, do not help our problem. I do not share the doubts of Page (*G.L.P.*, no. 20) and Lloyd Jones (Loeb, *Aeschylus*, no. 286) about the authorship of *P.S.I.*, no. 1211.

(XII) and three fragments can be related to *Iliad* XVIII.[1] The change of title is no more surprising than Pacuvius renaming the Euripidean *Oeneus* as *Periboea*. Of the Sophoclean plays too little is left of original or copy of the *Antenoridai*, *Erigone* (but Accius' play was certainly about Erigone, daughter of Aigisthos), *Athamas*, *Atreus* (certainly on the feast of Thyestes, but it is not clear whether it translates Sophocles' *Atreus* or Euripides' *Cretan Women*), *Epigoni*, *Eurysaces*, *Tereus*, *Oenomaus* (whether derived from Sophocles or Euripides) for any useful comparison to be made. The fragments of the *Antigone* are difficult: neither Euripides nor Astydamas is likely to have included Ismene, and therefore as Accius writes 'what are you doing? You are upsetting and twisting everything, sister', he is probably following Sophocles and this fragment (I) is a loose translation of Ismene's 'Why do you grieve me thus, profiting nothing yourself?' (550). The other fragments also can be explained as free translations.[2] It is not unexpected that Accius should translate Sophoclean iambics into trochaics, but on two occasions he chooses a more obviously lyric metre for a moment of excitement: dactyls for Creon's summons to his guards (IV) and anapaests for the passage of the messenger speech where Creon hears Haemon's voice (III). He seems therefore to have been just as free as Ennius in his use of metre. Accius' *Andromeda* was not founded on Euripides: this was a version in which apparently Kepheus appealed to Phineus to help Andromeda (III, IV, VI) and Perseus only arrived later. Sophocles has been claimed as the inspiration of three mid-fifth-century vase-paintings[3] in which Andromeda is shown being exposed with a post on either side of her, and this may be Pacuvius' source, as presumably the appeal to Phineus was made before Andromeda was tied to the posts.[4]

Of the Euripidean plays *Alcestis*, *Chrysippus*, *Meleager*, *Troades*, *Hecuba* do not survive in sufficient fragments to make comparison

[1] Cf. I with *Il.* XVIII, 114 f.; III with 155 f.; VI with 318.

[2] Cf. II with *Ant.* 98, III with 1217, IV with 1108, V with 922.

[3] Whiteground kalyx krater in Agrigento (Giudice); I owe my knowledge of this to Professor P. E. Corbett. Hydria in British Museum E 169, Séchan, op. cit., 149, fig. 47. Pelike, *Boston Museum Bulletin*, 61, 1963, 108.

[4] Two other possibilities are that *Deiphobus* derives from Sophocles' *Sinon* and *Aegisthus* = *Clytemnestra* from Sophocles' *Clytemnestra* (here again the names may have been duplicated but the evidence for both is very weak.)

useful. The *Alcumeo* and the *Alphesiboea* both fit well into the fragments of the *Alcmaeon in Psophis* and evidently derive from it; the
*Telephus* also fits into the fragments of Euripides' *Telephus*.[1] The
*Diomedes* may derive from the *Oeneus*. The *Bacchae* and *Phoenissae*
fragments can be compared with the Euripidean texts. In the *Bacchae*
he sometimes translates iambics into trochaics (VIII, X, XIV, XV)
and once apparently iambics of a messenger speech into cretics, if
*agite modico gradu, iacite nisus levis* is really an adaptation of Agave's
summons (689–94). In the *Phoenissae* he certainly twice translates
iambics into trochaics (VII, X). Certainly also one fragment (XI) in
which Eteocles visits wounded soldiers has no place in the original
and is an addition to suit Roman taste. Three fragments are unclear:
III, 'he handed on change of rule' and V 'that the son might safely
possess the sceptre of the father' were taken by Leo[2] to imply a
different version in which Oedipus instead of cursing his sons
arranged alternate rule: but possibly Polynices, not Oedipus, is the
subject of 'handed on' and the fragments are an expansion of the
brief description of the arrangement in Euripides (69 f.). The other
(IV) in trochaics 'lest their discord should scatter the riches of the
city' may perhaps be a prayer of the chorus from the context of l. 240,
but again it expands the simple Greek: 'may it not happen . . .'. The
*Amphitruo* may perhaps be derived from the *Hercules Furens*, if fr. IV
and V describe Megara in her distress and fr. VIII and XIII belong to
scene with Theseus.

Some of the other plays are for one reason or another worthy of
note. The *Armorum Judicium* seems to cover the same stretch of story
as the like-named play of Pacuvius, from the Judgment of Arms to
the burial of Ajax; but two lines come very close to the *Ajax* of
Sophocles: 'May you be equal in valour but unequal in fortune to
your father' (X, with S. *Aj.* 550) and 'may the guilt of the Pelopidai
be extinguished' (XV, with 839). We cannot tell whether it was
Pacuvius or the Greek poet of his original who introduced these
Sophoclean scenes. The fragments of the *Philoctetes* also show a close
relationship to Sophocles—with the prologue (IV, VI), the parodos

[1] On the *Alcmaeon* see Schadewaldt, *Hermes* 80, 1952, 57 ff.; on the *Telephus*,
E. W. Handley and J. Rea, op. cit., 40 f.

[2] Op. cit., 395.

(V), the first epeisodion (XIII, XI, XIV) of the Sophoclean play; but Accius' play started with a dialogue in anapaests between Odysseus and another, Leo assumes that they were the chorus of Odysseus' sailors, but Neoptolemos or Diomedes remain a possibility; he rightly compares the anapaests of the *Rhesus*, to which, of course, the anapaests of the *Iphigenia in Aulis* should be added. Philoctetes says (XVI): 'Alas, Mulciber, you made invincible arms for a coward'; this proves that someone told Philoctetes about the Judgment of Arms but not whether it was Odysseus in disguise or another. As in Sophocles, Philoctetes was tortured by his wound (XII, XXI) and in a monody (XIX), which recalls Sophocles, asked to be killed; here again Accius seems to be translating a poet who was greatly influenced by Sophocles.[1] Both Antiphon and Theodektes wrote a *Philoctetes* and either of these is a possible source for Accius.

Antiphon also comes in question as the source of Accius' *Astyanax*. There is no reason why Accius should not have translated the same original as Ennius; Morel[2] made a good case for identifying the original of Ennius' *Andromache Aichmalotis* with a papyrus fragment and suggested Antiphon as the author, and we know from Aristotle that Antiphon's Andromache tried to save her child by giving him to someone else to bring up, and Servius preserves a version in which Calchas ordered the murder of Astyanax and Ulysses found him in the hiding place prepared by his mother. Accius' fragments certainly refer to Calchas (IV, V) and to someone discovered in hiding in the mountains (IX–XI). The papyrus fragment apparently gives the initial warning to Andromache, and this may be the scene depicted on the funeral relief of Numitorius, to which I shall return later:[3] there an elderly man brings bad news to an Oriental woman who holds a boy by the hand.

The *Medea* raises difficult problems. The arrival of the Argo is observed by a shepherd (I–IV) who has never seen a ship before and

---

[1] Friedrich, *Hermes* 76, 1941, 121 argues for contamination of Sophocles and Euripides.

[2] *Ph. W.* 1937, 558. For details, cf. *Hermes* 82, 1954, 299.

[3] Cf. below, p. 302. Professor Bieber suggested the *Astyanax* of Accius and saw Odysseus in the man; but Odysseus should be younger and cheerful; this is an elderly bringer of bad news.

thinks it may be a rocky mass thrown up by Triton; this speech must have some relation to Apollonios Rhodios' account of the shepherds who left their sheep in fear, thinking that Apsyrtos' ships were sea-monsters (IV, 313 ff.). Apollonios' account is simpler and should therefore be earlier. In any case as Medea is still on the Argo, this part of Accius' play must belong to the period between the capture of the Fleece and the arrival at Iolkos. If fr. XVI, *pernici orbificor liberorum leto et tabificabili*, refers either to the death of Kreousa or to the death of Medea's children, the play had a very long time-span and a change of locality. It is perhaps worth hazarding the guess that it refers to the death of Apsyrtos and that this was put late as in Apollonios. The scene is presumably the island of Brygaean Artemis and her priestess had expected Medea (XII, XIV). Then possibly the story ran much as in Apollonios, but Aietes arrived late in the play to find that Apsyrtos had been killed (XVI). At least a Hellenistic original seems likely here. It may be chance that Accius shares the title *Hellenes* with Apollodoros of Tarsos, who is known for his comments on Euripides' *Medea*. Finally the *Nyktegresia*, as Leo says, covers the subject matter of the *Rhesus*, but the description of Hektor's success by a Greek (I, II) and the very clear reminiscence of Diomedes' speech in the planning of the raid (VI = *Iliad* X, 243) show that the play was set in the Greek camp and must derive from another original.

Accius visited South Italy and Asia and thus had ample opportunity to see productions of Greek tragedy. The one possible indication that some of the plays for which we do not know the original may have been written in Asia is the coincidence of title, *Hellenes*, with Apollodoros of Tarsos, but it is a slender link. Otherwise his plays are adaptations partly of classics which we have reason to suppose were often revived, such as *Alcestis, Antiope, Meleager, Tereus, Telephus*, partly of plays which we suspect to be Hellenistic and which he may have found on the stage in South Italy or in Asia, such as the new versions of the *Philoctetes* and the *Medea*. For both these classes he may have used acting texts rather than book texts. But there is a third class of plays: the originals of these have only come down to us in scanty fragments and we have no evidence for revivals either from vases or inscriptions or for earlier adaptations by Latin authors. Such are the *Andromeda, Antenoridae, Niptra, Erigone, Eury-saces*, of Sophocles. But Accius may have used book texts rather than actors' texts and his journey to Asia, presumably to Pergamon in the last years of the Attalids, may have been in search of texts, just as Terence went to Greece to find texts of Menander.

Accius was also interested in the history of poetry and revives in Rome the Alexandrian combination of scholar and poet. Leo[1] has plausibly suggested that his *Didascalica* was a dialogue partly in prose and partly in verse, sotadean and trochaic. The fragments of the *Pragmatica* are trochaic. The meaning of the titles and the relation between the two works are obscure. Probably the *Didascalica* dealt at length with the chronology of Roman drama including the dating of Livius Andronicus (16 M), the canon of Plautus' plays (17 M), Accius' own production in the same year as Pacuvius (18 M). But in the first book (6 M), he agreed against Eratosthenes and Aristar-chos that Hesiod was earlier than Homer; this may have been the Pergamene view. Two paraphrases of the *Iliad* (7, 8 M) recall Sotades,[2] and it is difficult to see in what context they fitted. In the second book Euripides was criticized for his use of the chorus (11 M); in the eighth book (12 M) tragic actors are said to have sleeves, belts, and daggers; whether this comes from a manual or Accius' own observation is unknown. Then in the ninth book (13 M) Baebius, presumably one of the speakers in the dialogue, is to be told of the different kinds of poetry. Leo argues that the past history led up to the chronology of Roman drama in the middle books and this may be right, but the paraphrases of single lines in the *Iliad* seem out of scale with this intention and the transition to other kinds of poetry is unexpected. Of the *Pragmatica* three interesting fragments survive: the first (23 M) speaks of describing bad citizens in the theatre; Leo assumes that the reference is to Greek Old Comedy but it could equally well apply to Naevius. The second (24 M): 'Therefore poets are plagued more often by your gullibility and folly than by their own faults', might be a translation of an Aristophanic parabasis or an echo of a Terentian prologue. In the third fragment (25 M) the reference can only be Greek: 'They sang dancing what they now

[1] *Gesch.*, 386 ff. Texts in W. Morel, *Fragmenta poetarum Latinorum*, 34.
[2] Cf. above, p. 126.

sing standing and they call them by the dark name of sikinnistai'. The name is dark because the Greeks argued about the origin of the sikinnis, the dance of the satyr-play; Athenaeus quotes Aristokles for the equation sikinnistai = satyrs (presumably choruses of men dressed as satyrs rather than satyrs).[1] The Accius fragment evidently refers to a stage before the stasimon (*quae nunc stantes canunt*) and it is tempting to connect this with the notice on Arion in the Suda lexikon; 'he was the first to make the chorus stationary'. In any case Accius is giving a piece of theory on the history of drama, which we do not have in this form anywhere else.

Here then was a dramatist, who also put literary history and theory into verse. In this he runs parallel to his critic and contemporary Lucilius,[2] who was writing from at least as early as 132 and died in 101: he had visited Athens probably about 140. What models for the form of his critical works Accius had is not clear, the Suda records that Theodektes wrote *Rhetoric* in metre and some such work may have provided an ancestor. Lucilius' literary criticism is joined with invective and is therefore more in the tradition of Kallimachos, the Kallimachos of the prologue to the *Aitia* and of the first and thirteenth *Iamboi*.[3] Some of it is criticism of tragic style including Accius, and some of it criticism of Accius' grammar; perhaps also a criticism of Accius' statue. Pliny says: 'the writers note also that L. Accius the poet had an enormous statue of himself put in the temple of the Camenae because he was extremely short': the fragment of Lucilius: 'Therefore in view of his face and figure Accius . . .' must surely be from a poem on Accius' statue.[4] Lucilius follows Kallimachos also in the poem on his own poetry: he is writing for the middle-brows (not that Kallimachos ever did that but he also defined his audience); profitable poetry is epics on campaigns, but he can only write his own kind; the critics must know the rules and realize the difference between *poiesis* and *poiema*.[5] His

---

[1] Ath. 622b. Pickard-Cambridge, *Festivals*, 259. Aristokles, an Alexandrian, is dated later than 117 B.C. by Athenaeus 174b. He cannot have been Accius' source.

[2] Leo, *Gesch.*, 406 f.        [3] Cf. above, p. 99 ff.

[4] Tragedy: 587, 605–6, 653, 875. Grammar: Book IX. Statue: 794. Cf. Pliny, *N.H.*, 34, 19.

[5] 588–96, 620–3; 341–8. Cf. also 462 f. and C. O. Brink, *Horace on Poetry*, 64.

middle-brows are expected to know a lot of Greek: Socrates, Isocrates, Phryne, Epicurus, Polemon, Aristippus, and Archilochus are all named and named, as far as we can see, allusively. Archilochos is indeed the most obvious model for his attacks on public figures (but this tradition was still alive, as we have seen, in the late third-century epigrammatists as well as in comedy).[1] One moralizing poem seems to have been almost a translation of Archilochos' poem to his *thymos*, but the attacks on luxury and the deposition of virtue are more in the tradition of Kerkidas.[2] The journey to Capua may have a remote ancestor in Theokritos' *Thalysia* (VII) but the flavour is more like that of Herodas. The cruel poem in which the council of the Gods condemn L. Cornelius Lentulus Lupus is a parody of Ennius and no Greek parallel is preserved since Aristophanes. Lucilius clearly made very good use of his time in Greece and knew the whole range of Greek poetry, particularly the range of satiric poetry from Archilochos through Old Comedy to Kallimachos and Kerkidas. He assumes a knowledge of this range in his audience and he transmutes his models into something peculiarly personal and Roman. The plays of Accius and Terence survived because they were read and revived; but Lucilius was the father of the whole line of Roman Satura.

The cross connections between the Roman dramatists and between Accius and Lucilius is the justification for treating them together and so carrying the history of poetry down to the end of the second century. Meanwhile the plundering of the Greek world had continued. In 146 Mummius brought marbles, bronzes, and paintings back from Corinth for the adornment of Rome and Italian cities.[3] He also, according to Tacitus,[4] was the first person to give a dramatic display at his triumph; this is obviously untrue, but Mummius' triumph must have been remembered for some particular dramatic reason which is lost to us. Mummius' attention was called to painting when Attalos II of Pergamon bought from Mummius' booty a picture of Dionysos by the fourth-century Theban painter Aristeides

---

[1] Cf. above, p. 236.
[2] 699–700 with Archilochos 67D; 515, 440 ff., 1228 ff., 1326 ff. with Kerkidas.
[3] Livy, *Perioch.*, 52–3; Vessberg, op. cit., 33.
[4] *Annals* XIV, 21, Cf. above, p. 277.

for a very large sum. According to Polybios the painting had been thrown on the floor and the soldiers were using it as a gambling board. Mummius was moved by the price to think that the picture must have some merit; so he withdrew it from the sale and dedicated it in the temple of Ceres in Rome.[1] Another work which found its home in a Roman temple, the temple of Felicitas, was the group of Thespiades, which he moved from Thespiai; these were probably Muses by Praxiteles.[2] The temple as Art Gallery has already met us in Syracuse; the Romans were merely following Greek custom. Q. Caecilius Metellus, also in 146, moved from Macedonia the bronze group of horsemen made by Lysippos to commemorate Alexander's victory at the Granikos and set it up in the porticus Metelli in Rome; the porticus Metelli enclosed the temple of Jupiter and the temple of Juno, for which two Athenian sculptors, Dionysios and Polykles, sons of Timarchides, made the cult statues.[3] Works of art in great quantity came to Italy when the property of Attalos III was auctioned in 133/2.

Pliny's note on the two temples in the porticus Metelli shows that Metellus not only collected old masters but also brought living Greek artists to work in Rome. The terracotta figures[4] from the pediment of a temple on the Caelian hill recall in design and scale the pediment in Samothrace, and fragments of a colossal statue[5] found in Rome have been connected in style with the Zeus of Aigeira and the group at Lykosoura. Thus besides classical masterpieces of the fifth and fourth centuries the Romans also knew the new classical style as it was practised in contemporary Greece. The same Attic sculptor Dionysios with his nephew, Timarchides son of Polykles, made a portrait statue in Delos of C. Ofellius Ferus; the Italian was given the body of a fourth-century Hermes and presumably a realistic portrait head like another statue of a Roman in Delos (pl. XXIIa).[6] This extraordinary mixture of realistic Roman

---

[1] Pliny, N.H., 35, 24; Strabo, 8, 381.
[2] Cicero, In Verr., II, iv, 4; Pliny, N.H., 36, 39; Roscher, II, 3248.
[3] Pliny, N.H., 34, 64; Plut., Alexander 16, 8. Porticus Metelli: Pliny, N.H., 36, 35.
[4] Rome, Conservatori, Braccio Nuovo. Strong, Roman Imperial Sculpture, figs. 11–12; Riis, Etruskiske Kunst, 248; Stuart-Jones, pl. 121.
[5] Bieber, Hell. Sc., 171, fig. 725.      [6] Cf. above, p. 247.

features with idealized Greek body presumably appealed to something in Roman taste. The portraits in Delos prove that Greek
sculptors were responsible for such work and many portraits in
Italy are signed by Greek sculptors. The two portraits in Delos have
an analogy in a portrait of a Roman commander (pl. XXIIb),
probably of the early first century, found in Tivoli;[1] again the heroic
body contrasts with the realistic elderly face; this sculptor did however choose a rather more suitable body, not a young athletic
Hermes but a Zeus or Poseidon rather in the style of the Poseidon of
Melos. When Greek portraiture was realistic, as, for instance, in the
portrait of Chrysippos, it was consistently realistic; the demand for
this curious hybrid art may well be Roman and faintly parallel to
Lucilius' purely Roman use of Hellenistic poetic models.

Delos and the warehouse in the Peiraeus provide the earliest
examples of exact copies of earlier masterpieces, and the two copies
of the Alkamenes herm in the warehouse were almost certainly
waiting shipment to Rome with earlier bronze originals.[2] The ship
wrecked off Tunis was bringing Neo-Attic kraters (pl. XXIIIa) to
Italy.[3] Two names can be connected with this kind of art in Rome:
Pasiteles and Arkesilaos – Pasiteles is quoted by Pliny as a silver-
worker in the time of Pompey the Great (106/48); he was a Greek
from South Italy, who was given Roman citizenship, presumably in
89; he wrote five books on famous works of art in the whole world;
among his statues was an ivory Jupiter in Metellus' temple; he said
that modelling was the mother of engraving and statuary and
sculpture (presumably this means metal vessels, bronzes, and marble
statues) and that he never made anything without first making a
model for it.[4] He can therefore certainly be connected with the
fine silver-work of the late Republic. Miss Richter[5] has argued that
he possibly invented exact copying with the use of casts and the
pointing process. It seems at least certain that he was an academic
artist who based his art on famous works, whether the result was

[1] Rome, Terme 106513. Bieber, *Hell. Sc.*, 173, fig. 732; Vessberg, op. cit.,
209 f., pl. 48–9.
[2] Cf. above, p. 247.      [3] Cf. above, p. 248.
[4] Pliny, *N.H.*, 33, 156; 36, 39–40; 35, 156.
[5] *Three Periods*, 44; cf. Vessberg, op. cit., 65, 109; Bieber, *Hell. Sc.*, 181.

exact copies or adaptations in the style which we should call Neo-Attic. His pupil Stephanos signed a marble youth (pl. XXIV*a*),[1] which is obviously inspired by early classical art but is perhaps an adaptation rather than a mechanical copy – it is, at least, a modernized copy, and one version was combined by Stephanos himself or a later artist with a late fifth-century Aphrodite to make a group of Orestes and Elektra.

Arkesilaos was a friend of Lucullus, who brought Kalamis' colossal Apollo from Apollonia Pontica to Rome in 72;[2] this was an early classical work and testifies, like Stephanos' youth, which may be contemporary, to a liking for this earlier style among the Romans. Arkesilaos may have been brought to Rome from Athens by Lucullus in 88. He made the Venus Genetrix in the forum of Julius Caesar in 46. His clay models (*proplasmata*) were sold for more to artists than the completed works of others and he sold a plaster mould (*exemplar*) for a talent to an *eques* who wanted to make a krater. If, as seems probable, the krater was to be cast in precious metal, Arkesilaos had the same range as Pasiteles. The two men seem to be at the centre of an industry producing academic art, copies and adaptations, in all sizes and materials for Roman patrons. Their activities explain why a set of plasters evidently belonging to a metal-worker in Afghanistan[3] contains figures and groups which are known elsewhere as paintings, relief carvings, and free sculpture. The plaster and the clay model were the artists' stock in trade and could be mechanically enlarged or reduced as the job for the particular patron required.

No work of Pasiteles has survived but the marble youth of Stephanos (pl. XXIV*a*) is probably a fair guide to what his marble sculpture looked like. Dohrn has pointed out that, although inspired by early classical work, it is meant to be seen from a three-quarter view and so loses the frontality of Greek early classical work. He may not be right in seeing a specifically Italian trait here; more probably

---

[1] Rome, Villa Albani 317. Richter and Bieber, loc. cit.; Dohrn, *Festschrift A. Rumpf*, 63.

[2] Pliny, *N.H.*, 35, 155–6; 34, 39. On the Apollo, Studniczka, *Kalamis*, 68, 85. On Arkesilaos, Bieber and Richter, loc. cit.

[3] Cf. above, p. 172.

this is simply natural adaptation by an artist who had the whole experience of classical, fourth-century, and Early Hellenistic art behind him. The pose is shared by other works which have often been taken for Greek originals but have been shown by Rumpf to be adaptations of early classical or classical statues to make them into lampstands for Roman dining rooms. Presumably the creator of the fashion remembered the golden boys with torches in their hands who gave light to the banqueters in Alkinoos' palace. One of the best known of these is the so-called Idolino (pl. XXIVb),[1] which is an adaptation of an athletic statue by Polykleitos. The artists who made these adaptations took classical works or even parts from different classical works and composed them with minor modifications to suit their purposes. The procedure is not essentially different from the combination of classical figures from different sources in different scenes by the artists of Neo-Attic reliefs.

The Neo-Attic marble vases signed by Sosibios of Athens and Salpion of Athens have been dated to the first half of the first century. They were found in Italy and are presumably the work of artists who immigrated after Sullas' sack. But as we have already seen, similar works were being made in Greece before they came.[2] The group of Dionysos supported by a satyr followed by three other satyrs, one of whom supports a falling maenad, which we noted as out of context on one of the Greek kraters found in the Mahdia wreck, occurs again on a first-century relief on a marble base in the Vatican,[3] where it makes sense because Dionysos is visiting a poet in his house and therefore the little satyr who unties Dionysos' sandals is relevant. In the late and much more elaborate example[4] in the British Museum the artist has misunderstood both the woman on the poet's couch and the group of satyr supporting maenad. It looks as if his model was unclear in these respects, and one wonders if he was working with a small plaster cast. The connection between

---

[1] Florence, Museo Archeologico 143. Lippold, *Gr. Pl.*, 165; Winter, *K.i.B.*, 254; Rumpf, *Critica d'Arte* 19/20, 1939, 17 ff.; Dohrn, loc. cit.; Van Buren, *A.J.A.*, 67, 1963, 33, compares Lucretius, II, 24.

[2] Cf. above, p. 247; Richter, op. cit., 50 f.; Bieber, *Hell. Sc.*, 182 ff.

[3] Rome, Vatican, Amelung II, 509; Strong, *Roman Imperial Sculpture*, fig. 24.

[4] British Museum 2190, Webster, *M.N.C.*, no. AS 3. Cf. above, p. 249.

Neo-Attic reliefs and silver-work is given not only by the interpretation here adopted for the texts on Pasiteles and Arkesilaos but by the recurrence of Neo-Attic themes on Arretine vases of the late first century. The dance with the basket headdress,[1] which derives ultimately from a Greek original of the late fifth century, is found both in Arretine and on Neo-Attic reliefs, and the likeness between the Victories with archaistic drapery on Arretine and on a limestone frieze of the early first century found below the Capitoline Hill is worth noting;[2] presumably both derive from an archaistic remodelling of the Nike balustrade. On the other side the relation of Arretine to silver ware is established by a small number of direct repetitions in both media.[3]

The great Neo-Attic vases clearly copy models in metal for shape and ornament, and in one case at any rate a fairly close connection between the decoration of a marble cup and a silver cup can be shown. A marble cup[4] found on the Esquiline is decorated with extraordinarily beautiful floral ornament, tendrils bearing different flowers and fruit rising out of beautifully executed acanthus leaves. Very similar decoration is seen on a silver cup (pl. XX*b*)[5] in the British Museum: there the flowers, leaves, and fruits belong to no fewer than fourteen different plants. Both the silver cup and the marble cup have been dated on style in the first half of the first century. This kind of floral ornament has a long history behind it, which goes back, perhaps but not necessarily only through Pergamon, to the mixed flowers and scrolls rising from an acanthus kalyx on the Pella mosaics.[6]

The silver cup with floral decoration belongs to the same set as the cup (pl. XX*a*)[7] with Chryseis and Chryses, which has similar

[1] Cf. Fuchs, *J.D.A.I.*, 20 Ergänzungsheft, 91; Christine Alexander, *C.V.A.*, Metropolitan Museum, i, pl. 1, 1 and p. 12.

[2] Arretine, *C.V.A.*, Metropolitan Museum, pl. 1, 2; Limestone, Rome Conservatori, Braccio Nuovo, Strong, op. cit., figs. 17–18.

[3] See K. Friis Johansen, *Acta Arch.* 31, 1960, 185 ff.; P. E. Corbett, *B.M.Q.* 23, 1961, 83.

[4] Strong, *Roman Imperial Sculpture*, fig. 20; Museo Nuovo Capitolino, Rome, Stuart Jones, pl. 51, no. 22.

[5] British Museum 1960. 2—1.3. P. E. Corbett, *B.M.Q.* 23, 1961, 77 ff.

[6] Cf. above, p. 22.          [7] Cf. above, p. 285.

floral decoration at the bottom. There we have suggested a model of the Early Hellenistic age for the figure decoration. The rather later Philoktetes cup from Hoby[1] goes back to a late fifth-century original. The silver cups from Boscoreale, which probably also date from the mid-first century, seem to go back to Alexandrian originals of the third century.[2] This elegant, eclectic art takes its models where it likes in the range of Greek art from the early classical period to the second century, sometimes copying, sometimes adapting, sometimes modernizing, sometimes archaizing, to make attractive but not necessarily meaningful new compositions.

Pasiteles and Arkesilaos were clearly central figures in the production of temple sculpture, bronzes, marble statues and reliefs, and metal-work. An interesting fringe-figure is Cicero's victim, Verres, who according to Cicero used his official positions abroad for wholesale plundering of works of art. He was in Asia in 80/79 and in Sicily from 73 to 70. He even took paintings and statues from the Heraion at Samos.[3] The most interesting works which he got hold of in Sicily were the following: (1) a statue of Himera and a portrait of Stesichoros, which had been moved by the Carthaginians and restored by Scipio.[4] (2) Heius of Messana had an ancestral shrine in his house, which contained a marble Eros by Praxiteles like the Eros of Thespiai, a bronze Herakles by Myron, and two bronze girls with baskets on their heads by Polykleitos. None of these artists are known to have made works for the West (the signed Apollo by Myron, which Verres took from the temple of Asklepios at Agrigentum, was a gift of Scipio, and may therefore have been brought from Greece). The Eros sounds like a copy, and the rest may also have been copies or comparatively recent acquisitions. (3) Silanion's portrait of Sappho from the Prytaneion in Syracuse; how it came there we do not know but there is no reason to doubt that it was a late fourth-century original.

So far Verres only appears as an unscrupulous collector, but he also used the enormous number of reliefs from gold vessels which he had collected for making up new vessels:[5] 'he set up a large workshop

---

[1] K. Friis Johansen, loc. cit.  [2] Cf. above, p. 172.
[3] Cic., *In Verr.*, II, i, 50.  [4] Cf. Schefold, *Bildnisse*, 172, 220.
[5] Himera, Cic., *In Verr.*, II, ii, 87; Heius, Cic., *In Verr.*, II, iv, 4–5; Agrigentum, ibid., 93; Syracuse, ibid., 126–7. The workshop, ibid, 54.

in the palace at Syracuse. He openly gave orders for all artists, en-
gravers and vase-makers, to come there, and he had several of his
own. He shut them up there, a large number of men. For eight
months on end they had no lack of work, although only gold vessels
were made. He so skilfully incorporated the reliefs which he had
taken from thuribles and dishes into cups and drinking vessels that
you would say that they had been made for that purpose. The
praetor who says that his vigilance kept peace in Sicily spent the
greater part of the day in this workshop wearing Greek dress.' The
story of this antique-factory makes the worthy orator exclaim
'o tempora, o mores'. Whether Verres' activities extended to copying
as well as making up, we do not know but it seems highly probable.
Verres' antique-factory will not have been any different from the
relevant department of Pasiteles' workshop.

The history of painting is not quite so simply brought under the
heading classicistic. It is true that we have ample evidence for the
import of originals and the making of copies. Sulla in 81 left a copy
of Zeuxis' Centaur family in Athens and sent the original to Greece
(it was sunk off Cape Malea). Lucullus brought a copy of Pausias'
wreath-seller in Athens, perhaps in 88. M. Junius Silanus brought
another fourth-century painting, Nikias' Nemea, from Asia to
Rome in 76; the painting must have been painted for a victor in the
Nemean games who may himself have come from Asia.[1] The
magnificent Alexander mosaic[2] in the Casa del Fauno at Pompeii
belongs to this period and is an accurate copy of a great late fourth-
century picture. The two small mosaics[3] of comic scenes by Dioskorides of Samos are dated by the inscription to about 100, but
seem to be accurate copies of third-century originals in Teos or
Pergamon. One of these mosaics was in fact copied on an enlarged
scale in another Campanian house. It is unfortunate that we know
nothing more of the use of small mosaics as painters' copy books. It
is very likely that the mask and garland mosaic[4] from the Casa del

---

[1] Sulla, Lucian, *Zeuxis*, 3. Lucullus, Pliny, *N.H.*, 35, 125. Silanus, Pliny, *N.H.*,
35, 131, cf. 27.

[2] Naples 10020, Pfuhl, *M.u.Z.*, fig. 648; Rumpf, *M.u.Z.*, pl. 49; *A.A.L.*, pl. 12.

[3] Cf. above, p. 185.

[4] Cf. above, p. 197. Bronze satyr: Naples, M. N. 814; Bieber, *Hell. Sc.*, figs. 95–6.

Plate I*a*. Plastic vase. Agora, P 12822. Dionysos child in cave covered with vines. *Photo: American School of Classical Studies.*

Plate I*b*. Terracotta statuette. Agora, T 2276. Girl. *Photo: American School of Classical Studies.*

Plate I*c*. Terracotta statuette. Agora, T 2180. Maenad seated with tympanon. *Photo: American School of Classical Studies.*

Plate I*d*. Terracotta statuette. Agora, T 2280. Eros. *Photo: American School of Classical Studies.*

Plate II. Kantharos. Agora, P 6878. Artemis hunting before a country shrine. *Photo: American School of Classical Studies.*

Plate IIIa. Marble statue. Athens,
N.M. 231. Themis. *Photo: German
Archaeological Institute.*

Plate IIIb. Bronze statuette. Naples,
M.N. 1606. Demetrios Poliorketes.
*Photo: Alinari.*

Plate IV. Marble relief. British Museum, 2191. Apotheosis of Homer.
*Photo: British Museum.*

Plate V*a*. 'Megarian' bowl. Private collection. Vines. *Photo: E. E. Hitchcock.*

Plate V*b*. 'Homeric' bowl. British Museum, G 104. Euripides, *Phoenissae*, with Antigone, Kreon, Teiresias, Manto, Poly-neikes. *Photo: British Museum.*

Plate VI*a*. Terracotta statuette. Alexandria, 24160. Herakles with wreath, club, himation. *Photo: Alexandria Museum.*

Plate VI*b*. Terracotta statuette. Boston, Fine Arts Museum, 13.155. Old man. *Photo: Boston Museum.*

Plate VII. Mosaic. Alexandria Museum. Erotes hunting. *Photo: Alexandria Museum.*

Plate VIIIb. Marble relief. Istanbul 1423. Man tying animal beneath tree. *Photo: Istanbul Museum.*

Plate VIIIa. Marble relief. Vienna, Kunsthistorisches Museum, I.873. Grave relief of Iomede, daughter of Diphilos. *Photo: Kunsthistorisches Museum.*

Plate IXb. Marble statue. Munich, 437. Drunken old woman. *Photo: Antikensammlungen.*

Plate IXa. Terracotta statuette. Alexandria, 24127. Negro boy asleep. *Photo: Alexandria Museum.*

Plate X. Bronze statuette. New York, Walter C. Baker. Veiled dancer. *Photo: Metropolitan Museum.*

Plate XI. Fayence oenochoe. Amsterdam, Allard Pierson Stichting, 7582.
Egyptian queen. *Photo: Allard Pierson Stichting.*

Plate XII. Fresco. Vatican. Odysseus' companions with the Laistrygones. *Photo: Alinari.*

Plate XIII. Marble sarcophagus. Istanbul 370. Alexander and the Persians. *Photo: Istanbul Museum.*

Plate XIV*b*. Marble statue. Vatican. Tyche of Antioch. *Photo: Alinari.*

Plate XIV*a*. Marble statue. Vatican. Niobid. *Photo: Alinari.*

Plate XV*b*. Marble statue. Louvre.
Victory. *Photo: Louvre.*

Plate XV*a*. Painted stele. Berlin 766a.
Funeral stele of Metrodoros. *Photo:
Berlin, Staatliche Museen.*

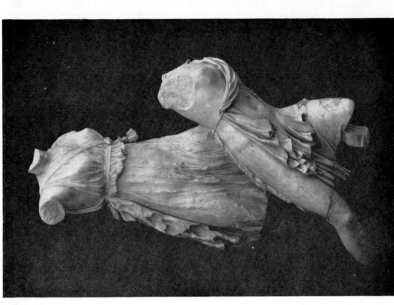

Plate XVIb. Marble group. Copenhagen, Ny Carlsberg Glyptotek, 104819. Artemis and Iphigenaia. *Photo: Ny Carlsberg Glyptotek.*

Plate XVIa. Marble group. Rome, Terme. Gaul and his wife. *Photo: Alinari.*

Plate XVII*a*. Marble relief. Berlin. Zeus and Porphyrion. *Photo: Berlin, Staatliche Museen.*

Plate XVII*b*. Marble relief. Berlin. Alkyoneus, Athena, Nike, and Oe. *Photo: Berlin, Staatliche Museen.*

Plate XVIIIb. Fresco. Naples, Museo Nazionale. Arcadia, Herakles and Telephos. *Photo: Alinari.*

Plate XVIIIa. Marble relief. Berlin. Herakles and Telephos. *Photo: Berlin, Staatliche Museen.*

Plate XIX*b*. Marble relief. Istanbul, 575. Maenad.
*Photo: Istanbul Museum.*

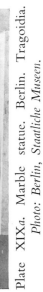

Plate XIX*a*. Marble statue. Berlin. Tragoidia.
*Photo: Berlin, Staatliche Museen.*

Plate XX*a*. Silver cup. British Museum. Chryseis, Chryses, Thoas.
*Photo: British Museum.*

Plate XX*b*. Silver cup. British Museum. Floral ornament. *Photo: British Museum.*

Plate XXI*b*. Marble head. Athens, N.M. 3377. Zeus.
Photo: *German Archaeological Institute.*

Plate XXI*a*. Marble head. Athens, N.M. 1736.
Anytos. Photo: *German Archaeological Institute.*

Plate XXII*a*. Marble statue. Athens, N.M. 1828. Portrait statue. *Photo: German Archaeological Institute.*

Plate XXII*b*. Marble statue. Rome, Terme 106513. Roman general. *Photo: Alinari.*

Plate XXIIIb. Marble relief. Athens, Agora S 7327. Dionysos. *Photo: American School of Classical Studies.*

Plate XXIIIa. Marble krater. Tunis, Musee Alaoui, C 1202. Satyrs and Maenad. *Photo: Musee Alaoui.*

Plate XXIV*b*. Bronze statue. Florence. Lampholder. *Photo: Alinari.*

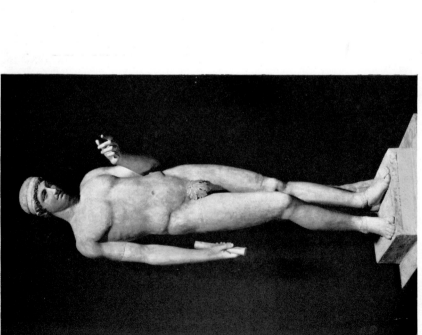

Plate XXIV*a*. Marble statue. Rome, Villa Albani, 317. Youth signed by Stephanos. *Photo: Alinari.*

Fauno is a copy of a Pergamene original (as also probably the bronze satyr which gives the house its name) and it is possible that the mystery pictures[1] of the Villa dei Misteri, which belongs to this time, are a copy of paintings in the Royal chapel at Pergamon: in the last case the coarseness of the execution shows that the artist was working from a much smaller model, whatever the relation of the model to the original may have been. Similarly the scene of the philosopher, Macedonia, and Greek Asia (if this is the right interpretation) at Boscoreale is a coarse enlargement of a model which perhaps copied an early third-century original from Pella.[2] The cubiculum at Boscoreale derives its decoration from theatrical scenery of the second century,[3] and belongs to a tradition of using theatrical scenery for house decoration which goes back before the earliest date proposed for Boscoreale, since Vitruvius attributes it to the *antiqui*, whose work preceded the more modern fashion of fantastic architecture exemplified by Augustan wall-decoration. (The dating of the Boscoreale paintings themselves varies from soon after the middle of the century to A.D. 12 and they may therefore fall outside our period.)[4] Alexandros of Athens,[5] who signed one of the four pictures on marble from Herculaneum, is dated by his signature in the first century B.C.; the pictures are true to the style of the late fifth century; the only question, which does not arise with the other three, is whether in his signed picture he combined two groups into one – the girls playing knuckle-bones as foreground and the three women as background.

What we know from literary sources suggests that the realistic tradition in scene-painting continued into the second quarter of the first century. In the games which Appius Claudius Pulcher[6] gave in 99 the background scenery was so realistic that crows tried to settle on the painted tiles; this must have been the kind of architecture

---

[1] Cf. above, p. 196.        [2] Cf. above, p. 25.

[3] Cf. above, p. 163. Vitruvius, VII, 5.

[4] Curtius, *Wandmalerei Pompeiis*, 123, dates 13/9 B.C.; Robertson, *J.R.S.* 45, 1955, 58, soon after 50 B.C.; Tanassia, *Arch. Class.* 11, 1959, 208, 12 A.D.

[5] Naples, M. N., Pfuhl, *M.u.Z.*, fig. 629; Rumpf, *M.u.Z.*, 122, pl. 39, 6; Kraiker, *Kentaurenbild des Zeuxis*, 1950, 21.

[6] Pliny, *N.H.*, 35, 23.

illustrated in the Boscoreale cubiculum. The scenery painted by Serapion was little later because he was a contemporary of the portrait-painter Dionysios and of Iaia of Kyzikos, who is dated in Varros' youth, i.e. the first quarter of the first century.[1] But in 58 Aemilius Scaurus built an elaborate architectural background in three storeys; he is said to have placed 3,000 statues in the intercolumniations and to have bought up and transferred to Rome all the paintings in Sikyon.[2] Three years later Pompey dedicated his theatre, and it seems clear that it also had an architectural background, since it also was adorned with works of art.[3] From this time onwards drama in the Roman world was deprived even of the modest possibilities of scenery allowed to the Greek theatre, and tragedy and comedy played before the same architectural background, as two terracotta reliefs of the mid-first-century show.[4]

The one original masterpiece of this period which may be preserved in copies is the Medea of Timomachos of Byzantium, who was given 80 talents for his Ajax and his Medea, when they were dedicated by Julius Caesar in the temple of Venus Genetrix.[5] If we did not know that this famous modern Medea was likely to be the inspiration of the copies, we should probably suppose that the original was a painting of the late fourth or early third century. The background with the open door can be paralleled on one of the Dioskorides mosaics; drapery and pose rather suggest the figures from the Mausoleum. If then this is the Medea of Timomachos, Timomachos, like his contemporary Arkesilaos, who provided this cult statue for the temple of Venus Genetrix, was a classicizing artist.

In the *Verrines* Cicero deliberately gives the impression of having learnt up enough art history to be able to point out the enormities of Verres, whose artistic enthusiasms awake no sympathy in him, but

---

[1] Pliny, *N.H.*, 35, 113 and 147.    [2] Pliny, *N.H.*, 36, 113; 34, 36; 35, 127.

[3] Cf. J. A. Hanson, *Roman Theater-Temples*, 43.

[4] *M.T.S.*, no. IT 7; *M.N.C.*, no. IT 65.

[5] Pliny, *N.H.*, 35, 136; Naples, M. N., Pfuhl, *M.u.Z.*, fig. 660; Rumpf, *M.u.Z.*, pl. 58, 2. Some have maintained that Pliny only dated Timomachos by the dedication of his pictures, and that Cicero refers to these paintings in *In Verr.*, II, iv, 135 as the pride of Kyzikos, in which case they would be much more likely to be Old Masters.

in other works he shows himself the educated man who can compare the history of art with the history of literature: he has read
some art historian which gives him the sequence Kanachos, Kalamis,
Myron, Polykleitos in bronzes and allows him to contrast Zeuxis
and Polygnotos with Aetion and Apelles, and he knows the obvious
anecdotes – that Pheidias included a portrait of himself on the shield
of the Parthenos and that Lysippos said that the Doryphoros of
Polykleitos was his master.[1] When in the letters he speaks of works
of art for his houses, his standard is simply the suitability of the subject for his literary pursuits. He has a statue of Plato in his garden and
Atticus has a statue of Aristotle.[2] Greek philosophical discussions had
taken place in the gymnasium or the palaestra, and he would like to
have the sort of works that they had there. He likes herms of Pen-
telic marble with bronze heads[3] (we think naturally of the bronze
head of Polykleitos' Doryphoros in the villa of Piso at Herculaneum
and we remember that a copy of the Doryphoros was found in the
palaestra at Pompeii).[4] He is pleased with herms of Hercules and a
herm of Minerva for the same reason. He likes Muses but he dislikes
Maenads. This is the sort of academic taste which the copyists
worked to satisfy.

In poetry also the strain of classicism is strong. In spite of the real
feeling of his epitaph on Corinth many of Antipater of Sidon's
epigrams were remodellings of Early Hellenistic epigrams.[5] In the
De Oratore (III, 194) of Cicero, of which the dramatic date was 92,
Crassus appeals to Q. Catulus' memory of Antipater as an extremely
fertile ex-tempore composer. Catulus was consul in 102 and his
memories may date from ten years or so earlier. Certainly therefore
Antipater was active in Rome in the late second century and may have
influenced the young Roman poets of that time. The two surviving
poems of Catulus are extremely accomplished epigrams in the
Greek manner. The first out-trumps an epigram of Kallimachos

---

[1] *Brutus* 70 f.; *De Oratore*, III, vii, 26; *Tusc.*, I, xv, 34; *Orator* 5.
[2] *Brutus* 24; *Ad Att.*, IV, 10.        [3] *Ad Att.*, I, viii, 2.
[4] Doryphoros herm: Naples, M. N. 854, Lippold 381; Winter, *K.i.B.*, 257/6;
Bieber, *Hell. Sc.*, fig. 755. Copy from Pompeii: Naples, M. N. 146; Lippold, 163,
pl. 59/1; Winter, *K.i.B.*, 257/5; Bieber, *Hell. Sc.*, fig. 754.
[5] Cf. above, p. 204.

(*Ep.* 41)[1] in just the same way as Antipater out-trumps Asklepiades. The second asserts that the mortal Roscius is more beautiful than the sun-god and recalls Artemon's equation of the young Echedemos with Apollo.[2] His contemporaries Valerius Aedituus and Porcius Licinus make different adaptations of the theme of the flame in the lover's heart which can illuminate the dark or set fire to a wood.

The next notable figure is Philodemos of Gadara,[3] who came to Italy between 80 and 70 and was established by Piso in Herculaneum. Cicero draws an unfair picture of him as corrupting the Roman senator and then celebrating his depravity in lascivious verse. His epigrams, as we have seen, were accomplished classicistic trifles and he was a competent and prolific Epicurean philosopher. Whether he had any influence on Lucretius as a philosopher is not known. If he had, Lucretius may also have got some poetic elegance from him, since his poem certainly shows acquaintance with Hellenistic poetry, and the group of Mars and Venus is clearly inspired by a picture with the same composition as the Dionysos and Ariadne in the Villa of the Mysteries;[4] this is just how Kallimachos adapted the statue of Serapis and Kerberos to his description of Hera and Iris.[5] The poetic tradition behind Lucretius' poem goes back through Aratos to Empedokles and Parmenides, and it is of these earlier Greek writers that his burning urgency reminds us, although he is a better poet than either. Cicero himself must not be judged only by the conceited effrontery of his autobiographical poems but rather by his extremely competent translations of Homer, Aeschylus, Sophocles, and Aratos, which show how perfect an instrument Latin had become for rendering Greek poetry in the original metre.

He evidently regards himself as representing a classical tradition in Roman poetry which went back to Ennius and despises the revolt of the younger generation of spondaizing poets, who extol the extremely obscure Euphorion.[6] The earliest of these criticisms is dated 49, when Catullus had been dead five years, Calvus and Cinna

---

[1] Morel, *Fragmenta Poetarum Latinorum*, 43. Cf. above, p. 205.
[2] Cf. above, p. 242.
[3] Cf. above, p. 213. Cicero, *In Pisonem* 68 ff.; *De Finibus*, III, 119.
[4] Cf. above, p. 301.       [5] Cf. above, p. 173.
[6] *Tusc.*, III, xix, 45; *De Div.*, II, 64; *Ad Att.*, VII, ii, 1.

were in their thirties, and Gallus already twenty. Something of the new direction, in so far as it was a new direction, was due to Parthenios of Nikaia.[1] It is uncertain whether he came to Rome as a prisoner of Cinna (whether the poet or not) when Nikaia was captured in 72 or slightly later; he was already established as a poet when he came to Rome and had already written his lament for his wife Arete. The fragments of his poems are unrevealing: they show that he was a learned poet and the very few surviving lines are elegant enough. But he also wrote a collection of prose-summaries of love affairs for Cornelius Gallus to use for hexameters or elegiac poetry. His sources for these included Alexander the Aetolian, Apollonios, Euphorion, Hermesianax, Nikainetos, Nikander, Philitas. He was therefore fully acquainted with Early Hellenistic poetry, and evidently himself wrote short narrative poetry in the tradition of Kallimachos. Euphorion was one of his sources, and Parthenios may have introduced him to the Romans. Lucian[2] brackets Parthenios, Euphorion, and Kallimachos together as long-winded poets in contrast to Homer: 'how many verses would they have needed to get the water up to Tantalos' lips?' This is a pretty and justifiable reversal of Kallimachos' own claim to be brief. His connection with Gallus, who may have been writing as early as 50, is clear from the dedication of the Love Affairs. His captor, Cinna, was either the poet Helvius Cinna or a relation. The poet Cinna spent nine years on a poem about Zmyrna, who fell in love with her father Cinyras,[3] and as a true follower of Kallimachos sent a friend a copy of Aratos with a four-line epigram, which starts with a reminiscence of Kallimachos (Ep. 37).

The only one of these poets of whom we can form any estimate is Catullus. Catullus the lover and Catullus the satirist hardly concern us, although even then the starting point in earlier Greek poetry can often be seen,[4] but these poems are the individual creations of a very individual poet: the death of Lesbia's sparrow (III) is a genuine

[1] Fragments in Loeb library volume with *Daphnis and Chloe*, and the new fragment of the Arete, Pfeiffer, C.Q. 37, 1943, 23.
[2] *Quomodo historiam* 86 (57).
[3] A tenuous connection with Parthenios is given by Parthenios fr. 23 and Catullus XCV, 5 (see Kroll, ad loc.).
[4] Kroll's edition gives the parallels.

experience, although Catullus may have been inspired to write the poem by the many Greek epitaphs for dead animals, and the death of his brother (*CI*) is a deeply felt sorrow even if it has a strong echo of Meleager's lament for Heliodora.[1] But he sees the poets who are his friends, particularly Cinna and Calvus, as upholding Kallimachos' ideal in Rome (*XCV*): the Zmyrna has taken nine years to write but will last for ever, but the annals of Volusius will be used for wrapping fish: 'may I like the small monuments of my friend, but let the people rejoice in swollen Antimachos'. Here the allusion to Kallimachos' dislike of the *Lyde* is clear.[2] The other friend, Calvus, wrote a poem on the death of his wife, which may owe something to Parthenios' poem for Arete, and Catullus sent him a consolation poem (*XCVI*), which perhaps takes off from the end of Antipater's epitaph on Anakreon (*A.P.* VII, 23).[3] The skill with which Catullus can hint at a model or even, as in the Sappho poem (*LI*), translate a model, and then preserving the manner of the original twist it into an entirely new poem shows not only great knowledge of Greek poetry but also long practice in translation. A specimen of his skill in translation, which can now be appreciated, is the *Coma Berenices* (*LXVI*).[4] The poem with which he sends the *Coma* to Ortalus (*LXV*) plays with the good Hellenistic idea of song as a consolation for misery and ends with the charming simile of the apple rolling from the girl's lap when her mother comes in, which may, as Kroll says, be an allusion to the apple in Kallimachos' *Akontion and Kydippe*.

Two other poems have been suspected of being translations, *Attis* (*LXIII*) and *Peleus and Thetis* (*LXIV*): they are placed between the marriage songs, which draw very heavily on Greek sources, and the *Coma*, but unlike the *Coma* they have no accompanying poem to introduce and explain them. The *Attis* is a brilliant adaptation of the Latin language to the difficult galliambic metre and tells the story of the Greek boy who left friends, parents, gymnasium, and

---

[1] CI, cf. *A.P.* VII, 476. Cf. also LI with Sappho 31 L–P, but Catullus gives it a completely different twist at the end and the major alteration that a *man* speaks; LXX with Kallimachos, *Ep.* 26; L with Hedylos ap. Athenaeus 473a.

[2] Cf. above, p. 103.

[3] On Catullus and Calvus see Fraenkel, *W.S.* 69, 1956, 279 ff.

[4] The text of Kallimachos fr. 110 is reprinted in Mynors, *Catulli Carmina*, 107 f.

country to serve Cybele as eunuch; after his first day of dancing he falls asleep and when he wakes repents of his action; Cybele hears him and sends a lion to attack him; this drives him mad and he spends the rest of his life as a servant of the goddess; the poem ends: 'Great goddess, goddess Cybele, goddess, queen of Dindymus, far from my home be all your madness, lady. Drive others with your spur, drive others with your fury.' The story of Attis seems then to be a story told by a ministrant of Kybele as a cautionary tale: it performs the same functions as the story of Erysichthon in Kalli-machos' *Hymn to Demeter*, which ends: 'Demeter, may that man who is hateful to you not be my friend or neighbour'.[1] The two galliambic lines (fr. 761 Pf.) about the devotees of Kybele attributed to Kallimachos could easily find a place in Catullus' poem, after '*agite, ite ad alta, Gallae*' (12), but we must assume that Catullus, the faithful translator, would have included them there if he had been translating that poem. It does however seem likely that he was translating a Greek poem in galliambics, which had a similar form to Kallimachos' *Hymn to Demeter*, whether this original was by Kalli-machos himself or another.[2]

The *Peleus and Thetis* is an Epyllion on the marriage of Peleus and Thetis in hexameters. The story shows strange divergences from the normal tradition. Peleus is not married to Thetis when the Argo sails; the Argo is the first ship that the Nereids have seen (they are astonished like the rustics in Apollonios and Accius); Peleus and Thetis fall in love, so that she is a willing bride; Cheiron brings flowers as a wedding present and *not* the famous spear; Apollo and Artemis refuse to attend the wedding, so that it is the Fates who sing the story of Achilles and (unlike Apollo in Aeschylus) tell also of his death. This account not only differs both expressly and by implica-tion from earlier accounts but also from Apollonios Rhodios, who makes Cheiron bring Achilles to watch the Argo sail.[3] The new

---

[1] Cf. above, p. 110.

[2] Gow, *J.H.S.* 80, 1960, 92 n. 33, notes the coincidence of the lion attacking a wavering Atys in Dioskorides (*A.P.* VI, 220, cf. above, p. 141). Dioskorides may therefore have been remodelling the original of Catullus' poem.

[3] For early accounts, cf. A. Lesky, *S.I.F.C.* 27–8, 1956, 216 ff. For the relation of this poem to Apollonios, cf. Wilamowitz, *Hell. Dicht.*, II, 299 f.

setting makes possible the pretty picture of the Nereids admiring the Argo and the Argonauts admiring the Nereids; it becomes a love story with a marriage and a prophecy, and only the slightest hints show that the poet was aware of Zeus' love for Thetis (26, 394). Into this is inserted a description of the tapestry on the nuptial couch, which accounts for more than half the poem. It is much more out of scale than the description of the basket in Moschos' *Europe*[1] and the subject represented, Theseus, Ariadne, and Dionysos, has not the relevance for the story of Peleus that the story of Io has for Europe. Unlike Moschos also, the poet is not much interested in the tapestry, its origin, or its technique: the picture (or relief) of which he is thinking evidently had Theseus departing on the left, Ariadne in the centre, Dionysos with satyrs and maenads arriving from the right, as on the 'Ikarios' reliefs,[2] which may well derive originally from such a scene. He is interested in the distress of Ariadne, who is evidently modelled on Apollonios' Medeia, and in the lengthy instructions of Aegeus, which Theseus forgets to carry out; here again the picture of the aged Aegeus owes something to Apollonios' Phineus. Finally at the end of the poem the poet explains the presents of the gods at the wedding of Peleus and Thetis, by saying that their visits to mortals took place in a time before men indulged in crimes, before human greed or concupiscence made brothers kill brothers, sons cease to mourn their parents, fathers wish for the death of their sons in order to marry again unhampered, mothers to lie with their sons.

One line of this curious poem (111) has been thought to be a translation of a Greek line quoted by Cicero; this has been ascribed to Kallimachos' *Hekale* (fr. 732). Cicero is, of course, likely to have quoted from a famous poem. But it must be pointed out first that there is no evidence for the ascription, secondly that Catullus is unlikely to have substituted the tame *jactantem* for the more literal *irascentem* which would have given him a spondaic ending like the

[1] Cf. above, p. 154.
[2] Cf. e.g. Pompeii, Helbig 1234; Reinach, R. P., III, 6. (On the 'Ikarios' relief see above, p. 297.) The position of the poet becomes intelligible if he has been substituted for a sleeping Ariadne, who was between the departing Theseus and the arriving Dionysos.

Greek θυμήναντα. The point is only important because Wilamowitz[1] says categorically: 'l. 111 is naturally from the *Hekale*: this is only doubted because it contradicts this perverse assumption that the whole poem is a translation'. It is more likely that a Greek poet transferred the *Hekale* line from the bull of Marathon and applied it with an altered verb to the Minotaur before Catullus used it. Wilamowitz[2] finds in the end of the poem a Roman speaking from his heart in a terrible time, when he sees his country plunging to disaster. Such a view naturally excludes the possibility that the whole poem is a translation. But Catullus was a satirist who described directly the immorality of his contemporaries when he wished. Would he criticize contemporary morality in this curiously generalized epilogue added to what Wilamowitz 'calls his masterpiece, comparable with the *Zmyrna* of his friend and fellow-countryman Cinna'? The mixture of genres is extraordinary. If however the poem is a translation, Catullus took the epilogue with the rest. Its background lies, of course, in Homer and Hesiod; in the Hellenistic period Aratos' description of Dike[3] naturally comes to mind, and then the curious mixture of moralizing and mythology in Euphorion.[4] If so, the generalized examples of crime need not conceal anyone more recent than Eteokles and Polyneikes, Phoinix and Amyntor, Iokaste and Oidipous, although doubtless Parthenios could provide many less well known examples. The source should therefore be sought in a poem which is certainly later than Apollonios and probably later than the *Hekale*, perhaps in what we have called the mainland moralizing tradition, to which Euphorion belonged. The poet was certainly more interested in the individual parts than the whole and elaborated some details out of scale. This tendency is unique in Catullus and is perhaps an additional argument for the poem being a translation rather than an original like the *Zmyrna*.

But we cannot prove whether the *Attis* and the *Peleus and Thetis* are translations or originals. We have the *Coma Berenices* as a certain example of translation and we know something about the *Zmyrna* as an original. But, as in contemporary art, the boundary between

---

[1] *Hell. Dicht.*, II, 300 n. 2.   [2] Op. cit., 304.
[3] Cf. above, p. 35.   [4] Cf. above, p. 227.

Y

original and copy is a narrow one. The original is an adaptation of earlier themes or simply a re-combination of earlier figures. What poets and artists gained by this kind of exercise was great technical proficiency; reader and spectator received works of great charm and needed considerable education to appreciate the allusions. It would probably be fair to say that the education of the Romans in Hellenistic poetry and art was the great achievement of the early first century and that this education was a necessary preparation for Augustan poetry and art, but in saying this it must not be forgotten that Lucretius and Catullus were by any standards great poets in their own right.

# Index